Using Mathematics in Economics

Second Edition

R. L. Thomas

 ADDISON-WESLEY

HARLOW, ENGLAND ▪ READING, MASSACHUSETTS ▪ MENLO PARK, CALIFORNIA

NEW YORK ▪ DON MILLS, ONTARIO ▪ AMSTERDAM ▪ BONN ▪ SYDNEY

SINGAPORE ▪ TOKYO ▪ MADRID ▪ SAN JUAN ▪ MILAN ▪ PARIS ▪ MEXICO CITY

SEOUL ▪ TAIPEI

Addison Wesley Longman Limited
Edinburgh Gate
Harlow
Essex CM20 2JE
England
and Associated Companies throughout the world

Visit Addison Wesley Longman on the world wide web at:
http://www.awl-he.com

© Addison Wesley Longman Limited 1999

First published 1989
Fourth impression 1996
Reprinted 1997
This edition published 1999

ISBN 0 201 36050 0

British Library Cataloguing in Publication Data
A catalogue record for this book is available from the British Library

Library of Congress Cataloging-in-Publication Data
Thomas, R. L. (Richard Leighton), 1942–
    Using mathematics in economics / R. L. Thomas. — 2nd ed.
       p.   cm.
    Includes bibliographical references (p.   ) and index.
    ISBN 0–201–36050–0 (ppr)
    1. Economics—Graphic methods.   I. Title.
HB135.T486   1999
510′.24′33—dc21   98–49112
                                                        CIP

Typeset by 32 in 10/12pt Times
Produced by Addison Wesley Longman Singapore (Pte) Limited.
Printed in Singapore

Contents

Preface to the Second Edition   page   ix
Preface to the First Edition   xi
Mathematical prerequisites   xiii

1   Functions and equations   1

   1.1   Variables and functions   1
   1.2   Coordinate systems   3
   1.3   The graphing of functions   4
   1.4   Linear functions and straight lines   9
   1.5   The algebraic solution of equations in one variable   11
   1.6   Inverse functions   18

2   Simultaneous linear equations   23

   2.1   Simultaneous equations in two variables   23
   2.2   Generalisation to more than two variables   30
   2.3   Non-linear systems   32
   2.4   Economic models, their completeness and their consistency   35

3   Stocks, flows and equilibrium in economics   42

   3.1   Stock and flow variables   42
   3.2   Some definitions relating to markets   45
   3.3   Flow markets for a single good   46
   3.4   Static and dynamic analysis   51
   3.5   Stable and unstable equilibrium   54

4   The reduced and structural forms of equation systems   58

   4.1   An indeterminate system   58
   4.2   Multi-good flow markets   60
   4.3   The reduced form of an equation system   62
   4.4   A difficulty   71
   4.5   A macro-economic example   73

5 Stock-flow markets 78

5.1 Net investment in stocks 78
5.2 Equilibrium in a stock-flow market 80
5.3 Exogenous variables and reduced forms 86
5.4 Stock-flow markets for more than one good 87
5.5 A macro-economic example 89

6 Geometric progressions and discounted cash flows 93

6.1 Geometric progressions 94
6.2 Present values 99
6.3 Discounted cash flows 103

7 The differentiation of functions of one variable 109

7.1 The gradients of non-linear functions 109
7.2 More about limits 110
7.3 The derivative of a function 114
7.4 General rules of differentiation I 117
7.5 Some economic applications 122
7.6 General rules of differentiation II 128

8 Higher-order derivatives 138

8.1 Stationary points 140
8.2 The relationship between average and marginal cost functions 147
8.3 Profit maximisation 149
8.4 Taxation and the profit-maximisation model 152
8.5 Reduced and structural forms of the profit-maximisation model 156

9 Integration 160

9.1 Notation and terminology 160
9.2 Rules for integration I 161
9.3 Total and marginal functions 163
9.4 Rules for integration II 164
9.5 Definite integrals 168
9.6 Consumer and producer surplus 172

10 Differentiations of functions of more than one variable 175

10.1 Functions of more than one variable 175
10.2 Partial differentiation 178
10.3 Partial differentiation and the *ceteris paribus* assumption 181
10.4 Production functions and utility functions 184
10.5 Higher-order partial derivatives 188

11 Total differentials and total derivatives 193

11.1 Differentials 193
11.2 The reduced form of a non-linear system 195
11.3 Total derivatives and implicit differentiation 201
11.4 Homogeneous functions and Euler's theorem 204

12 Unconstrained and constrained optimisation 211

12.1 The unconstrained optimisation of functions of more
than one variable 211
12.2 Profit maximisation again 215
12.3 Constrained optimisation 218
12.4 Distinguishing between constrained maxima and
constrained minima 225

13 Calculus in economics I: the firm 233

13.1 Isoquants and iso-cost lines 233
13.2 Constrained optimisation and the firm 235
13.3 Profit-maximisation and cost-minimisation models 238
13.4 The Cobb–Douglas production function 242
13.5 Cost and revenue functions in the profit-maximisation model 244

14 Calculus in economics II: the consumer 249

14.1 Utility maximisation 249
14.2 Demand functions 252
14.3 Maximising utility over time 257

15 Exponential and logarithmic functions 265

15.1 Exponential functions 265
15.2 Logarithmic functions 266
15.3 The natural exponential function 271
15.4 The differentiation of exponential and logarithmic functions 276
15.5 The natural exponential function in economics 278

16 Introduction to dynamics 282

16.1 Difference equations 282
16.2 Solving difference equations 288
16.3 The dynamic flow market model again 297
16.4 The simple Keynesian model again 298

17 Introduction to matrix algebra 303

17.1 Vectors and matrices 303
17.2 Further basic definitions and operations 310

17.3 Inverting a matrix   312
17.4 Determinants   314
17.5 Alternative method of inverting a matrix   317
17.6 Solution of equation systems by matrix inversion   319
17.7 Structural and reduced forms again   322

Answers to examples   327
Index   337

Preface to the Second Edition

I have made no major structural changes in this edition. However, I have realised that as the range of mathematical abilities of students taking economics courses is becoming broader, the need for a more basic introduction to mathematics has become necessary. One of the key changes I have made to this edition, therefore, is to include a section entitled 'Mathematical prerequisites'. I have also expanded some of the later chapters, particularly that on matrix algebra, and improved the clarity of other chapters. The most important change I have made in the second edition, though, is to greatly expand the number of examples, reflecting the value to students of practising the theory they learn. I am indebted to Joanne Lindley for her meticulous checking of answers to so many examples.

RLT
September 1998

Preface to the First Edition

Teachers of the typical 'mathematics for economists' first-year course at British universities and polytechnics invariably face a major problem – the varying mathematical background and ability of their students. Backgrounds tend to vary from those who obtain excellent A-level grades in both pure and applied mathematics to those who abandoned mathematics with a sigh of relief two or three years previously and now, with trepidation, realise they face a compulsory first-year mathematics course. One solution is the running of separate courses for the two types of student but this simply postpones the problem to the start of the second year by which time the disparity in mathematical aptitudes has often become even more marked.

The accommodation of varying mathematical backgrounds within a single course poses obvious problems. If too fast a pace is set then weaker students rapidly lose all hope, whereas if the pace is that of the slowest the interest of the mathematically more able is immediately lost. This book is the result of my efforts at Salford during the past 10 years to steer a middle course. Difficulties are particularly severe during the early part of a first-year course when some fairly basic ideas have to be revised. I have found that it is necessary, as far as possible, to teach the basics in a way that students with A-level mathematics may not have previously encountered and to introduce a substantial economics content into the course at the earliest possible stage. Even so, students with A-level maths should probably be set alternative tasks while the material in the first chapter of this book is being covered.

At A-level, mathematics and economics tend to be taught as entirely separate subjects and as a result many students keep them in separate 'boxes' at least during their first two years at university. A first-year mathematics course presents the perfect opportunity to start breaking down these barriers and by doing so retain the interest of the mathematically adept student. In fact if this is not done the student with A-level maths is likely to learn nothing new at all from his/her first-year mathematics course.

In the early part of this book I have spent considerable time on equation systems and their solution. As well as being a good starting-point for those with a weaker mathematical background, this also provides an excellent chance to introduce both the distinction between the structural and reduced forms of equation systems and that between stock and flow variables in economics. These distinctions are so crucial to much of economic model building that their early appreciation is vital for students; yet there is rarely room in the standard first-year economic theory course to spend sufficient time ramming home the differences. Since the obvious first example of the use of equation systems in economics involves the study of markets, the distinction between stock and flow variables is easily introduced at this stage. The derivation of reduced forms is a recurring theme throughout the book.

The last two-thirds of the book are more conventional, dealing as they do mainly with the differential and integral calculus. However, the differentiation of functions of two or more variables and particularly constrained optimisation are often unfamiliar even to students with A-level mathematics, so the problem of retaining interest is less severe here. Also, the less mathematically oriented student has great difficulty grasping the concepts involved at this point, particularly those of constrained optimisation. An intuitive rather than a thoroughly rigorous approach is therefore essential at first. In addition, many students find three-dimensional diagrams difficult to handle and I have almost entirely eschewed their use. A contour map approach is used which fits in well with the *ceteris paribus* approach so often used in economics. There are also separate chapters devoted to the mathematical economics of firm and consumer in a further effort to break down the barriers, referred to earlier, that students so often erect between mathematics and economics.

The final two chapters involve dynamic analysis and matrix algebra. Lack of space (and time in a first-year course) mean that only an introduction to these topics can be provided. The excellent mathematics for economists textbook by A. C. Chiang[1] can be consulted if a more extensive treatment is required. Indeed Chiang would make ideal background reading for the interested student. In the mathematical economics area, as opposed to mathematics for economists, the present book should serve as a good introduction to the text by Birchenhall and Grout.[2] Prerequisites for the book are no more than an adequate grasp of arithmetic and a familiarity with the elementary rules of algebra.

The author is greatly indebted to those friends and colleagues at the University of Salford who read and commented on various chapters of this book. For the thankless task of typing and amending various drafts, I am indebted to my wife Margaret and to Shirley Woolley in particular.

RLT
October 1988

References

1. A. C. Chiang (1984) *Fundamental Methods of Mathematical Economics*, 3rd edn, International Student Edition. McGraw-Hill, Tokyo.
2. C. Birchenhall and R. Grout (1984) *Mathematics for Modern Economists*. Philip Allen, Oxford.

Mathematical prerequisites

If the thought of studying mathematics as part of your economics course fills you with fore-
boding, this section is written to help you. The purpose of the section is to revise some simple,
basic arithmetic and algebra that you may not have encountered since your school days. The
material included is not exhaustive, but, once you have worked through it, you should be able
to tackle the rest of the text with more confidence.

Basic operations with integers

You should be familiar with the basic operations of addition, subtraction, multiplication and
division as far as integers (whole numbers) are concerned. Notice that, when performing a
series of calculations involving addition and subtraction alone, a basic rule of *working from left
to right* applies. For example,

(i) $12 - 5 + 3 = 7 + 3 = 10$

(ii) $8 + 3 - 7 + 2 - 5 = 11 - 7 + 2 - 5 = 4 + 2 - 5 = 6 - 5 = 1$

Notice, however, that we cannot evaluate (i) as $12 - 8 = 4$ nor can we evaluate (ii) as
$11 - 9 - 5 = -3$.

A basic left to right rule also applies when multiplication and division operations alone are
performed. For example,

(i) $24 \div 2 \times 6 = 12 \times 6 = 72$

(ii) $12 \times 6 \div 3 \times 4 = 72 \div 3 \times 4 = 24 \times 4 = 96$

In this case we cannot evaluate (i) as $24 \div 12 = 2$ nor can we evaluate (ii) as $72 \div 12 = 6$.
Again the left to right rule must be applied.

Notice next that, in the absence of brackets (see later), in more complicated 'mixed' multiple
operations involving both addition/subtraction and multiplication/division it is necessary to
perform multiplication and division calculations before addition and subtraction. For example,

(i) $8 \times 3 - 2 = 24 - 2 = 22$

(ii) $12 + 8 \div 4 = 12 + 2 = 14$

(iii) $40 + 20 \times 3 = 40 + 60 = 100$

(iv) $8 - 2 \times 3 - 5 = 8 - 6 - 5 = -3$

Observe that the need to perform multiplication/division first means that we need not now always follow the left to right rule if we are performing 'mixed' operations such as those in (i) to (iv) immediately above.

The use of brackets in arithmetic operations

Consider the following two simple examples.

Example 1

A woman goes shopping with £5. She buys 10 oranges at 40 pence each. How much money (in pence) has she left?

Solution

$$500 - 10 \times 40 = 500 - 400 = 100$$

Notice in obtaining the answer to Example 1 that we have used the rule that multiplication/division should be performed before addition/subtraction.

Example 2

Forty school children have £5 each. Each spends 10 pence in the school canteen. How much money (in pence) do the children now have left altogether?

Solution

$$(500 - 10) \times 40 = 490 \times 40 = 19\,600$$

Notice that the answer to Example 1 involves the same numbers as the answer to Example 2. However, to obtain the correct answer to Example 2 we have to break the rule that multiplication must be performed before subtraction. The way to ensure and signal this is to make use of brackets. In the answer to Example 2 the brackets indicate that the operation $500 - 10 = 490$ is to be performed first.

A general rule is that *operations in brackets are always performed first, even before multiplication/division*. In the absence of brackets then, as usual, multiplication and division are performed before addition and subtraction. For example,

(i) $16 \div 4 + 4 = 4 + 4 = 8$ but $16 \div (4 + 4) = 16 \div 8 = 2$

(ii) $3 \times 4 - 2 = 12 - 2 = 10$ but $3 \times (4 - 2) = 3 \times 2 = 6$

Note that the order in which you perform addition and subtraction does not matter and the order in which you perform multiplication and division does not matter. For example,

(i) $(8 - 3 + 5) \div 2 = (5 + 5) \div 2 = 10 \div 2 = 5$

or $= (8 + 2) \div 2 = 10 \div 2 = 5$

(ii) $8 + 3 \times 4 \div 2 = 8 + 12 \div 2 = 8 + 6 = 14$

$\quad\quad$ or $\quad = 8 + 3 \times 2 = 8 + 6 = 14$

Exercises 1

$\quad$ (i) $10 - 3 + 5 + 4 - 6 =$

$\quad$ (ii) $8 \times 3 \div 2 \times 4 =$

$\quad$ (iii) $5 + 3 \times 4 =$

$\quad$ (iv) $7 \times (2 + 5) =$

$\quad$ (v) $8 - 6 \div 2 =$

$\quad$ (vi) $12 \times 3 \div 4 - 5 =$

$\quad$ (vii) $(14 - 2) \times 4 \div 2 =$

(viii) $7 \times 3 \times (5 - 2) =$

Fractions and decimals

A fraction can always be expressed in the form

$$\frac{\text{numerator}}{\text{denominator}}$$

and is evaluated as numerator divided by denominator. For example,

$$\frac{25}{5} = 25 \div 5 = 5$$

We can also express a numerator divided by a denominator as a *decimal*. For example,

$$\frac{9}{2} = 4.5 \quad \frac{25}{3} = 8.3\dot{3} \quad \frac{1}{400} = 0.0025$$

You should be familiar with the computation of decimals even if you require a calculator to help. However, handling fractions is more difficult and this section is therefore mostly concerned with such operations.

$\quad$ It is often possible to *simplify* a fraction by exactly dividing both numerator and denominator by the same whole number. For example,

$$\frac{112}{21} = \frac{16 \times 7}{3 \times 7} = \frac{16}{3}$$

The sevens obviously 'cancel' out in both numerator and denominator. Similarly

$$\frac{54}{378} = \frac{9 \times 6}{7 \times 9 \times 6} = \frac{1}{7}$$

When adding or subtracting fractions it is necessary to convert each fraction in such a way that each has the same denominator. For example,

$$\frac{4}{5} + \frac{1}{6} = \frac{24}{30} + \frac{5}{30} = \frac{24+5}{30} = \frac{29}{30}$$

Similarly

$$\frac{2}{5} + \frac{3}{10} = \frac{4}{10} + \frac{3}{10} = \frac{4+3}{10} = \frac{7}{10}$$

or alternatively

$$\frac{2}{5} + \frac{3}{10} = \frac{20}{50} + \frac{15}{50} = \frac{35}{50} = \frac{7 \times 5}{10 \times 5} = \frac{7}{10}$$

If integers appear in computations involving fractions, it is possible to convert the integers into fractions with the same denominator. For example,

$$5\tfrac{3}{8} = \frac{43}{8} \quad \text{or} \quad 6\tfrac{3}{5} = \frac{33}{5} \quad \text{or} \quad 7\tfrac{1}{4} = \frac{29}{4}$$

This will often be necessary when adding or subtracting. For example,

(i) $$2\tfrac{4}{7} + \frac{2}{3} = \frac{18}{7} + \frac{2}{3} = \frac{54}{21} + \frac{14}{21} = \frac{68}{21} = 3\tfrac{5}{21}$$

(ii) $$3\tfrac{1}{4} - \frac{3}{5} = \frac{13}{4} - \frac{3}{5} = \frac{65}{20} - \frac{12}{20} = \frac{53}{20} = 2\tfrac{13}{20}$$

To multiply fractions it is necessary first to multiply the numerators together and then to multiply the denominators together. For example,

(i) $$\frac{7}{5} \times \frac{3}{8} = \frac{21}{40}$$

(ii) $$\frac{3}{4} \times \frac{5}{3} \times \frac{4}{7} = \frac{60}{84} = \frac{5}{7}$$

Notice that it is often easier to perform a computation by first cancelling out any integers that can be divided by both a numerator and a denominator. For example,

$$\frac{28}{15} \times \frac{25}{7} \times \frac{11}{24} = \frac{(7 \times 4) \times (5 \times 5) \times 11}{(5 \times 3) \times 7 \times (6 \times 4)} = \frac{5 \times 11}{3 \times 6} = \frac{55}{18}$$

Frequently you will see a mathematician performing the previous calculation by simply striking out any numbers that cancel out. That is

$$\frac{\overset{7}{\cancel{28}}}{\underset{3}{\cancel{15}}} \times \frac{\overset{5}{\cancel{25}}}{\cancel{7}} \times \frac{11}{\underset{6}{\cancel{24}}} = \frac{55}{18}$$

Dividing by a fraction involves multiplying by the inverse of that fraction. For example,

(i) $5 \div \dfrac{1}{4} = \dfrac{5}{1} \times \dfrac{4}{1} = 5 \times 4 = 20$

(ii) $\dfrac{8}{3} \div \dfrac{1}{5} = \dfrac{8}{3} \times \dfrac{5}{1} = \dfrac{8}{3} \times 5 = \dfrac{40}{3}$

(iii) $\dfrac{24}{11} \div \dfrac{32}{33} = \dfrac{24}{11} \times \dfrac{33}{32} = \dfrac{3}{1} \times \dfrac{3}{4} = \dfrac{9}{4}$

(iv) $\dfrac{3}{4} \div \dfrac{5}{8} = \dfrac{3}{4} \times \dfrac{8}{5} = \dfrac{3}{1} \times \dfrac{2}{5} = \dfrac{6}{5}$

Exercises 2

(i) Simplify $\dfrac{72}{27}, \dfrac{15}{20}, \dfrac{56}{24}, \dfrac{120}{144}$.

(ii) $\dfrac{1}{3} + \dfrac{1}{6} =$

(iii) $\dfrac{4}{7} + \dfrac{1}{5} =$

(iv) $2\dfrac{3}{8} + \dfrac{3}{4} =$

(v) $4\dfrac{1}{3} - 2\dfrac{5}{7} =$

(vi) $\dfrac{8}{3} \times \dfrac{9}{11} =$

(vii) $\dfrac{6}{5} \times \dfrac{5}{4} \times \dfrac{8}{9} =$

(viii) $2\dfrac{1}{3} \times 1\dfrac{3}{4} =$

(ix) $\dfrac{6}{7} \div \dfrac{3}{4} =$

(x) $\dfrac{8}{5} \times \dfrac{3}{4} \div \dfrac{7}{5} =$

(xi) $5\dfrac{2}{5} \div 3 =$

There are useful advantages to acquiring some skill in handling fractions. As we shall see later the rules for handling fractions are identical to those used when we manipulate algebraic expressions. Although computation on a calculator is a possible alternative when using the rules for dealing with fractions, no such alternative exists when handling algebraic expressions. Thus in the later section on algebra we shall have to make use repeatedly of the rules we have developed for handling fractions.

Negative numbers

We shall introduce this topic via some simple real-world examples. If a student has £30 in the bank we shall say the bank account is 30. However, if a student has an overdraft of £30, we shall say the bank account is −30.

If five students have amounts £20, £40, £15, £30 and £25 in their accounts then obviously their combined accounts are worth the sum of their individual accounts, $20 + 40 + 15 + 30 + 25 = £130$. Suppose, however, the five students have accounts +35, −15, −25, 60, −10 (i.e. three have overdrafts). Then the combined accounts are worth their sum

$$35 + (-15) + (-25) + 60 + (-10) = 35 - 15 - 25 + 60 - 10 = £45$$

Notice that to obtain a sensible answer we have to use the rule that *a positive and a negative make a negative* when brackets are removed.

Similarly, if five students have accounts −25, −40, 30, −40, 20, then their combined account is

$$-25 + (-40) + 30 + (-40) + 20 = -£55$$

That is, the combined account is in the red by £55.

Suppose the five students each have accounts −200. Their combined account is clearly −£1000 which we can obtain by taking 5×-200 or by taking -200×5. Notice again that a positive and a negative (or a negative and a positive) always make a negative.

Suppose next that student A has an account 80 and student B has an account 50. Obviously student A is better off by

$$\text{student A's account} - \text{student B's account} = 80 - 50 = £30$$

But what if both students have overdrafts? That is, suppose student A has an account −30 and student B has an account −60. Student A is again obviously better off by £30. But to obtain the sensible answer we must take

$$\text{student A's account} - \text{student B's account} = -30 - (-60)$$

$$= -30 + 60 = 30$$

That is, we have to use the rule that *a negative and a negative make a positive* when removing brackets. The rules for using negative numbers always apply either when removing brackets or when multiplying or dividing. For example,

(i) $5 + (-8) = 5 - 8 = -3$ (iv) $-3 \times -2 = 6$ (vii) $-12 \div -3 = 4$

(ii) $6 - (-5) = 6 + 5 = 11$ (v) $3 \times -7 = -21$ (viii) $15 \div -3 = -5$

(iii) $-4 \times 2 = -8$ (vi) $-8 \div 2 = -4$

That is,

    a positive and a negative give a negative

    a negative and a positive give a negative

    a negative and a negative give a positive

Exercises 3

(i) $12 \div -4 =$

(ii) $-5 \times -3 =$

(iii) $-\frac{3}{4} \times -2 =$

(iv) $-12 \div -3 =$

(v) $8 \div -5 =$

(vi) $-2 \times \frac{2}{5} =$

The powers of numbers

We often find ourselves performing calculations such as

(i) $8 \times 8 = 64$

(ii) $10 \times 10 \times 10 = 1000$

For example, a floor with sides each equal to 8 metres has an area of 64 square metres. Similarly, a room with sides and height all equal to 10 metres has a volume of 1000 cubic metres. Mathematicians use the following shorthand or *notation* when making such calculations. For example,

(i) 6×6 is written as $6^2 = 36$

(ii) $8 \times 8 \times 8$ is written as $8^3 = 512$

The superscripts 2 and 3 in (i) and (ii) are known as *powers*, *indices* or *exponents*. There are no real-world analogues of the powers 2 and 3 but we also write as shorthand

(i) $4 \times 4 \times 4 \times 4 \times 4 = 4^5 = 1024$

(ii) $3 \times 3 \times 3 = 3^3 = 27$

(iii) $12 \times 12 \times 12 \times 12 = 12^4 = 20\,736$

Note that $8^1 = 8$, $10^1 = 10$, $5^1 = 5$ and so on. Thus an exponent of 1 can be ignored.

Use of a calculator to work out the powers of numbers

The y^x or x^y button on a calculator can be used to evaluate the powers of numbers. For example,

(i) To calculate 9^5: press 9, press y^x, press 5, press $=$ and obtain $9^5 = 59\,049$.

(ii) To calculate 2^{15}: press 2, press y^x, press 15, press $=$ and obtain $2^{15} = 32\,768$.

(iii) To calculate $(1.8)^4$: press 1.8, press y^x, press 4, press $=$ and obtain $(1.8)^4 = 10.4976$.

Rules for handling powers

Rule 1

$$6^3 \times 6^5 = (6 \times 6 \times 6) \times (6 \times 6 \times 6 \times 6 \times 6)$$
$$= 6 \times 6 \times 6 \times 6 \times 6 \times 6 \times 6 \times 6 = 6^8 = 1\,679\,616$$

Similarly

$$4^7 \times 4^2 = (4 \times 4 \times 4 \times 4 \times 4 \times 4 \times 4) \times (4 \times 4) = 4^9 = 262\,144$$

and

(i) $5^2 \times 5^4 = 5^6 = 15\,625$

(ii) $3^{11} \times 3^4 = 3^{15} = 14\,348\,907$

(iii) $7^8 \times 7 = 7^9 = 403\,536\,007$

In such situations we have the general rule 1 that when multiplying we must *add the powers*.

Rule 2

$$5^7 \div 5^3 = \frac{5^7}{5^3} = \frac{5 \times 5 \times 5 \times 5 \times 5 \times 5 \times 5}{5 \times 5 \times 5} = 5 \times 5 \times 5 \times 5 = 5^4 = 625$$

Similarly

$$7^5 \div 7^3 = \frac{7^5}{7^3} = \frac{7 \times 7 \times 7 \times 7 \times 7}{7 \times 7 \times 7} = 7 \times 7 = 7^2 = 49$$

and

(i) $8^6 \div 8^3 = \dfrac{8^6}{8^3} = 8^3 = 512$

(ii) $4^{10} \div 4^6 = \dfrac{4^{10}}{4^6} = 4^4 = 256$

(iii) $6^9 \div 6 = \dfrac{6^9}{6} = 6^8 = 1\,679\,616$

In such situations we have the general rule 2 that when dividing we must *subtract the powers*.

Rule 3

$$(5^4)^2 = 5^4 \times 5^4 = 5^8 \quad \text{(using rule 1)}$$
$$= 390\,625$$

Similarly

$$(2^2)^5 = 2^2 \times 2^2 \times 2^2 \times 2^2 \times 2^2 = 2^{10} \quad \text{(using rule 1)}$$
$$= 1024$$

and

(i) $(4^2)^3 = 4^6 = 4096$

(ii) $(3^3)^2 = 3^6 = 729$

(iii) $(6^1)^5 = 6^5 = 7776$

In such situations we have the general rule 3 that we *multiply the powers*.

Exercises 4

(i) $(3.4)^3 =$

(ii) $(1.5)^5 =$

(iii) $3^2 \times 3^5 =$

(iv) $4^6 \div 4^2 =$

(v) $5^6 \times 5^2 \div 3^4 =$

(vi) $8^3 \div 8^5 =$

(vii) $(2^3)^4 =$

(viii) $(4^2)^3 =$

(ix) $4^3 \div (3^3)^2 =$

Zero and negative powers

Using rule 1 above, $8^6 \times 8^0 = 8^6$, that is we add the powers $6 + 0 = 6$. Thus, since $8^6 \times 1 = 8^6$ also, it must be the case that $8^0 = 1$. In fact *any number raised to the power 0 must equal one*. For example,

(i) $4^0 = 1$ (ii) $238^0 = 1$ (iii) $3.76^0 = 1$

Check this by using the y^x button on your calculator.

Suppose we wish to interpret the quantity 3^{-3}. Again using rule 1 above

$$3^8 \times 3^{-3} = 3^5 \quad \text{(adding the powers gives } 8 + (-3) = 5)$$

But using rule 2 above

$$\frac{3^8}{3^3} = 3^5 \quad \text{(subtracting the powers gives } 8 - 3 = 5)$$

However,

$$\frac{3^8}{3^3} = 3^8 \times \frac{1}{3^3}$$

Hence it must be the case that $3^{-3} = 1/3^3$. That is, 3^{-3} must simply be another way of writing $1/3^3$. Similarly

(i) $6^{-2} = \dfrac{1}{6^2}$ (ii) $8^{-4} = \dfrac{1}{8^4}$ (iii) $5^{-6} = \dfrac{1}{5^6}$

Thus, *a negative power of a number indicates the number of times we have to divide by the number.* For example,

(i) $4^{-3} \times 4^4 = \dfrac{4^4}{4^3} = \dfrac{4 \times 4 \times 4 \times 4}{4 \times 4 \times 4} = 4$

(ii) $8^2 \times 8^{-5} = \dfrac{8^2}{8^5} = \dfrac{8 \times 8}{8 \times 8 \times 8 \times 8 \times 8} = \dfrac{1}{8^3}$

The powers of negative numbers

These are handled in the same way as the powers of positive numbers. The only problem is deciding what sign to attach to the answer. For example,

(i) $(-4)^5 = (-4) \times (-4) \times (-4) \times (-4) \times (-4) = -(4^5) = -1024$

(ii) $(-3)^4 = (-3) \times (-3) \times (-3) \times (-3) = +3^4 = 81$

(iii) $(-5)^3 = (-5) \times (-5) \times (-5) = -(5^3) = -125$

Since an *even* number of negatives make a positive, the answer will be *positive* when the power is an *even* number (see e.g. (ii) above). However, since an *odd* number of negatives make a negative, the answer will be *negative* when the power is an *odd* number (see e.g. (i) and (iii) above).

Fractional or decimal powers

How should we interpret quantities such as $8^{1/5}$ or $6^{0.5}$? Let us consider $6^{0.5}$. It must be the case that, applying rule 1 for powers,

$6^{0.5} \times 6^{0.5} = 6^{0.5+0.5} = 6^1 = 6$ (adding the powers)

Thus $6^{0.5}$ is that number which, when you multiply it by itself, yields 6. That is, $6^{0.5}$ is simply the *square root* of 6, also written $\sqrt{6}$. That is,

$6^{0.5} = 6^{1/2} = \sqrt{6} = 2.449$

Similarly, consider $8^{1/5} = 8^{0.2}$. Again, applying rule 1,

$8^{1/5} \times 8^{1/5} \times 8^{1/5} \times 8^{1/5} \times 8^{1/5} = 8^{1/5+1/5+1/5+1/5+1/5}$

$$= 8^1 = 8 \quad \text{(adding the powers)}$$

Thus $8^{1/5}$ is that number which, when multiplied by itself five times, yields 8. That is, it is the *fifth root* of 8, also written $\sqrt[5]{8}$. That is,

$$8^{1/5} = 8^{0.2} = \sqrt[5]{8}$$

Similarly,

(i) $7^{1/4} = \sqrt[4]{7}$ (ii) $24^{1/3} = \sqrt[3]{24}$ (iii) $56^{1/10} = \sqrt[10]{56}$

Unless the answer to a root is a whole number, roots are difficult to work out by hand. However, they can easily be computed using the y^x button on a calculator in the usual way. For example,

(i) $10^{1/5} = 10^{0.2} = 1.585$

(ii) $5^{1/3} = 5^{0.33} = 1.710$

(iii) $(8.45)^{1/4} = (8.45)^{0.25} = 1.705$

Notice that a non-integer power can be written as either a fraction or a decimal. Any fractional power has to be converted to the corresponding decimal power if a calculator is to be used.

Sometimes we can get fractional/decimal powers that do not correspond to an exact root. For example, how can we interpret $8^{0.8}$ or its equivalent $8^{4/5}$? Making use of rule 3 on powers, we can write

$$8^{4/5} = (8^{1/5})^4 \quad \text{(multiplying the powers)}$$

$$= (\sqrt[5]{8})^4$$

Thus $8^{4/5}$ is simply the fifth root of 8 multiplied by itself four times! Similarly

(i) $5^{2/3} = (5^{1/3})^2 = (\sqrt[3]{5})^2$

(ii) $6^{0.625} = 6^{5/8} = (6^{1/8})^5 = (\sqrt[8]{6})^5$

(iii) $4^{8/7} = (4^{1/7})^8 = (\sqrt[7]{4})^8$

(iv) $2^{0.57} = 2^{57/100} = (2^{1/57})^{100} = (\sqrt[57]{2})^{100}$

When attempting to *interpret* powers such as (i) to (iv) above it is preferable to express powers in terms of fractions. However, such powers can be best *computed* using the y^x button on a calculator. For example, $(5.4)^{0.64} = 2.943$ and $45^{2.34} = 7387.84$. The y^x button is very easy to use even if sometimes you may have difficulty interpreting what is being asked for!

It is possible to combine fractional/decimal powers with negative powers. For example,

(i) $5^{-3/2} = \dfrac{1}{5^{3/2}} = \dfrac{1}{5^{1.5}} = 0.725$

(ii) $24^{-0.32} = \dfrac{1}{24^{0.32}} = \dfrac{1}{2.765} = 0.362$

Exercises 5

(i) $5^{-3} \times 5^4 =$

(ii) $4^3 \times 4^{-4} \times 3^2 =$

(iii) $(-2)^7 =$

(iv) $(-1)^{10} =$

(v) $8^4 \times 8^{-4} =$

(vi) $16^{1/4} =$

(vii) $125^{-1/3} =$

(viii) $10^{1/4} =$

(ix) $8^{0.6} =$

(x) $3^{6/5} =$

(xi) $4^{1/3} \times 4^{2/3} =$

(xii) $9^{-1/2} =$

Revision of basic algebra

Algebra is basically a *shorthand*. Symbols are used to represent *variables* that can take different values. For example, in economics we usually employ the symbol Y as a shorthand for income. However, before we can employ the algebra shorthand usefully, we need to recall some basic rules.

Basic rules of the algebra shorthand

1. We write $p \times q = pq$, $6 \times q = 6q$ and $a \times b \times c = abc$.
   Thus when we use the algebra shorthand we frequently omit the multiplication '$\times$' sign. Notice also that the order in which quantities are multiplied together does not matter. Obviously $3 \times 4 = 4 \times 3$. Thus, for example,

   $$pq = qp \quad \text{and} \quad abc = bac = cab \quad \text{etc.}$$

2. We write $a \times a \times a = aaa = a^3$ and $b \times b \times b \times b \times b = bbbbb = b^5$.
   Thus the power notation we used when manipulating numbers is also made use of in algebra. Similarly,

   (i) $a \times a \times c \times c \times c = a^2 \times c^3 = a^2 c^3$

   (ii) $p \times p \times p \times q \times r \times r = p^3 \times q \times r^2 = p^3 q r^2$

3. We write $a \times (b + c) = a(b + c) = ab + ac$.
   Thus, as with numbers, the brackets imply that the 'b' and 'c' are first to be added and then their sum multiplied by 'a'. That is, the 'a' is multiplied by both the 'b' and the 'c'. Similarly,

   (i) $(a + b) \times c = (a + b)c = ac + bc$

   (ii) $6 \times (a + b) = 6(a + b) = 6a + 6b$

4. The rules concerning brackets and otherwise performing multiplication/division before addition/subtraction apply in algebra just as they apply when handling numbers. For example,

   (i) $a \times b + c = ab + c$ but $a \times (b + c) = ab + ac$

   (ii) $p + q \times r = p + qr$ but $(p + q) \times r = pr + qr$

5. We write $a \div b = \dfrac{a}{b}$ and $w \div z = \dfrac{w}{z}$.

Thus we use the same notation for algebra as we used when dividing with numbers. Notice that we also write

(i) $a \div (b + c) = \dfrac{a}{b + c}$

(ii) $(p - q) \div r = \dfrac{p - q}{r}$

Note, in particular, that

$$a + \frac{b}{c} \quad \text{is } not \text{ the same as} \quad \frac{a + b}{c}$$

This is the case because

$$a + \frac{b}{c} = a + b \div c \quad \text{but} \quad \frac{a + b}{c} = (a + b) \div c$$

In the second case the brackets take precedence over the division sign. To understand this, suppose $a = 3$, $b = 4$ and $c = 2$. Then

$$a + \frac{b}{c} = 3 + \frac{4}{2} = 3 + 2 = 5$$

but

$$\frac{a + b}{c} = \frac{3 + 4}{2} = \frac{7}{2} = 3.5$$

Remember that the rules for handling negative quantities apply when using algebra. That is, *two negatives make a positive*, and *one negative and one positive make a negative*. For example,

(i) $-a \times -a = a^2$

(ii) $-p^2 \times p^3 = -p^5$

(iii) $m^{-2} \times -m^5 = -m^3$

(iv) $-3(a - b) = -3a + 3b$

(v) $-y(2z - y) = -2yz + y^2$

(vi) $-(u - v) = -u + v$

(vii) $-3c(ab - c) = -3cab + 3c^2$

In particular be careful with negative signs when multiplying out brackets.

Exercises 6

(a) Simplify the following:

(i) $5y + 8y - 4y =$

(ii) $3z + 4y - 2z + 3y =$

(iii) $3zy + 2yz =$

(iv) $2a^2 + 5ab + 2a^2 - 3ba =$

(v) $3pqr - rpq + 4prq =$

(b) Expand the following:

(i) $(p + 3)p =$

(ii) $-3(4z - 2y) =$

(iii) $a^2(2a^2 + b^2) =$

(iv) $-m(n - m^2) =$

(v) $-(z^2 - y^3)y^2 =$

Some examples of the use of the algebra shorthand

Example 3

A factory makes wooden chairs. Each chair needs 0.05 tonnes of wood, 0.2 hours of machine time and 1.3 hours of labour time. If q chairs are constructed, write down algebraic expressions for the quantities of wood, machine time and labour time required.

Solution

wood required $= 0.05 \times q = 0.05q$ tonnes

machine time required $= 0.2 \times q = 0.2q$ hours

labour time required $= 1.3 \times q = 1.3q$ hours

Suppose that the price of wood is p per tonne, the price of machine time is r per hour and the price of labour is w per hour. Obtain an algebraic expression or 'formula' for the total cost of making q chairs.

Solution

cost of wood $= 0.05q \times p = 0.05qp$

cost of machine time $= 0.2q \times r = 0.2qr$

cost of labour time $= 1.3q \times w = 1.3qw$

If we let C be the total cost of making q chairs, then

$C = 0.05qp + 0.2qr + 1.3qw$

or

$C = q(0.05p + 0.2r + 1.3w)$

We have the required formula for total cost C, which we could now make use of. For example, if $p = 10$, $r = 15$ and $w = 5$, we can use the formula for C to find the total cost of making $q = 100$ chairs. For these values

$$C = 100(0.05 \times 10 + 0.2 \times 15 + 1.3 \times 5) = \pounds1000$$

Example 4

A woman has a husband, n sons and m daughters. When she dies she leaves a sum of money, $\pounds k$, to be shared out among her family. The woman's will says that her husband and sons are to get $\pounds c$ each and the rest of the money is to be shared equally between her daughters. Find an algebraic expression for the amount, M, that each daughter gets.

Solution

The sons get $c \times n = cn$ altogether. The husband also gets c. Thus

amount received by sons and husband $= cn + c = c(n + 1)$

amount left for daughters $= k - c(n + 1)$

Hence

Each daughter receives $M = \dfrac{k - c(n + 1)}{m}$

If necessary, we can make use of the expression or 'formula' for M above. For example, suppose the woman has $n = 3$ sons and $m = 2$ daughters, and leaves $k = \pounds50\,000$ altogether with $c = 5000$ going to the husband and each son. Each daughter will now receive

$$M = \frac{50\,000 - 5000(3 + 1)}{2} = \pounds15\,000$$

Example 5

A firm manufactures wooden chairs which it can sell any number of at a fixed cost of £30 per chair. The factory's costs are a fixed or overhead cost of £8000, plus a variable cost of £20 per chair that is made. Using the symbol q for output (in chairs) find an expression for the factory's total profit, Π, in terms of q. Hence find the firm's profit (a) when output $q = 2000$, (b) when output $q = 500$.

Solution

the firm's total revenue $=$ price $\times$ output $= 30 \times q = 30q$

the firm's total cost $=$ fixed cost $+$ variable cost

$$= 8000 + 20 \times q = 8000 + 20q$$

the firm's total profit $\Pi =$ total revenue $-$ total cost or

$$\Pi = 30q - (8000 + 20q) = 10q - 8000$$

Using the 'formula' for profit Π, we have

when $q = 2000$, $\quad \Pi = 10(2000) - 8000 = £12\,000$

when $q = 500$, $\quad \Pi = 10(500) - 8000 = -£3000$

Notice the value $\Pi = -£3000$ implies that the firm makes a loss when output is as low as 500.

More about expanding brackets in algebra

When a bracket with a single term inside is squared then *everything* inside the bracket must be squared. For example,

(i) $(2p)^2 = 2p \times 2p = 2 \times 2 \times p \times p = 4p^2$

(ii) $(4y)^2 = 4y \times 4y = 4 \times 4 \times y \times y = 16y^2$

Similarly $(3z)^2 = 9z^2$, $(8t)^2 = 64t^2$, etc.

Note the difference between $4p^2$ and $(4p)^2$. With $4p^2$ only the 'p' has to be squared. For example, if $p = 2$ then

$$4p^2 = 4 \times 2^2 = 16 \quad \text{but} \quad (4p)^2 = (4 \times 2)^2 = 64$$

Everything inside a bracket must also be squared in cases like

(i) $(pq)^2 = pq \times pq = p^2q^2$

(ii) $(ab^2)^2 = ab^2 \times ab^2 = a^2b^4$

(iii) $(z^3y^4)^2 = z^3y^4 \times z^3y^4 = z^6y^8$

(iv) $(2u^2v)^2 = 2u^2v \times 2u^2v = 4u^4v^2$

Powers other than 2 can be applied to brackets containing a single term. For example,

(i) $(ab)^4 = ab \times ab \times ab \times ab = a^4b^4$

(ii) $(p^2q^2)^3 = p^2q^2 \times p^2q^2 \times p^2q^2 = p^6q^6$

(iii) $(n^3m)^3 = n^3m \times n^3m \times n^3m = n^9m^3$

(iv) $(a^4c^2)^4 = a^{16}c^8$

(v) $(y^2z^3)^5 = y^{10}z^{15}$

Notice that in these last examples we are really applying an extension of rule 3 in the section on the powers of numbers.

Exercises 7

(i) $(5p)^2 =$

(ii) $(-3q)^2 =$

(iii) $(a^3b)^2 =$

(iv) $(p^3q^3)^2 =$

(v) $(z^2y)^4 =$

(vi) $(-m^4n^2)^6 =$

Multiplying bracketed terms together

When faced with an expression like $(p + 2)(q + 4)$, each term in one bracket has to be multiplied in turn by each term in the other bracket. This will give four quantities in all which then are added up. This is most easily done by forming a 'square':

	p	2
q	pq	$2q$
4	$4p$	8

Thus $(p + 2)(q + 4) = pq + 4p + 2q + 8$

Similarly, when faced with $(y + 2z)(3p + z)$, form the 'square':

	y	$2z$
$3p$	$3yp$	$6pz$
z	yz	$2z^2$

Thus $(y + 2z)(3p + z) = 3yp + yz + 6pz + 2z^2$

Let us check that the above is true when, for example, $y = 2$, $z = 1$ and $p = 3$. Firstly

$(y + 2z)(3p + z) = (2 + 2)(9 + 1) = 40$

Alternatively

$3yp + yz + 6pz + 2z^2 = 3 \times 2 \times 3 + 2 \times 1 + 6 \times 3 \times 1 + 2 \times 1 \times 1 = 40$

Notice that the same answer of 40 is obtained in each case but that the answer is more quickly found when the expression is kept in bracketed terms.

Sometimes you can *group terms when forming squares*. For example, consider $(2p + 5)(3p + 2)$. In this case

	$2p$	5
$3p$	$6p^2$	$15p$
2	$4p$	10

$(2p + 5)(3p + 2) = 6p^2 + 4p + 15p + 10 = 6p^2 + 19p + 10$

Thus, in this example, we have to group the terms $4p$ and $15p$ to make the $19p$.

It is important to *watch out for negative signs* when forming 'squares'. For example, consider $(3p - 2q)(p - 3)$:

	$3p$	$-2q$
p	$3p^2$	$-2pq$
-3	$-9p$	$+6q$

$(3p - 2q)(p - 3) = 3p^2 - 9p - 2pq + 6q$

Squaring more complicated bracketed terms

We have seen that $(4y)^2 = 16y^2$ etc. To square more complicated bracketed terms, note that, for example, we can write

$$(y + 4)^2 = (y + 4)(y + 4)$$

We can now form a 'square' in the usual way.

	y	4
y	y^2	$4y$
4	$4y$	16

$(y + 4)^2 = y^2 + 4y + 4y + 16 = y^2 + 8y + 16$

where the two $4y$'s can be grouped together.

When you are squaring terms such as $(y + 4)$, you will always have to group two terms that are the same. For example, to square $(2p + q)$ we have

$$(2p + q)^2 = (2p + q)(2p + q)$$

	$2p$	q
$2p$	$4p^2$	$2pq$
q	$2qp$	q^2

$(2p + q)^2 = 4p^2 + 2qp + 2pq + q^2 = 4p^2 + 4pq + q^2$

Be careful not to fall into the trap of writing

$$(2p + q)^2 = 4p^2 + q^2$$

It is easy to fail to include the terms $2pq = 2qp$.

Finally, again remember to watch out for negative signs and the rules for handling them. For example, to form $(3v - 2u)^2$, we have

	$3v$	$-2u$
$3v$	$9v^2$	$-6vu$
$-2u$	$-6uv$	$4u^2$

$(3v - 2u)^2 = 9v^2 - 6vu - 6uv + 4u^2 = 9v^2 - 12uv + 4u^2$

Exercises 8

Multiply out the following by forming 'squares'.

(i) $(x + 4)(2y + 2) =$

(ii) $(3m + n)(3n + m) =$

(iii) $(2p - 3)(q + 2p) =$

(iv) $(2x + 4)^2 =$

(v) $(3x - 4)(3x + 4) =$

Algebraic fractions

Just like an ordinary fraction, an algebraic fraction takes the form

$$\frac{\text{numerator}}{\text{denominator}}$$

For example,

$$\frac{p}{q}, \quad \frac{3a}{a+c}, \quad \frac{6}{y}, \quad \frac{mn}{uv}$$

are all algebraic fractions. The rules for handing algebraic fractions are exactly the same as for ordinary fractions.

Multiplication

Just as

$$\frac{5}{3} \times 7 = \frac{35}{3} \quad \text{and} \quad 5 \times \frac{11}{4} = \frac{55}{4}$$

so we write, for example,

$$\frac{p}{q} \times r = \frac{pr}{q} \quad \text{or} \quad y \times \frac{c}{d} = \frac{yc}{d}$$

Remember, though, to make use of brackets when necessary:

(i) $\quad s \times \dfrac{u+v}{w} = \dfrac{s(u+v)}{w}$

(ii) $\quad \dfrac{b+c}{a} \times d = \dfrac{d(b+c)}{a}$

(iii) $\quad 5 \times \dfrac{p}{p+q} = \dfrac{5p}{p+q}$

(iv) $\quad \dfrac{m}{n} \times (a+b) = \dfrac{m(a+b)}{n}$

Just as

$$\frac{5}{3} \times \frac{3}{7} = \frac{15}{21} \quad \text{and} \quad \frac{2}{3} \times \frac{5}{9} = \frac{10}{27}$$

so we can write

$$\frac{a}{b} \times \frac{x}{z} = \frac{ax}{bz}$$

Similarly, again using brackets when required:

(i) $\dfrac{p}{q} \times \dfrac{m+n}{r} = \dfrac{p(m+n)}{qr}$

(ii) $\dfrac{3}{b} \times \dfrac{a}{4} = \dfrac{3a}{4b}$

(iii) $\dfrac{z}{a} \times \dfrac{y}{a+b} = \dfrac{zy}{a(a+b)}$

(iv) $\dfrac{y-z}{z} \times \dfrac{p}{p+q} = \dfrac{p(y-z)}{z(p+q)}$

(v) $\dfrac{u}{2a} \times \dfrac{v}{3a} = \dfrac{uv}{6a^2}$

(vi) $\dfrac{y}{p+q} \times y = \dfrac{y^2}{p+q}$

Just as $a \times a = a^2$ so we can write

$$\frac{a}{b} \times \frac{a}{b} = \left(\frac{a}{b}\right)^2 = \frac{a^2}{b^2}$$

Similarly,

(i) $\left(\dfrac{3}{p}\right)^2 = \dfrac{9}{p^2}$

(ii) $\left(\dfrac{mn}{p}\right)^2 = \dfrac{m^2 n^2}{p^2}$

(iii) $\left(\dfrac{y}{2b}\right)^3 = \dfrac{y^3}{8b^3}$

Exercises 9

(i) $\dfrac{p}{q} \times \dfrac{p^2}{p+q} =$

(ii) $\dfrac{a}{b+c} \times \dfrac{a^2}{c} \times \dfrac{b}{b+c} =$

(iii) $\left(\dfrac{mn}{pq}\right)^2 \times \dfrac{m}{q} =$

(iv) $\dfrac{3m}{n} \times \dfrac{2m(n+3)}{3n(m+4)} =$

(v) $\dfrac{z+y}{z^3} \times \dfrac{(z+y)^2}{z} \times \dfrac{y}{z^2} =$

Simplifying fractions

The ordinary fraction $\frac{12}{18}$ can be simplified to

$$\frac{12}{18} = \frac{6 \times 2}{6 \times 3} = \frac{2}{3}$$

This is possible because both numerator and denominator can be divided by the *factor* 6, which may be 'cancelled out'. The six is referred to as a factor because it can be divided exactly into both numerator and denominator.

The same procedure may be followed to simplify algebraic fractions. For example,

$$\frac{ab}{bd} = \frac{a \times b}{b \times d} = \frac{a}{d} \quad \text{or} \quad \frac{pq}{rq} = \frac{p \times q}{r \times q} = \frac{p}{r}$$

In the first case the factor b can be cancelled out and in the second case the factor q. Often a mathematician will miss out one of the steps and just write, for this example,

$$\frac{a\cancel{b}}{\cancel{b}d} = \frac{a}{d}$$

It is possible to cancel out more than one factor at the same time and also to cancel out the same factor more than once. For example,

(i) $\dfrac{f\cancel{g}h}{f\cancel{h}j} = \dfrac{g}{j}$

(ii) $\dfrac{w^2 yz}{wyx} = \dfrac{wz}{x}$

(iii) $\dfrac{6yz}{3ya} = \dfrac{2z}{a}$

(iv) $\dfrac{4a^2 b}{3ca^2} = \dfrac{4b}{3c}$

(v) $\dfrac{5p^3 q^2}{p^2 q} = 5pq$

(vi) $\dfrac{4a^2}{5b} \times \dfrac{5b^2}{2a} = \dfrac{20a^2 b^2}{10ab} = 2ab$

Note carefully that a number or letter can only be cancelled out *if it is a factor of both numerator and denominator*. For example,

$$\frac{4 \times 3}{4 \times 2} = \frac{3}{2} \quad \text{but we cannot write} \quad \frac{4+3}{4 \times 2} \quad \text{as} \quad \frac{3}{2}$$

This is because 4 is a factor of 4×3 but it is not a factor of $4 + 3$.

Similarly,

$$\frac{a \times b}{a \times c} = \frac{b}{c} \quad \text{but we cannot write} \quad \frac{a+b}{a \times c} \quad \text{as} \quad \frac{1+b}{1 \times c}$$

In the first case the a can be cancelled because a is a factor of both $a \times b$ and $a \times c$, but in the second case the a is not a factor of $a + b$ and therefore cannot be cancelled.

Also,

$$\frac{a(y + b)}{ac} = \frac{y + b}{c} \quad \text{but we cannot write} \quad \frac{ay + b}{ac} \quad \text{as} \quad \frac{y + b}{c}$$

Again, in the first case the a is a factor of $a(y + b)$ and can be cancelled, but in the second case the a is not a factor of $ay + b$.

Thus it is only possible to simplify algebraic fractions by the correct cancelling out of factors. For example,

(i) $\dfrac{ac}{a(z + y)} = \dfrac{c}{z + y}$

(ii) $\dfrac{wx}{w + y}$ cannot be simplified

(iii) $\dfrac{b^2}{2bc} = \dfrac{b}{2c}$

(iv) $\dfrac{7w + u}{3w}$ cannot be simplified

(v) $\dfrac{m^2}{m(n + 2)} = \dfrac{m}{n + 2}$

(vi) $\dfrac{y^2 w}{y^2} = w$

(vii) $\dfrac{a^2 b + c}{ab^2}$ cannot be simplified

Exercises 10

Simplify the following when possible. If simplification is not possible simply write 'will not simplify'.

(i) $\dfrac{y^2}{3y + 3}$

(ii) $\dfrac{n(m + n)}{3n^2}$

(iii) $\dfrac{p^2 q}{pq + r}$

(iv) $\dfrac{a^2 b + 4a}{abc}$

(v) $\dfrac{x^2 y}{x^3 y^2 + xy}$

(vi) $\dfrac{xyz}{x + y + z}$

Reciprocals and division

The reciprocal of a number is obtained by dividing unity (i.e. 1) by that number. Thus the reciprocal of 5 is $1/5 = 0.2$, the reciprocal of $1/3$ is 3 and the reciprocal of 0.25 is 4. Obviously if we multiply a number by its reciprocal we always obtain unity. For example, $5 \times 1/5 = 1$,

$1/3 \times 3 = 1$ and $0.25 \times 4 = 1$. Since multiplying something by its reciprocal always yields unity, the reciprocal of an ordinary fraction can always be obtained by turning the fraction 'upside down'. For example, $\frac{3}{4}$ is the reciprocal of $\frac{4}{3}$ and $\frac{7}{5}$ is the reciprocal of $\frac{5}{7}$.

The reciprocal of an algebraic fraction is also obtained by dividing unity by that fraction. Again, the reciprocal of an algebraic function can always be found by turning the fraction 'upside down'. For example,

(i) since $\dfrac{a}{b} \times \dfrac{b}{a} = 1$, the reciprocal of $\dfrac{a}{b}$ is $\dfrac{b}{a}$

(ii) since $\dfrac{m}{m+n} \times \dfrac{m+n}{m} = 1$, the reciprocal of $\dfrac{m}{m+n}$ is $\dfrac{m+n}{m}$

(iii) since $\dfrac{1}{p} \times p = 1$, the reciprocal of $\dfrac{1}{p}$ is p

(iv) since $\dfrac{r^2}{s} \times \dfrac{s}{r^2} = 1$ the reciprocal of $\dfrac{r^2}{s}$ is $\dfrac{s}{r^2}$

Division

It should be clear that *dividing by a number is equivalent to multiplying by its reciprocal.* For example, dividing 10 by 5 is the same as multiplying 10 by 1/5. Similarly, $20 \div \frac{1}{4}$ is equivalent to 20×4 since 4 is the reciprocal of $\frac{1}{4}$. The same rule can be applied when dividing with algebraic fractions. Dividing by an algebraic fraction is the same as multiplying by its reciprocal. For example,

(i) $\dfrac{a}{b} \div \dfrac{p}{q} = \dfrac{a}{b} \times \dfrac{q}{p} = \dfrac{aq}{bp}$

(ii) $\dfrac{m}{p} \div \dfrac{n}{3} = \dfrac{m}{p} \times \dfrac{3}{n} = \dfrac{3m}{pn}$

(iii) $\dfrac{4}{c} \div \dfrac{a}{b} = \dfrac{4}{c} \times \dfrac{b}{a} = \dfrac{4b}{ac}$

(iv) $\dfrac{a^2}{b} \div \dfrac{a}{c} = \dfrac{a^2}{b} \times \dfrac{c}{a} = \dfrac{ac}{b}$

(v) $\dfrac{mv^2}{r} \div \dfrac{2r}{a} = \dfrac{mv^2}{r} \times \dfrac{a}{2r} = \dfrac{amv^2}{2r^2}$

(vi) $\dfrac{4q^2}{p} \div qp^2 = \dfrac{4q^2}{p} \times \dfrac{1}{qp^2} = \dfrac{4q}{p^3}$

Exercises 11

(i) $\dfrac{mn}{pq} \div \dfrac{ma}{rq} =$

(ii) $\dfrac{(a-c)^2}{c^3} \div \dfrac{a-b}{c^2} =$

(iii) $\dfrac{(ab)^3}{a+c} \div \dfrac{ab}{(a+c)^2} =$

(iv) $\dfrac{pq}{rs} \div \dfrac{p^2}{(rs)^2} =$

The solution of simple equations

On a number of previous occasions we have found it necessary to substitute values for a variable into an algebraic expression, thus finding a specific numerical value for the expression. For example, suppose a consumer makes an 80p return bus journey and buys x oranges at a price of 20p per orange. The consumer's total expenditure is therefore $20x + 80$ pence. If 10 oranges are purchased then total expenditure is

$$20x + 80 = 20(10) + 80 = 280p$$

Similarly, if $x = 5$, then total expenditure is

$$20x + 80 = 20(5) + 80 = 180p$$

Frequently, however, we may find that we wish to reverse the process. Suppose, knowing that total expenditure is actually 240p, we wish to find the number of oranges bought. That is, we require the value of x that makes total expenditure $20x + 80$ equal to 240. A mathematician would say that we wish to *solve the equation*

$$20x + 80 = 240 \tag{1}$$

for the value of x. That is, we have to find the value for x that makes the equation 'correct', in the sense that the quantities on the left- and right-hand sides of the equality sign become the same.

One way of solving such an equation is to try substituting different values of x into the equation until we find a value for x that makes the left- and right-hand sides of the equation equal. Eventually this 'trial and error' method will lead us to the answer $x = 8$ oranges, which yields the value 240p for both sides of the equation. The value $x = 8$ which makes the equation 'correct' is known as a *solution to the equation.*

Rather than finding a solution to an equation by 'trial and error' methods, mathematicians prefer more systematic methods, making use of the rules of algebra. Consider again the equation [1]. Suppose we subtract the number 80 from either side of the equation. This yields

$$20x + 80 - 80 = 240 - 80$$

Thus

$$20x = 160 \tag{2}$$

If we now divide both sides of [2] by 20 we obtain

$$20x \div 20 = 160 \div 20$$

or

$$x = 8 \qquad\qquad [3]$$

Rather than using a trial and error method, we have found the solution [3] to the equation [1] by a systematic process. When solving an equation in this way, it is permissible to perform any algebraic operation (e.g. addition, multiplication, etc.) to the left-hand side of an equation provided we perform the identical operation to the right-hand side. Clearly, if the left and right sides of the equation are originally equal, then they must remain equal if identical operations are performed on both sides of the equation. Although we consider only very simple equations in this subsection, it is possible to apply these ideas to far more complicated equations.

As a further simple example, we find a solution to the equation

$$5x - 5 = 2x + 4 \qquad\qquad [4]$$

Firstly adding 5 from each side of eqn [4] gives

$$5x = 2x + 4 + 5 = 2x + 9 \qquad\qquad [5]$$

Next, subtracting $2x$ from either side

$$5x - 2x = 9 \quad \rightarrow \quad 3x = 9 \qquad\qquad [6]$$

Finally dividing both sides by 3 gives the solution

$$x = 3$$

Note that it is always sensible to bring all terms in x to the left-hand sign of the equality sign and to bring all numbers to the right. Notice also that the process of adding or subtracting quantities to both sides of an equation can be regarded as the taking of quantities 'across the equality sign', provided we remember to change their sign. For example, to move from [4] to [5] above, we take the -5 across the equality sign to the right-hand side, making it $+5$. Similarly, to move from [5] to [6] above, we take the $2x$ across the equality sign to the left-hand side, making it $-2x$.

Sometimes equations can look more complicated than they really are. For example, consider the equation

$$2(3x + 2) - 12 = 2x - 5(2x - 4) \qquad\qquad [7]$$

To solve an equation, always remember that we are seeking a value that makes the left- and right-hand sides of the equation equal after substitution of a solution value for x. The first step in solving equations such as [7] is to remove all brackets. Hence [7] becomes

$$6x + 4 - 12 = 2x - 10x + 20$$

Taking all terms in x to the left gives

$$6x - 2x + 10x + 4 - 12 = 20$$

Taking all numbers to the right gives

$$6x - 2x + 10x = 20 - 4 + 12$$

or

$$14x = 28$$

We therefore obtain the solution $x = 2$ to the original equation [7]. Of course, if necessary, when solving equations such as [7], many of the steps required can be performed simultaneously, once the process has become familiar.

Finally, once a solution has been obtained to an equation, it is always a worthwhile arithmetic check to see whether substitution of the solution into the original equation does indeed give the same values for both left- and right-hand sides! For example, for eqn [7] when $x = 2$,

left-hand side $= 2(6 + 2) - 12 = 4$

right-hand side $= 4 - 5(4 - 4) = 4$

This verifies that eqn [7] does have the solution $x = 2$.

Exercises 12

Solve the following equations:

(i) $2x - 5 = 4x - 11$.
(ii) $0.5x = 0.25x - 8$.
(iii) $4(x - 3) - 2(3x - 2) = 5(3 - 2x)$.
(iv) A factory has fixed costs of £5000. For every unit the factory produces it faces variable costs of £120 per unit. If the factory has total costs of £11 000 how many units are being produced?
(v) A college course involves coursework and an end of term examination. The aggregate mark for the course is determined by a 40:60 weighting between coursework and examination. If a student is given 64 per cent for coursework, what mark is required in the examination to obtain an aggregate mark of 50 per cent?
(vi) A factory has a marginal cost schedule $MC = 10 + 3q$, where q is output. Its marginal revenue schedule is $MR = 130 - 5q$. If profits are maximised when $MC = MR$, what is the factory's profit-maximising output?

Answers to exercises

1 (i) 10 (ii) 3 (iii) 17 (iv) 49 (v) 5 (vi) 4 (vii) 24 (viii) 63

2 (i) 8/3, 3/4, 7/3, 5/6 (ii) 1/2 (iii) 27/35 (iv) 25/8 (v) 34/21 (vi) 24/11 (vii) 4/3 (viii) 49/12 (ix) 8/7 (x) 6/7 (xi) 9/5

3 (i) –3 (ii) 5/3 (iii) 3/2 (iv) 4 (v) –8/5 (vi) –4/5

4 (i) 39.304 (ii) 7.594 (iii) 2187 (iv) 256 (v) 4822.53 (vi) 0.0156 (vii) 4096 (viii) 4096 (ix) 0.0878

5 (i) 5 (ii) 2.25 (iii) –128 (iv) 1 (v) 1 (vi) 4 (vii) 0.2 (viii) 1.778 (ix) 3.482 (x) 3.737 (xi) 4 (xii) 0.333

6 (a) (i) $9y$ (ii) $z + 7y$ (iii) $5zy$ (iv) $4a^2 + 2ab$ (v) $6pqr$ (b) (i) $p^2 + 3p$ (ii) $-12z + 6y$ (iii) $2a^4 + a^2b^2$ (iv) $-mn + m^3$ (v) $-z^2y^2 + y^5$

7 (i) $25p^2$ (ii) $9q^2$ (iii) a^6b^2 (iv) p^6q^6 (v) z^8y^4 (vi) $m^{24}n^{12}$

8 (i) $2xy + 2x + 8y + 8$
(ii) $10mn + 3m^2 + 3n^2$
(iii) $2pq + 4p^2 - 3q - 6p$
(iv) $4x^2 + 16x + 16$ **(v)** $9x^2 - 16$

9 (i) $\dfrac{p^3}{q(p+q)}$ **(ii)** $\dfrac{a^3 b}{a(b+c)^2}$

(iii) $\dfrac{m^3 n^2}{p^2 q^3}$ **(iv)** $\dfrac{2m^2(n+3)}{n^2(m+4)}$ **(v)** $\dfrac{y(z+y)^3}{z^6}$

10 (i) will not simplify **(ii)** $\dfrac{m+n}{3n}$

(iii) will not simplify **(iv)** $\dfrac{ab+4}{abc}$

(v) $\dfrac{x}{x^2 y + 1}$ **(vi)** will not simplify

11 (i) $\dfrac{nr}{pa}$ **(ii)** $\dfrac{(a-c)^2}{c(a-b)}$ **(iii)** $a^2 b^2 (a+c)$

(iv) $\dfrac{q^4 rs}{p}$

12 (i) $x = 3$ **(ii)** $x = -32$ **(iii)** $x = 2.875$
(iv) $x = 50$ units **(v)** 41 per cent
(vi) $q = 15$

1 Functions and equations

1.1 Variables and functions

When a measurable quantity, for example the level of unemployment, can take a number of different values we refer to it as a *variable*. Obviously, if we observed the level of unemployment in different countries we would obtain, almost certainly, different measurements. Similarly, if we observed the level of unemployment in a particular country over successive years, we would again obtain variations in our measurements. This is in complete contrast to measurements of, for example, the speed of light. Provided our experiments were accurate, we would find that, regardless of when and where we measured it, the speed of light was 3×10^{10} cm per second. We therefore refer to this quantity as a *constant*.

Students of economics will be familiar with the fact that variables tend to be related to each other. The rate of money wage inflation normally declines as the level of unemployment rises. Consumer expenditure usually rises when disposable income rises. The demand for a good falls when its price rises. When such relationships are 'systematic' in the sense that a given value for one such variable always results in the same unique value for the other variable, we say that the one variable is a *function* of the other and that, hence, there is a functional relationship between them. for example, suppose

$$y = 2x^2 + 3x \qquad [1.1]$$

If y and x are related in this way, then whenever x takes the value 2, for example, y always takes the value $y = 2(2)^2 + 3(2) = 14$. Similarly when $x = -5$, y will always take the value 35, and whenever $x = 2000$, y always takes the value 8 006 000. y is therefore said to be a function of x (the function being $2x^2 + 3x$) and [1.1] describes the functional relationship between them.

Notice that if [1.1] holds then for every value of x there is a corresponding value of y. What this functional relationship does is provide *a rule by which we can transform x-values into their corresponding y-values*. Functions can, of course, take many forms. For example, we could have any of the following functional relationships

$$y = x^3 \qquad [1.2]$$

$$y = 10x + 3 \qquad [1.3]$$

$$y = 8x^2 + 5 \qquad [1.4]$$

Equations [1.2]–[1.4] all provide rules by which x-values are transformed into y-values. In the first case, y-values are obtained by 'cubing' the relevant x-value, in the second case by multiplying the x-value by 10 and adding 3 and in the third case by multiplying the square of the x-value by 8 and adding 5.

Notice that it is mathematically possible to have an equation or relationship involving x and y which is not a functional relationship in the sense we have just defined. For example, if

$$y = \sqrt{x} \qquad\qquad [1.5]$$

then if x takes the value 9, since the square root of 9 is either $+3$ or -3, the corresponding value of y is not unique but can be either $y = +3$ or $y = -3$. Similarly, if $x = 25$ then $y = +5$ or -5. Since for a given x-value there is not a unique y-value, [1.5] is not a function under our definition.[1] However, we shall not be concerned much with relationships of the kind [1.5] in this book.

It is often the case in economics that we believe or are aware that one variable is a function of another but are unable or do not wish to specify the exact functional relationship between them. For example, we may know that y is a function of x but not know whether the precise form of the function is [1.1], [1.2], [1.3] or [1.4]. When this is the case we simply write

$$y = f(x) \qquad\qquad [1.6]$$

The relationship [1.6] is simply a shorthand way of writing 'y is a function of x'. The form of the function is unspecified. It could be [1.1], [1.2], [1.3] or [1.4] or something entirely different. Notice that [1.6] does *not* mean that y equals f times x! A variety of letters, both English and Greek, can be used to express the fact that y is a function of x. For example,

$$y = y(x); \quad y = a(x); \quad y = \varphi(x)$$

are all regarded by mathematicians as acceptable shorthand notations for the statement 'y is a function of x'. It is also customary to refer to y as the *dependent variable* and x as the *independent variable* (y depends on x).

It is not difficult to think of situations in economics when we might want to make use of this notation. For example, other things being equal, the demand for a good is a function of its price. We can write this in shorthand as

$$d = f(p) \quad \text{or} \quad d = d(p)$$

where $d =$ demand and $p =$ price. Similarly, other things being equal, the level of fixed capital investment in an economy depends on the rate of interest. We can write this in shorthand as

$$I = f(r) \quad \text{or} \quad I = I(r) \qquad\qquad [1.7]$$

where $I =$ fixed investment and $r =$ rate of interest.

For example, we might have the functional relationship between I in £ billion and r in percentage points,

$$I = 200 + \frac{1000}{r^2} \qquad\qquad [1.8]$$

We can then use [1.8] to obtain the exact unique value for I for any given value of r. For example, if the rate of interest $r = 5$, then we obtain $I = 200 + 1000/(5)^2 = £240$ billion. Alternatively, if $r = 10$ then $I = 200 + 1000/(10)^2 = £210$ billion.

Example 1.1

Consider the following functional relationships:

(a) $y = 8x^2 - 5x + 3$

(b) $y = \dfrac{5}{x} + 10$

(c) $y = (2x + 3)^3$

Find in each case the corresponding value of y when x takes the value:

(i) $x = 2$　(ii) $x = -3$　(iii) $x = 100$.

Example 1.2

If $z = 6t^4 + 3t^2 + 10$, find the corresponding values of z when $t = 4$ and when $t = -6$.

Example 1.3

Express in the function shorthand the following statements:

(a) Consumption depends on income.
(b) The demand for money depends on the rate of interest.
(c) Average cost depends on output.

1.2　Coordinate systems

Most readers will be familiar with the concept of a coordinate system. The horizontal and vertical 'axes' drawn in Fig. 1.1 intersect at a point called the *origin*. Values of a variable y are measured on the vertical axis (known as the *y-axis*) and values of a variable x measured on the horizontal axis (known as the *x-axis*). Positive values of y are measured above the origin and negative values below. Positive values of x are measured to the right of the origin and negative values to the left.

Any pair of values for the variables x and y can now be represented by a point in such a coordinate system. For example, the pair of values $x = 3$ and $y = -2$ can be represented by point A in Fig. 1.1 obtained by moving rightwards 3 units from the origin along the x-axis and downwards 2 units along the y-axis.

It is customary to refer to point A as the point $(3, -2)$. The numbers in brackets are the x-value (placed first) and the y-value of point A. The x-value is known as the x-*coordinate* (sometimes called the abscissa) and the y-value as the y-*coordinate* (sometimes called the ordinate).

Further points are plotted in Fig. 1.1. For example, B is the point $(7, 4)$ – that is, the point with an x-coordinate of 7 and a y-coordinate of 4. It represents that pair of values $x = 7$ and $y = 4$. Similarly, point C on the x-axis has the coordinates $(-3, 0)$ and point D on the y-axis has the coordinates $(0, 5)$.

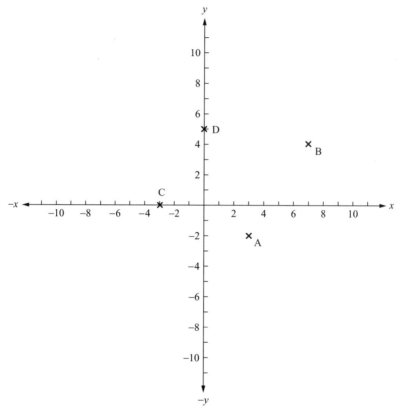

Fig. 1.1 A coordinate system

Example 1.4

Plot the points $(-5, -8)$, $(6, -4)$, $(0, -6)$, $(-3, 2)$, $(0, 0)$, $(2, 0)$ on the coordinate system.

1.3 The graphing of functions

Given the above coordinate system, it is possible to graph or illustrate any function of the kind described previously. For example, consider the functional relationship

$$y = x^2 + 3x - 4 \qquad\qquad [1.9]$$

We know we can use this function to transform any x-values into corresponding y-values. For example, when $x = 3$ the corresponding value is

$$y = (3)^2 + 3(3) - 4 = 14$$

x	−6	−5	−4	−3	−2	−1	0	1	2	3	4
x^2	36	25	16	9	4	1	0	1	4	9	16
3x	−18	−15	−12	−9	−6	−3	0	3	6	9	12
y	14	6	0	−4	−6	−6	−4	0	6	14	24

$(= x^2 + 3x − 4)$

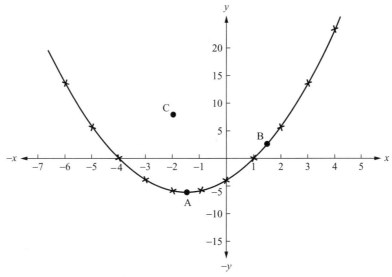

Fig. 1.2 Graph of $y = x^2 + 3x − 4$

This pair of values can be represented by a point (3, 14) in our coordinate system. We can therefore use the function to generate a whole series of pairs of associated values for x and y and hence a whole series of points in the coordinate system. Such a series of points for values of x between −6 and +4 are derived in the table in Fig. 1.2. These points are plotted as crosses on the coordinate system in Fig. 1.2. Notice that it is conventional to measure the dependent variable on the vertical axis and the independent variable on the horizontal axis. That is why previously we labelled these axes the y-axis and the x-axis respectively.

We obtain the graph of the functional relationship [1.9] by sketching a smooth curve through the points in Fig. 1.2. We have not, of course, sketched the whole graph, but only its most interesting part − that between $x = 4$ and $x = −6$. As x increases beyond $x = 4$, y increases indefinitely, and as x decreases beyond $x = −6$, y again increases indefinitely. However, from the section we have sketched we can see the main property of the function. As the value of x falls, the corresponding value of y also falls at first, but at a decreasing rate, eventually reaching a minimum value at point A and then increasing. Since the graph is symmetrical its minimum point occurs when $x = −1.5$. We can find the minimum value of y by substituting $x = −1.5$ into [1.9]. This yields

$$y = (−1.5)^2 + 3(−1.5) − 4 = −6.25$$

Thus the minimum value of y is −6.25 and the coordinates of point A are (−1.5, −6.25).

It is worth emphasising the close relationship between the functional relationship [1.9] and its graph in Fig. 1.2. Clearly *any pair of values for x and y generated by the function can be represented by a point on the graph.* Conversely *any point on the graph in Fig. 1.2 must represent a pair of values for x and y satisfying the functional relationship [1.9].* For example, when $x = 1.5$, [1.9] yields $y = 2.75$, and the point (1.5, 2.75) is point B on the graph in Fig. 1.2.

It is also the case that any pair of values for x and y which do *not* satisfy the functional relationship [1.9] will represent a point that is *not* on the graph in Fig. 1.2. Conversely any point *not* on the graph in Fig. 1.2 will *not* satisfy the functional relationship [1.9]. For example, point C in Fig. 1.2 has the coordinates (−2, 8) but clearly does not satisfy the functional relationship which implies $y = -6$ when $x = -2$.

Example 1.5

Graph the functional relationship $y = 2x^2 + 7x - 4$ from $x = -5$ to $x = 2$ and hence find the minimum value of *y*. Verify that the point $(\frac{1}{2}, 0)$ both satisfies the functional relationship and lies on the graph, but that the point (2, 10) neither satisfies the relationship nor lies on the graph.

Notice that the graph of the functional relationship [1.9] cuts or *intersects* the x-axis at two points. In fact $y = 0$ when either $x = -4$ or $x = 1$. Since, from [1.9], $y = 0$ implies that $x^2 + 3x - 4 = 0$, it follows that we have found the values of x which make $x^2 + 3x - 4 = 0$. Mathematicians refer to this process as solving the *equation*

$$x^2 + 3x - 4 = 0 \qquad\qquad [1.10]$$

The values of x for which eqn [1.10] is 'true' are known as the *solutions* or *roots* of the equation. That is, $x = -4$ and $x = 1$ are the solutions to eqn [1.10] because they are the only values of x which satisfy the equation in the sense that they make its left-hand side equal to its right-hand side. Those who worked through the section on mathematical prerequisites at the beginning of the text will have encountered the notion of the solution to an equation before.

Example 1.6

Use the graph drawn in Example 1.5 to solve the equation $2x^2 + 7x - 4 = 0$.

The function in the relationship [1.9] is a particular case of what is known as a *quadratic function*. The general form of a quadratic function is $f(x) = ax^2 + bx + c$, yielding a functional relationship

$$y = ax^2 + bx + c \qquad\qquad [1.11]$$

It is easily seen that [1.9] is a special case of [1.11] with $a = 1$, $b = 3$ and $c = -4$. The graphs of quadratic functional relationships like [1.11] all have a shape essentially similar to that illustrated in Fig. 1.2, except that, for negative values of a, they have an inverted 'U-shape' rather than a 'U-shape' and have maximum values rather than minimum values. For example,

$$y = -2x^2 + 8x - 13 \qquad\qquad [1.12]$$

has $a = -2$ and is graphed in Fig. 1.3. It has a maximum value of $y = -5$ occurring when $x = 2$.

x	-2	-1	0	1	2	3	4	5	6
$-2x^2$	-8	-2	0	-2	-8	-18	-32	-50	-72
$8x$	-16	-8	0	8	16	24	32	40	48
y	-37	-23	-13	-7	-5	-7	-13	-23	-37

$(= -2x^2 + 8x - 13)$

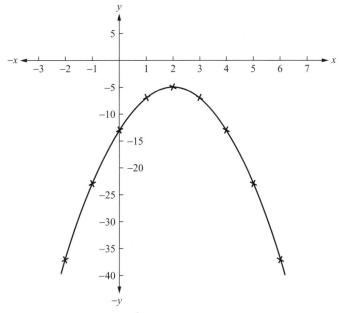

Fig. 1.3 Graph of $y = -2x^2 + 8x - 13$

It should be clear that graphs of quadratic relationships will normally intersect the x-axis either at two points as in Fig. 1.2 or not at all as in Fig. 1.3. Since at such points of intersection, $y = 0$, we see from [1.11] that equations of the form

$$ax^2 + bx + c = 0 \qquad\qquad [1.13]$$

will normally have either two solutions or no solution at all. That is, either there will be two values of x which satisfy eqn [1.13] or there will be no such values. For example, we know that eqn [1.10] has the two solutions $x = -4$ and $x = 1$. However, from Fig. 1.3 we deduce that the equation

$$-2x^2 + 8x - 13 = 0 \qquad\qquad [1.14]$$

has no solution since the graph in Fig. 1.3 does not intersect the x-axis.

Equations of the general form [1.13] are known as *quadratic equations*. We have seen that normally such equations have either two solutions or no solution. However, there is an exception to these normal cases. Have you realised what this exception is and how graphically it can come about?[2]

q	0	1	2	3	4	5
q^2	0	1	4	9	16	25
$2q$	0	2	4	6	8	10
TC	8	11	16	23	32	43

$(= q^2 + 2q + 8)$

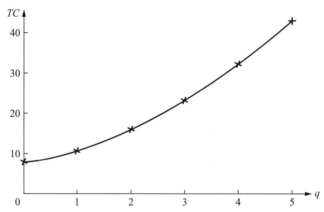

Fig. 1.4 Graph of total cost function [1.15]

Example 1.7

Graph $y = -3x^2 - 2x + 5$ from $x = -2$ to $x = 2$. find the maximum value of y. Use the graph to solve the equation $3x^2 + 2x - 5 = 0$.

Quadratic functions are often used in economics to represent a firm's total cost curve. If a firm produces a quantity q of a single good then total cost TC is written as

$$TC = aq^2 + bq + c \quad q > 0 \qquad [1.15]$$

Such a function is sketched in Fig. 1.4 for the case $a = 1$, $b = 2$ and $c = 8$. Since the dependent variable is now TC, this appears on the vertical axis with q on the horizontal axis. Notice that the function is such that not only do total costs rise as output rises but they rise at an increasing rate as would be expected if one of the factors of production were fixed. Since, when output $q = 0$, $TC = c = 8$ we see that fixed costs are equal to 8. In general fixed or overhead costs are given by the c-term in [1.15].

Strictly speaking, of course, the functional relationship [1.15] also extends to the left of the vertical axis. However, since the firm cannot produce a negative output we are not interested in this part of the function. For this reason, in [1.15] we have restricted the 'range' or *domain* of the relationship to $q > 0$. That is, [1.15] only yields values of total costs for positive outputs. We shall find that we often need to restrict the domain of functions if we are to use them to represent economic relationships.

q	0.25	0.5	1	2	3	4	5	6	7	8
$q + 2$	2.25	2.5	3	4	5	6	7	8	9	10
$8/q$	32	16	8	4	2.67	2	1.6	1.33	1.14	1
AC	34.25	18.5	11	8	7.67	8	8.6	9.33	10.14	11

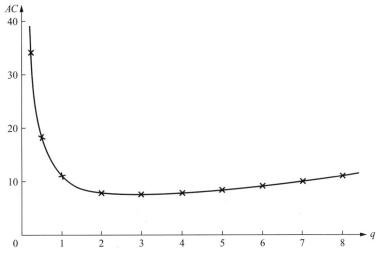

Fig. 1.5 Graph of average cost function [1.16]

Quadratic cost functions of the type [1.15] have the advantage that they imply average cost curves with the traditional U-shape. We obtain the *average cost function* from [1.15] by dividing total cost by output q:

$$AC = \frac{TC}{q} = aq + b + \frac{c}{q} \tag{1.16}$$

where AC is average cost. Such a curve is sketched in Fig. 1.5 for the case $a = 1$, $b = 2$ and $c = 8$. Notice that as output q becomes closer and closer to zero, average cost AC becomes larger and larger. Why is this?

Example 1.8

If the firm's total cost function is $TC = 2q^2 + 5q + 20$, graph its average cost curve and find the level of output q at which average costs are minimised.

1.4 Linear functions and straight lines

The simplest form of function is a *linear function*. A function is said to be linear if it takes the form $f(x) = mx + c$, yielding a functional relationship

$$y = mx + c \tag{1.17}$$

x	−4	−3	−2	−1	0	1	2	3	4
$3x$	−12	−9	−6	−3	0	3	6	9	12
y	−8	−5	−2	1	4	7	10	13	16

$(= 3x + 4)$

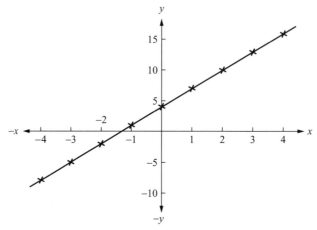

Fig. 1.6 Graph of $y = 3x + 4$

where m and c are constants. For example, if $m = 3$ and $c = 4$, then we have the linear functional relationship

$$y = 3x + 4 \qquad\qquad [1.18]$$

The graph of this relationship is shown in Fig. 1.6. When graphing this function it is immediately apparent that we are graphing a straight line. For every increase of 1 unit in x, y increases by 3 units. For this reason [1.17] is referred to as *the equation of a straight line*. No matter what the values of m and c, the graph of eqn [1.17] will be a straight line. Hence when graphing such a relationship it is only necessary to plot two points and use a straight edge to draw a line passing through these points.[3]

The coefficient m in eqn [1.17] tells us the *slope* or *gradient* of the straight line. Specifically, m measures the increase in y per unit change in x or b/a in Fig. 1.7. A positive value for m therefore implies a line sloping upwards from left to right. A negative value for m implies a line sloping downwards from left to right, as illustrated in Fig. 1.8.

The coefficient c in eqn [1.17] is the value of y when $x = 0$. It therefore indicates the point where the straight line intercepts the y-axis. For this reason, c is referred to as the *intercept*. A negative value for c simply implies a straight line intercepting the y-axis below the origin, as illustrated in Fig. 1.8.

Two special cases should perhaps be noted. If $m = 0$ in eqn [1.17] then the equation represents a horizontal straight line (i.e. with zero gradient) intersecting the y-axis at $y = c$. If $a = 0$ in Fig. 1.7 then m is infinite and we have a vertical straight line which never intersects the y-axis.

It is clear that except for the special case of a horizontal line, straight lines will intersect the x-axis at one point and one point only. For example, in Fig. 1.6, the straight line [1.18]

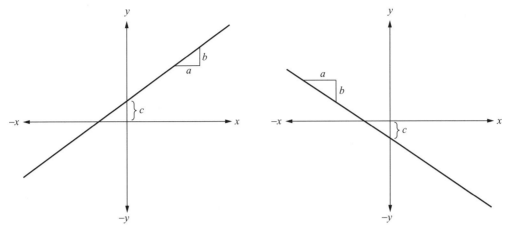

Fig. 1.7 Positive slope and intercept   **Fig. 1.8** Negative slope and intercept

intersects the x-axis when $x = -\frac{4}{3}$. $x = -\frac{4}{3}$ is therefore the solution to the equation $3x + 4 = 0$. In general the *linear equation*

$$mx + c = 0 \quad \text{with } m \neq 0 \tag{1.19}$$

will have one solution and one solution only.

Example 1.9

Find the intercept on the y-axis and the slope or gradient of the following straight lines:

(a) $y = 6x + 8$;
(b) $2x - 3y = 8$;
(c) $7x = 2y - 5$.

What is the equation of the straight line with gradient $\frac{1}{4}$ and intercept 3 on the y-axis?
    Sketch the straight line given by (b) above and check which of the following points both satisfy the equation and lie on the line: $(4, 0)$; $(3, 1)$; $(4, 2)$; $(-1, 2)$; $(-3, -3)$.

1.5 The algebraic solution of equations in one variable

We have seen that one method of solving equations such as [1.13] or [1.19] is to sketch graphs of the corresponding functional relationships and to determine the points where these graphs intersect the x-axis. However, this can be a tedious business and accurate answers require very careful graph drawing. For this reason it is often more convenient to find solutions by the use of a little algebra.

Solution of linear equations

Anyone who has looked at the introductory section on mathematical prerequisites will have come across linear equations earlier. However, we now look briefly at such equations in a more formal way.

The algebraic solution of linear equations such as [1.19] is a simple matter. Since $mx + c = 0$, it follows that

$$mx = -c \qquad\qquad\qquad [1.20]$$

and hence that

$$x = -c/m \qquad\qquad\qquad [1.21]$$

Thus [1.21] gives the single unique solution to the linear [1.19]. For example, if $m = 3$ and $c = 4$ as in [1.18] then the solution is $x = -\frac{4}{3}$, as was found graphically in Fig. 1.6.

Obviously equations which can be reduced to the form [1.20] can be solved in a similar manner. For example, consider the equation

$$3(x + 5) + 2x = 7 + 5(2x - 1) \qquad\qquad\qquad [1.22]$$

Multiplying out the brackets and bringing all terms in x to the left-hand side (LHS) and all constants to the right-hand side (RHS) yields

$$3x + 2x - 10x = 7 - 5 - 15$$

or

$$-5x = -13$$

The solution to eqn [1.22] is therefore $x = 13/5$.

At this point it is worth drawing the reader's attention to the difference between equations and *identities*. Consider the 'equation'

$$5(2 - x) + x = 2(3 - 2x) + 4 \qquad\qquad\qquad [1.23]$$

At first sight [1.23] appears similar to eqn [1.22], so we might expect to solve it in the same way. In fact, multiplying out the brackets and collecting terms yields

$$-5x + x + 4x = 6 + 4 - 10$$

which reduces to

$$0 = 0$$

This is obviously correct but hardly very illuminating. Our solution procedure appears to have broken down. This is because [1.23] is in fact not an equation but an *identity*. That is, *it is identically true for all possible values of x*, not just for one solution value. The reader may check this by substituting alternative values for x into [1.23] and verifying that the value of the RHS of [1.23] always equals that of the LHS. In fact, whenever attempts at solving an 'equation' reduce to the unhelpful statement $0 = 0$ this is a sure sign that the original 'equation' was not an equation at all but an identity. So as not to confuse them with genuine equations, we normally write identities such as [1.23] as

$$5(2 - x) + x \equiv 2(3 - 2x) + 4 \qquad [1.24]$$

where the sign $\equiv$ means 'identically equal to'.

Identities are relatively common in economics. The most well-known examples are probably the famous 'equation of exchange' relating the money stock to the level of money income, and the various national income identities.

Example 1.10

Which of the following are identities and which are equations? Solve those which are equations.

(a) $3(x + 4) + 2(x - 5) = 3x$;
(b) $2x + 5(2 - x) = 2(x + 5) - 5x$;
(c) $3x - 5(x - 3) = 2(2x - 3)$;
(d) $2x(x + 4) + 3(x - 1) = x(8 + 2x) + 3(x - 1)$;
(e) $x(x - 5) + 6(x - 1) = x(x - 3) + 6$.

Quadratic equations

There are two possible algebraic methods of solving quadratic equations of the kind [1.13]. Firstly it is sometimes possible to 'factorise' the LHS of such equations. For example, consider again eqn [1.10]:

$$x^2 + 3x - 4 = 0 \qquad [1.10]$$

In this case it is possible to replace the LHS of this equation by the product of two bracketed terms and write

$$(x + 4)(x - 1) = 0 \qquad [1.25]$$

The reader can easily verify that the LHSs of [1.10] and [1.25] are the same by multiplying out the brackets in [1.25].

We require values of x which satisfy [1.25] and which will, hence, satisfy [1.10]. However, [1.25] can only be satisfied if either[4]

$$x + 4 = 0 \quad \text{in which case} \quad x = -4$$

or

$$x - 1 = 0 \quad \text{in which case} \quad x = 1$$

Hence there are just two values of x, $x = -4$ and $x = 1$, that satisfy [1.25] and hence [1.10]. The solutions to eqn [1.10] are therefore $x = -4$ and $x = 1$. Of course, these are exactly the same solutions obtained graphically in Fig. 1.2.

The 'knack' of factorisation is one that some find difficult, so such readers will be relieved to know that there is an alternative method of attempting to solve quadratic equations of the kind

$$ax^2 + bx + c = 0 \qquad [1.13]$$

This is by using the famous formula

$$x = \frac{-b \pm \sqrt{(b^2 - 4ac)}}{2a}$$

[1.26]

For example, eqn [1.10] has $a = 1$, $b = 3$ and $c = -4$, so that substituting these values into [1.26] yields

$$x = \frac{-3 \pm \sqrt{[9 - 4(1)(-4)]}}{2} = \frac{-3 \pm \sqrt{25}}{2} = \frac{-3 \pm 5}{2}$$

The + or − sign means we can take either the positive value of $\sqrt{25}$ or the negative value so that we obtain as solutions either

$$x = \frac{-3 + 5}{2} = 1$$

or

$$x = \frac{-3 - 5}{2} = -4$$

Hence we again obtain the solutions found previously, first graphically and then by factorisation.

When solutions to a quadratic equation exist they can always be found by the application of the formula [1.26]. The method of factorisation, however, is not always feasible even when solutions exist. Consider, for example, the equation

$$x^2 + 2x - 5 = 0$$

[1.27]

It is not possible to factorise the LHS of eqn [1.27] so we must resort to the formula [1.26]. In this case $a = 1$, $b = 2$ and $c = -5$, so we have

$$x = \frac{-2 \pm \sqrt{[4 - 4(1)(-5)]}}{2} = \frac{-2 \pm \sqrt{24}}{2} = \frac{-2 \pm 4.90}{2}$$

Thus the solutions to eqn [1.27] are $x = 1.45$ and $x = -3.45$.

Example 1.11

Solve algebraically the quadratic equations you solved graphically in Examples 1.6 and 1.7. (Both these equations can be solved by factorisation but you may use the formula if you wish.) Compare your answers with those obtained algebraically.

Example 1.12

Solve the following quadratic equations:

(a) $x^2 - 5x + 6 = 0$;

(b) $2x^2 = 3 - 5x$;

(c) $3x^2 + 8x - 5 = 0$.

The number of solutions to a quadratic equation

We saw when using graphical methods to solve quadratic equations that we normally expect to obtain either two solutions or no solutions at all. We can make use of the formula [1.26] to derive the conditions under which these two cases occur. Suppose we attempt to solve eqn [1.14] by using the formula. For this equation, $a = -2$, $b = 8$ and $c = -13$, so we obtain

$$x = \frac{-8 \pm \sqrt{[64 - 4(-2)(-13)]}}{-4} = \frac{-8 \pm \sqrt{-40}}{-4}$$

However, the square root of -40 does not exist. The square root of 40 is approximately 6.324 and certainly exists. But the square root of -40 is not -6.324 since $(-6.324)^2$ also equals $+40$ (minus times minus equals plus). Hence, since $\sqrt{-40}$ does not exist, solutions to the eqn [1.14] do not exist. This of course is exactly the situation we found graphically in Fig. 1.3.

Since it is never possible to find the square root of a negative number, we will encounter the case of no solutions whenever the expression under the square root sign in [1.26] yields a negative number. Thus, *a quadratic equation will have no solution if* $b^2 < 4ac$. When this is the case, the graph of the equation has no points of intersection with the x-axis.

Strictly speaking, we should have stated in the last paragraph that a quadratic equation will have no '*real* solutions' if $b^2 < 4ac$. Mathematicians regard equations such as [1.14] as having solutions which are 'unreal' or 'complex'. These solutions involve a quantity denoted by 'i' which equals the 'imaginary' square root of -1. Although such 'complex numbers' have uses in certain areas of economics we shall not have cause to make use of them in this book.[5] For our purposes we can regard a quadratic equation for which $b^2 < 4ac$ as having no solutions.

The case of two solutions will arise whenever the expression under the square root sign in [1.26] yields a positive number as it did in eqns [1.10] and [1.27]. Thus *a quadratic equation will have two solutions if* $b^2 > 4ac$. When this is the case the graph of the equation intersects the x-axis at two points.

There remains the rather unlikely case where b^2 and $4ac$ happen to be exactly equal. Consider, for example, the equation

$$x^2 - 6x + 9 = 0 \tag{1.28}$$

In this case $a = 1$, $b = -6$ and $c = 9$, so that $b^2 = 4ac$ and the formula [1.26] yields

$$x = \frac{6 \pm \sqrt{[36 - 4(1)9]}}{2} + \frac{6 \pm \sqrt{0}}{2} = 3$$

Equation [1.28] *has only one solution*,[6] $x = 3$. The graph of the functional relationship $y = x^2 - 6x + 9$ is shown in Fig. 1.9. Notice that it happens to touch the horizontal x-axis at just one point – hence the single solution. We can therefore say that *a quadratic equation will have just one solution if* $b^2 = 4ac$. We stress, however, that this is the unlikely special case. Normally a quadratic equation will have either two solutions or no solution at all. In summary

if $b^2 > 4ac$, a quadratic equation will have two solutions

if $b^2 = 4ac$, a quadratic equation will have one solution

if $b^2 < 4ac$, a quadratic equation will have no solution

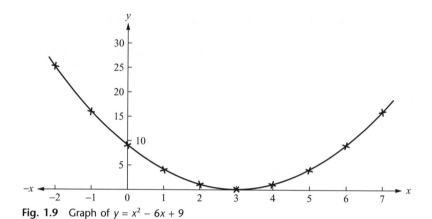

Fig. 1.9 Graph of $y = x^2 - 6x + 9$

Example 1.13

Which of the following quadratic equations have solutions?

(a) $x^2 - 3x + 3 = 0$;

(b) $2x^2 + 11x - 21 = 0$;

(c) $9x^2 - 24x + 16 = 0$;

(d) $2x^2 + 5x - 6 = 0$;

(e) $3x^2 + 2x + 3 = 0$.

Find the solutions to the equations that have solutions.

Polynomial equations

Both linear and quadratic equations are special cases of the general polynomial equation in one variable:

$$a_n x^n + a_{n-1} x^{n-1} + \ldots + a_2 x^2 + a_1 x + a_0 = 0 \qquad [1.29]$$

where n is some positive integer or whole number and the a's are all constants. For example, if $a_1 = m$ and $a_0 = c$, while all the other a's are zero, then $n = 1$ and [1.29] reduces to

$$mx + c = 0$$

which we know is the equation of a straight line. Similarly, if $a_2 = a$, $a_1 = b$ and $a_0 = c$, while all the other a's are zero, then $n = 2$ and we obtain

$$ax^2 + bx + c = 0$$

the general form for a quadratic equation.

x	-3	-2	-1	0	1	2	3	4	5
x^3	-27	-8	-1	0	1	8	27	64	125
$-4x^2$	-36	-16	-4	0	-4	-16	-36	-64	-100
x	-3	-2	-1	0	1	2	3	4	5
y	-60	-20	0	6	4	0	0	10	35

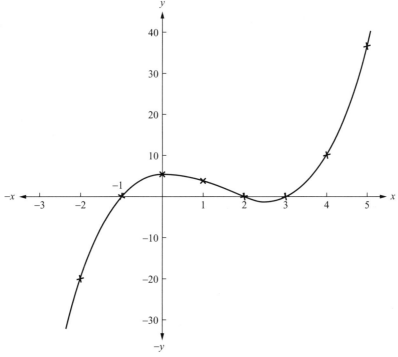

Fig. 1.10 Graph of $y = x^3 - 4x^2 + x + 6$

If a_0, a_1, a_2 and a_3 are non-zero while all other a's are zero then $n = 3$ and we obtain the general form of what is known as a *cubic or third-order equation*

$$a_3x^3 + a_2x^2 + a_1x + a_0 = 0 \qquad [1.30]$$

There is unfortunately no convenient algebraic formula for finding solutions to cubic equations, unlike the case of quadratic or linear equations. Solution by factorisation is sometimes possible but we shall adopt a graphical approach. For example, consider the cubic equation

$$x^3 - 4x^2 + x + 6 = 0 \qquad [1.31]$$

The graph of the functional relationship $y = x^3 - 4x^2 + x + 6$ is shown in Fig. 1.10. We see that it intersects the x-axis in three places giving three solutions to eqn [1.31]: $x = -1$, $x = 2$ and $x = 3$.

The solution to higher-order equations (e.g. containing terms in x^4 or x^5) may be obtained graphically in a similar manner.

Example 1.14

Graph the functional relationship $y = 2x^3 + 7x^2 + 2x - 3$. Hence solve the equation $2x^3 + 7x^2 + 2x - 3 = 0$. Can you verify your answer algebraically?

1.6 Inverse functions

Consider the linear functional relationship [1.18] reproduced below:

$$y = 3x + 4 \qquad\qquad [1.18]$$

For any value of x, this function yields a unique corresponding value of y. For example, when $x = 1$, $y = 7$ and when $x = -3$, $y = -5$. Manipulation of [1.18] enables us to express x in terms of y:

$$y = 3x + 4 \quad \rightarrow \quad 3x = y - 4 \quad \rightarrow \quad x = \tfrac{1}{3}y - \tfrac{4}{3} \qquad [1.32]$$

The final version of [1.32] is also a functional relationship, since for any given value of y it yields a unique corresponding value of x. For example, when $y = 7$, $x = 1$ and when $y = -5$, $x = -3$.

Consider, however, the functional relationship

$$y = x^2 + 3 \qquad\qquad [1.33]$$

It is possible to manipulate [1.33] to express x in terms of y:

$$y = x^2 + 3 \quad \rightarrow \quad x^2 = y - 3 \quad \rightarrow \quad x = \sqrt{(y - 3)} \qquad [1.34]$$

The last version of [1.34], however, is not a functional relationship because if, for example, y takes the value 19 then $x = \sqrt{16}$ and may take the value $+4$ or -4. For the given y-value there is not a unique corresponding x-value. Thus we do not have a functional relationship in the way we defined one in section 1.1.

When the manipulation of a functional relationship, $y = y(x)$, to yield x in terms of y results in another functional relationship, $x = x(y)$, then the function $x(y)$ is known as the *inverse function* of $y(x)$. For example, the function in [1.32] is the inverse function of that in [1.18]. As a further example, consider

$$y = -4x + 8 \qquad\qquad [1.35]$$

Since manipulation of [1.35] yields the functional relationship

$$x = 2 - \tfrac{1}{4}y \qquad\qquad [1.36]$$

the function in [1.36] is the inverse of that in [1.35].

Notice that since manipulation of [1.33] to express x in terms of y did *not* yield a functional relationship, the function in [1.33] does *not* have an inverse.

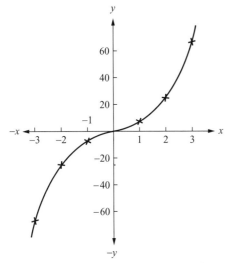

Fig. 1.11 Graph of $y = 2x^3 + 4x$

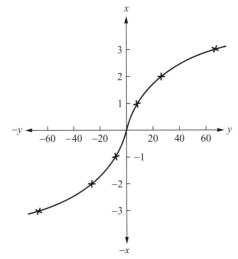

Fig. 1.12 Graph of inverse function

It is sometimes the case that a function $y = y(x)$ has an inverse but it is impossible to write out the inverse function, $x = x(y)$, in an explicit form. For example, the function in

$$y = 2x^3 + 4x \qquad\qquad [1.37]$$

has an inverse but manipulation of [1.37] to obtain an expression for x in terms of y is not possible (try it!). It is, however, possible without too much difficulty to obtain the graph of the inverse function $x = x(y)$. The function in [1.37] is graphed in Fig. 1.11.

To obtain the graph of the inverse function we need simply to 'invert the axes' in Fig. 1.11. That is, we replot the graph with the x-variable on the vertical axis and the y-variable on the horizontal axis. The result is shown in Fig. 1.12. We can see that the inverse function $x = x(y)$ is indeed a functional relationship since for any given value of y, the graph indicates that there is only one corresponding value of x.

Notice that to obtain the graph of the inverse function, all one has to do is to rotate the axis in Fig. 1.11 anticlockwise through 90° and then take a 'mirror image' of the result (e.g. try viewing Fig. 1.11 from the reverse side of the page). This is often a useful way of getting a quick idea of the shape of an inverse function.

It is not difficult to think of examples of inverse functions in economics. For example, the function in [1.7] has the inverse $p = p(d)$ and for any given level of demand d yields the price at which that level of demand is forthcoming. Similarly, the function in [1.8] has the inverse $r = r(I)$ and for any given level of investment, I, yields the rate of interest r necessary to bring forth such investment.

Example 1.15

Graph the inverse function of $y = x^3 - 3x^2 + 5x - 5$.

Revision examples

Example R1.1

Graph the functional relationship $y = 2x^2 + 6x - 4$ between $x = -4$ and $x = +3$. Find the coordinates of the point where y takes its minimum value.

(a) Verify that the values $x = 1.5$ and $y = 9.5$ satisfy the given functional relationship and that the point (1.5, 9.50) lies on the graph of the relationship. Verify that the values $x = 3$ and $y = 15$ do not satisfy the relationship and that the point (3, 15) does not lie on its graph.

(b) Find graphically solutions (if they exist) to the following equations:

(i) $2x^2 + 6x - 4 = 0$;

(ii) $2x^2 + 6x - 8 = 0$;

(iii) $2x^2 + 6x + 8 = 0$.

(c) Check algebraically which of the equations in (b) have solutions. Verify algebraically the solutions found in (b).

Example R1.2

(a) Find the intercept on the y-axis and the gradient of the following straight lines:

(i) $3x + 5y = 10$;

(ii) $3y = 8 + 2x$;

(iii) $2y + 4x = -5$.

Without using any graph paper, make rough sketches of the lines (i), (ii) and (iii).

(b) Find the equations of the following straight lines:

(i) that with intercept -2.5 and gradient 0.5;

(ii) that with intercept 5 and gradient -1.25;

(iii) that with intercept 2 and gradient 0.

What is the equation of the vertical line passing through the point (4, 0) on the x-axis?

Example R1.3

(a) Determine which of the following are equations and which are identities. Find the solution for each equation.

(i) $4(2x - 3) - 2(3x + 2) = 5x$;

(ii) $5x - 6 = 3(x - 4) - 3(2x + 4)$;

(iii) $3(x - 2) = 6(x - 1) - 3x$;

(iv) $0.5(2x + 6) = 1.5(x - 3)$.

(b) Can you find a solution to the following equation?

$$3(2x + 4) = 2(3x + 3)$$

Example R1.4

Determine algebraically which of the following quadratic equations have solutions. Find any solutions.

(a) $3x^2 + 14x - 5 = 0$;

(b) $x^2 - 7x + 11 = 0$;

(c) $x^2 = 3x - 10$;

(d) $x^2 + 8x + 12 = 0$;

(e) $2x^2 + 5x = 7$;

(f) $9x^2 = 30x - 25$;

(g) $4x^2 + 4x - 13 = 0$.

Example R1.5

Graph the function $y = 2x^3 - 6x + 4$ from $x = -3$ to $x = +3$. Hence

(a) Solve graphically the equation $2x^3 - 6x + 4 = 0$.
(b) Solve graphically the equation $2x^3 - 6x + 10 = 0$.

Graph the inverse function of $y = 2x^3 - 6x + 4$.

Solution

x	-3	-2	-1	0	1	2	3
$2x^3$	-54	-16	-2	0	2	16	54
$-6x$	18	12	6	0	-6	-12	-18
y	-32	0	8	4	0	8	40

(a) Two solutions at intersection with x-axis: $x = 1$, $x = -2$.
(b) One solution at intersection with line $y = 6$: $x = -2.3$ approx.

The inverse function is sketched below, using the figures in the above table.

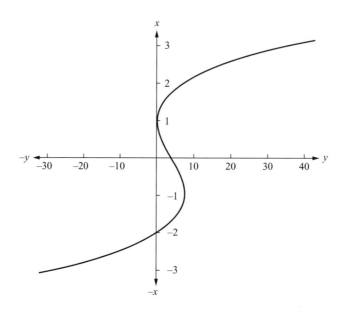

Notes

1. Some mathematicians regard relationships such as [1.5] as functions even though they do not yield unique values of y. They would then refer to functions of the special type [1.1], [1.2], [1.3] and [1.4] as 'single-valued' functions of x since they yield a unique single value for y.

2. See section 1.5.

3. In practice it is advisable to plot three points to guard against minor (or major!) errors in the plotting of the first two points.

4. The product ab of two quantities a and b can be zero if either a or b or both are zero. That is, if $ab = 0$ then either $a = 0$ or $b = 0$ or both a and b are zero. If both a and b were non-zero then ab could not be zero. In eqn [1.25] the a is $x + 4$ and the b is $x - 1$.

5. For an introduction to complex numbers see A. C. Chiang (1984) *Fundamental Methods of Mathematical Economics*, 3rd edn, International Student Edition. McGraw-Hill, Tokyo, p. 511.

6. A mathematician would say that eqn [1.28] has two 'coincident' solutions, that is two solutions which happen to be identical.

2 Simultaneous linear equations

Recall that by a solution to eqn [1.10] we meant a value for x which makes the LHS of eqn [1.10] equal to its RHS. Equations can involve more than one variable. For example,

$$x^2 + 2xy + 1 = z^2 \qquad [2.1]$$

is an equation in three variables x, y and z. By a solution to eqn [2.1] we mean a set of values, one for each of the variables x, y and z, which make the LHS of [2.1] equal to the RHS. For example, $x = 2$, $y = 1$ and $z = 3$ represents a solution since, on substitution of these values into [2.1], we obtain the value 9 for both LHS and RHS. The values $x = 4$, $y = 1$ and $z = 5$ constitute another solution. It should be clear that there are in fact very many solutions to this equation.

2.1 Simultaneous equations in two variables

Consider the equations

$$3x + 4y = 6 \qquad [2.2]$$

$$2x + 6y = 14 \qquad [2.3]$$

By a solution to this *system* of equations we mean a pair of values for x and y which satisfy these equations *simultaneously* in the sense that the LHS of each equation is made equal to the RHS. For example, consider the values $x = 2$ and $y = 4$. This pair of values is *not* a solution because on substituting them into the LHSs of [2.2] and [2.3] we obtain the numbers 22 and 28 respectively. These are obviously not the same as the respective RHSs.

To obtain a solution we shall adopt the following procedure. We take one of the equations, for example [2.2], and use it to express one variable in terms of the other, for example x in terms of y:

$$3x + 4y = 6 \quad \rightarrow \quad 3x = 6 - 4y \quad \rightarrow \quad x = 2 - \tfrac{4}{3}y \qquad [2.4]$$

We now use [2.4] to substitute for x in the other equation [2.3]:

$$2(2 - \tfrac{4}{3}y) + 6y = 14$$

On simplifying we now have an equation for y alone which we can solve for y:

$$4 - \tfrac{8}{3}y + 6y = 14 \quad \rightarrow \quad \tfrac{10}{3}y = 10 \quad \rightarrow \quad y = 3 \qquad\qquad [2.5]$$

Given that $y = 3$, we can now use [2.4] to find a solution value for x:

$$x = 2 - \tfrac{4}{3}(3) = -2 \qquad\qquad [2.6]$$

The values we have obtained, $x = -2$ and $y = 3$, constitute a solution to the equation system [2.2] and [2.3]. We can check this by substituting these values into the LHSs of eqns [2.2] and [2.3]. This yields the numbers 6 and 14 which equal the respective RHSs. So we have a solution.

Example 2.1

Solve the following pairs of simultaneous equations algebraically:

(a) $2x + 4y = 10$ (b) $3x - 5y = -1$ (c) $x = 5y - 10$

$\quad\;\; 3x - y = 1$ $\quad\;\; -2x + 3y = -11$ $\quad\;\; y = 2x - 7$

Readers may well have encountered an alternative way of solving simultaneous equations which we shall look at briefly in a moment. The alternative approach is fine for tackling simultaneous equations of the kind [2.2] and [2.3] but unfortunately this approach is not always viable for systems which contain what are called 'non-linear' equations.[1] The approach outlined above, however, is always viable whether an equation system contains linear or non-linear equations.

The alternative solution procedure involves, if necessary, multiplying one or both equations by appropriate constants. Given the resultant equations, it is then possible to eliminate one of the variables (x or y), either adding or subtracting these equations. A solution can then easily be found. For example, taking eqns [2.2] and [2.3], let us multiply [2.2] by the constant 2 and multiply [2.3] by the constant 3. This yields

$$6x + 8y = 12$$

$$6x + 18y = 42$$

Taking the first of the above equations from the second gives

$$10y = 30 \quad \rightarrow \quad y = 3$$

We now have the solution value for y. Substituting $y = 3$ into either [2.2] or [2.3] then gives the solution value of $x = -2$. We thus obtain the same solution obtained earlier for eqns [2.2] and [2.3]. The reader should now resolve the equation systems in Example 2.1 above using the alternative approach.

The interesting question now arises of whether there exist any other solutions to the equation system [2.2] and [2.3]. That is, are there any other pairs of values for x and y (apart from -2 and 3) which will satisfy both equations? We shall approach this problem graphically.

Let us rearrange eqns [2.2] and [2.3] so that in each case y is expressed in terms of x:

$$3x + 4y = 6 \quad \rightarrow \quad 4y = 6 - 3x \quad \rightarrow \quad y = 1.5 - 0.75x \qquad\qquad [2.7]$$

$$2x + 6y = 14 \quad \rightarrow \quad 6y = 14 - 2x \quad \rightarrow \quad y = 2.33 - 0.33x \qquad\qquad [2.8]$$

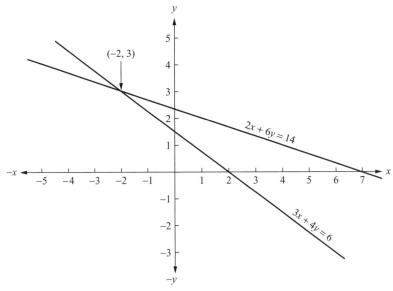

Fig. 2.1 Intersection of two straight lines

Notice that in the final versions of [2.7] and [2.8] the original eqns [2.2] and [2.3] have been re-expressed as linear functional relationships, giving in each case y as a function of x. These functional relationships are graphed in Fig. 2.1. (Remember that, since the functions are linear, their graphs are straight lines, so we need to plot just two points in each case.) We have labelled each straight line in Fig. 2.1 by the original equations they represent rather than by [2.7] and [2.8]. Although, strictly speaking, they are the graphs of the functional relationships [2.7] and [2.8] we shall also refer to the straight lines as the graphs of eqns [2.2] and [2.3].

For a solution to eqns [2.2] and [2.3] we require a pair of values for x and y that satisfy both these equations and hence both the functional relationships [2.7] and [2.8]. From our discussion in Chapter 1, however, we know that such a pair of values will only satisfy a functional relationship if they represent the coordinates of a point lying on its graph. Hence we require a point which lies on *both* the straight lines drawn in Fig. 2.1. There is, of course, only one such point – the point at which they intersect. This has coordinates (−2, 3), so by graphical means we obtain the same solution, $x = -2$ and $y = 3$, as that found above algebraically. What is also clear from Fig. 2.1 is that, since there is only one point of intersection, the eqns [2.2] and [2.3] have *one solution only.*

Equations [2.2] and [2.3] both have the general form

$$\alpha x + \beta y = \gamma \tag{2.9}$$

Since such equations can always be re-expressed as linear functional relationships such as [2.7] and [2.8], they are referred to as *linear equations* in two variables. Clearly, the graphs of such linear equations will always be straight lines. A set of such linear simultaneous equations (there may be more than two, as we shall see in a moment) is known as a linear *system* of equations.

Since two straight lines will normally have a single intersection point, we can therefore say that *a system of two linear simultaneous equations in two variables will normally have one solution and one solution only.*

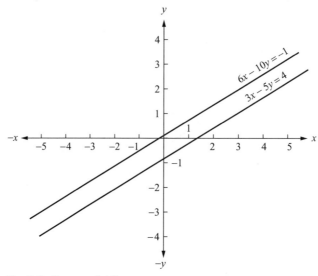

Fig. 2.2 Two parallel lines

Example 2.2

Solve the simultaneous equations in Example 2.1 graphically and check whether you get the same solutions as before.

There is one obvious exception to the above general rule. This occurs when the implied straight lines are parallel. For example, consider the linear system

$$3x - 5y = 4 \qquad\qquad [2.10]$$

$$6x - 10y = 1 \qquad\qquad [2.11]$$

Expressing y in terms of x for each equation yields

$$3x - 5y = 4 \quad \rightarrow \quad -5y = 4 - 3x \quad \rightarrow \quad y = 0.6x - 0.8 \qquad [2.12]$$

$$6x - 10y = -1 \quad \rightarrow \quad -10y = -1 - 6x \quad \rightarrow \quad y = 0.6x + 0.1 \qquad [2.13]$$

From [2.12] and [2.13] we see that both straight lines have, in this case, the same gradient of 0.6 but different intercepts on the y-axis. They are in fact graphed in Fig. 2.2.

Since such parallel lines have no intersection point, it is clear that eqns [2.10] and [2.11] have no solution – that is, there exists no pair of values for x and y that will satisfy both equations. In fact if we attempt to solve [2.10] and [2.11] algebraically we will soon run into trouble. For example, from [2.12] we know that $y = 0.6x - 0.8$. Substituting for y in [2.11] yields

$$6x - 10(0.6x - 0.8) = -1 \quad \text{or} \quad 8 = -1 \qquad\qquad [2.14]$$

which is obviously not true. In fact, as we shall see, whenever we attempt to 'solve' equation systems which actually have no solution, the absence of a solution is always signalled by the derivation of nonsensical statements such as [2.14].

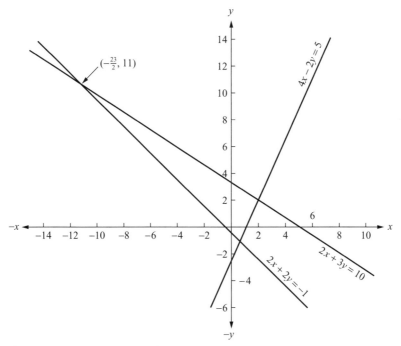

Fig. 2.3 No common intersection point

Next we consider systems of more than two simultaneous linear equations, but again involving just two variables. For example, consider the linear system

$$2x + 3y = 10 \qquad [2.15]$$

$$4x - 2y = 5 \qquad [2.16]$$

$$2x + 2y = -1 \qquad [2.17]$$

By a solution to [2.15]–[2.17] we now mean a pair of values for x and y which will satisfy *all three* equations. Does such a solution exist? We can again tackle this problem graphically by first expressing y in terms of x for each of the equations in turn:

$$2x + 3y = 10 \quad \rightarrow \quad 3y = 10 - 2x \quad \rightarrow \quad y = -0.67x + 3.33$$

$$4x - 2y = 5 \quad \rightarrow \quad -2y = 5 - 4x \quad \rightarrow \quad y = 2x - 2.5$$

$$2x + 2y = -1 \quad \rightarrow \quad 2y = -1 - 2x \quad \rightarrow \quad y = -x - 0.5$$

The three implied straight lines are graphed in Fig. 2.3.

It is immediately clear that there is no point which lies on all three straight lines, that is the lines have no common intersection point. Hence, adopting our usual argument, we can say that there is no pair of values for x and y which will satisfy all three eqns [2.15]–[2.17]. The system has no solution.

An algebraic approach will lead us to the same conclusion. For example, we can find a solution to the first two equations in the usual way without difficulty. In fact $x = 35/16$ and $y = 15/8$ will satisfy both [2.15] and [2.16]. However, if we substitute these values into [2.17] we obtain

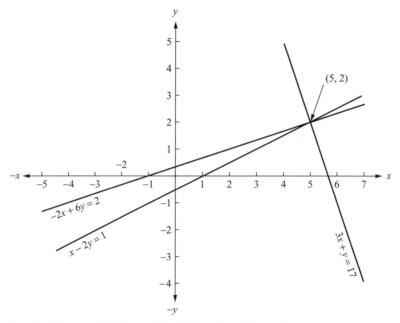

Fig. 2.4 Three straight lines with a single intersection point

$$2(35/16) + 2(15/8) = -1 \quad \text{or} \quad 8.125 = -1 \qquad [2.18]$$

which is clearly untrue. So again a nonsensical statement signals the absence of a solution.

We obtain untrue statements such as [2.14] and [2.18] because the equations in each of the systems we started from were inconsistent with one another. The lack of a solution is simply another way of saying it is impossible for all eqns [2.15]–[2.17] to hold true at the same time. Such a system of equations is said to be an *inconsistent system*.

Since it is usually the case that three straight lines will have no common intersection point, we can say that, *normally, a system of three linear simultaneous equations in two variables will have no solution and will be an inconsistent system*. While we can always find a solution satisfying any two of the equations, it is highly unlikely that the solution values will also satisfy the third equation. There is, again, an obvious exception to the general rule we have just stated. Although unlikely, it is of course possible that three straight lines could pass through a common intersection point. For example, consider the system

$$-2x + 6y = 2 \qquad [2.19]$$

$$x - 2y = 1 \qquad [2.20]$$

$$3x + y = 17 \qquad [2.21]$$

Solving any two of the eqns [2.19]–[2.21] will yield the values $x = 5$ and $y = 2$. The third equation is also always satisfied when these values are substituted into it. Hence, this three-equation system does have a solution: $x = 5$ and $y = 2$. The graphs of eqns [2.19]–[2.21] are sketched in Fig. 2.4. They have, of course, a common intersection point at (5, 2).

It should be stressed that, as with parallel straight lines, the case of a common intersection point is very much a special case which is unlikely to occur often. Normally we expect a two-equation system in two variables to have one solution only and a three-equation system to have no solution.

Linear systems in two variables that contain more than three equations are now easily dealt with. Clearly four, five or more straight lines are even less likely to have a common intersection point than are three straight lines. Hence we do not expect systems with four, five or more equations in two variables to have solutions.

Example 2.3

Determine graphically which of the following systems of equations have solutions and which are inconsistent.

(a) $3x + 4y = 11$ (b) $x + y = 1$ (c) $y + 3x = 6$ (d) $2x - 5y = 11$

      $2x + 3y = 8$ $-2x + 3y = 13$ $3y + x = 6$ $x + y = 2$

      $4x - 2y = 0$ $3x + y = -2$ $y + x + 2 = 0$ $-3x + 2y = -11$

                                                                                  $2x + y = 3$

Example 2.4

Verify your answers to Example 2.3 algebraically.

Finally, for completeness, consider the linear 'system' consisting of the single equation

$$4x - 5y = 10 \qquad\qquad [2.22]$$

In asking the question whether this 'system' has any solutions we are asking whether there are any pairs of values for x and y which will satisfy eqn [2.22]. There are in fact an infinite number of such pairs. To find a solution to [2.22], all we have to do is to choose a value of x, substitute that value into [2.22] and find the corresponding value for y. For example, if $x = 3$, then [2.22] implies that $y = 0.4$. Hence $x = 3$ and $y = 0.4$ is a solution to [2.22]. Similarly, $x = 4$ and $y = 1.2$ is a solution, $x = 2$ and $y = -0.4$ is a solution, etc.

Graphically, of course, [2.22] represents a single straight line and there will be an infinite number of points that lie on this line, including those with coordinates (3, 0.4), (4, 1.2), (2, −0.4). Hence, we can safely say that any linear 'system' with just one equation in two variables will have an infinite number of solutions.

Bringing together everything we have deduced in this section, we have, ignoring any special cases, the following general rules for linear systems:

     three or more equations in two variables will have no solutions   [2.23]

     two equations in two variables will have one solution and one solution only   [2.24]

     one equation in two variables will have an infinite number of solutions   [2.25]

2.2 Generalisation to more than two variables

It is quite possible to have systems of linear equations which involve more than two variables. For example, consider the system

$$5x - 2y + 3z + 3w = -6 \qquad\qquad\qquad [2.26]$$

$$4x + 3y - 2z - 7w = 10 \qquad\qquad\qquad [2.27]$$

By a solution to this system we mean a set of values, one for each of the variables, x, y, z and w, that will satisfy both eqns [2.26] and [2.27]. For example, the values $x = -1$, $y = 2$, $z = 3$ and $w = -2$ constitute a solution.

The question naturally arises of whether there exist general rules, similar to those derived above for two-variable equations, which can tell us whether systems in more than two variables have solutions or not. Let us first reformulate rules [2.23]–[2.25] as follows. Ignoring any special cases,

a system in which the number of equations > the number of variables will have no solutions $\qquad\qquad\qquad [2.28]$

a system in which the number of equations = the number of variables will have one solution only $\qquad\qquad\qquad [2.29]$

a system in which the number of equations < the number of variables will have an infinite number of solutions $\qquad\qquad\qquad [2.30]$

For systems in two variables, the rules [2.28]–[2.30] are identical to rules [2.23]–[2.25]. The point is that, special cases apart, the rules [2.28]–[2.30] *can be shown to hold for any linear system no matter how many variables it contains.*[2] For example, consider the system

$$\begin{aligned} 4x + 3y + z &= 3 \\ 6x - 5y \phantom{{}+ 2z} &= 11 \\ -3x + 7y + 2z &= -6 \end{aligned} \qquad\qquad\qquad [2.31]$$

Since in system [2.31] both the number of equations and the number of variables equal three, we can say immediately that we expect this system to have *one solution and one solution only.* We shall describe a systematic way of obtaining this solution in Chapter 17 and merely note for now that the single solution to this equation is in fact $x = 1$, $y = -1$ and $z = 2$. (Check that these values make LHS = RHS for each equation.)

Systems such as [2.31], with an equal number of equations and unknowns and a single unique solution, are sometimes called *determinate systems* since they 'determine' the values of the system's variables for us. For example, [2.31] 'determines' the values of x, y and z to be 1, -1 and 2 respectively. A determinate system 'tells' us what the values of its variables are.

Consider next the linear system[3]

$$\begin{aligned} 3a + 2b - c \phantom{{}+ 3d} &= 8 \\ -3a + b + 2c - 3d &= 14 \\ a - \phantom{2b +{}} 4c + d &= -3 \\ 2a - 2b + 3c - 4d &= 12 \\ 4b + 2c - 2d &= 7 \end{aligned} \qquad\qquad\qquad [2.32]$$

The system [2.32] contains just four variables, a, b, c and d, but has five equations. Applying rule [2.28] above we can say immediately that we do not expect this system to have a solution. We could find values that would satisfy the first four equations, for example, but these values are most unlikely to satisfy the fifth equation as well.

We have already noted that equation systems that have no solution are referred to as *inconsistent systems*. They are also sometimes called *overdeterminate systems*.

As a final illustration of the use of the rules [2.28]–[2.30] consider the linear system

$$8u + 3w + x - 2y + 3z = 20$$

$$2w + 2x + y - 2z = 30 \qquad\qquad [2.33]$$

The system [2.33] obviously contains more variables (five) than equations (two). Applying rule [2.30] we can therefore say that it will have an infinite number of solutions. That is, there will be any number of sets of values for u, w, x, y and z which will satisfy both equations in [2.33]. In fact we can select any arbitrary values we like for three of the variables, substitute these values into [2.33] and solve for the remaining two values to obtain a solution. For example, if we select $x = 1$, $y = 0$ and $z = -1$, substitution of these values into [2.33] yields

$$8u + 3w = 22$$

$$2w = 26$$

which on solving gives $w = 13$ and $u = -2.125$. It follows that a solution to the system [2.33] is given by the values $u = -2.125$, $w = 13$, $x = 1$, $y = 0$ and $z = -1$. However, since we could have selected any arbitrary values we like for x, y and z, it should be clear that we can generate as many solutions to the system [2.33] as we wish.

Systems such as [2.33] which have an infinite number of solutions are often called *indeterminate systems* because they do not 'determine' the values of variables for us. Since there are an infinite number of solutions to system [2.33] it does not 'tell us' what the actual values of the variables should be.

Example 2.5

Which of the following systems of equations would you expect to have one solution and one solution only?

(a) $3w + 2x + 4z = 4$ (b) $3x + 2y = 8$ (c) $2p + 3q = 2m - 6$

    $2x - 3y + z = -8$ $2y - 4z = 7$ $5p = q + m$

    $w - 3x + 2y = 5$ $4x - 2z = 3$

Before leaving indeterminate systems we should note the possibly obvious point that if, for some reason, we happen to 'know' beforehand the values of a sufficient number of variables then we can always find determinate values for the remaining variables. For example, in the system [2.33], if we 'know' that the values of x, y and z are 1, 0 and −1 respectively, then the values of u and w are 'determined' as −2.125 and 13. Alternatively, if we 'knew' that the values of x, y and z were 3, 2 and 1 respectively then, in this situation, the values of u and w are determined as −2.25 and 12.

We shall develop this method of handling indeterminate systems at some length in Chapter 4. For the moment we note that if an indeterminate linear system has n equations and k variables, where $k > n$, then *provided values of $k - n$ of the variables are known, we can use the system to determine values for the remaining n variables*. In system [2.33] for example, $n = 2$ and $k = 5$. So it is necessary that $k - n = 3$ of the variables have values known beforehand if it is to be possible to determine the values of the remaining $n = 2$ variables. Similarly in the system comprising eqns [2.26] and [2.27] above, $n = 2$ and $k = 4$. In this system if any two of the variables have given values, then we can always determine values for the remaining two variables (check this).

Example 2.6

Consider the system

$$5a + 2b - 3c + d = 8$$

$$2a - b + 4c + 3d = 4$$

(a) If $a = 1$ and $b = 2$ find the solution to the system.
(b) If $a = -3$ and $b = 10$ find the solution to the system.
(c) Generate 10 further solutions to the system.

Example 2.7

Consider the systems

(a) $3x + 4y + w = 5$ (b) $3x + y = 5$
     $2x - 3y + 2w = 3$ $2x + z + 2w = -3$
     $x + y - z = 4$ $4x - 2z + 3w = 10$

By selecting arbitrary values for w, find five solutions to each of the systems. Check that each solution satisfies every equation in its system.

2.3 Non-linear systems

We have applied the rules [2.28]–[2.30] to the analysis of linear systems of simultaneous equations. The next question, naturally, is whether these clear-cut rules can be applied to systems in which at least one of the equations is non-linear. For example, consider the two-equation system

$$3x^2 - 5x - 3y = -4 \qquad\qquad [2.34]$$

$$2x + 3y = 10 \qquad\qquad [2.35]$$

The first of the equations in this system is clearly non-linear, since it contains a term in x^2 and, hence, cannot be reduced to the general form for a linear equation given by [2.9]. Any system containing at least one non-linear equation is referred to as a *non-linear system*.

Firstly, we will solve this non-linear system algebraically. Using [2.35] to obtain an expression for y in terms of x

$$2x + 3y = 10 \quad \rightarrow \quad 3y = 10 - 2x \quad \rightarrow \quad y = \frac{10}{3} - \frac{2}{3}x \qquad \qquad [2.36]$$

Substituting this expression for y into [2.34], we obtain

$$3x^2 - 5x - 3y = -4 \quad \rightarrow \quad 3x^2 - 5x - 3\left(\frac{10}{3} - \frac{2}{3}x\right) = -4$$

$$\rightarrow \quad 3x^2 - 3x - 6 = 0$$

This is a quadratic equation in x alone which can be solved by factorisation

$$3x^2 - 3x - 6 = 0 \quad \rightarrow \quad x^2 - x - 2 = 0 \quad \rightarrow \quad (x - 2)(x + 1) = 0$$

Solution values for x are therefore $x = 2$ and $x = -1$. To find corresponding values for y we can use the final equation in [2.36]:

$$\text{when } x = 2 \quad y = \frac{10}{3} - \frac{2}{3}(2) = 2$$

$$\text{when } x = -1 \quad y = \frac{10}{3} - \frac{2}{3}(-1) = 4$$

There are therefore *two solutions* to the system of eqns [2.34] and [2.35]. One solution is $x = 2$ and $y = 2$ and the other $x = -1$ and $y = 4$. Both pairs of values will satisfy both [2.34] and [2.35].

To illustrate these solutions graphically, first rearrange [2.34] to express y as a function of x:

$$3x^2 - 5x - 3y = -4 \quad \rightarrow \quad -3y = -3x^2 + 5x - 4$$

$$\rightarrow \quad y = x^2 - \frac{5}{3}x + \frac{4}{3} \qquad \qquad [2.37]$$

In [2.37], eqn [2.34] has been re-expressed as a quadratic functional relationship. The graph of this quadratic is sketched in Fig. 2.5 together with that of the straight line [2.35]. The two graphs intersect at two points (2, 2) and (−1, 4), confirming the two solutions found algebraically.

Obviously the non-linear system of eqns [2.34] and [2.35] does not obey the rules for linear systems outlined in [2.28]–[2.30]. Furthermore, suppose instead that [2.35] were replaced by

$$2x + 3y = -11 \qquad \qquad [2.38]$$

Equation [2.38] is also graphed in Fig. 2.5 and it should be clear that the two-equation system comprising [2.34] and [2.38] has *no solution*.

We have now examined two non-linear systems in which the number of equations equalled the number of variables and in neither case was the simple rule [2.29] followed. In one case we obtained two solutions and in the other no solution at all. Unfortunately this is the situation with each of the rules [2.28]–[2.30]. In general, *none of them hold for non-linear systems*. Strictly speaking, only if all of the equations in a system are linear can we make use of these rules.

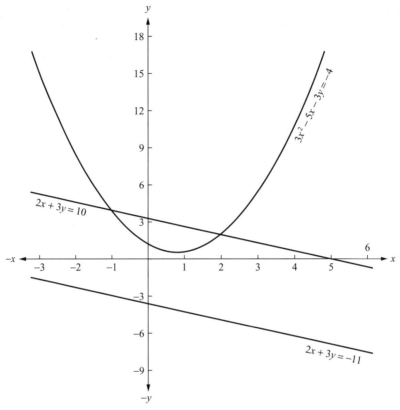

Fig. 2.5 Graph of eqn [2.34] and alternative straight lines

Example 2.8

Find graphically whether the following pairs of simultaneous equations have solutions:

(a) $y = -3x^2 + 5x + 3$ (b) $y = 2x^2 + 3x + 4$

    $y = 4x + 1$ $y = x + 3$

Verify your answers algebraically.

Example 2.9

Sketch the curve $y = 3x^2 + 5x - 8$ and the straight line $7x + y + 20 = 0$ from $x = -4$ to $x = 3$. Hence determine how many solutions (if any) there are to the systems of equations

    $y = 3x^2 + 5x - 8$

    $7x + y + 20 = 0$

Do you consider your answer to be unusual in any way? If so, why?

Example 2.10

Sketch the function $y = x^3 - 12x + 4$ from $x = -4$ to $x = +4$. Hence

(a) Solve graphically the equation $x^3 - 12x + 4 = 0$.
(b) Solve graphically the simultaneous equations

$$y = x^3 - 12x + 4$$

$$y = 2x + 10$$

2.4 Economic models, their completeness and their consistency

It is possible to express any theory or model of the workings of an economic system in terms of a set of relationships or equations. This is the case whether the model is intended to represent the whole economy or simply an individual consumer or firm. Let us take, as an example, the simple Keynesian theory of the determination of the level of national income. This is depicted in the familiar 'Keynesian cross' diagram of Fig. 2.6 with income/output, Y, on the horizontal axis and expenditure, E, on the vertical axis.

The line labelled C in Fig. 2.6 graphs the so-called consumption function, indicating levels of consumers' expenditure for various levels of national income. This has been drawn as a straight line but, since the consumption function need not necessarily be linear, we shall represent it algebraically as

$$C = f(Y) \tag{2.39}$$

Remember that we are now using the function notation introduced in Chapter 1. Equation [2.39] is simply shorthand for the statement 'consumption is a function of income'.

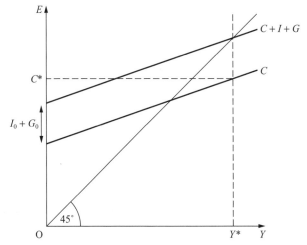

Fig. 2.6 The 'Keynesian cross'

In this simple model both types of non-consumption expenditure – private capital invest-ment, I, and government expenditure, G – are assumed to be equal fixed constants, I_0 and G_0, which are independent of the level of income. We therefore write

$$I = I_0 \tag{2.40}$$

$$G = G_0 \tag{2.41}$$

Equilibrium income is determined by the condition that total expenditure $C + I + G$ equals income. In Fig. 2.6 this occurs when the $C + I + G$ line intersects the $45°$ line, giving an equilibrium level of income Y^* and an equilibrium level of consumption, C^*. Algebraically we write the equilibrium condition:

$$Y = C + I + G \tag{2.42}$$

The simple Keynesian model in Fig. 2.6 does what it is supposed to do – it tells us, or determines for us, what the equilibrium levels of income and consumption are. Its algebraic representation, eqns [2.39]–[2.42], is a four-equation simultaneous system in the four variables C, Y, I and G (remember: I_0 and G_0 are just numbers). From the rules for simultaneous systems, developed in the last two sections, we see that it is a determinate system with just one solution, the equilibrium values of its variables. Thus, an algebraic version of the model will also tell us what the equilibrium values are.

Two points concerning this simple model should be noted. Firstly, the fact that the model is 'determinate' does not necessarily mean that it is an adequate description of how national income is actually determined in the real world. Its 'determinacy' simply means that it is at least internally consistent and complete, in the sense that it 'does what it is supposed to do'. Whether it does it sufficiently well is another matter!

Secondly, eqns [2.40] and [2.41] state that I and G are known given numbers and, it could be argued, are hardly worth calling equations at all. Without them we have a two-equation system, consisting of [2.39] and [2.42] in the four variables C, Y, I and G, which by rule [2.30] is indeterminate. However, we saw in the last section that we can handle such systems provided we 'know' beforehand the values of a sufficient number of variables. In this case, since we know $I = I_0$ and $G = G_0$, the system reduces to two equations in two variables C and Y which we can solve to yield equilibrium values. In fact, 'knowing' values of certain variables in an indeterminate system is equivalent to adding extra equations to the system; for example, knowing I and G is equivalent to adding the equations $I = I_0$ and $G = G_0$ to the above system.

Let us now generalise the above Keynesian model in two ways. Firstly we assume that consumption depends not only on the level of income but also on the rate of interest, R. For example, it may be the case that as R rises, more is saved, so, at a given level of income, less is consumed. We write our more general consumption function as

$$C = f(Y, R) \tag{2.43}$$

Here we are simply extending slightly the function notation introduced in Chapter 1. Equation [2.43] is shorthand for the statement 'C is a function of both Y and R' – that is, consumption depends on both income and the rate of interest.

We next allow for the fact that fixed capital investment, I, may also depend on the interest rate. As the rate falls, investment expenditure is likely to rise. We therefore replace eqn [2.40] by

$$I = g(R) \tag{2.44}$$

If we retain the equilibrium condition [2.42] we now have a four-equation system consisting of eqns [2.41]–[2.44] containing five variables, C, Y, I, G and R. Clearly, as it stands this system is indeterminate and cannot have a single unique solution. We can expect an infinite number of sets of values for C, Y, I, G and R which will satisfy all four equations. Thus our model is in some sense incomplete since it cannot tell us the equilibrium values of all its variables.

We consider three possible ways in which we can 'complete' the above model. We stress that neither of the ways is necessarily the 'right' way in the sense of turning the model into an adequate representation of reality. However, each renders the model determinate and leaves it internally consistent.

Firstly, we could simply postulate that the monetary authorities maintain the interest rate constant. If R is 'known' then the four-equation system can be solved for unique values of the remaining four variables C, Y, I and G. This is, of course, equivalent to adding a fifth equation, $R = R_0$, to the system. Effectively, for given G and R, the system determines equilibrium values for Y, C and I.

Alternatively, suppose the labour market was sufficiently flexible for changes in wage rates automatically to ensure full employment. This would mean that national income, Y, was always at its full employment level. Under such conditions we can add an alternative fifth equation $Y = Y_F$ to the model, where Y_F is the given full employment income level. This could replace the equation $R = R_0$. For given G and Y, the model would then yield determinate values of C, I and R.

If we require a model that provides determinate values without the necessity of assuming R or Y is known, then we have to extend the model beyond the four equations [2.41]–[2.44]. The traditional Keynesian way of completing the model is to add money demand and supply equations together with a condition for equilibrium in the money market:

$$L = L(R, Y) \tag{2.45}$$

$$M = M_0 \tag{2.46}$$

$$L = M \tag{2.47}$$

Equation [2.45] states that the demand for money, L, is a function of the rate of interest, R (speculative motive), and the level of income, Y (transactionary motive). Equation [2.46] simply states that money supplied, M, is a fixed quantity determined by the monetary authorities. Equation [2.47] is the equilibrium condition specifying that the demand for and supply of money have to be equal for equilibrium in the money market.

We now have a seven-equation system consisting of eqns [2.41]–[2.47] in the seven variables C, Y, I, G, R, L and M. We can therefore expect this to be a determinate system with one solution only, telling us the equilibrium values of all variables.

Readers may be more familiar with the above Keynesian model when it is presented in diagrammatic form. Economics textbooks refer to it as the IS–LM model. We have deliberately eschewed the use of diagrams, firstly to illustrate how any economic model can be expressed as a system of equations and, secondly, to demonstrate the use of the rules [2.28]–[2.30]. Before we leave the model let us again briefly consider the labour market.

If we were now to postulate a flexible labour market in which real wages always adjusted to ensure full employment, then we would face a problem when attempting to integrate such a labour market into the above model. The labour market would determine a value for Y, the income level corresponding to full employment output. However, there could be no guarantee that this value for Y would coincide with the value obtained as a solution to eqns [2.41]–[2.47]. Our combined model would start giving us inconsistent statements like [2.14] or [2.18]. *It would no longer be internally consistent* but would be overdeterminate or inconsistent. In fact, if we were to add to eqns [2.41]–[2.47] the necessary equations describing the labour market, we would find we have a model in which the number of equations *exceeded* the number of variables. We do not have the time or space in this book to consider the various answers to this dilemma.

The reader no doubt will already have objected that whereas the rules [2.28]–[2.30] specifically apply only to linear systems, we cannot normally expect economic relationships to be of linear form. However, it is very often the case that economic relationships can be fairly well approximated by linear functions. For example, the consumption function [2.39], even if it is not linear, can be expected to slope continually upwards – we do not expect it to be U-shaped! Similarly we normally expect demand curves to slope continually downwards and not be spiral shaped! We can therefore expect the rules [2.28]–[2.30] to apply to most economic systems, even if they are not exactly linear. We must therefore ensure that our models never contain more equations than they do variables, otherwise we can be fairly certain that they will be internally inconsistent in some way. Perhaps it must seem that, ideally, we should construct only models in which the number of equations equals the number of variables. However, we have already noted that we can handle indeterminate systems that appear to have too many variables provided we can treat a sufficient number of the variables as 'given' or 'known'. In practice this is often the case. Some variables can be considered as 'determined by the government'. Tax rates are an obvious example. Other variables such as import prices can be regarded as 'determined abroad by the world economy'. We shall discuss this approach at greater length in Chapter 4 when we deal with the reduced forms of equation systems.

Revision examples

Example R2.1

Determine algebraically whether the following systems of equations have solutions or not.

(a) $x + y = 5$ (b) $4x - 2y = 3$ (c) $2x + 3y = 37$
    $3x - y = 5$ $2x + \ y = 9$ $3x + 2y = -2$
    $-2x + y = 4$ $2x + 5y = 24$ $x + \ y = 7$
                                $4x + 3y = 10$

Verify your answers geometrically.

Solution

The procedure for tackling each system of equations is, in each case, to select any pair of the equations and solve for x and y. These values may then be substituted into the *remaining* equation(s). If these values also satisfy any remaining equation(s) then we have a solution. If these values do not satisfy any of the remaining equation(s) then we have an inconsistent system with no solution.

(a) From the first equation

$$y = 5 - x$$

Substituting for y in the second equation gives

$$3x - (5 - x) = 5 \quad \rightarrow \quad 4x = 10 \quad \rightarrow \quad x = 2.5$$

Hence

$$y = 5 - 2.5 = 2.5$$

Thus the first two lines intersect at the point (2.5, 2.5). Substituting these values into the third equation gives

$$-2(2.5) + 2.5 = -2.5 = 4$$

Thus the third equation is not satisfied and there is no solution to the system which is inconsistent. The third line does not pass through the intersection of the first two.

(b) From the second equation

$$y = 9 - 2x$$

Substituting for y in the first equation gives

$$4x - 2(9 - 2x) = 3 \quad \rightarrow \quad 8x = 21 \quad \rightarrow \quad x = 2.625$$

Hence

$$y = 9 - 2(2.625) = 3.75$$

Thus the first two lines intersect at the point (2.625, 3.75). Substituting into the third equation gives

$$2(2.625) + 5(3.75) = 24$$

Thus the third equation is satisfied and there is a single solution, $x = 2.625$, $y = 3.75$, to the system which is determinate. All three lines pass through the single intersection point.

(c) From the third equation

$$y = 7 - x$$

Substituting for y in the second equation gives

$$3x + 2(7 - x) = -2 \quad \rightarrow \quad x = -16$$

Hence

$$y = 7 - (-16) = 23$$

Thus the second and third lines intersect at the point (−16, 23). Substituting into the first equation gives

$$2(-16) + 3(23) = 37$$

Thus the first equation is satisfied so the third line also passes through the intersection point (−16, 23).

However, substituting into the fourth equation gives

$$4(-16) + 3(23) = 5 \neq 10$$

Thus the fourth equation is not satisfied and the fourth line does not pass through the intersection of the other three lines. The system is inconsistent and has no solution.

Example R2.2

Consider the system

$$3w - 2x + 4y - z = 20$$

$$2w + 3x - 2y = 18$$

(a) By selecting arbitrary pairs of values for w and x find five solutions to the system.
(b) By selecting arbitrary pairs of values for y and z find five further solutions.

If you selected arbitrary values for all three variables x, y and z, would you expect to find a solution?

Example R2.3

Graph the function $y = 2x^2 + 6x - 4$ and the straight line $y = 3x - 2$ between $x = -4$ and $x = +3$. Hence find graphically the solutions (if any) to the systems of equations

(a) $y = 2x^2 + 6x - 4$ (b) $y = 2x^2 + 6x + 6$
    $y = 3x - 2$ $y = 3x - 2$

Verify your answer to (b) algebraically.

Example R2.4

Graph the functional relationship $y = x^3 + 3x^2 - 9x$ from $x = -5$ to $x = 3$. Hence

(a) Solve graphically the equation $x^3 + 3x^2 - 9x = 0$.
(b) Solve graphically the simultaneous equations

$$y = x^3 + 3x^2 - 9x$$

$$y + 5x + 10 = 0$$

Example R2.5

Graph the curve $y = 3x^2 + 12x + 5$ from $x = -5$ to $x = 2$. Hence find the minimum value of y. Graph the straight lines $y = 2x + 2$, $y = 2x - 6$ and $y = 2x - 10/3$ on the same diagram as the curve. Hence determine which of the following pairs of simultaneous equations have solutions and find any such solutions.

(a) $y = 3x^2 + 12x + 5$ (b) $y = 3x^2 + 12x + 5$ (c) $y = 3x^2 + 12x + 5$

   $y = 2x + 2$ $y = 2x - 6$ $y = 2x - 10/3$

Verify your answers algebraically.

Example R2.6

In a simple macro-economic model, Y is GDP, C is consumer expenditure, I is investment expenditure, G is government expenditure and R is the rate of interest. Suppose

$$C = 20 + 0.8Y$$

$$I = 10 + 0.1Y - 2R$$

$$Y = C + I + G$$

Determine whether this system is determinate, indeterminate or inconsistent

(a) if the government fixes G but allows all other variables to vary freely;
(b) if the government fixes G and R but allows all other variables to vary freely;
(c) if the government allows all five variables to vary freely.

Notes

1. Linear equations only contain terms such as x or y apart from the constants, so their graphs are straight lines. Equations containing terms such as x^2, y^3 or xy are referred to as non-linear equations.
2. Since a linear equation in three variables can be represented by a plane surface in three-dimensional space, readers who are able to think in terms of three dimensions should be able to appreciate why the rules hold for systems containing three variables. Three equations in three variables can be represented by three planes in three-dimensional space. Any two of the planes will intersect in a straight line. Normally, the third plane will intersect this straight line in a single point. Hence three planes will normally intersect in a single point and hence three equations in three variables will normally have one solution only. This verifies rule [2.29]. A little thought should reveal that rules [2.28] and [2.30] also hold for systems in three variables.
3. Do not be concerned that variables are missing from some of the equations. The first equation could be rewritten as

   $$3a + 2b - c + 0d = 8$$

   Similarly the coefficient of b in the third equation is simply zero, as is that of a in the fifth equation.

3 Stocks, flows and equilibrium in economics

3.1 Stock and flow variables

Readers will be aware that the 'variables' we deal with in economics are all 'prices' or 'quantities' in one sense or another. What is less obvious is that there are two distinct types of quantity-type variables – *flow variables* and *stock variables*. Let us consider flow variables first.

Typical examples of flow variables in economics are 'income', 'consumption', 'output', etc. As their name suggests, these variables refer to flows *over time*. They have to be measured per unit of time, for example per year or per week. The value of a flow variable is meaningless unless the time period over which it is measured is specified. Clearly a statement that the output of a large automobile manufacturer is 2000 cars has little meaning unless we know whether output is 2000 per week, 2000 per month or 2000 per year! Similarly, to know that a family's income is £5000 tells us virtually nothing about how well off that family is if we do not know whether its income is £5000 per week or £5000 per year.

In contrast, stock variables cannot be measured over time but have to be measured at particular moments in time. Typical examples of stock variables are 'money supply', 'capital equipment', 'land', etc. Obviously to say that agricultural land in an English county is 8 million hectares *per year* is a completely nonsensical statement. Similarly, the UK money supply, however defined, has to be measured at particular points in time (e.g. at the end of each year). We may find that the money supply was £20 billion on 31 December 1986 – we certainly do not measure it as £20 billion per year!

The distinction between stock and flow variables is crucial to much of economics and it is helpful if a student can get the distinction clear in his/her mind very early in the study of the subject. The consideration of specific examples will help clarify the distinction, so consider the following list of economic-type variables. In each case, make sure you attach to the variable the meaning normally given to it in an introductory economics textbook. For example, do not envisage 'exports' as a pile of crates lying on a dock-side!

(a) sales (flow);
(b) saving (flow);
(c) the labour force (stock);
(d) exports (flow);
(e) foreign exchange reserves (stock);
(f) wealth (stock);

Table 3.1 Inhabitable dwellings in a city

Year	Begin-year stock	Dwellings completed	Dwellings demolished	Net flow	End-year stock
1980					60 000
1981	60 000	2000	800	1200	61 200
1982	61 200	500	800	−300	60 900
1983	60 900	1000	800	200	61 100
1984	61 100	800	800	0	61 100

(g) profits (flow);
(h) inventories (stock).

Confusion as to whether we are dealing with a stock or a flow can exist for several reasons. Firstly, most economic literature does not explicitly specify the unit of time involved when discussing flow variables. This is either because it is implicitly assumed that the time unit is a year or because, in a purely theoretical model, although flow variables still have to be measured per unit of time, it is irrelevant whether the time unit used is a week, a month or a year. Another reason for confusion is that for every stock variable in economics there are corresponding related flow variables. Some examples should make this clear.

Suppose we take as our stock variable the number of completed and inhabitable dwellings in a city. Suppose, further, that on 31 December 1980 (i.e. end-year 1980) this stock was 60 000 dwellings. The value of this stock will have changed by end-year 1981 for two reasons. Firstly, new dwellings are being built and completed and, secondly, old dwellings are being demolished. Hence there are two flow variables related to our stock variable – the number of new dwellings completed *per year* and the number of old dwellings demolished *per year*. The relationship between the stock variable and the two flow variables is illustrated in Table 3.1 for a four-year period.

We have assumed in Table 3.1 that dwellings get demolished at a constant rate of 800 per year, but that completions vary from year to year, depending maybe on the availability of finance and on weather conditions. Obviously whether the stock of inhabitable dwellings falls, rises or remains unchanged from one end-year to another depends on the balance of dwellings completed and dwellings demolished during the year. We refer to this balance as a *net flow*. When dwellings completed exceed those demolished, net flow is positive and the stock of houses increases. When net flow is negative, as in 1982, stock decreases. Only when net flow is zero as in 1984 does end-year stock remain unchanged.

As a further example, let us take as our stock variable a country's foreign exchange reserves. When the country's residents pay for goods or financial assets purchased abroad they must obtain foreign currency to do so and this depletes their country's reserves. We shall refer to such purchases as 'imports', whether they refer to goods or assets. However, when residents sell goods or financial assets abroad, they receive foreign currency in exchange and this increases their country's reserves. We shall refer to such sales as 'exports'. The relationship between the stock variable, foreign exchange reserves, and the two flow variables 'imports' and

Table 3.2 Exports, imports and foreign exchange reserves

Month	Begin-month reserves	Imports	Exports	Net flow	End-month reserves
Jan.					2000
Feb.	2000	500	400	−100	1900
Mar.	1900	450	450	0	1900
Apr.	1900	400	450	50	1950
May	1950	450	500	50	2000

'exports' is illustrated in Table 3.2 over a sequence of months. The net flow in this case can be referred to as the 'balance of payments'. Figures can be treated as millions of pounds.

Notice again that when net flow is positive (i.e. 'exports' exceed 'imports'), the stock of reserves increases and when net flow is negative (i.e. 'imports' exceed 'exports') the stock decreases. *Only when net flow is zero does a stock variable remain constant.*

In the remainder of this chapter and in the following two chapters we shall make use, firstly, of the above distinction between stocks and flows, and, secondly, of the 'rules' concerning simultaneous systems of equations developed in Chapter 2, to analyse a sequence of markets of gradually increasing complexity.

Example 3.1

The value in constant 1975 prices of an economy's total capital stock on 1 January 1975 is £10 billion. Depreciation or capital consumption occurs at a rate per annum equal to 4 per cent of the value of the beginning-of-year capital stock. If average gross fixed investment per annum during the years 1975–80 (again measured in 1975 prices) is £400m, £200m, £1000m, £300m, £600m and £800m respectively, calculate the value of the economy's total capital stock in millions of pounds on 1 January of each year from 1976 to 1981.

Example 3.2

Stocks of a firm's product equal 5000 items at the beginning of January. The firm follows a policy of producing each month an output equal to $3000 - 0.1S$ where S is the stock in hand at the beginning of the month. All this output is added to stocks initially. If, during the first six months of the year, sales are such that stock is depleted at a rate of 2300 a month, find the stock level at the beginning of each month from February to July.

Define the net flow variable that is associated with the stock variable S. Under what condition will net flow be zero? At what value will stock in hand S remain constant?

3.2 Some definitions relating to markets

Readers will be familiar with the concept of a *market*. We shall define it simply as any organisation whereby buyers and sellers of a 'good' are kept in sufficiently close touch to arrive at 'prices'. A market need not be confined to one site of course – we are not thinking just of the village-street-type market. For example, the markets for many basic commodities – tin, wheat, oil, etc. – are world-wide with buyers and sellers in touch by telephone or telex.

Let us consider the market for a particular good – it could be matchboxes or automobiles. We shall define *stock demand* as the total stock of the good that individuals (consumers or producers) *wish to hold* at particular moments in time. This is obviously a stock variable as its name suggests. Stock demand for matchboxes might be 200 000 on 31 December 1998, for example. In contrast, we define *stock supply* as the total stock of the good in existence at particular moments in time. Since all stocks must be held by someone, stock supply is simply the total stock of the good that individuals *actually hold*. For example, if, on 31 December 1998, stock supply is not 200 000 but 250 000 matchboxes, this means people are actually holding more matchboxes than they wish to.

We next define two flow variables. We shall refer to total *desired* consumption per unit of time as *flow demand*. Similarly, we define *flow supply* as total *desired* production per unit of time. Thus flow demand for matchboxes might be 20 000 *per week* and flow supply 25 000 *per week*. Since we are describing flow variables, we have to specify the time unit over which we are measuring them.

We can also define *excess flow demand* as the excess of flow demand over flow supply – that is, the excess of desired consumption over desired production. This variable can be negative. For example, if flow demand is 20 000 and flow supply 25 000 then excess flow demand is *minus* 5000 per week. Alternatively, of course, we could describe this as an excess flow supply of 5000 per week.

Assume for the moment that consumers always consume what they want to consume and that producers always produce what they want to produce. If desires are always fulfilled in this way, then flow demand (desired consumption) will be equal to actual consumption and flow supply (desired production) will equal actual production. Under such conditions there is now a definite relationship between flow demand, flow supply and the stock supply variable defined earlier. If production of a good exceeds consumption of that good then the total stock of the good in existence (i.e. stock supply) must increase. Similarly, if consumption exceeds production then stock supply must fall. Stock supply can only remain constant when production and consumption are equal. The balance of consumption and production provides us with the net flow variable (similar to the net flows in Tables 3.1 and 3.2), which determines changes over time in stock supply. Summarising, we can say that, assuming that the desires of consumers and producers are always realised,

stock supply = constant if and only if flow demand = flow supply   [3.1]

We conclude this section by defining the flow variables *market demand* and *market supply*. These in fact are the variables normally being referred to when the rather vague terms 'demand' and 'supply' are used in introductory economics textbooks. Firstly, we define market demand for a good as total *desired purchases* per unit of time. Purchases can be made either for the purpose of immediate consumption or because it is wished to increase stocks of the goods held for future consumption. Hence we can write

market demand = flow demand + desired additions to stocks   [3.2]

We define market supply as total *desired sales* per unit of time. Sales can either be made out of current production or be met by running down existing stocks. Hence we can write

market supply = flow supply + desired depletions to stocks   [3.3]

It is possible for market demand to be less than flow demand. For example, if consumers wish to consume 20 000 matchboxes in total per week but also plan to run down or consume stocks at a rate of 4000 per week then desired additions to stocks in eqn [3.2] will be negative and desired purchases per week (market demand) will be 16 000 only. Similarly, market supply will be less than flow supply if producers decide that they want to add to their stocks. Desired depletions to stocks in eqn [3.3] will then be negative and part of current production will be added to producers' stocks rather than being offered for immediate sale.

We can also define a net flow variable, excess market demand, which is simply the excess of market demand over market supply:

excess market demand = market demand − market supply   [3.4]

or, using eqns [3.2] and [3.3],

excess market demand = excess flow demand + net investment in stocks   [3.5]

where we use the expression *net investment in stocks* to represent the excess of desired additions over desired depletions of stocks. Net investment in stocks could of course be negative if, in aggregate, consumers and producers wish to deplete rather than add to their stocks.

Market demand and market supply, as their names suggest, are the variables whose influence is actually felt in the market place. A common assumption is that the balance of market demand and market supply is what determines the behaviour of the price of a good. This stems from the idea that, for example, if excess market demand is positive then, since this implies that the quantity of the good people want to buy exceeds the quantity people want to sell, the price of the good will be 'bid' upwards. Similarly, when excess market demand is negative, the price of the good will be bid downwards. Whether markets do in fact behave in this way is the subject of much debate in modern economics.[1] However, there will be a number of occasions in this book when we will need to make some assumption about the relationship between excess market demand and prices and we will normally assume that markets behave as just described. In particular we shall assume that *the price of a good can only remain constant and will remain constant when excess market demand is zero*. The reasoning here is that only when what people want to buy equals what people want to sell will there be no tendency for the price of the good to be bid either upwards or downwards.

3.3 Flow markets for a single good

We consider in this section the simplest type of market – that for a perishable good. Since the good is perishable, there is no point in either consumers or producers holding stocks. If it is not sold and consumed immediately, the good becomes unfit for consumption. Under such assumptions, since the good is only purchased for the sake of immediate consumption, [3.2] becomes

market demand = flow demand = desired consumption per unit of time   [3.6]

Also, since all production has to be sold immediately, eqn [3.3] becomes

market supply = flow supply = desired production per unit of time   [3.7]

Hence, from eqns [3.6] and [3.7]

excess market demand = excess flow demand

= desired consumption – desired production   [3.8]

We shall assume for the moment that both flow demand and flow supply are functions of the price of the good only. That is, we assume that variables such as the prices of other goods, the incomes of consumers and the prices of factors of production remain constant during our analysis. The reader should be familiar with such assumptions – the demand and supply curves in introductory economics textbooks are always drawn up under the so-called *ceteris paribus* assumption, which implies that all variables other than price are assumed to remain unchanged.

The flow supply function

If p is the price of the good and s is flow supply, then using the function notation introduced in Chapter 1 we can write

$$s = s(p) \qquad [3.9]$$

The law of diminishing marginal productivity[2] leads us to expect that, at least in the short run, this function will slope 'upwards'. Let us suppose that we can approximate it by the linear function

$$s = -700 + 300p \qquad [3.10]$$

The function [3.10] is graphed in Fig. 3.1.

Notice that, contrary to usual mathematical procedure, we have placed the dependent variable, s, on the horizontal axis. Economists, being perverse creatures, have always placed the independent variable p on the vertical axis in demand/supply diagrams. This can be a little confusing, but in this case we will follow the custom of the economists.

In Fig. 3.1 we have drawn the supply function [3.10] just for values of price greater than $\frac{7}{3}$. This is because for $p < \frac{7}{3}$ the function yields negative values of s (e.g. when $p = 0$, $s = -700$). The actual supply function is in fact shown by the heavy line in Fig. 3.1. For values of p below $\frac{7}{3}$, production is unprofitable and no supply is forthcoming at all.[3] In general *the flow supply function tells us what producers want to produce* (and hence want to sell, since no stocks are held) *at various levels of p, the price of the good*. For example, if $p = 4$ then desired production is $s = 500$ per unit of time.

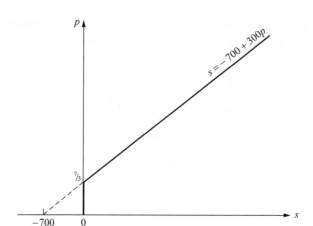

Fig. 3.1   A flow supply function

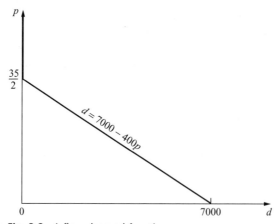

Fig. 3.2   A flow demand function

The flow demand function

If we use the symbol d for flow demand, then under the *ceteris paribus* assumption we can write flow demand as

$$d = d(p) \tag{3.11}$$

If consumers experience diminishing marginal utility from consumption of our good, we can expect the flow demand function [3.11] to slope downwards.[4] Suppose it can be approximated by the linear function

$$d = 7000 - 400p \tag{3.12}$$

This function is graphed in Fig. 3.2, again with price on the vertical axis.

Notice that we have graphed the function [3.12] for values of price, p, between 0 and $\frac{35}{2}$ only. This is because price cannot be negative and because for values of p greater than $\frac{35}{2}$, the function [3.12] yields negative values for d. The actual flow demand function is shown by the heavy line in Fig. 3.2 which implies that when price rises above $\frac{35}{2}$, consumers no longer wish to consume the good. In general, *the flow demand function tells us what consumers want to consume* (and hence want to purchase, since no stocks are held) *at various possible levels of p, the price of the good.* For example, when $p = 10$, then desired consumption is $d = 3000$ per unit of time.

Equilibrium in a flow market

When we speak of *equilibrium* in an economic system we normally mean a situation in which some or all of the variables in the system remain constant over time.[5] It is, in fact, possible to distinguish between two such types of equilibrium. *A flow equilibrium* is said to exist when all flow variables in the system or model remain constant over some specified time interval. A more fundamental type of equilibrium occurs, however, when not only the flow variables in the system but also all the stock variables remain constant over time. Such an equilibrium is known as a *full stock equilibrium* and we shall see later that a flow equilibrium position cannot be expected to persist for long unless it is also a full stock equilibrium. However, since stocks do not exist in the market we are at present discussing, we can limit our discussion for the moment to simple flow equilibria.

Since the two flow variables in our market, flow demand and flow supply, have been assumed to be functions of price alone, a flow equilibrium will exist; that is, d and s will show no tendency to change, provided price, p, remains constant. We can now invoke the assumption introduced at the end of section 3.2, that price will remain unchanged only when excess market demand is zero. From eqn [3.8], we see that, for the simple flow market we are at present considering, excess market demand will be zero only when flow demand equals flow supply. That is, when

$$d = s \tag{3.13}$$

Equation [3.13] ensures that there is no tendency for price to be bid upwards or downwards and once price becomes constant eqns [3.10] and [3.12] tell us the constant flow equilibrium values for d and s. The system is easily solved by substituting for d and s in eqn [3.13] to obtain

$$7000 - 400p = -700 + 300p$$

an equation which can be solved to yield the flow equilibrium value $p = 11$. Substitution of this value for p into [3.10] and [3.12] then yields the flow equilibrium values for flow demand and flow supply as $d = s = 2600$. Only for these values of its variables will this system or market be in equilibrium with its flow variables remaining constant over time.

Notice that regardless of the precise forms for the flow supply and flow demand functions, it is always possible to represent a market of the present type by the three-equation system [3.9], [3.11] and [3.13]. Since the system contains just three variables, d, s and p, we have, applying the rules of Chapter 2, a determinate system in which the number of equations and the number of variables are equal. We know that such a system will always have a single unique solution and that solution gives us the flow equilibrium values for all the variables. The equation system will always 'tell' us what these equilibrium values are.

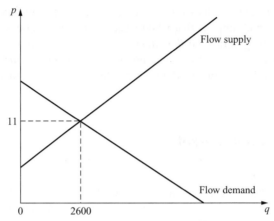

Fig. 3.3 The determination of flow equilibrium

We can, of course, solve such systems graphically. Since in equilibrium flow demand always equals flow supply, we can replace both d and s in eqns [3.10] and [3.12] by the single variable, q, representing 'quantity':

$$q = -700 + 300p \tag{3.10a}$$

$$q = 7000 - 400p \tag{3.12a}$$

Equations [3.10a] and [3.12a] represent a two-equation system in two variables, q and p, which is solved graphically in Fig. 3.3. The solution to the system is given by the intersection point in Fig. 3.3. This again gives flow equilibrium values of 11 for price and 2600 for quantity (i.e. for both flow demand and flow supply). Notice that this approach will always lead to the representation of the market by a two-equation system in two variables, again always with a single determinate solution.

Finally, we can analyse the market in terms of eqn [3.8]. Using eqns [3.10] and [3.12] we can write eqn [3.8] as

excess market demand = excess flow demand

$$= d - s$$

$$= 7000 - 400p - (-700 + 300p)$$

or, using the symbol x to represent excess market demand,

$$x = 7700 - 700p \tag{3.14}$$

The *excess demand function* [3.14] tells us the excess of desired purchases over desired sales (or in the absence of stocks, the excess of desired consumption over desired production) for various possible levels of price, p. For example, when $p = 15$, $x = -2800$, indicating that at this price desired sales in fact exceed desired purchases. On the other hand, when $p = 6$, $x = 3500$, indicating an excess of desired purchases over desired sales.

To determine the equilibrium price level, we simply invoke the assumption that price remains constant only when excess market demand is zero, that is when $x = 0$. From eqn [3.14] this gives us the equation

$$7700 - 700p = 0 \qquad\qquad\qquad [3.15]$$

Solving [3.15] gives us the same flow equilibrium price level, $p = 11$, that we obtained previously.

Notice that, for this type of market, whatever the precise form of the flow demand and flow supply functions, this approach will always lead to an equation such as [3.15] in just one variable, p. The point is that however we analyse this market we always end up with a determinate system of equations yielding a single unique solution. The system [3.10], [3.12] and [3.13] has three equations and three variables, the system [3.10a] and [3.12a] two equations and two variables, the system [3.15] just one equation and one variable. Each approach leads to a single solution which tells us the flow equilibrium values of variables in the market.

Example 3.3

Consider the following single-good flow markets:

(a) $d = 80 - 5p$ (b) $d = 25 - p$ (c) $d = -2p^2 - 4p + 14$

     $s = 30 + p$ $s = 40 - 4p$ $s = -1 + 3p$

Determine for each market (both algebraically and geometrically) the flow equilibrium values of p, d and s.

3.4   Static and dynamic analysis

The analysis of the previous section is often referred to as a static form of analysis. In economics by a *static analysis* we mean a method of analysis which enables us to determine the equilibrium values of variables, that is an analysis which 'tells' us where the equilibrium position is. In the previous section we determined the equilibrium position in the simple market considered by solving a system of equations. However, our analysis told us nothing about how this market behaved when it was in a state of disequilibrium. Moreover, it said nothing about whether (starting from a state of disequilibrium) the market would ever reach the equilibrium position that we found.

To make these problems clearer, suppose that the market is, in fact, in the equilibrium position given by $p = 11$, $d = s = 2600$, that we found in the previous section. Suppose further that, because of a change in consumer tastes, the flow demand function [3.12] suddenly 'shifts' to

$$d = 8400 - 400p \qquad\qquad\qquad [3.16]$$

That is, desired consumption, and hence desired purchases, are now 1400 greater at all levels of price, p.

We can find the market's new equilibrium position easily enough by applying the static-type analysis of the previous section and solving the three-equation system consisting of [3.10], [3.13] and the *new* flow demand function [3.16]. This yields new flow equilibrium values of $p = 13$ and $d = s = 3200$. The question we have to ask is whether the market will now move to

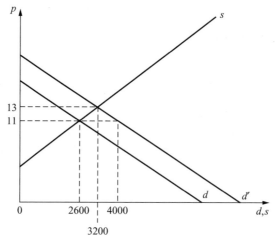

Fig. 3.4 A shift in the demand curve

this new equilibrium position. The new situation is represented in Fig. 3.4 where we measure both flow demand and flow supply on the horizontal axis.

The original flow demand and flow supply functions are labelled d and s in Fig. 3.4 and intersect at the 'old' equilibrium point $p = 11$ and $d = s = 2600$. The new flow demand function is labelled d' and it is clear from the diagram that once the shift from d to d' has occurred, flow demand will exceed flow supply at the 'old' price $p = 11$. In fact, substituting $p = 11$ into [3.10] and [3.16] yields a flow supply value of 2600 and a flow demand value of 4000. The new 'equilibrium point' is given by the intersection of the s and d' curves at $p = 13$ and $d = s = 3200$. When we compare an original equilibrium point with a new equilibrium point, as above, the analysis is referred to as a *comparative static* analysis. Our analysis therefore tells us where the new equilibrium point is. However, whether or not the market moves to this new equilibrium will depend on how it behaves when it is in a position of disequilibrium, as it is now that flow demand and flow supply are no longer equal.

One possible set of assumptions about how the market will behave in disequilibrium was indicated at the end of section 3.2. There it was suggested that when excess market demand was positive price would rise, and when excess market demand was negative price would fall. In the absence of stockholding this is equivalent to saying

    if flow demand > flow supply then price rises   [3.17]

    if flow demand < flow supply then price falls   [3.18]

Under these assumptions it is not difficult to deduce that the market will indeed move to its new equilibrium. In Fig. 3.5 we have omitted the original flow demand curve and just indicated the 'old' price $p = 11$ and the new equilibrium price $p = 13$.

At the 'old' price $p = 11$, flow demand exceeds flow supply so that, under assumption [3.17], price will rise. Moreover, since for any price below the new equilibrium, $p = 13$, flow demand exceeds flow supply, price will continue to rise until the new equilibrium point is reached. Once price attains the value $p = 13$, flow demand and flow supply are equal and there will be no tendency for price to change further.

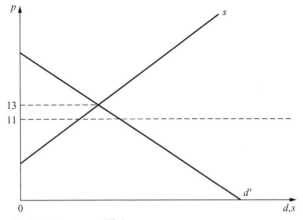

Fig. 3.5 A new equilibrium

An analysis of how a system behaves in situations of disequilibrium is referred to in economics as a *dynamic* analysis, as opposed to the static or comparative static analysis above. Assumptions such as [3.17] and [3.18] about how a system behaves in disequilibrium are called *dynamic assumptions*. It must be stressed, however, that [3.17] and [3.18] are not necessarily plausible assumptions. They arise from the idea of price being bid upwards whenever desired purchases exceed desired sales and being bid downwards when desired sales exceed desired purchases. This presupposes a sufficiently strong competitive element in the market which might not in practice be present. Some economists would argue that the typical immediate response to disequilibrium in a market is not a change in price but a change in the quantity actually bought and sold. However, this is a subject of much current debate and we shall not pursue it further here.

Example 3.4

Suppose flow demand is given by

$$d = 40 - 5p + 2q$$

where q is the price of a substitute good. That is, as q falls, consumers switch to the substitute and purchase less of the original good, so that d falls. Thus if $q = 20$, then the flow demand function becomes $d = 80 - 5p$ as in Example 3.3(a). Suppose q falls to 10. Find the new flow demand function and hence the new flow equilibrium position for Example 3.3(a). If assumptions [3.17] and [3.18] hold, will the market move to the new equilibrium?

Example 3.5

Suppose the flow demand function in Example 3.3(b) shifts to $d = 30 - p$. Determine the new flow equilibrium position. If assumptions [3.17] and [3.18] hold, will the market move to the new equilibrium?

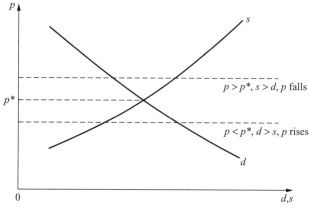

Fig. 3.6 A stable equilibrium

3.5 Stable and unstable equilibrium

An equilibrium in an economic system is said to be *stable* if, once the system is displaced from its equilibrium, forces are brought into play that lead to a restoration of the original equilibrium. On the other hand, if, once the system is displaced from equilibrium, forces are brought into play that drive the system even further from its equilibrium position, then that equilibrium is said to be *unstable*. We shall have more to say about the stability or instability of equilibrium in Chapter 16, but the concepts can be illustrated in terms of the simple flow market of this chapter.

In Fig. 3.6, the customary upward-sloping flow supply function intersects the customary downward-sloping flow demand function at an equilibrium price p^*. Suppose that by 'accident' price is pushed above its equilibrium level p^*. If the assumptions [3.17] and [3.18] hold, then since at prices higher than p^* flow supply exceeds flow demand, price will fall back towards its equilibrium level. Similarly, if price were pushed below p^* then flow demand would exceed flow supply and price would rise back towards its equilibrium level. Clearly, given assumptions [3.17] and [3.18], the equilibrium of Fig. 3.6 is stable in the sense that we have defined it.

It is occasionally the case that a flow demand function slopes upwards, either because the relevant good is a 'Giffen good'[6] or maybe because of reasons related to 'conspicuous consumption'.[7] An upward-sloping flow demand function, together with an upward-sloping flow supply function, is drawn in Fig. 3.7. Again, the equilibrium price is p^*.

Close study of Fig. 3.7 should make it obvious that the equilibrium depicted there is an unstable one. If price is pushed above p^* then it will continue to rise, whereas if price is pushed below p^* it will continue to fall. In either case, market forces drive the price of the good further and further from its equilibrium level.

It should be clear from the above that whether an equilibrium is stable or not depends very much on *dynamic* factors – that is, on how a system or market behaves when it is no longer in equilibrium. If we had adopted somewhat different dynamic assumptions from [3.17] and [3.18] we might have come to different conclusions about the stability of equilibrium in the above case.

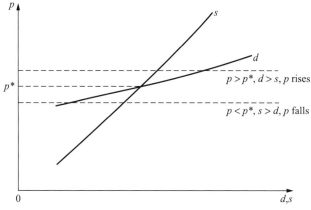

Fig. 3.7 An unstable equilibrium

Obviously an unstable equilibrium is rather unlikely in the simple flow market we are at present considering. However, in more complicated economic systems the stability of equilibrium can by no means be taken for granted.

Example 3.6

Which of the equilibrium positions found in Example 3.3 are stable and which unstable?

Revision examples

Example R3.1

Which of the following are flow variables and which are stock variables: (a) bank balances; (b) imports; (c) dividends; (d) gross domestic product; (e) money in circulation; (f) fixed capital; (g) investment; (h) unemployment?

Example R3.2

Interest is accredited to a building society account at a rate of 5 per cent per annum. The interest is paid at the beginning of each year on the sum in the account at the time. Each year the account holder withdraws an amount equal to $0.25A - 300$, where A is the sum in the account at the beginning of the year before interest is accredited. If $A = £2000$ at the beginning of 1992, how much will there be in the account at the beginning of the years 1993, 1994 and 1995? At what level will the sum in the account eventually stabilise?

Example R3.3

Consider the single-good flow market

$d = 250 - 10p$

$s = 100 + 5p$

$d = s$

Graph the flow demand and supply schedules and use your diagram to find the flow equilibrium values. Verify your solution algebraically.

Suppose the demand schedule shifts to $d = 280 - 10p$. Find the new flow equilibrium values. Next, suppose the supply schedule changes to $s = 100 + 8p$. Find the new flow equilibrium levels.

Example R3.4

The flow demand for a good is given by $d = 50 - 5p + 2q$, where p is the price and q is the price of a close substitute. Graph the demand curve for the good when $q = 5$.

(a) Illustrate on your graph the effect on d of a rise in p from $p = 6$ to $p = 8$, with q constant at 5. What is the size of this effect?

(b) If p now remains constant at 8, illustrate the effect on d of a rise in q from $q = 5$ to $q = 15$. What is the size of this effect?

Example R3.5

The flow market for good (1) has a flow demand function

$d = 21 - 2p + 3q$

and a flow supply function

$s = -5 + 6p - 2q$

where p is the price of good (1) and q is the price of a substitute good (2). If $q = 2$, find the flow equilibrium values for d, s and p.

If the price of the substitute good rises to 3, find the new flow equilibrium values for d, s and p. What type of analysis have you just performed? Suggest some dynamic assumptions which will help to determine whether the new flow equilibrium will be reached. Given your dynamic assumptions, will the new equilibrium be stable or unstable?

Notes

1. The labour market is an obvious example. Many would argue that money wage rates do not fall in response to a negative excess demand for labour reflected in high unemployment levels.

2. See, for example, R. S. Lipsey (1989) *An Introduction to Positive Economics*, 7th edn. Weidenfeld and Nicolson, London, p. 180.
3. We shall see that it is often the case that economic relationships hold only for certain values of their RHS independent variables. In this case we say that the supply function is 'defined only for $p > \frac{7}{3}$'.
4. See, for example, Lipsey, op. cit., p. 140. Alternatively we could argue that since the 'substitution effect' of a price change is always negative and since, for non-inferior goods, the 'income effect' is also negative, a rise in prices will always lead to a fall in flow demand.
5. Sometimes a 'moving' form of equilibrium is defined as holding when variables are growing at a constant rate over time.
6. See, for example, Lipsey, op. cit., p. 135.
7. See, for example, Lipsey, op. cit., p. 191.

4 The reduced and structural forms of equation systems

We shall be concerned in this chapter firstly with relaxing the *ceteris paribus* assumptions made in our analysis of the flow market for a single good and, secondly, with expanding the analysis to cover the case of more than one good. However, we shall retain, for the moment, the assumption that the goods we deal with are perishable. We therefore continue to abstract from problems of stockholding, leaving such problems until Chapter 5.

4.1 An indeterminate system

Consider again the flow market for the single perishable good discussed in section 3.3. We shall refer to this good as good 1 with flow demand d_1, flow supply s_1 and price p_1. Suppose that this good has a close substitute, good 2, the price of which, p_2, has a major influence on the flow demand and flow supply of good 1. This second good is also assumed to be perishable. If we retain, for the moment, the assumption that the income of consumers and the factor prices facing producers remain unchanged during our analysis, then we can write for good 1

$$\text{market demand} = \text{flow demand } d_1 = d_1(p_1, p_2) \qquad [4.1]$$

$$\text{market supply} = \text{flow supply } s_1 = s_1(p_1, p_2) \qquad [4.2]$$

In [4.1] and [4.2] we are again using an extension of the function shorthand introduced earlier. Equation [4.1] simply states that d_1 is a function of both the variables p_1 and p_2 appearing in brackets. That is, d_1 depends on both p_1 and p_2. Similarly [4.2] states that s_1 is also a function of p_1 and p_2. However, because the precise form of the functions will obviously differ, we have written that in [4.1] as $d_1(p_1, p_2)$ and that in [4.2] as $s_1(p_1, p_2)$. Since the good is perishable, market demand consists solely of flow demand (desired consumption) and market supply consists solely of flow supply (desired production).

For an equilibrium price level, we require as usual that excess market demand be zero or, in this case, that flow demand equal flow supply. That is,

$$d_1 = s_1 \qquad [4.3]$$

Equations [4.1]–[4.3] make up a three-equation simultaneous system in *four* variables, d_1, s_1, p_1 and p_2. Applying the rules for simultaneous systems developed in Chapter 2, we see that we have an *indeterminate* system which we can expect to have an infinite number of solutions.

Since it has no unique solution this system cannot tell us what the flow equilibrium values of its variables are and, hence, must be incomplete in some sense. It is easy to see what the problem is. While eqn [4.3] ensures a constant price level, p_1, [4.1] and [4.2] state that flow demand and flow supply depend not only on p_1 but also on p_2, the price of the substitute good. Since there is nothing in our system to ensure a constant p_2, constancy in p_1 is insufficient to ensure constant equilibrium levels for the two flow variables.

The above problem will become clearer if we give specific forms to the functions [4.1] and [4.2]. Suppose, for example,

$$d_1 = 8000 - 200p_1 + 300p_2 \qquad\qquad [4.4]$$

$$s_1 = -200 + 500p_1 - 100p_2 \qquad\qquad [4.5]$$

Notice the signs on the coefficients of the p_2-variable in eqns [4.4] and [4.5]. As p_2 rises d_1 rises provided there is no change in p_1. This should indeed be the case if good 2 is a close substitute for good 1 and vice versa, since as the price of good 2 rises relative to good 1 consumers will switch their purchases from good 2 to good 1. Similarly in [4.5] as p_2 rises s_1 falls provided there is no change in p_1. This should be the case because as p_2 rises relative to p_1, good 2 becomes relatively more profitable than good 1 produce, so that desired sales of good 2 increase while desired sales of good 1 decline.

The problem is that we cannot graph the flow demand and flow supply curves for good 1, as we did in Chapter 3, unless we know p_2, the price of good 2. The positions of these demand and supply curves depend on the value of p_2 and hence we cannot determine their intersection point unless we know p_2. For example, *if* $p_2 = 4$ then substituting this value into [4.4] and [4.5] yields the flow demand and flow supply functions

$$d_1 - 9200 - 200p_1 \qquad\qquad [4.6]$$

$$s_1 = -600 + 500p_1 \qquad\qquad [4.7]$$

The functions [4.6] and [4.7] are sketched as the solid lines in Fig. 4.1.

Equations [4.3], [4.6] and [4.7] comprise a three-equation system in three variables which can be solved to yield the values $p_1 = 14$, $d_1 = s_1 = 6400$. This is represented by the intersection point A in Fig. 4.1. Thus *if* $p_2 = 4$ then the market will have a flow equilibrium point at the above values.[1]

Suppose, however, $p_2 = 11$ and not 4. Equations [4.4] and [4.5] then become

$$d_1 = 11\,300 - 200p_1 \qquad\qquad [4.8]$$

$$s_1 = -1300 + 500p_1 \qquad\qquad [4.9]$$

These flow demand and flow supply functions are graphed as the dashed lines in Fig. 4.1. They intersect at point B where $p_1 = 18$ and $d_1 = s_1 = 7700$. These values can also be obtained by solving the three-equation system [4.3], [4.8] and [4.9]. Thus *if* $p_2 = 11$ then the market has a flow equilibrium point at these new values.

Clearly since we could have started by choosing any arbitrary value for p_2 we can generate as many flow equilibrium positions as we wish. This reflects the fact that the original system [4.3]–[4.5] has an infinite number of solutions. Only if we know the 'actual' value of p_2 can we find the true flow equilibrium position. The system is indeterminate because it contains nothing that can tell us what the value of p_2 is.

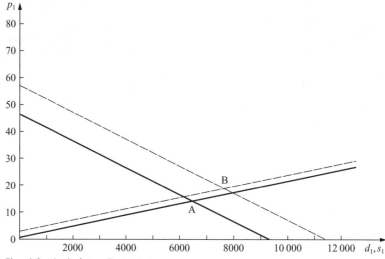

Fig. 4.1 An indeterminate system

One important principle of diagrammatic analysis can be illustrated by a careful study of Fig. 4.1. Notice that we represent the effect on d_1 and s_1 of changes in p_1 (the variable on the vertical axis) by *movements along* stationary d_1 and s_1 curves. However, the effect of a change in p_2 (a variable not measured on either axis) has to be represented by *shifts* in the *whole* d_1 and s_1 curves. This is a quite general principle. Changes caused by a variable *shown on one of the axes* can always be represented by movements along curves whereas changes caused by any variable *not shown on either axis* have to be represented by shifts in curves.

Example 4.1

Consider the flow demand function

$$d_1 = 12 - 3p_1 + 4p_2$$

Suppose $p_2 = 3$. Graph the demand function $d_1(p_1)$ under this assumption and hence illustrate:

(a) the effect on d_1 of a fall in p_1 from 4 to 3 with p_2 remaining constant at 3;
(b) the effect on d_1 of a fall in p_2 from 3 to 2 with p_1 remaining constant at 3.

4.2 Multi-good flow markets

The system of eqns [4.1]–[4.3] has been seen to be indeterminate. Provided we retain the *ceteris paribus* assumption that the income of consumers and the factor prices facing producers remain unchanged during our analysis, one method of making our system determinate is to add to it flow demand and flow supply functions for good 2, together with a second equilibrium condition to ensure a constant value for p_2, the price of the second good. We then have the following expanded system of equations:

$$\text{good 1} \quad \begin{cases} d_1 = d_1(p_1, p_2) & [4.1] \\ s_1 = s_1(p_1, p_2) & [4.2] \\ d_1 = s_1 & [4.3] \end{cases}$$

$$\text{good 2} \quad \begin{cases} d_2 = d_2(p_1, p_2) & [4.10] \\ s_2 = s_2(p_1, p_2) & [4.11] \\ d_2 = s_2 & [4.12] \end{cases}$$

Equations [4.10] and [4.11] state that flow demand for good 2, d_2, and flow supply of good 2, s_2, are functions of the prices of both goods, p_1 and p_2. Equation [4.12] states that flow demand and flow supply of good 2 must be equal if the price, p_2, of good 2 is to remain constant. It is an equilibrium condition similar to eqn [4.3].

We now have a *six*-equation simultaneous system in the *six* variables d_1, s_1, p_1, d_2, s_2 and p_2, which is determinate. We can therefore expect this system to have a single unique solution which tells us the flow equilibrium values of all its variables. Equation [4.3] ensures a constant p_1 and eqn [4.12] a constant p_2. Given constant values for p_1 and p_2 the remaining equations ensure constant values for all the flow variables d_1, s_1, d_2 and s_2.

As an example, suppose the system takes the following specific form:

$$d_1 = 8000 - 200p_1 + 300p_2 \qquad [4.13]$$

$$s_1 = -200 + 500p_1 - 100p_2 \qquad [4.14]$$

$$d_1 = s_1 \qquad [4.15]$$

$$d_2 = 1000 + 200p_1 - 150p_2 \qquad [4.16]$$

$$s_2 = 6200 - 200p_1 + 50p_2 \qquad [4.17]$$

$$d_2 = s_2 \qquad [4.18]$$

This system is most easily solved by substituting [4.13] and [4.14] into [4.15] to yield

$$8200 - 700p_1 + 400p_2 = 0 \qquad [4.19]$$

and substituting [4.16] and [4.17] into [4.18] to yield

$$-5200 + 400p_1 - 200p_2 = 0 \qquad [4.20]$$

Equations [4.19] and [4.20] can be solved to yield the flow equilibrium values of p_1 and p_2. From [4.20]

$$-200p_2 = 5200 - 400p_1 \quad \rightarrow \quad p_2 = -26 + 2p_1 \qquad [4.21]$$

Substituting for p_2 in eqn [4.19] yields

$$8200 - 700p_1 + 400(-26 + 2p_1) = 0 \quad \rightarrow \quad -2200 + 100p_1 = 0 \quad \rightarrow \quad p_1 = 22 \qquad [4.22]$$

If $p_1 = 22$, then using eqn [4.21] $p_2 = -26 + 2(22) = 18$.

The flow equilibrium price values are therefore $p_1 = 22$ and $p_2 = 18$. Substituting these values into [4.13], [4.14], [4.16] and [4.17], we obtain flow equilibrium values for the remaining variables as $d_1 = s_1 = 9000$ and $d_2 = s_2 = 2700$. Since this system has just one solution, only when its variables take these values can it be in flow equilibrium.

Example 4.2

Consider the following two-good flow markets:

(a) $d_1 = 12 - 3p_1 + 4p_2$ (b) $d_1 = 27 - 3p_1 + 2p_2$

    $s_1 = -5 + 4p_1 - 2p_2$ $s_1 = 9 + 3p_1 - 3p_2$

    $d_2 = 2 + 2p_1 - p_2$ $d_2 = 10 + p_1 - 4p_2$

    $s_2 = 18 - 3p_1 + 2p_2$ $s_2 = 3 - p_1 + 2p_2$

Find the flow equilibrium values for p_1, p_2, d_1, d_2, s_1 and s_2 in each of these markets.

It is not difficult to see how our system could be extended to include more than two goods. For example, if a third good has flow demand d_3, flow supply s_3 and price p_3, then retaining the *ceteris paribus* assumption about income and factor prices we can write

$$\text{good 1} \quad \begin{cases} d_1 = d_1(p_1, p_2, p_3) \\ s_1 = s_1(p_1, p_2, p_3) \\ d_1 = s_1 \end{cases}$$

$$\text{good 2} \quad \begin{cases} d_2 = d_2(p_1, p_2, p_3) \\ s_2 = s_2(p_1, p_2, p_3) \\ d_2 = s_2 \end{cases}$$

$$\text{good 3} \quad \begin{cases} d_3 = d_3(p_1, p_2, p_3) \\ s_3 = s_3(p_1, p_2, p_3) \\ d_3 = s_3 \end{cases}$$

The above system consists of nine equations in nine variables so again we can expect it to have just one unique flow equilibrium solution. The three equilibrium conditions ensure constant prices, p_1, p_2 and p_3, and since all the flow variables are functions of these prices, constant prices ensure constant values for flow demands and flow supplies.

It should now be clear that we could expand our analysis to cope with as many goods as we like but always find that the system we have to deal with is determinate with a single unique solution. Such an approach is the basis of what is known as general equilibrium analysis first envisaged by the nineteenth-century economist Leon Walras. Although we shall not pursue it further, this approach conceives the whole economy as one massive system of simultaneous equations.

4.3 The reduced form of an equation system

Consider again the two-good flow market introduced at the beginning of section 4.2. We now relax the assumption that the income of consumers remains constant during our analysis although, purely for expository purposes, we shall retain the assumption about the prices of factors of production remaining constant. If consumer incomes vary then this is likely to be an important factor determining flow demand (i.e. desired consumption) for any good. We therefore need to rewrite the two-good system of section 4.2 as

$$
\text{good 1} \quad
\begin{cases}
d_1 = d_1(p_1, p_2, Y) & \text{[4.23]} \\
s_1 = s_1(p_1, p_2) & \text{[4.24]} \\
d_1 = s_1 & \text{[4.25]}
\end{cases}
$$

$$
\text{good 2} \quad
\begin{cases}
d_2 = d_2(p_1, p_2, Y) & \text{[4.26]} \\
s_2 = s_2(p_1, p_2) & \text{[4.27]} \\
d_2 = s_2 & \text{[4.28]}
\end{cases}
$$

Equations [4.23] and [4.26] state that flow demands now depend not only on the prices of the two goods, p_1 and p_2, but also on the aggregate income, Y, of people that consume the goods.

The system [4.23]–[4.28] consists of just *six* equations in the *seven* variables d_1, s_1, p_1, d_2, s_2, p_2 and Y. As it stands then it is an indeterminate system with an infinite number of solutions. It cannot tell us what the flow equilibrium values of its variables will be.

It may seem that the simplest way to resolve the above indeterminacy is to add another equation to the system 'to help determine Y'. Unfortunately it is by no means obvious what this equation should be and we shall adopt another approach. We shall treat Y as a predetermined or *exogenous variable*. That is, we shall regard Y as being determined 'outside' the two-good market we are analysing. This is a not implausible assumption because, although some of the consumers of goods 1 and 2 may earn their income from the production and sale of these goods, the aggregate income of all consumers will not be much affected by the behaviour of the market for just these two goods.

Once Y is treated as exogenous, it is then possible to find flow equilibrium values for the remaining variables *for given values of* Y. We treat the remaining variables d_1, s_1, p_1, d_2, s_2 and p_2 as having their values determined 'inside' the two-good system we are analysing. Such variables are said to be endogenous to the system and hence are referred to as *endogenous variables*. This approach will become clearer if we take a specific numerical example. Suppose eqns [4.23]–[4.28] take the form

$$
\text{good 1} \quad
\begin{cases}
d_1 = -2000 + 7Y - 200p_1 + 300p_2 & \text{[4.23a]} \\
s_1 = -200 + 500p_1 - 100p_2 & \text{[4.24a]} \\
d_1 = s_1 & \text{[4.25a]}
\end{cases}
$$

$$
\text{good 2} \quad
\begin{cases}
d_2 = -1000 + 4Y + 200p_1 - 100p_2 & \text{[4.26a]} \\
s_2 = -800 - 100p_1 + 300p_2 & \text{[4.27a]} \\
d_2 = s_2 & \text{[4.28a]}
\end{cases}
$$

The positive sign on the coefficients of the Y-variable in eqns [4.23a] and [4.26a] indicates that as consumer income rises desired purchases of each good also rise. That is, we are dealing with normal rather than inferior goods.

In Table 4.1 flow equilibrium values for all the endogenous variables in the system are calculated for various given values of the exogenous variable, Y. For example, in the first section of the table, Y is assumed to be 'determined elsewhere' as 600, the value $Y = 600$ is substituted into the equation system [4.23a]–[4.28a] and the resulting system solved for d_1, s_1, p_1, d_2, s_2 and p_2 in exactly the same manner as we solved the determinate two-good system in section 4.2. In the second section of the table we derive the flow equilibrium values that would occur *if Y* were 400. Finally in the third section of the table similar calculations are performed for a given Y-value of 800. When we compare flow equilibrium positions in this way, it should be clear that we are performing a comparative static analysis of the type defined in the last chapter.

Obviously we could carry out the above procedure of finding flow equilibrium values for any given value of Y. What should be apparent from Table 4.1 is that once we accept a given value for Y, 'determined elsewhere', we are *always left with a determinate six-equation system in the six endogenous variables which we can solve to find flow equilibrium values*. This suggests a general way in which we can handle systems which contain fewer equations than variables. Such systems are normally indeterminate. However, we saw in Chapter 2 that in an n-equation system with $k > n$ variables, provided we could assign, beforehand, values to $k - n$ of the variables, we could then solve such systems for the remaining n variables. What we need to be able to do, then, is to treat $k - n$ of the variables in the system as exogenous. If we are able to do this, we can then always solve the system for the remaining n endogenous variables. For example, we can handle an $n = 5$ equation system in $k = 8$ variables, provided we can treat $k - n = 3$ of the variables as exogenous. For given values of three exogenous variables we are always left with a determinate five-equation system in five variables. For such an approach to be feasible it should be clear that we must be able to treat a sufficient number of variables as exogenous for it to be the case that

number of equations = number of endogenous variables [4.29]

If the condition [4.29] holds then we can handle simultaneous systems in which the *total* number of variables exceeds the number of equations. When representing economic systems algebraically *we must always aim to construct systems of equations such that the condition [4.29] holds*. We were able to do this for our two-good market because although we represented it as a six-equation system in seven variables we were able to treat one of the variables, income, as exogenous.

The technique of treating certain variables in an economic system as exogenous is a powerful and useful one. Effectively we treat the exogenous variables as the 'levers' that 'drive' the system. For example, the system [4.23a]–[4.28a] can be regarded as being 'driven' by the exogenous income variable, Y. As Table 4.1 demonstrates, changes in Y result in changes in the flow equilibrium values of the system's endogenous variables. That is, the table enables us to carry out a comparative static analysis. If it should so happen that a system's exogenous variables are under the control of the economic authorities then the attractiveness of the technique should be clear.

Example 4.3

In the following simple macro-model of an economy, C, Y, I and R represent consumption, national income, investment and the rate of interest respectively:

Table 4.1 Flow equilibrium values for alternative values of Y

Exogenously determined Y-value	System becomes	Equating excess market demands to zero	Flow equilibrium solution
$Y = 600$	$d_1 = 2200 - 200p_1 + 300p_2$ $s_1 = -200 + 500p_1 - 100p_2$ $d_1 = s_1$ $d_2 = 1400 + 200p_1 - 100p_2$ $s_2 = -800 - 100p_1 + 300p_2$ $d_2 = s_2$	→ $2400 - 700p_1 + 400p_2 = 0$ → $2200 + 300p_1 - 400p_2 = 0$	$p_1 = 11.5 \quad p_2 = 14.125$ $d_1 = s_1 = 4137.5$ $d_2 = s_2 = 2287.5$
$Y = 400$	$d_1 = 800 - 200p_1 + 300p_2$ $s_1 = -200 + 500p_1 - 100p_2$ $d_1 = s_1$ $d_2 = 600 + 200p_1 - 100p_2$ $s_2 = -800 - 100p_1 + 300p_2$ $d_2 = s_2$	→ $1000 - 700p_1 + 400p_2 = 0$ → $1400 + 300p_1 - 400p_2 = 0$	$p_1 = 6 \quad p_2 = 8$ $d_1 = s_1 = 2000$ $d_2 = s_2 = 1000$
$Y = 800$	$d_1 = 3600 - 200p_1 + 300p_2$ $s_1 = -200 + 500p_1 - 100p_2$ $d_1 = s_1$ $d_2 = 2200 + 200p_1 - 100p_2$ $s_2 = -800 - 100p_1 + 300p_2$ $d_2 = s_2$	→ $3800 - 700p_1 + 400p_2 = 0$ → $3000 + 300p_1 - 400p_2 = 0$	$p_1 = 17 \quad p_2 = 20.25$ $d_1 = s_1 = 6275$ $d_2 = s_2 = 3575$

$$C = 20 + 0.8Y$$

$$I = 10 + 0.1Y - 0.5R$$

$$Y = C + I$$

If the rate of interest can be regarded as exogenous apply a comparative static analysis to find the effect on the endogenous variables of a rise in R from 5 to 10.

A note of caution must be sounded at this point. One cannot arbitrarily choose which variables in a system should be treated as exogenous. Considering the system [4.23a]–[4.28a] from a purely mathematical point of view, we could just as easily have selected, for example, p_2 as the 'exogenous' variable. For given values of p_2 we could always solve the system for its remaining variables d_1, s_1, p_1, d_2, s_2 and Y, just as we solved it for given values of Y. However, such a procedure would make little sense from an economic point of view. It would hardly be sensible to regard the price of good 2 as being determined 'outside' the markets for goods 1 and 2. This may be plausible for Y but is not for p_2. Ideally we want our exogenous variables to be such that they influence the system but are not themselves influenced by the system. This will not always be possible but we must at least require that causality runs in the main from the exogenous variables to the system and not vice versa.

The comparative static analysis carried out in Table 4.1 for determining flow equilibrium values for given alternative values of Y is clearly a tedious one. We have to 'solve the system' for each given value of Y. A more convenient and practical approach is first to derive the *reduced form* of the system. The original equations [4.23a]–[4.28a] are referred to as *structural equations* and constitute the so-called *structural form* of the system. To obtain the reduced form we 'solve' the structural equations *treating the symbol, Y, whenever it occurs just as if it were a constant or number.* The reduced form will, as we shall see, therefore consist of:

(a) an equation for each endogenous variable in the system;
(b) equations with only the exogenous Y-variable on the RHS.

The simplest way to find the reduced form of the system [4.23a]–[4.28a] is as follows. Substituting [4.23a] and [4.24a] into [4.25a] yields

$$-2000 + 7Y - 200p_1 + 300p_2 = -200 + 500p_1 - 100p_2$$

or

$$-700p_1 + 400p_2 = 1800 - 7Y \qquad\qquad [4.30]$$

Similarly, substituting [4.26a] and [4.27a] into [4.28a] yields

$$-1000 + 4Y + 200p_1 - 100p_2 = -800 - 100p_1 + 300p_2$$

or

$$-300p_1 - 400p_2 = 200 - 4Y \qquad\qquad [4.31]$$

Notice that in [4.30] and [4.31] we have treated the symbol Y as if it were an ordinary number and taken it over to the RHS in each case. Since Y is being treated as a constant, [4.30] and [4.31] can be regarded as two equations in just two variables, p_1 and p_2. They can therefore be solved in the usual way to yield

$$p_1 = -5.00 + 0.0275Y \qquad [4.32]$$

$$p_2 = -4.25 + 0.030\,625Y \qquad [4.33]$$

Equations [4.32] and [4.33] are the reduced form equations for p_1 and p_2. As required, they express these variables in terms of the exogenous variable Y only. To obtain the remaining reduced form equations we simply substitute these expressions for p_1 and p_2 into [4.23a], [4.24a], [4.26a] and [4.27a] and obtain

$$d_1 = -2275 + 10.6875Y \qquad [4.34]$$

$$s_1 = -2275 + 10.6875Y \qquad [4.35]$$

$$d_2 = -1575 + 6.4375Y \qquad [4.36]$$

$$s_2 = -1575 + 6.4375Y \qquad [4.37]$$

Equations [4.32]–[4.37] constitute the full reduced form of the system [4.23a]–[4.28a]. Notice that *all* the endogenous variables are now expressed in terms of the single exogenous variable, Y.

Uses of the reduced form

One use of the reduced form equations [4.32]–[4.37] should be immediately obvious. If we want to obtain flow equilibrium values of the system for a given value of Y, all we need now do is to substitute that value of Y into the reduced form equations. For example, if Y is determined 'elsewhere' as 400, then substituting $Y = 400$ into eqns [4.32]–[4.37] yields.

$$p_1 = 6 \quad p_2 = 8 \quad d_1 = s_1 = 2000 \quad d_2 = s_2 = 1000$$

This is, of course, the same flow equilibrium solution as we obtained in the second section of Table 4.1. The point is that, whatever the given value of Y, we no longer need to 'solve the system' to find the flow equilibrium values. We simply have to substitute the given Y-value into the reduced form equations. Thus use of the reduced form is a particularly convenient way to carry out a comparative static analysis.

The most important use of the reduced form equations is less obvious. Consider, for example, the reduced form equation for d_2, eqn [4.36]:

$$d_2 = -1575 + 6.4375Y \qquad [4.36]$$

We can deduce from eqn [4.36] that an increase of 1 unit in consumer income Y (it matters not whether the increase is from 300 to 301, or 550 to 551, or 399 to 400) will eventually lead to an increase of 6.4375 units in equilibrium flow demand for good 2. It would be extremely difficult to deduce this simply by considering the structural equations [4.23a]–[4.28a]. Indeed, eqn [4.26a] might seem to suggest that an increase of 1 unit in Y will result in a rise of just 4 units in d_2. However, a rise in consumer income, Y, in fact sets off a 'chain reaction' of events in the markets for goods 1 and 2. The 4-unit rise in d_2 is but the initial movement in this chain of events. The initial rise in d_2 will result in an excess market demand for good 2 and hence a rise in its price, p_2. But from eqns [4.23a], [4.24a], [4.26a] and [4.27a] we see that a rise in p_2 means changes in d_1, s_1, s_2 and a *further* change in d_2. In turn, these changes in the flow variables mean changes in the excess market demands for both goods which have consequences for their prices. But further price changes mean further changes in the flow variables etc.

What the coefficient 6.4375 in eqn [4.36] tells us is the *total* effect on flow demand for good 2 of this chain of events. It tells us what will have happened to d_2 once the chain reaction resulting from the increase in Y has fully worked itself out. Similarly, for example, eqn [4.32] tells us that the eventual total effect of a rise of 1 unit in Y will be to increase the flow equilibrium price of the good 1 by 0.0275 units.

The constants in the reduced form equations [4.32]–[4.37], for example the −5.00 and the 0.0275 in eqn [4.32], are for obvious reasons referred to as *reduced form coefficients*. In contrast the numbers in the original structural equations [4.23a]–[4.28a] are referred to as *structural coefficients*. In economic jargon the reduced form coefficients that are attached to any exogenous variables, for example the 0.0275 on Y in eqn [4.32], are also sometimes referred to as *multipliers*.[2]

We should note at this point that the above analysis implicitly assumes that a new flow equilibrium point is in fact reached after a change in the exogenous Y-variable. In terms of the discussion of section 3.4 our analysis has been a purely *static* one. Following a change in the exogenous Y-variable, we can use the reduced form to tell us what the new flow equilibrium values are, but we have not discussed the question of whether a new equilibrium is ever actually reached. Whether it is or not will firstly depend obviously on what dynamic assumptions are valid for describing the behaviour of the system when in disequilibrium. However, even if we can plausibly make dynamic assumptions of the kind [3.17] and [3.18] this alone will not guarantee that a new equilibrium position will be reached. What also matters is the nature of the coefficients or 'numbers' in the original structural equations [4.23a]–[4.28a]. The size of these coefficients will determine the nature of the chain reaction that is set off by a change in the exogenous Y-variable. This chain reaction will not necessarily 'peter out' with the endogenous variables converging on their equilibrium values. While it does in fact do so in the above example, it is feasible that, for certain values of the coefficients in the structural equations, the chain reaction will be an 'explosive' one with the endogenous variables moving further and further away from their equilibrium values. However, we will defer any analysis of this type of situation until Chapter 16.

Example 4.4

Consider the following two-commodity system. Both commodities are perishable and income y is exogenous.

$$d_1 = -15 + 5y - 2p_1 + 2p_2$$

$$s_1 = 3 + 4p_1 - p_2$$

$$d_2 = -2 + 10y + p_1 - 3p_2$$

$$s_2 = -2 - 3p_1 + 2p_2$$

Given that for flow equilibrium $d_1 = s_1$ and $d_2 = s_2$, find the reduced form of the system. Hence find the flow equilibrium values of the endogenous variables when $y = 9$ and the *change* in flow equilibrium values that results from a *change* in y of 1 unit.

A further example

It is quite possible to have two or more exogenous variables in a system or model. For example, in the two-market system just examined, if it was implausible to assume that factor prices remained constant during the analysis, then we could include them as exogenous variables in the flow supply functions. However, as an example of a system with two exogenous variables, let us consider again the indeterminate system examined in section 4.1. This described the flow market for a single good with a close substitute and here we extend it to allow for the fact that flow demand for the good also depends on consumer income Y. Suppose we have

$$d_1 = -2600 + 7Y - 200p_1 + 300p_2 \qquad [4.38]$$

$$s_1 = -200 + 500p_1 - 100p_2 \qquad [4.39]$$

$$d_1 = s_1 \qquad [4.40]$$

The above is a *three*-equation system in *five* variables, d_1, s_1, p_1, p_2 and Y, and is clearly indeterminate. Using [4.29] we know that to handle it we need to be able to treat two of its variables as exogenous and thereby reduce it to a three-equation system in three *endogenous* variables. Consumer income, Y, could obviously be regarded as exogenous but it is not so easy to find a second variable that could be treated in this way. Indeed the most appropriate way of resolving the indeterminacy in this system would be to expand it by including flow demand and supply functions for the second good together with an equilibrium condition $d_2 = s_2$. We would then have a system akin to that of eqns [4.23a]–[4.28a]. However, let us suppose we have no information on the precise form of the flow demand and flow supply functions for good 2. Then, if we wish to be able to handle the system, we have to select a second exogenous variable in addition to Y.

We shall treat p_2 as the second exogenous variable. Although it is hardly satisfactory to treat the price of good 2 as being determined independently of the market for its close substitute, good 1, we have no alternative in the absence of knowledge concerning the flow demand and supply functions for good 2. We have in fact broken the rule, discussed on page 66, that we should treat as exogenous only variables that influence a system but are not influenced by that system. However, it is clearly more plausible to treat p_2 as being determined 'outside' the market for good 1 than it would be to apply the same assumption to any of the other variables in the system. For example, it would be obvious nonsense to treat the price of good 1 as being determined outside the market for good 1.

Once Y and p_2 are taken as exogenous it becomes possible to solve the system in the usual way for given values of Y and p_2. For example, if $Y = 500$ and $p_2 = 6$ then eqns [4.38]–[4.40] reduce to

$$d_1 = 2700 - 200p_1$$

$$s_1 = -800 + 500p_1$$

$$d_1 = s_1$$

Solving yields flow equilibrium values of $p_1 = 5$ and $d_1 = s_1 = 1700$. Obviously, to carry out a comparative analysis, we could follow this procedure for any given pair of values of Y and p_2 but it is again less tedious and more useful to derive the reduced form.

To derive the reduced form in this case we 'solve the system' in the usual way, treating the symbols for the exogenous variables, Y and p_2, just as if they were constants. Substituting [4.38] and [4.39] into [4.40] yields

$$-2600 + 7Y - 200p_1 + 300p_2 = -200 + 500p_1 - 100p_2 \qquad [4.41]$$

or

$$-700p_1 = 2400 - 7Y - 400p_2 \qquad [4.42]$$

Notice that in [4.42] we have moved all terms in Y and p_2 as well as the constants to the RHS. From [4.42] we have

$$p_1 = -3.43 + 0.01Y + 0.571p_2 \qquad [4.43]$$

Equation [4.43] is our first reduced form equation and expresses the endogenous p_1 in terms of the exogenous variables only. The remaining reduced form equations are obtained by substituting eqn [4.43] into eqns [4.38] and [4.39]. This yields

$$d_1 = -1914.29 + 5.0Y + 185.71p_2 \qquad [4.44]$$

$$s_1 = -1914.29 + 5.0Y + 185.71p_2 \qquad [4.45]$$

Notice that the reduced form equations [4.43]–[4.45] again consist of one equation for each of the endogenous variables in the system. Also, the reduced form equations again contain only exogenous variables on their RHSs. The numbers in the reduced form are again known as reduced form coefficients and those attached to the exogenous variables are again referred to as multipliers.

Now we have obtained the reduced form, it is a simple matter to obtain flow equilibrium values of the endogenous variables for any pair of given values for the exogenous Y and p_2. For example, if $Y = 500$ and $p_2 = 6$, then substituting these values into eqns [4.43]–[4.45] yields the values $p_1 = 5$ and $d_1 = s_1 = 1700$, identical values to those obtained above. Similarly, if Y were 400 and p_2 were 4 then flow equilibrium values would be $p_1 = 2.857$ and $d_1 = s_1 = 828.5$.

Again, however, the reduced form is most useful for what it tells us about the overall effect of changes in the exogenous variables. For example, [4.45] tells us that the final effect on s_1 of a rise of 1 unit in p_2 is an *increase* of 185.71 units in the flow equilibrium value of output and sales of good 1. This is by no means obvious from a study of the structural equations [4.38]–[4.40]. Indeed [4.39] indicates that the initial effect of a rise in p_2 is a decline in desired output and sales of good 1 as resources are switched from the production of good 1 to the production of good 2. However, this is again but the initial effect in a whole chain reaction of events. The rise in the price of good 2 also increases flow demand for its close substitute, good 1. Excess market demand for good 1 forces up p_1 and this leads to an *increase* in desired sales and output of good 1. Changes in the flow demand and supply variables have further implications for the price of p_1 and so the chain reaction continues. It is the overall effect of this chain of events that is reflected in the reduced form equations.

Example 4.5

Consider the following market for a good, no stocks of which are ever held:

$$d_1 = 10 + 2y - 3p_1 + p_2$$

$$s_1 = 12 + 2p_1 - 3p_2$$

$$d_1 = s_1$$

Income y and p_2, the price of a substitute commodity, may be regarded as exogenous.

(a) Find the reduced form of the system. Hence, by performing a comparative static analysis, find the flow equilibrium values of p_1, d_1 and s_1 when: (i) $y = 20$ and $p_2 = 5$; (ii) $y = 20$ and $p_2 = 4$; (iii) $y = 15$ and $p_2 = 4$.
(b) The demand equation suggests that a fall in p_2, the price of the substitute, leads to a *fall* in demand. Explain why, then, a fall in p_2 from 5 to 4 with y constant at 20 leads to a *rise* in the *equilibrium* level of demand.

Example 4.6

In the market for a perishable good, desired consumption, d, and desired production, s, are determined as

$$d = -25 + 6y - 2p + q$$

$$s = -5 + 5p - 2q$$

where p is the price of the good. The income of consumers, y, and the price of a substitute good, q, are exogenous. If flow equilibrium occurs when $d = s$, determine the effect on the flow equilibrium values of d, s and p of a fall of 7'units in y accompanied by a rise of 14 units in q. Describe the economic interactions that bring about the change in flow equilibrium values.

4.4 A difficulty

We have made considerable use in this chapter of the fact that, provided condition [4.29] holds, we can always find a single unique solution to a system for given values of its exogenous variables. However, we have, so far, ignored the possibility that the solution might involve negative values of some or all of its variables. For example, consider again the system [4.38]–[4.40] with reduced form given by eqns [4.43]–[4.45]. Suppose we assign the values $Y = 100$ and $p_2 = 7$ to the exogenous variables. The reduced form then yields the 'solution'

$$p_1 = 1.57 \quad d_1 = s_1 = -114.3$$

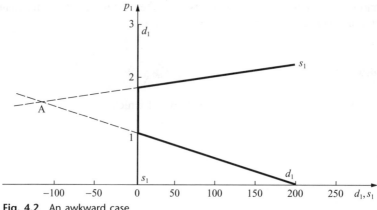

Fig. 4.2 An awkward case

Since desired sales and purchases can hardly be negative, we cannot regard these values as representing the flow equilibrium position in the market when income is 100 and the price of the second good is 7.

The easiest way to see what has gone 'wrong' is to substitute the values $Y = 100$ and $p_2 = 7$ into the flow demand and supply functions [4.38] and [4.39]. This results in

$$d_1 = 200 - 200p_1 \qquad\qquad [4.46]$$

$$s_1 = -900 + 500p_1 \qquad\qquad [4.47]$$

These functions are graphed in Fig. 4.2 and they do indeed intersect at the point $p_1 = 1.57$ and $d_1 = s_1 = -114.3$, designated as point A in Fig. 4.2. However, just as in Figs 3.1 and 3.2, the true flow supply and flow demand functions are shown by the heavy lines in Fig. 4.2. For prices below 1.8 production is unprofitable and no supply at all is forthcoming. Similarly at prices greater than 1 consumers no longer wish to consume the good. The true functions do not therefore intersect at point A. There is in fact no single intersection point since the true functions coincide along the vertical price axis between $p_1 = 1$ and $p_1 = 1.8$. Hence if $Y = 100$ and $p_2 = 7$, price p_1 in the market for good 1 could be anything between $p_1 = 1$ and $p_1 = 1.8$, and for any value of p_1 within the range flow demand and flow supply will both be zero.

The lesson to be remembered from the above is that all the economic functions we have been dealing with are only defined (i.e. they are only valid) over certain values of their independent variables. For example, the first function we defined (eqn [3.10]) only yielded the 'correct' value of flow supply for values of price $p > \frac{7}{3}$. Consequently, the reduced form equations which we derive from our original functions can only be expected to tell us 'correct' flow equilibrium values for values of the exogenous variables within specified ranges. In the above example, the values $Y = 100$ and $p_2 = 7$ clearly lay outside these ranges and hence the reduced form equations did not yield the 'correct' flow equilibrium values. In fact whenever a reduced form yields values for endogenous variables which do not make 'economic sense' (e.g. negative values for flow demand or flow supply) we will know that the selected values for the exogenous variables are outside the allowable range. When this occurs, determining the true equilibrium position becomes, as Fig. 4.2 indicates, a rather more difficult matter.

4.5 A macro-economic example

The approach of handling indeterminate systems by designating certain variables as exogenous and then deriving the reduced form can be equally useful in macro-economics. As an example, consider again the simple Keynesian system described by eqns [2.42]–[2.44]. Suppose the consumption function [2.43] takes the form

$$C = 80 + 0.8Y - 0.5R \tag{4.48}$$

while private investment expenditure, I, is related to the interest rate as follows:

$$I = 2000 - 2R \tag{4.49}$$

The equilibrium condition for the model is given by eqn [2.42] which we reproduce below:

$$Y = C + I + G \tag{4.50}$$

Equations [4.48]–[4.50] constitute a three-equation system in five variables, Y, C, I, G and R, which as such is indeterminate. However, if we are prepared to assume that both the interest rate, R, and government expenditure, G, are under the control of the economic authorities, then we can treat both these variables as exogenous. This will leave us with three equations in the three endogenous flow variables Y, C and I. We can therefore determine flow equilibrium values for this system for any given values of G and R.

Let us derive the reduced form of the above system. Remember that we require one reduced form equation for each endogenous variable, Y, C and I. Also these equations may only contain exogenous variables on the RHS. Since eqn [4.49] already contains only the exogenous R on the RHS, it will serve as the reduced form equation for I.

To obtain the remaining reduced form equations it is simplest to substitute for I and C into eqn [4.50]:

$$Y = 80 + 0.8Y - 0.5R + 2000 - 2R + G$$

We can now solve this equation for Y, treating the exogenous R and G as if they were constants:

$$0.2Y = 2080 - 2.5R + G$$

or

$$Y = 10\,400 - 12.5R + 5G \tag{4.51}$$

Equation [4.51] is the reduced form equation for Y. To find that for C we simply use eqn [4.51] to substitute for Y in eqn [4.48]:

$$C = 80 + 0.8(10\,400 - 12.5R + 5G) - 0.5R$$

or

$$C = 8400 - 10.5R + 4G \tag{4.52}$$

We can now use the reduced form eqns [4.49], [4.51] and [4.52] to obtain flow equilibrium values for Y, C and I given any pair of values for R and G. For example, if $G = 300$ and $R = 6$ per cent then the system is in flow equilibrium when $Y = 11\,825$, $C = 9537$ and $I = 1988$. Alternatively, if $G = 500$ and $R = 4$ then flow equilibrium values are $Y = 12\,850$, $C = 10\,358$ and $I = 1992$. As usual, a comparative static analysis becomes straightforward once the reduced form has been obtained.

Again, however, the most useful role of the reduced form is what it tells us about the overall effect on the endogenous variables of changes in the exogenous variables. Thus we see from eqn [4.51] that a 1 per cent rise in the rate of interest, R, will lead to a fall of 12.5 in the equilibrium level of income. Similarly a rise of 1 unit in government expenditure, G, will lead to a rise of 5 units in the equilibrium level of income.

What we have in the second of the above effects is in fact the famous Keynesian 'multiplier'. From eqn [4.48] we see that a rise in income of 1 unit leads (assuming a constant interest rate) to an increase in consumption of 0.8 units. The *marginal propensity to consume* is therefore 0.8 and the *marginal propensity to save* is 0.2. Readers should be familiar with the fact that the Keynesian 'multiplier' equals the reciprocal of the marginal propensity to save. In this case $1 \div 0.2 = 5$. This is in fact what eqn [4.51] tells us – any increase in government expenditure G leads, in this model, to an increase five times as large in income, Y. It is left to the reader to check that whatever coefficient appears on the Y-variable in eqn [4.48] (i.e. whatever the marginal propensity to consume), the coefficient on the G-variable in eqn [4.51] (i.e. the multiplier) will always equal the reciprocal of the marginal propensity to save.

Example 4.7

Find the reduced form of the macro-model in Example 4.3. Hence check your answer about a rise in R from 5 to 10.

Example 4.8

In the following simple macro-model consumption, C, investment, I, and national income, Y, are endogenous, while government expenditure, G, and the rate of interest, R, are exogenous. C, I, Y and G are all measured in £ billions.

$$C = 10 + 0.8Y$$

$$I = 5 + 0.1Y - 50R$$

$$Y = C + I + G$$

Find the reduced form of the model. Hence

(a) find the equilibrium levels of the endogenous variables when $G = £20$ billion and $R = 0.1$;
(b) deduce the effect on the endogenous variables of a rise of £1 billion in the level of government expenditure.

Revision examples

Example R4.1

In the market for two perishable goods, flow demand and flow supply functions are as follows:

$d_1 = -15 + 8y - 2p_1 + 2p_2$

$s_1 = 8 + 3p_1 - 2p_2$

$d_2 = -4 + 4y + 3p_1 - p_2$

$s_2 = 3 - 2p_1 + p_2$

Interpret the signs on the price variables in the demand and supply functions.

Flow equilibrium occurs when $d_1 = s_1$ and $d_2 = s_2$. If income $y = 2$, substitute for y into the demand and supply equations and find the flow equilibrium values for all other variables.

Example R4.2

Explain the difference between the structural and reduced forms of an equation system. In a two-good flow market demand and supply functions are

$d_1 = -20 + 10y - 3p_1 + 2p_2$

$s_1 = 10 + 3p_1 - 2p_2$

$d_2 = -5 + 5y + 4p_1 - p_2$

$s_2 = 4 - 2p_1 + p_2$

Flow equilibrium occurs when $d_1 = s_1$ and $d_2 = s_2$. If income can be regarded as exogenous, find the reduced form of the system. *Hence* find the flow equilibrium values for all endogenous variables when $y = 2$. Suppose y changes to $y = 1.5$. What are the new equilibrium values? What type of analysis have you just carried out?

Example R4.3

For the market in Example R4.1, assume income y is exogenous. Find the reduced form for this system. Use the reduced form to find flow equilibrium values for all endogenous variables when $y = 2$. Hence check your answer to Example R4.1.

Use the reduced form to find the *change* in flow equilibrium values for all endogenous variables when there is a rise of 0.1 units in the value of y. (Note that y does not necessarily have an initial value of 2.)

Example R4.4

Distinguish clearly between endogenous and exogenous variables. Are exogenous variables always truly exogenous?

In a market in which stocks are never held, desired consumption of a good, d, and desired production, s, are determined as

$$d = -30 + 8y - 3p + 2q$$

$$s = -4 + 6p - 2q$$

where p is the price of the good. If the income of consumers, y, and the price of a substitute good, q, are exogenous, and if flow equilibrium occurs when $d = s$, find the reduced form of the system. Determine the effect on the flow equilibrium values of d, s and p of a fall of 2 units in y accompanied by a rise of 4 units in q.

Example R4.5

In a simple model of the market for money, M and L are the supply and demand for money in £ billions, Y is national income in £ billions and R is the rate of interest in percentage points.

$$L = 5 + 8Y - 2R$$

$$M = 4 + R$$

The level of national income can be regarded as exogenous and the market is in equilibrium when $L = M$. Find the reduced form for the system. Hence find market equilibrium values when $Y = 4$. If Y falls by 1 unit what is the effect on the equilibrium rate of interest?

Example R4.6

In the following model of a simple economy, C, Y, I and G are consumption, national income, investment and government expenditure in the current year, respectively, while Y_{-1} is national income in the previous year.

$$C = 20 + 0.6Y$$

$$I = 5 + 0.1(Y - Y_{-1})$$

$$Y = C + I + G$$

Government expenditure G is exogenous and Y_{-1} can be treated similarly as an exogenous variable. C, Y and I are endogenous. Find the reduced form of the model.

If during 1994 income was 180 and during 1995 government expenditure was 50, use the reduced form to find the values of C, Y and I in 1995. If government expenditure remains constant at 50, hence determine what happens to C, Y and I during 1996–8.

If G remains constant at 50 can you deduce at what value national income Y will stabilise?

Notes

1. Again, do not be concerned about the units involved. Here $p_1 = 14$ and $p_2 = 4$ could be prices of 4p and 14p, or they could be prices of £4000 and £14 000. Similarly s_1 and d_1 could be measured in 'numbers of matchboxes' or 'millions of tonnes'.
2. Students will no doubt be familiar with the term 'multiplier' from their elementary macro-economics. The Keynesian investment 'multiplier' is in fact a reduced form coefficient obtained from the simple Keynesian macro-model $C = cY$, $Y = C + I$, where c is the marginal propensity to consume. If I is regarded as exogenous then the resultant reduced form equation for Y is $Y = I/(1 - c)$, the multiplier being $1/(1 - c)$.

5 Stock-flow markets

We have so far made the very convenient assumption that goods are perishable. This enabled us to abstract from the problem of stockholding and meant that the only equilibria we needed to concern ourselves with were flow equilibria. Once we accept that goods are non-perishable we have to allow for the fact that stocks can be held and this complicates the analysis considerably. Before proceeding the reader should ensure the definitions given in section 3.2 are thoroughly understood.

5.1 Net investment in stocks

We begin by considering the stock-flow market for a single non-perishable good under the usual *ceteris paribus* assumptions that such factors as the prices of other goods, the incomes and tastes of consumers and the prices of factors of production remain constant during our analysis. Under these conditions flow demand (desired consumption) and flow supply (desired production) can be regarded as functions of one variable only – the price of the good whose market we are analysing. Using d, s and p for flow demand, flow supply and price, we therefore write

$$d = d(p); \quad s = s(p) \tag{5.1}$$

We can also assume that *stock demand*, for which we use the symbol, D, will also be a function of price only:

$$D = D(p) \tag{5.2}$$

It is important to note, however, that *stock supply*, for which we use the symbol, S, will not be directly dependent on price. As explained in section 3.2, the behaviour of stock supply (total stock in existence) will depend on whether production exceeds consumption or vice versa. Thus provided producer and consumer desires are met the behaviour of S will depend on the balance of flow supply and flow demand. The point is that while a change in price can cause an *instantaneous* change in the stock of the good people *want* to hold (stock demand) it cannot cause an *instantaneous* change in the stock in existence (stock supply).

Since it is market demands and market supplies which ultimately determine the behaviour of price, we take as the starting-point in our analysis eqn [3.5], reproduced here as eqn [5.3]:

excess market demand = excess flow demand + net investment in stocks $\qquad$ [5.3]

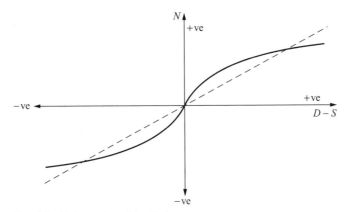

Fig. 5.1 Net investment in stocks

Equation [5.3] states that the excess of desired purchases over desired sales is the sum of two components. Excess flow demand is the excess of desired consumption over desired production while net investment in stocks is the excess of desired additions over desired depletions in stocks. Under our *ceteris paribus* assumptions flow demand and flow supply are functions of the price of the good alone. We therefore rewrite [5.3] as

$$x = d(p) - s(p) + N \tag{5.4}$$

where x again represents excess market demand and we have used the symbol N for net investment in stocks.

Perhaps the first thing to be noted about N is that it is a flow variable describing desired additions to stocks over time. For example, if $N = 500$ we have to specify whether this means an addition to stocks of 500 per week of 500 per year. We can say something immediately about the behaviour of N. If we take our time unit as a week, for example, then, if *at the beginning* of a week stock demand D exceeds stock supply S, we can expect people in general to want to add to stocks *during* that week. Hence

if $D > S$, that is $D - S > 0$, then $N > 0$ [5.5]

Similarly, if, at the beginning of the week, the stocks people actually hold, S, exceed the stocks they want to hold, D, then we can expect N to be negative and stocks to be run down. Hence

if $D < S$, that is $D - S < 0$, then $N < 0$ [5.6]

Clearly net investment in stocks will depend on the balance of stock demand and stock supply. For example, the relationship might look like the solid curve drawn in Fig. 5.1. The curve must pass through the origin since if $D - S = 0$, and the stocks people actually hold equal those they want to hold, then $N = 0$ and there is no desire either to run down or to add to stocks. The problem is that although we know it passes through the origin we have no idea of the precise form of the functional relationship graphed in Fig. 5.1. We shall assume that we can adequately approximate it by the linear relationship

$$N = k(D - S) \tag{5.7}$$

where k is some *constant* with a value between 0 and 1, known as a *stock adjustment coefficient.*

What we are doing is approximating the unknown function in Fig. 5.1 by the dashed straight line. Since there is no intercept term in eqn [5.7] the line passes through the origin, implying $N = 0$ when $D - S = 0$ as required. The slope of the line is given by the k in eqn [5.7].

To understand the economic behaviour underlying [5.7] suppose, for the moment, that $k = \frac{1}{5}$. If, at the beginning of the week, $D = 500$ and $S = 400$, then this would mean that producers and consumers in aggregate wished to hold 100 units more of the good than they actually hold. Clearly they will wish to add to stocks during the following week. However, eqn [5.7] with $k = \frac{1}{5}$ implies that producers/consumers are unable or unwilling to add the full 100 to their stocks during the week. Desired additions to stock are only $\frac{1}{5}$ of $100 = 20$ units during the week. The implication is that it takes time to bring actual stocks to the desired level. For consumers to add to stocks, purchases must exceed consumption and with a given income purchases are naturally limited. For producers to add to stocks output must exceed sales and with given productive capacity there is a limit to which this is possible. A complete adjustment of stocks to their desired level is not possible in the limited time available. A partial adjustment is all that is possible and that is why k is also sometimes referred to as a partial adjustment coefficient.

The actual size of k will depend on the length of the time unit specified. Obviously a larger adjustment is possible in a year than in a week. If the time unit is long enough, complete adjustment is possible and k takes its maximum possible value which is unity. Provided the time unit is long enough for at least some adjustment to take place, k will exceed zero.

Substituting [5.7] into [5.4], we have for excess market demand

$$x = d(p) - s(p) + k[D(p) - S] \qquad [5.8]$$

where the $D(p)$ expresses the fact that stock demand is a function of price.

Example 5.1

Suppose net additions to stock are determined by [5.7] with the stock adjustment coefficient $k = \frac{1}{3}$ when the time unit is one month. What will happen to stocks held if at the beginning of the month:

(a) $S = 500$, $D = 1100$;
(b) $S = 800$, $D = 800$;
(c) $S = 700$, $D = 400$;
(d) $S = 200$, $D = 500$;
(e) $S = 400$, $D = 400$?

5.2 Equilibrium in a stock-flow market

Recalling section 3.3, we have to consider two types of equilibrium in a stock-flow market. A *flow equilibrium* exists whenever flow demand and flow supply remain constant over time, regardless of the behaviour of the stock variables. However, the more fundamental *full stock equilibrium* only exists when not only the flow variables but also stock demand and stock supply remain constant over time.

Since flow demand and flow supply are functions of price alone, *the condition for flow equilibrium* in the present market is the same as that for a constant equilibrium price. If we make our usual assumption that only when excess market demand is zero will there be no tendency for price to change, then from [5.8] this condition is

$$d(p) - s(p) + k[D(p) - S] = 0 \qquad [5.9]$$

Since stock demand, D, is also a function of price, p, alone, a constant price level implies a constant stock demand. However, full stock equilibrium also requires a constant stock supply, S. We already know that the behaviour of stock supply depends on the relationship between production and consumption. Stock supply can only remain constant when production equals consumption. Hence provided consumer and producer desires are realised, as they will be in equilibrium, the condition for a constant stock supply is that flow demand (desired consumption) and flow supply (desired production) should be equal. That is, net flow demand should be zero, or

$$d(p) - s(p) = 0 \qquad [5.10]$$

Only if eqns [5.9] and [5.10] hold simultaneously will the market be in full stock equilibrium. Equation [5.10] ensures a constant S and eqn [5.9] ensures a constant price and hence constant values for d, s and D. Equations [5.9] and [5.10] are therefore *the conditions for full stock equilibrium* in the present market. They consist of just two equations in just two variables S and p (see example below) and hence can be solved for determinate equilibrium values for p and S. Given the equilibrium value of p, full stock equilibrium values for the remaining variables d, s and D can then be found. A numerical example should make this clearer. Suppose

stock demand	$D = -2p + 8$	[5.11]
flow demand	$d = -4p + 10$	[5.12]
flow supply	$s = 3p + 6$	[5.13]
	$k = \frac{1}{2}$	[5.14]

Substituting these expressions into eqn [5.9] yields

$$-4p + 10 - (3p + 6) + \tfrac{1}{2}[(-2p + 8) - S] = 0$$

or

$$-8p - \tfrac{1}{2}S + 8 = 0$$

or

$$S = 16 - 16p \qquad [5.15]$$

Similarly, substituting in eqn [5.10] yields

$$-4p + 10 - (3p + 6) = 0$$

or

$$-7p + 4 = 0 \qquad [5.16]$$

Notice that eqns [5.15] and [5.16] are indeed two equations in just two variables p and S. In fact [5.16] contains p alone and can be immediately solved to give a full stock equilibrium value for $p = 0.57$. Substituting for p in [5.15] then yields a full stock equilibrium value for $S = 6.86$. Finally p can be substituted into [5.11]–[5.13] to yield values for D, d and s. The full stock equilibrium solution is in fact

$$p = 0.57 \quad d = s = 7.71 \quad D = S = 6.86 \tag{5.17}$$

Note that in full stock equilibrium, stock demand and stock supply are, not surprisingly, equal. This reflects the fact that only when people hold the stock they want to hold will there be no adding to or running down of stocks. Only then can stock supply remain constant.[1]

The relationship between flow and full stock equilibrium

The demand and supply curves drawn in elementary economics textbooks almost always refer to what we have defined as *market demand* and *market supply* – that is, desired purchases and desired sales. Together they determine the equilibrium price in the 'market period'. We define a market period as simply the interval between the time the market 'opens for business' and the time when it (temporarily) 'closes'. The next market period begins when the market 'reopens'.

Taking the simple model of the previous section as an example, market demand and supply curves for 'market period 1' are shown in Fig. 5.2. The intersection of these curves determines the equilibrium price level, p^*, for market period 1. Only at this price is excess market demand equal to zero and will there be no tendency for price to be bid upwards or downwards.

The first point to be noted about the equilibrium of Fig. 5.2 is that it is a flow equilibrium, but not necessarily a full stock equilibrium. A constant equilibrium price, p, implies, from eqn [5.1], that d and s, flow demand and flow supply in market period 1, have also attained constant values since they depend on p alone. Thus clearly *the market period equilibrium is a flow equilibrium*. However, just because flow demand and flow supply are *constant* does not necessarily mean they are equal. If they are unequal then the condition [5.10], necessary for a constant stock supply, is not met. But if stock supply is changing then the *market will not be in full stock equilibrium*.

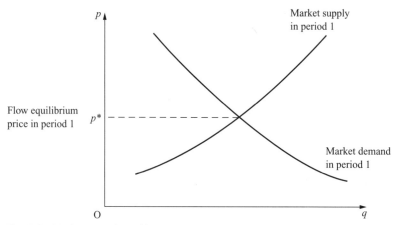

Fig. 5.2 Market period equilibrium

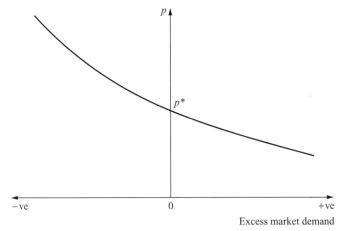

Fig. 5.3 An excess market demand function

We now consider the conditions under which the equilibrium price in the following period, 'market period 2', turns out to be identical to that in period 1. We shall in fact show that only when the first period equilibrium is not merely a flow equilibrium but also a full stock equilibrium will the equilibrium price level remain unchanged.

Consider the market excess demand function [5.8] reproduced here:

$$x = d(p) - s(p) + k[D(p) - S] \qquad [5.8]$$

Since k is a constant, excess market demand during any period depends on price and the level of stock supply at the beginning of that period. Such an excess market demand function is graphed in Fig. 5.3 *for a given level of stock supply.*

The excess market demands in Fig. 5.3 are obtained by subtracting the market supplies from the market demands in Fig. 5.2. Excess market demand is zero only at the equilibrium price p^*. It is positive for price levels below p^* and negative (i.e. there is an excess market supply) for price levels above p^*.

The important point is that a change in stock supply will shift the excess market demand function graphed in Fig. 5.3. For example, a rise in stock supply with price, and hence stock demand, constant, will lead to a fall in net additions to stocks (the $k[D(p) - S]$-component in eqn [5.8]) and hence to a fall in excess market demand. This implies a shift to the left in the curve drawn in Fig. 5.3. Similarly a fall in stock supply will lead to an increase in excess demand and a shift to the right in the curve.

Suppose now that the equilibrium in market period 1 is merely a flow equilibrium but not a full stock equilibrium. That is, flow demand and flow supply are constant but not equal at the equilibrium price. Since condition [5.10], necessary for a constant stock supply, is not met, this means that stock supply at the beginning of market period 2 must differ from that at the beginning of market period 1. But this means that there will be a shift in the excess market demand curve of Fig. 5.3 between the two periods. The intersection point on the vertical price axis must therefore change, implying a *different equilibrium price in the second period.*

By contrast, if the equilibrium of the first period is a full stock equilibrium then stock supply will be the same at the beginning of market period 2 as it was at the beginning of the previous period. There will therefore be no shift in the excess market demand function between the two periods and *no change in the equilibrium price*. Moreover, since there has been no change between the two periods, the second period equilibrium will also be a full stock equilibrium and this implies an unchanged equilibrium price in 'market period 3'.

Clearly equilibrium price can only remain unchanged from period to period when we are in full stock equilibrium. A flow equilibrium that is not also a full stock equilibrium is necessarily temporary. *Only a full stock equilibrium can persist from period to period*. We can use the example introduced as eqns [5.11]–[5.14] to make this clearer. This market had full stock equilibrium values given by eqn [5.17].

Suppose at the beginning of market period 1 stock supply $S = 6$. Note that this is *not* the full stock equilibrium value of stock supply. Price will be at its equilibrium value in period 1 when excess market demand is zero. Substituting eqns [5.11]–[5.14] and $S = 6$ into eqn [5.19], this implies

$$-4p + 10 - (3p + 6) + \tfrac{1}{2}[(-2p + 8) - 6] = 0 \qquad [5.18]$$

Solving eqn [5.18] for p gives a value for equilibrium price $p^* = 0.625$. This is the flow equilibrium value for price in market period 1.[2] Given a price of 0.625, we can use [5.12] and [5.13] to find the resultant values for flow demand and flow supply. We then have the flow equilibrium values for market period 1 which are

$$p^* = 0.625 \quad d = 7.5 \quad s = 7.875 \qquad [5.19]$$

Notice that flow demand and flow supply are unequal. There is in fact an excess flow supply of 0.375 units. Or, looking at it another way, production exceeds consumption by 0.375 in market period 1.

We can also use the fact that equilibrium $p^* = 0.625$ to obtain the flow equilibrium value of stock demand. Substituting in [5.11] yields a value of $D = 6.75$ whereas we know that stock supply at the beginning of the period was $S = 6$. Since stock demand exceeds stock supply there will be net additions to stock during market period 1. Using [5.7] with $k = \tfrac{1}{2}$, net investment in stocks will in fact be

$$N = \tfrac{1}{2}(6.75 - 6) = 0.375 \qquad [5.20]$$

The addition to stocks is, of course, exactly equal to the excess of production over consumption found above. Since additions are being made to stocks during market period 1, the equilibrium for this period is clearly not a full stock equilibrium and stock supply at the beginning of market period 2 will differ from that at the beginning of period 1. In fact since $S = 6$ at the beginning of the first period, and 0.375 is added to stocks during this period, stock supply at the beginning of market period 2 will be $S = 6.375$.

To determine the equilibrium price level in market period 2, we again substitute eqns [5.11]–[5.14] into eqn [5.9] but this time use the value $S = 6.375$. This gives

$$-4p + 10 - (3p + 6) + \tfrac{1}{2}[(-2p + 8) - 6.375] = 0 \qquad [5.21]$$

which yields an equilibrium price level for market period 2 of $p^* = 0.6015$. Notice that this differs from the equilibrium price for the first period because we have a different value for stock supply. Thus we see that because the first period equilibrium was merely a flow equilibrium and not a full stock equilibrium, the equilibrium price level changes.

Stock supply at the beginning of market period 2, $S = 6.375$, is still not at the full stock equilibrium level given by [5.17]. Hence the market cannot attain full stock equilibrium in this period either and this implies a further change in the equilibrium price level for market period 3. Suppose, however, that at the beginning of market period 1 stock supply had not been $S = 6$ *but had been at its full stock equilibrium value* $S = 6.86$. To obtain equilibrium price we would now substitute $S = 6.86$ into eqn [5.9] and obtain not eqn [5.18] but

$$-4p + 10 - (3p + 6) + \tfrac{1}{2}[(-2p + 8) - 6.86] = 0 \tag{5.22}$$

Solving [5.22] yields an equilibrium price level of $p^* = 0.57$. Substituting this price value into eqns [5.11]–[5.13] yields equilibrium values for market period 1 of $D = 6.86$, $d = 7.71$ and $s = 7.71$. Notice from [5.17] that we are, in fact, in full stock equilibrium. Consequently, since $d = s$, production and consumption are identical and, since $D = S$, there are no additions to stock during the period. It follows that stock supply at the beginning of market period 2 will be identical to that in period 1, and that to obtain the equilibrium price level for market period 2 we will again have to solve eqn [5.22]. Not surprisingly this again yields the value $p^* = 0.57$ – no change from the full stock equilibrium value of the previous period. Since we are again in full stock equilibrium, there will again be no change in stock supply and hence to obtain the equilibrium price level for market period 3 we must again solve eqn [5.22]. Clearly, while we remain in full stock equilibrium, price will remain unchanged from period to period.

Example 5.2

Find the full stock equilibrium value for the following stock-flow market for a single good:

flow demand	$d = -2p + 15$
flow supply	$s = 3p - 5$
stock demand	$D = -5p + 30$

Net investment in stock per period is equal to one-third of the excess of the demand for stocks over the supply available.

Find market period equilibrium values for p, d, s and D when stock supply, S, at the beginning of the market period is: (a) 20; (b) 0; (c) 10.5; (d) 9.5. Hence, in each case, find stock supply at the beginning of the next market period. What do your answers suggest about the stability of full stock equilibrium in this market?

Example 5.3

Flow demand and flow supply functions for a commodity are respectively

$$d = -3p + 10 \quad \text{and} \quad s = 2p + 5$$

where p is the price of the commodity. Stock demand for the commodity is given by $D = -2p + 8$, while net additions to stocks during any period are equal to half the excess of stock demand over stock supply at the beginning of that period (i.e. $k = \tfrac{1}{2}$).

(a) Determine full stock equilibrium values for all variables.

(b) Given that stock supply at the beginning of a period is 10, determine the flow equilibrium values for d, s, D and p: (i) during this period; and (ii) during the next period.

(c) If $k = \frac{1}{4}$ how does this affect your answers to (a) and (b)?

Example 5.4

Find what you think are 'economically realistic' full stock equilibrium values for price and all other variables in a single-good stock-flow market where

flow demand	$d = -3p^2 + 8p + 6$
flow supply	$s = 2p^2 + 2p - 2$
stock demand	$D = -3p + 16$
stock investment coefficient	$k = 0.2$

5.3 Exogenous variables and reduced forms

In the simple stock-flow model of the last section all the variables were endogenous, that is all values for the variables were determined by the model itself. However, there is no reason why exogenous variables should not also appear in stock-flow models. For example, both flow demand and stock demand could be dependent on an exogenously determined level of consumer income, Y. Suppose, using the notation of the last section, we have the following single-good stock-flow market:

flow demand	$d = 10 - 2p + 5Y$	[5.23]
flow supply	$s = 2p + 5$	[5.24]
stock demand	$D = 12 - 3p + 6Y$	[5.25]
	$k = \frac{1}{3}$	[5.26]

As with any models containing exogenous variables, it is always sensible first to find the reduced form. In this case the reduced form will give full stock equilibrium values as functions of the exogenous Y. To obtain the reduced form we handle the model in just the same manner as in the last section, except that whenever we encounter the symbol Y we treat it as if it were a constant.

Substituting into [5.9], the condition for flow equilibrium, and using [5.23]–[5.24], we obtain

$$10 - 2p + 5Y - (3p + 5) + \tfrac{1}{3}(12 - 3p + 6Y - S) = 0$$

or, remembering to take any terms in Y onto the RHS,

$$-2p - 3p - p - \tfrac{1}{3}S = -4 - 2Y - 10 - 5Y + 5$$

or

$$6p + \tfrac{1}{3}S = 9 + 7Y \qquad\qquad [5.27]$$

Substituting into [5.10] then gives

$$10 - 2p + 5Y - (5 + 3p) = 0$$

$$5p = 5 + 5Y \quad \rightarrow \quad p = 1 + Y \tag{5.28}$$

Equation [5.28] is the first reduced form equation obtained, giving the full stock equilibrium value for price in terms of exogenous income, Y.

Substituting for p in [5.27] then gives

$$6(1 + Y) + \tfrac{1}{3}S = 9 + 7Y$$

or

$$\tfrac{1}{3}S = 3 + Y \quad \rightarrow \quad S = 9 + 3Y \tag{5.29}$$

Equation [5.29] is the reduced form equation for stock supply, S.

The remaining reduced form equations can be obtained by substituting for p into eqns [5.23]–[5.25], giving

$$d = s = 8 + 3Y \tag{5.30}$$

$$D = 9 + 3Y \tag{5.31}$$

Notice that, since $D = S$ in full stock equilibrium, the reduced form equations [5.29] and [5.31] are identical.

5.4 Stock-flow markets for more than one good

It is a relatively simple matter to extend our stock-flow analysis to cover markets for more than one good. Suppose, for example, we have two substitute goods. Retaining the *ceteris paribus* assumption of constant consumer tastes and incomes and of constant factor prices, we can write, for the first good,

flow demand $d_1 = d_1(p_1, p_2)$ [5.32]

flow supply $s_1 = s_1(p_1, p_2)$ [5.33]

stock demand $D_1 = D_1(p_1, p_2)$ [5.34]

where p_1 and p_2 are the prices of the first and second goods respectively. Similarly for the second good we can write

flow demand $d_2 = d_2(p_1, p_2)$ [5.35]

flow supply $s_2 = s_2(p_1, p_2)$ [5.36]

stock demand $D_2 = D_2(p_1, p_2)$ [5.37]

The stock supplies S_1 and S_2 of the two goods are, of course, not directly dependent on prices but will depend on the balance of production and consumption for the respective goods.

Net investment in stocks of each good will depend on the rates at which actual stocks are brought up to desired levels. There is no reason why rates of adjustment should be the same for both goods, so we shall assume an adjustment parameter k_1 for the first good and k_2 for the second good. Net investment in stocks of the first good is therefore

$$N_1 = k_1[D_1(p_1, p_2) - S_1] \tag{5.38}$$

and for the second good

$$N_2 = k_2[D_2(p_1, p_2) - S_2] \tag{5.39}$$

As usual we assume that prices of goods only become constant at equilibrium levels when excess market demands are zero. We therefore have an equation similar to eqn [5.9] for each good:

$$d_1(p_1, p_2) - s_1(p_1, p_2) + k_1[D_1(p_1, p_2) - S_1] = 0 \tag{5.40}$$

$$d_2(p_1, p_2) - s_2(p_1, p_2) + k_2[D_2(p_1, p_2) - S_2] = 0 \tag{5.41}$$

Equations [5.40] and [5.41] ensure constant price levels. Given constant prices, eqns [5.32]–[5.37] determine constant values for d_1, s_1, D_1, d_2, s_2 and D_2. There remain the stock supply variables S_1 and S_2. Stock supplies will only be constant when production equals consumption. Therefore, for a full stock equilibrium we also require equality of flow demand and flow supply for each good:

$$d_1(p_1, p_2) - s_1(p_1, p_2) = 0 \tag{5.42}$$

$$d_2(p_1, p_2) - s_2(p_1, p_2) = 0 \tag{5.43}$$

Equations [5.40]–[5.43] represent the conditions for full stock equilibrium in this two-good market. They consist of four equations in just four variables, p_1, p_2, S_1 and S_2, and hence we can expect them to yield unique full stock equilibrium values. Given the equilibrium values for p_1 and p_2 we can then use eqns [5.32]–[5.37] to find the full stock equilibrium values for the remaining variables.[3]

Example 5.5

Suppose in the two-good stock-flow market

$$d_1 = -4p_1 + 2p_2 + 6 \qquad d_2 = 5p_1 - 2p_2 + 7$$

$$s_1 = 3p_1 - p_2 + 5 \qquad s_2 = -2p_1 + 3p_2 + 4$$

$$D_1 = -2p_1 + 3p_2 + 4 \qquad D_2 = 3p_1 - p_2 + 2$$

$$k_1 = \tfrac{1}{2} \qquad k_2 = \tfrac{1}{4}$$

(a) Find the full stock equilibrium values for all variables.
(b) If at the beginning of a market period stock supplies are $S_1 = 6$ and $S_2 = 5$, determine the flow equilibrium values for the price variables during this period.

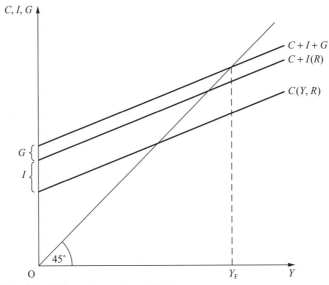

Fig. 5.4 Full employment equilibrium

5.5 A macro-economic example

Let us consider again the simple Keynesian macro-economic model of eqns [4.48]–[4.50] which we reproduce here in general functional notation as

$$C = C(Y, R) \tag{5.44}$$

$$I = I(R) \tag{5.45}$$

$$Y = C + I + G \tag{5.46}$$

where G is the exogenous level of government expenditure and I is private fixed capital investment expenditure which depends on the exogenous rate of interest, R.

Suppose that the levels of the exogenous variables G and R are such that the resultant equilibrium values of Y, C and I result in full employment. In particular, $Y = Y_F$ where Y_F is the 'full employment level of income'. Since Y, C and I are all flow variables it is clear that we have a flow equilibrium. The equilibrium is illustrated in Fig. 5.4.

Since the model [5.44]–[5.46] does not contain any stock variables as it stands, it may seem that we need not be concerned with full stock equilibria. However, a fuller specification of the consumption function [5.44] might allow for the fact that consumer expenditure depends not only on consumer income, Y, but also possibly on consumers' total physical and financial wealth, W. That is, we should rewrite eqn [5.44] as

$$C = C(Y, R, W) \tag{5.47}$$

The question now arises of whether in the flow equilibrium depicted in Fig. 5.4, the stock variable, W, remains constant. The answer is almost certainly not. In the equilibrium of Fig. 5.4 income clearly exceeds consumption so that consumers' saving is non-zero and positive. But saving adds to consumer wealth, W. Provided this saving is not counterbalanced by a depreciation in existing wealth, wealth must therefore increase.[4] But a rise in consumer wealth with given levels of Y and R will lead to an increase in consumption according to eqn [5.47]. That is, the consumption function in Fig. 5.4 will shift upwards, altering the flow equilibrium position. Thus again we have a situation where a flow equilibrium cannot persist over time because it is not also a full stock equilibrium.

The flow equilibrium of Fig. 5.4 will, almost certainly, involve changes not only in W but also in another important stock variable. The flow equilibrium level of I is positive in Fig. 5.4. But fixed capital investment means an addition to capital stock provided it is not offset by a depreciation in the existing stock.[5] An increase in an economy's capital stock implies an increase in the full employment level of income. The flow equilibrium level of income in Fig. 5.4 will therefore no longer be sufficient to maintain full employment. Increasing levels of unemployment may cause money wages and eventually the general price level to fall. This would lead to a rise in the real value of consumer wealth and, hence, to a further upward shift in the consumption function. This, then, is a further reason why the flow equilibrium of Fig. 5.4 cannot persist for long. Because it completely ignores stock variables the simple Keynesian model of eqns [5.44]–[5.46] can at best provide only a short-run explanation of the level of national income.[6]

Revision examples

Example R5.1

Explain what is meant by the stock adjustment coefficient for a non-perishable good. Why must the coefficient always take a value between 0 and 1 inclusive? Why is it unlikely that it will actually take the value 0 or 1?

Find full stock equilibrium values for all variables for the following market:

flow demand	$d = 10 - p$
flow supply	$s = 4 + 2p$
stock demand	$D = 16 - 2p$

where p is price and the stock adjustment coefficient $k = 0.25$.

If actual stock, S, is 8 units at the start of a market period, what will the market equilibrium values be: (a) at the end of the current market period; (b) at the end of the next market period? Explain your result. How would your answer differ if the stock adjustment coefficient equalled zero?

Example R5.2

In a stock-flow market for a single good

flow demand	$d = 32 - 2p$
flow supply	$s = 7 + 3p$
stock demand	$D = 40 - 4p$

Net additions to stock during any period are equal to a half of the difference between stock demand and stock supply at the beginning of that period.

At the beginning of a market period, stock supply S is 16. Find the flow equilibrium values of d, s, D and p for this period. Hence find the value of S at the beginning of the next period. Carry out similar analyses for market periods in which S takes the values: (a) 20; (b) 24. Comment on your results.

Example R5.3

Consider an isolated stock-flow market in which

$$\text{flow demand} \quad d = -3p + 22$$

$$\text{flow supply} \quad s = 2p + 2$$

$$\text{stock demand} \quad D = -4p + 20$$

$$\text{stock adjustment coefficient } k = 0.25$$

(a) Determine full stock equilibrium values for all variables. If k changes to 0.5, will there be any change in full stock equilibrium values?
(b) During a given market period, the market equilibrium price is $p = 3$. What was stock supply at the beginning of this period?

Example R5.4

In a stock-flow market for a single perishable good

$$\text{flow demand} \quad d = 20 - 3p$$

$$\text{flow supply} \quad s = 26 - 4w + 2p$$

$$\text{stock demand} \quad D = 42 - 2p$$

The variables d, s, D and p are defined as usual and w is an index of wage costs. Thus, as wage costs rise, the desired production of firms in the market falls. w can be regarded as an exogenous variable, whereas all other variables are endogenous. Net investment in stocks per period is equal to half of the excess of stock demand over stock supply, S, at the beginning of the period. Find reduced form full stock equilibrium equations for d, s, D, S and p.

(a) Find full stock equilibrium values for all variables when $w = 6$ units.
(b) What is the effect on the full equilibrium values of $D = S$ when w rises by 1 unit?

Notes

1. The conditions for full stock equilibrium could in fact be written as

$$d(p) - s(p) = 0$$

$$D(p) - S \quad = 0$$

That is, the equilibrium values are independent of the value of k, the stock adjustment coefficient. However, as we shall see, the value of k has an important effect on how the market behaves when it is not in full stock equilibrium.

2. Notice that the flow equilibrium values depend very much on the value of k. The solution to eqn [5.18] would have been different had k, for example, been equal to $\frac{1}{4}$ rather than $\frac{1}{2}$. Thus, while the full stock equilibrium position is independent of k (see note 1), the value of k is important when the market is not in full stock equilibrium.

3. The conditions for full stock equilibrium could also be written as $d_1 = s_1$, $d_2 = s_2$, $D_1 = S_1$ and $D_2 = S_2$. As in the single-good market, full stock equilibrium values are independent of the values of stock adjustment coefficients. However, k_1 and k_2 again influence the behaviour of the market when it is not in full stock equilibrium.

4. Existing wealth could lose value either because of a depreciation in physical assets held or because financial assets which have a fixed money value (e.g. bank deposits) lose real value as prices rise. The difference between saving and depreciation in existing wealth, which we can call net saving, is the net flow variable which determines the behaviour of the stock variable, wealth.

5. Fixed capital (e.g. plant and machinery) physically depreciates with use. The difference between fixed capital investment and depreciation in the existing capital stock is known as net fixed investment. Net investment is the net flow variable which determines the behaviour of capital stock.

6. A full stock equilibrium, in the sense we have defined it, could only exist in this model if net saving and net investment were both zero. However, it is possible to define a stock equilibrium in which stock variables are not constant but, instead, are growing at a constant rate.

6 Geometric progressions and discounted cash flows

Most people are familiar with the idea of compound interest. Suppose, for example, a person places £500 in a deposit account at a bank and a year later receives interest of 8 per cent on the deposit. The account will now contain an amount

$$D_1 = £500 + \left(\frac{8}{100} \times £500\right) = £500\left(1 + \frac{8}{100}\right) = £500(1.08)$$

Provided no cash is withdrawn from the account, at the end of the second year interest will be received both on the original deposit and on the interest earned in the first year – that is, on the entire amount D_1 in the account at the end of the first year.[1] Provided the interest rate remains unchanged the account will therefore contain at the end of the second year, an amount

$$D_2 = £500(1.08) + \left[\frac{8}{100} \times £500(1.08)\right] = £500(1.08)\left(1 + \frac{8}{100}\right)$$

$$= £500(1.08)^2$$

Similarly, provided no cash is withdrawn so that interest continues to be 'compounded', the account will contain at the end of the third year an amount

$$D_3 = £500(1.08)^3$$

and at the end of the fourth year an amount

$$D_4 = £500(1.08)^4$$

In general if the initial deposit is A and the rate of interest is r per annum (notice that, for example, if the rate of interest is 12 per cent then $r = 0.12$), then

$$D_1 = A(1 + r)$$
$$D_2 = A(1 + r)^2$$
$$D_3 = A(1 + r)^3$$
$$D_4 = A(1 + r)^4 \text{ etc.}$$

It is clear from the above sequence that at the end of x years the account will contain an amount

$$D_x = A(1 + r)^x \qquad \qquad [6.1]$$

We shall make considerable use of eqn [6.1] later in this chapter.

The above sequence of D's forms what is known as a geometric progression because each D can be obtained from the preceding D by multiplying by the constant quantity $1 + r$. Geometric progressions arise fairly frequently in economics so it is worth spending a little time on them.

6.1 Geometric progressions

A *geometric progression* is simply a sequence of terms in which each term is obtained from the preceding term by multiplying by a constant known as the *common ratio*. For example, the sequence

1, 3, 9, 27, 81, 243, . . .

is a geometric progression (GP) with common ratio 3 since each term is three times the preceding one. Similarly, the sequence

$4, -2, 1, -\frac{1}{2}, \frac{1}{4}, -\frac{1}{8}, \dots$

is a GP with a common ratio of $-\frac{1}{2}$ since each term in this sequence is obtained by multiplying its predecessor by $-\frac{1}{2}$.

If we let the first term of a GP be a and the common ratio c, then the GP has the general form

$a, ac, ac^2, ac^3, ac^4, ac^5, \dots$ [6.2]

Clearly, the fifth term of the sequence [6.2] is ac^4 while the seventh is ac^6 and it is not difficult to see that the fifty-seventh term, for example, will be ac^{56}. In general then we can say that

the nth term of a GP $= ac^{n-1}$ [6.3]

The sum to n terms of a geometric progression

The sum of the first n terms in a GP is referred to as the 'sum to n terms' and we shall refer to it as S_n. That is,

$S_n = a + ac + ac^2 + ac^3 + \dots + ac^{n-1}$ [6.4]

It is often convenient to have a compact expression for [6.4] and we obtain it as follows. Multiplying [6.4] throughout by c yields

$cS_n = ac + ac^2 + ac^3 + ac^4 + \dots + ac^{n-1} + ac^n$ [6.5]

Subtracting [6.5] from [6.4], we obtain

$S_n - cS_n = a - ac^n$

or

$S_n(1 - c) = a(1 - c^n)$

Hence we have

sum to n terms of a GP $= \dfrac{a(1-c^n)}{1-c}$ [6.6]

To illustrate the use of [6.3] and [6.6] consider the following examples.

Worked example 1

Find the eighth term and the sum to six terms of the GP

$\frac{1}{2}$, 1, 2, 4, 8, . . .

This GP has $a = \frac{1}{2}$ and $c = 2$. Hence using eqn [6.3]

eighth term $= ac^{n-1} = \frac{1}{2}(2)^7 = 64$

and using eqn [6.6]

sum to six terms $= \dfrac{a(1-c^n)}{1-c} = \dfrac{\frac{1}{2}(1-2^6)}{1-2} = \dfrac{\frac{1}{2}(1-64)}{-1} = 31.5$

Notice that for simple examples the answers provided by [6.3] and [6.6] can easily be checked by adding terms to the given GP. For example, in the present case the progression can be extended to $\frac{1}{2}$, 1, 2, 4, 8, 16, 32, 64, ... The eighth term is obviously 64 and simple addition gives S_6 as 31.5.

Worked example 2

Find the sixth term and the sum to six terms of the GP

9, −3, 1, $-\frac{1}{3}$, . . .

This has $a = 9$ and $c = -\frac{1}{3}$. Hence, using eqns [6.3] and [6.6],

sixth term $= ac^{n-1} = 9(-\frac{1}{3})^5 = 9(-\frac{1}{243}) = -0.037$

sum to six terms $= \dfrac{a(1-c^n)}{1-c} = \dfrac{9\left[1-(-\frac{1}{3})^6\right]}{1-(-\frac{1}{3})} = \dfrac{9(1-\frac{1}{729})}{\frac{4}{3}} = 6.741$

Example 6.1

Which of the following sequences are geometric progressions and which are not?

(a) 12, 6, 3, 1.5, 0.75, . . .
(b) −2, 6, −18, 54, −162, . . .
(c) 3, 8, 13, 18, 23, . . .
(d) 0.45, 1.8, 7.2, 28.8, 115.2, . . .
(e) $\frac{1}{2}, \frac{1}{3}, \frac{1}{4}, \frac{1}{5}, \frac{1}{6}, \ldots$

Example 6.2

Consider the following GPs:

(a) $\frac{1}{9}, \frac{1}{3}, 1, 3, 9, \ldots$

(b) $\frac{2}{3}, \frac{2}{9}, \frac{2}{27}, \frac{2}{81}, \ldots$

(c) 0.7, 0.56, 0.448, 0.3584, ...

(d) −2, 4, −8, 16, −32, ...

(e) 50, −25, 12.5, −6.25, ...

For each series find the 10th term and the sum to five terms.

The sum to infinity of a geometric progression

All GPs contain an unlimited or infinite number of terms. For example, the progression

$$8, 4, 2, 1, \tfrac{1}{2}, \tfrac{1}{4}, \ldots \qquad [6.7]$$

continues indefinitely. The question arises of whether it is possible to sum or add up the infinite number of terms in a GP and obtain an answer which is not itself infinite but is a finite number. In the table next to Fig. 6.1, the expression [6.6] has been used to calculate the sum of the gradually increasing numbers of terms of the GP [6.7]. For GP [6.7] $a = 8$ and $c = \tfrac{1}{2}$ so that eqn [6.6] yields

$$S_n = \frac{8\left[1 - (\tfrac{1}{2})^n\right]}{1 - \tfrac{1}{2}} = 16\left[1 - (\tfrac{1}{2})^n\right] \qquad [6.8]$$

It should be clear, both from the table and from Fig. 6.1, that as the number of terms being summed gets larger and larger, their sum gets closer and closer to the number 16. It should now

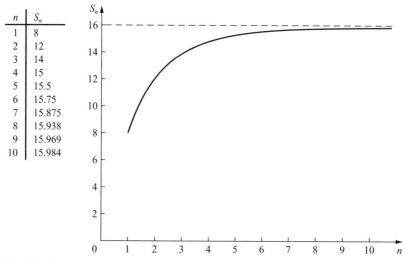

n	S_n
1	8
2	12
3	14
4	15
5	15.5
6	15.75
7	15.875
8	15.938
9	15.969
10	15.984

Fig. 6.1 A convergent GP

be clear that it *is* possible to obtain a finite number for the sum of the infinite number of terms in the GP [6.7]. The finite sum in this case is obviously 16.

It is instructive to examine why such a finite sum exists in this case. We can rewrite eqn [6.8] as

$$S_n = 16 - 16(\tfrac{1}{2})^n \qquad [6.9]$$

Clearly, as we make the number of terms, n, larger and larger, the first part of the RHS of [6.9], that is the 16, remains unchanged. However, as n becomes larger and larger, the quantity $(\tfrac{1}{2})^n$ becomes smaller and smaller. For example, $(\tfrac{1}{2})^2 = 0.25$, $(\tfrac{1}{2})^4 = 0.0625$, $(\tfrac{1}{2})^6 = 0.015\,625$, etc. This means that the second part of the RHS of [6.9], which is simply 16 times $(\tfrac{1}{2})^n$, also becomes continually smaller as n increases. Hence we see that as n increases, S_n gets closer and closer to 16. Mathematically we say 'as n tends to infinity, S_n tends to 16' or

$$\text{as } n \rightarrow \infty \quad S_n \rightarrow 16 \qquad [6.10]$$

where the arrow sign in [6.10] is shorthand for 'tends to' and the symbol ∞ represents infinity.

Another way of expressing [6.10] is to say that 'the *limit* of S_n as n tends to infinity is 16'. In mathematical shorthand this is written as

$$\underset{n \rightarrow \infty}{\text{Limit }} S_n = 16 \qquad [6.10a]$$

Equations [6.10] and [6.10a] are just alternative ways of expressing the same thing. The limit of S_n is just the number that S_n gets closer and closer to as n gets larger and larger.

When a GP has a finite sum that sum is known as the *sum to infinity* of the GP. The GP is then described as *convergent* since S_n converges to a finite values as n increases.

Many GPs, however, are not convergent and do not have sums to infinity. For example, consider the GP

$$3, 9, 27, 81, 243, \ldots \qquad [6.11]$$

Again, using [6.6], values of S_n for gradually increasing n have been worked out in the table next to Fig. 6.2 and plotted in Fig. 6.2. It is clear that in this case as n, the number of terms, becomes larger and larger, S_n, the sum of these n terms, also continually increases. We can see why by considering [6.6] which for $a = 3$ and $c = 3$ yields

$$S_n = \frac{3(1 - 3^n)}{1 - 3} = -\frac{3}{2} + \frac{3}{2}(3)^n$$

Since $(3)^n$ gets larger as n gets larger, clearly S_n increases without limit as n gets larger and larger. Mathematically we write

$$\text{as } n \rightarrow \infty \quad S_n \rightarrow \infty \quad \text{or} \quad \underset{n \rightarrow \infty}{\text{Limit }} S_n = \infty \qquad [6.12]$$

Clearly the GP [6.11] does not have a sum to infinity. That is, we cannot sum its infinite number of terms and obtain a finite answer. Such a GP is described as *divergent* as opposed to convergent.

To deduce the condition which must hold if a GP is to be convergent and have a sum to infinity, consider again the general GP [6.2]. The sum to n terms of this GP is given by the expression [6.6] which we develop as we did for the GPs [6.7] and [6.11]:

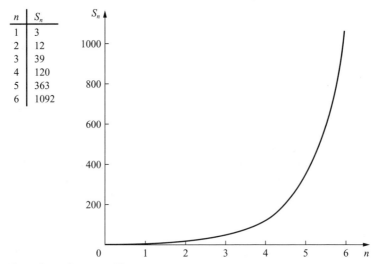

n	S_n
1	3
2	12
3	39
4	120
5	363
6	1092

Fig. 6.2 A divergent GP

$$S_n = \frac{a(1-c^n)}{1-c} = \frac{a-ac^n}{1-c} = \frac{a}{1-c} - \frac{ac^n}{1-c}$$

Hence

$$S_n = \frac{a}{1-c} - \left(\frac{a}{1-c}\right)c^n \qquad\qquad [6.13]$$

The first term in eqn [6.13], $a/(1-c)$, is a constant but consider the c^n-term at the end of [6.13]. If the common ratio, c, lies between 1 and -1, as it did in the GP [6.7], then

$$\text{as } n \to \infty \quad c^n \to 0 \qquad\qquad [6.14]$$

As further examples, let $c = \frac{1}{3}$ or $-\frac{1}{4}$, and see what happens to c^n and n becomes larger and larger. Examining [6.13] it follows, using eqn [6.14], that

$$\text{as } n \to \infty \quad S_n \to \frac{a}{1-c} \quad \text{or} \quad \underset{n \to \infty}{\text{Limit }} S_n = \frac{a}{1-c} \qquad\qquad [6.15]$$

Equation [6.15] states that as the number of terms in this GP increases their sum gets closer and closer to the finite expression $a/(1-c)$ where a is the first term and c the common ratio. Hence we can say that

if $-1 < c < 1$ then a GP is convergent with a sum to infinity of $\dfrac{a}{1-c}$ $\qquad\qquad [6.16]$

Suppose, however, that c is either greater than 1 or less than -1 (as was the case for the GP [6.11]). We now have in [6.13]

$$\text{as } n \to \infty \quad c^n \to \pm\infty \qquad\qquad [6.17]$$

For example, if $c = 3$ or -4, see what happens to c^n and n becomes larger and larger. From [6.13] we now have as $n \to \infty$ $S_n \to \pm\infty$

Thus for this type of GP, as the number of terms increases, their sum most certainly does not approach a finite number. Hence

if $c > 1$ or < -1 then a GP is divergent and has no sum to infinity   [6.18]

Summarising, a GP is convergent only if its common ratio lies between $+1$ and -1. Otherwise it is divergent. For example, the GP [6.7] has $c = \frac{1}{2}$ and hence is convergent, while the GP [6.11] has $c = 3$ and hence is divergent. Also, using eqn [6.16], the sum to infinity of GP [6.7] which has $a = 8$ and $c = \frac{1}{2}$ is

$$\frac{a}{1-c} = \frac{8}{1-\frac{1}{2}} = 16$$

This, of course, is the same figure as derived in Fig. 6.1.

Example 6.3

Which of the GPs in Example 6.1 are convergent and which are divergent?

For series (b), (c) and (e) find: (i) the sum to 10 terms; (ii) the sum to 15 terms; (iii) the sum to infinity. (Remember that $c^{10} = c^5 \times c^5$ and $c^{15} = c^{10} \times c^5$.)

For series (b) and (e) sketch the path taken by the sum of the series as the number of terms is increased.

Example 6.4

Find the sum to infinity of the following GPs:

(a) $1, -x^2, x^4, -x^6, x^8, \ldots$ where $-1 < x < 1$;

(b) $\dfrac{x+3}{y+1}, \dfrac{(x+3)^2}{(y+1)^2}, \dfrac{(x+3)^3}{(y+1)^3}, \ldots$ where $y > x + 2$.

Under what conditions will the following geometric progression be convergent?

$$x^8 y^8, x^6 y^9, x^4 y^{10}, x^2 y^{11}, \ldots$$

6.2   Present values

In Chapter 3 we stressed the very important difference between stock and flow variables in economics. Because of this difference it is not a straightforward matter to make a comparison between a stock at a given point in time and a flow over a period of time. For example, suppose a person is given a choice between receiving a payment of £5000 immediately (stock) and receiving £500 per annum for the rest of his/her lifetime (flow). It is not immediately obvious how a rational choice can be made. Also the problem becomes more difficult if the value of the flow payments varies over time. The vital tool in tackling problems of this sort is the concept of present value.

We saw at the beginning of this chapter that if the sum of money A is invested at a compound rate of interest r then in x years' time it will have accumulated to a sum of $A(1 + r)^x$. Obviously if we invested four times as much, that is $4A$, it would accumulate to $4A(1 + r)^x$. Similarly if we invested only one-third as much, that is $A/3$, then it would accumulate to only $A(1 + r)^x/3$. In particular, if we invested $A/(1 + r)^x$ it would accumulate to $A(1 + r)^x/(1 + r)^x = A$ in x years' time. The sum

$$\frac{A}{(1 + r)^x} \quad \text{is known as the } \textit{present value} \text{ of a payment } A \text{ to be made in } x \text{ years' time} \quad [6.19]$$

By present value in [6.19] we mean the value today of an unshakeable promise to make such a payment in x years' time. To see exactly why this promise should be worth $A(1 + r)^x$ it will help if we introduce some numbers. Suppose the rate of interest is 5 per cent, that is $r = 0.05$, $x = 5$ years and $A = £100$. We know from [6.1] that

£100 invested today will accumulate to

$$£100(1.05)^5 = £100(1.276) = £127.6 \text{ in 5 years' time} \quad [6.20]$$

It follows that

$$\frac{£100}{1.276} = \frac{£100}{(1.05)^5} = £78.4 \text{ invested today will accumulate to £100 in 5 years' time} \quad [6.21]$$

According to [6.19] we can interpret the £78.4 as the value today of a promise to make a payment of £100 in five years' time. We can regard the promise as an IOU from a completely trustworthy person which is redeemable in five years' time. The value of this IOU or promise is worth no more and no less than £78.4 for two reasons.

Firstly, *no rational person would pay more for such a promise*. For example, no one would be prepared to pay £80 for the promise. If they did so, they would indeed receive their £100 in five years' time, but from [6.21] we can deduce that if, instead, they invest the £80 elsewhere at the 5 per cent rate of interest it will have accumulated to more than £100 in five years' time. All rational persons will prefer the second option provided the 5 per cent interest rate is universally available and remains unchanged.

Secondly, *no rational person would sell such a promise for less than £78.4*. For example, no one would sell it for £75. Once sold the promise has to be redeemed and this involves paying out £100 in five years' time. But from [6.21] the £75 received for the promise when invested at 5 per cent will have accumulated to something less than £100 in five years' time. When it comes to redeeming the promise the seller will therefore be out of pocket on the transaction.

Since no one will purchase the promise for more than £78.4 and no one will sell it for less, the only price at which the promise will change hands is £78.4. This then is the value today of such an unshakeable promise and in general [6.19] must hold.

It must be stressed at this point that the above analysis assumes a world of complete certainty. The promise to pay must be 'unshakeable' in the sense that the purchaser knows with certainty that the promise will be kept in five years' time. If there was anything less than complete certainty the value of the promise would be less than £78.4. The extent to which the price falls below £78.4 will depend on the degree of uncertainty attached to the promise.

Example 6.5

Find the present values of

(a) £1300 payable in 8 years' time when the rate of interest is 3 per cent;
(b) £700 payable in 6 years' time when the rate of interest is 7 per cent.

If the present value of £600 payable in 4 years' time is only £300, what must be the rate of interest?

Annuities

We can return now to the problem posed at the beginning of this section – that of making a rational choice between stocks and flows. Suppose a person were given the choice between an immediate payment of £4000 and an 'annuity' consisting of £1000 payable immediately and £1000 payable after each of the next four years. What we are now able to do is to calculate the present value, that is the immediate value of each of the five payments making up the annuity. If the interest rate is 8 per cent, that is $r = 0.08$, then using [6.19]

$$\text{present value of £1000 payable in 4 years' time} = \frac{1000}{(1.08)^4}$$

$$\text{present value of £1000 payable in 3 years' time} = \frac{1000}{(1.08)^3}$$

$$\text{present value of £1000 payable in 2 years' time} = \frac{1000}{(1.08)^2}$$

$$\text{present value of £1000 payable in 1 year's time} = \frac{1000}{(1.08)}$$

Since the present value of the immediate payment of £1000 is obviously £1000, it follows that the total present value (PV) of the annuity is

$$PV = 1000 + \frac{1000}{1.08} + \frac{1000}{(1.08)^2} + \frac{1000}{(1.08)^3} + \frac{1000}{(1.08)^4} \qquad [6.22]$$

It should be easy to see that [6.22] consists of the sum of the first five terms in a GP with first term $a = 1000$ and common ratio $c = 1/1.08 = 0.926$. Hence using [6.6]

$$PV = \frac{1000(1 - 0.926^5)}{1 - 0.926} = \frac{1000(1 - 0.681)}{0.074} = £4311$$

Since the value 'today' of the payments making up the annuity is £4311, the annuity is obviously to be preferred to the offer of an immediate £4000. Note again, however, that this conclusion rests on the assumption that we can be absolutely certain about the future payments making up the annuity. The provider of the annuity must be completely trustworthy!

It should be clear that in calculating the present value of an annuity we will always be summing terms in a GP and that the common ratio in the GP will be $1/(1 + r)$.

Perpetual annuities

It is possible to purchase annuities involving payments which extend indefinitely into the future. For example, suppose an annuity involved payment of £500 immediately and a further £500 after each year in perpetuity (i.e. for ever). If the interest rate is 4 per cent then the present value of such a perpetual annuity is

$$PV = 500 + \frac{500}{1.04} + \frac{500}{(1.04)^2} + \frac{500}{(1.04)^3} \cdots \qquad [6.23]$$

Equation [6.23] involves a GP with a common ratio $c = 1/1.04 = 0.961\,54$. Thus by eqn [6.16] the GP is convergent and to find the required present value we have to sum the GP to infinity. Using [6.16]

$$PV = \frac{a}{1-c} = \frac{500}{1-0.961\,54} = £13\,000$$

Hence the value of the perpetual annuity is £13 000. It is worth considering why in practice this is so.

Firstly, no one would be prepared to pay more than £13 000 for the annuity. They would not pay £13 130, for example. With such a sum they could, instead, set aside £505 for example, and then by investing the remaining £12 625 at the interest rate of 4 per cent earn $0.04(12\,625) = £505$ every year in perpetuity. Such a stream of payments is clearly preferable to the annuity.

Secondly, no one would be prepared to sell such an annuity for less than £13 000. They would not sell it for only £12 870, for example. With such a sum they could only pay out £495 immediately, for example, and by investing the remaining £12 375 at 4 per cent interest they could only earn enough to make payments of $0.04(12\,375) = £495$ per annum. These payments would not be sufficient to meet the promises in the annuity. Since no one will purchase it for more than £13 000 or sell it for less than £13 000, the value of the annuity must equal this sum.

Clearly finding the present value of a perpetual annuity as in [6.23] will always involve summing to infinity a convergent GP. The common ratio will always be $1/(1 + r)$ which is less than unity. If the annual payment involved is A, then the present value will be, using [6.16],

$$PV = \frac{a}{1-c} = \frac{A}{1-1/(1+r)} = \frac{A(1+r)}{r} \qquad [6.24]$$

Example 6.6

Find the present value of the following:

(a) £500 payable in three years' time when the rate of interest is 6 per cent per annum.
(b) An annuity consisting of £500 now and £500 after each of the next 10 years if the rate of interest is 12 per cent per annum.
(c) An annuity consisting of £2000 now and £2000 after each year, payable in perpetuity, if the rate of interest is 8 per cent per annum.

6.3 Discounted cash flows

Equation [6.19] can also be used to assess the value of a stream of unequal payments occurring over time. For example, suppose a firm expects, from a certain project, a net return of £800 in the first year after initiation and net returns of £1200, £700, £500 and £300 in the succeeding second, third, fourth and fifth years. After the fifth year no returns are expected. Suppose we regard the first year's return as being received immediately, the second year's return as being received after one year and the third year's after two years, etc.[2] The present value of the stream of returns, assuming an interest rate of 5 per cent for example, is then

$$PV = 800 + \frac{1200}{1.05} + \frac{700}{(1.05)^2} + \frac{500}{(1.05)^3} + \frac{300}{(1.05)^4} \qquad [6.25]$$

Notice that in [6.25], since the returns vary from year to year, we are not, this time, dealing with a GP. We have, therefore, to work out each term in [6.25] separately. This yields

$$PV = 800 + 1143 + 635 + 432 + 247 = £3257 \qquad [6.26]$$

Provided the returns are expected with complete certainty and the rate of interest is not expected to change, the firm will therefore value the returns arising from the project at £3257. Hence if the investment required to initiate the project were less than £3257, then provided the firm had the funds to spare and had no better alternative use, it would make sense to undertake this project.

Example 6.7

Find the present value of the following streams of payments:

(a) £500 now, £800 after one year, £600 after two years and £400 after three years if the rate of interest is 10 per cent per annum;
(b) £800 now, £2000 after each of the next five years and £1000 after each of the following five years if the rate of interest is 5 per cent per annum.

The technique of finding the present value of a future payment is known as 'discounting' that payment. A series of discounted payments such as those summed in eqn [6.26] is often referred to as a *discounted cash flow*. The method of discounted cash flows can also be used to compare one stream of future payments with another. For example, recall our firm, which was faced with the stream of returns expected from the project introduced at the beginning of this section. The present value of the expected returns from this project was computed as £3257 in eqn [6.26]. Suppose, however, our firm also had the option of investing in a second project, net returns from which were £900 in the first year, £1800 in the second year and £600 in the third year. Unlike the first project, no returns are expected from the second project in the fourth and fifth years. At the 5 per cent interest rate we can easily discount this cash flow to find the present value of the second project:

$$PV = 900 + \frac{1800}{1.05} + \frac{600}{(1.05)^2} = 900 + 1714 + 544 = £3158 \qquad [6.27]$$

The firm will therefore value the returns from this project at £3158. Hence, provided the initial investment required by this project is less than £3158, it is a project worth considering.

Suppose that the initial investment required by both projects is £2500. That is, if the firm wishes to 'acquire' either of the streams of returns it has to 'pay a price' of £2500 for each project. Obviously, if the firm had sufficient funds available it would invest in both projects since from [6.26] and [6.27] both are 'worth' more than £2500. However, if the firm had insufficient funds to invest in both projects, it would select the first since this has the larger present value.

All the above calculations have been based on an interest rate of 5 per cent. Suppose the interest rate suddenly rose sharply to 15 per cent. Would this affect the firm's choice of project? We can easily work out present values with $r = 0.15$. For the first project

$$PV = 800 + \frac{1200}{1.15} + \frac{700}{(1.15)^2} + \frac{500}{(1.15)^3} + \frac{300}{(1.15)^4} = £2873 \qquad [6.28]$$

and for the second project

$$PV = 900 + \frac{1800}{1.15} + \frac{600}{(1.15)^2} = £2919 \qquad [6.29]$$

The first point to note is that the rise in the rate of interest from 5 to 15 per cent has led to a fall in the value placed by the firm on each of the projects. The reason for this is simply that the firm can now earn a far greater return if it invests elsewhere than it could when the interest rate was only 5 per cent.[3] It is therefore prepared to 'pay' far less for the projects than previously because of this increase in the returns from elsewhere that it forgoes if it invests in either of the projects.

Because the present values of each project still exceed their 'price' of £2500, the firm would still invest in both if it had the funds available. However, if the firm could only afford to invest in one of the projects it would now select the second project rather than the first. At first sight this may seem baffling, so let us consider carefully why a rise in interest rates from 5 to 15 per cent should bring about this change in preferences.

In choosing between the two projects, two factors must be allowed for. Firstly, the firm always prefers larger total returns to smaller total returns. The sum of the *undiscounted* returns from the first project over the five years is £3500, whereas the sum of the undiscounted returns for the second project is only £3300. Thus if the rate of interest is zero, the first project is preferable.[4] Secondly, however, the firm prefers returns which arise in the near future rather than those which occur later. This is because the rate of interest is not zero and hence returns received early can be reinvested to earn further returns. Clearly, returns on the second project are expected earlier than those on the first project, so by this criterion the second project is preferable. Notice that *the higher the rate of interest the greater the preference for early returns* since the greater are the further returns of reinvestment.

We can now see why a rise in the rate of interest causes the firm to switch from preferring the first project to the second. At the 5 per cent interest rate, the larger total returns of the first project outweigh the earlier returns of the second project so that the firm prefers the first. However, at the 15 per cent interest rate, the early returns factor becomes more important and, hence, now outweighs the larger total returns of the first project. The firm therefore switches its preference.

Example 6.8

A firm has to choose between two projects. The first involves an immediate investment of £1000 and provides net returns over the next four years of £1500, £1300, £1200 and £200 respectively. The second involves an immediate investment of £500 and provides net returns over the next five years of £1200, £800, £600, £600 and £600 respectively. If the rate of interest is 5 per cent per annum, which project should the firm choose? (No discounting procedure need be applied to net returns during the first year.) If the rate of interest rises to 8 per cent per annum should the firm change its decision? If so, what is it about the two streams of net returns that makes this the case?

Example 6.9

A firm is considering two independent projects, both of which involve an initial investment of £1000. The first project yields net returns over the next three years of £500, £500 and £400 respectively and the second project net returns of £900, £400 and £50 over the same years. If the rate of interest is 10 per cent, which project should the firm undertake if it has: (a) £2000 available for investment; (b) only £1000 available? If the rate of interest were only 5 per cent show that the firm's decision should be different in case (b) above and explain why this is so.

(Interest is paid once per year and no discounting procedure need be applied to net returns during the first year.)

Revision examples

Example R6.1

Which of the following are geometric progressions and which are not?

(a) 10, 5, 2.5, 1.25, 0.625, . . .
(b) 30, 24, 18, 12, 6, . . .
(c) −3, 6, −12, 24, −48, . . .
(d) 128, 64, −32, −16, 8, . . .
(e) 0.9, 0.63, 0.441, 0.3087, 0.21609, . . .

Of the series that are geometric progressions, which are convergent? Find the sum to infinity of any convergent series. Find the sum to 10 terms of any geometric series that is divergent.

Example R6.2

Find an expression for the sum to n terms of a geometric progression with first term a and common ratio c. Hence find an expression for the sum to infinity of a convergent geometric progression. Hence find the sum to infinity of the following series:

(a) $600, 400, \dfrac{800}{3}, \dfrac{1600}{9}, \ldots$

(b) $1, \dfrac{(y+3)^2}{x^2}, \dfrac{(y+3)^4}{x^4}, \dfrac{(y+3)^6}{x^6}, \ldots$ where $x - y > 3$

(c) $pq^6, p^2q^5, p^3q^4, p^4q^3, \ldots$ where $p/q < 1$

Example R6.3

If the current rate of interest is 6 per cent, what is the present value of an annuity consisting of £300 payable now and £300 payable after the next four years? What assumptions have you made in making your calculation?

Show that, if the above annuity was payable in perpetuity, its present value would be £5300. Explain carefully why no one would be prepared to pay more for such an annuity and why no one would be prepared to sell it for less.

Example R6.4

A firm is considering a project which involves an immediate investment of £1500. The project provides net returns of £500, £450 and £630 during the first, second and third years following the investment. If the rate of interest is r, write down an expression for the present value of the returns from the project. Hence find the rate of interest that makes this present value exactly equal to the initial investment. (Interest is paid annually and no discounting procedure need be applied to net returns during the first year.)

Example R6.5

A firm can invest in two projects if it wishes. Each project involves an immediate investment of £5000. The first provides an immediate return of £4200 with a further return of £900 in a year's time. The second project provides an immediate return of only £500 but a further return of £4800 in a year's time.

(a) Find for each project the rate of interest that makes the present value of returns equal to the initial investment.
(b) Find the rate of interest which equates the present value of returns from the first project to that from the second project.
(c) If the firm has £10 000 available for investment, deduce, without making any further calculations, what project(s) the firm would invest in at the rate of interest (i) 4 per cent; (ii) 8 per cent.

How would the firm's decisions differ if it had only £5000 available for investment?

Solution

Present value of returns from first project is

$$PV_1 = 4200 + \frac{900}{1+r}$$

Present value of returns from second project is

$$PV_2 = 500 + \frac{4800}{1+r}$$

(a) To find r for the first project, solve

$$5000 = 4200 + \frac{900}{1+r}$$

Thus

$$800 = \frac{900}{1+r} \quad \rightarrow \quad 1 + r = 1.125 \quad \rightarrow \quad r = 0.125$$

that is 12.5 per cent.
  To find r for the second project, solve

$$5000 = 500 + \frac{4800}{1+r}$$

Thus

$$4500 = \frac{4800}{1+r} \quad \rightarrow \quad 1 + r = 1.067 \quad \rightarrow \quad r = 0.067$$

that is 6.7 per cent.

(b) To find r that equates present values, solve

$$4200 + \frac{900}{1+r} = 500 + \frac{4800}{1+r}$$

Thus

$$3700 = \frac{3900}{1+r} \quad \rightarrow \quad 1 + r = 1.054 \quad \rightarrow \quad r = 0.054$$

that is 5.4 per cent.

(c) Recall that

$$5000 = PV_1 \text{ when } r = 0.125 \quad \text{and} \quad 5000 = PV_2 \text{ when } r = 0.067$$

Remember that as r rises (falls) the PV of any future stream of returns falls (rises). Thus if $r < 0.125$ then $PV_1 > 5000$ and if $r > 0.125$ then $PV_1 < 5000$. Similarly if $r < 0.067$ then $PV_2 > 5000$ and if $r > 0.067$ then $PV_2 < 5000$.
  Recall that when $r = 0.054$, $PV_1 = PV_2$. Remember that as r rises, earlier returns become more valuable than later returns. Since the first project has the earlier returns, it follows that

if $r > 0.054$ then $PV_1 > PV_2$ but if $r < 0.054$ then $PV_1 < PV_2$

It follows that if the firm has £10 000 for investment then if $r = 0.04$ the firm will invest in both projects since $PV_1 > 5000$ and $PV_2 > 5000$. However, if $r = 0.08$, then the firm will invest in only the first project since $PV_1 > 5000$ but $PV_2 < 5000$.

If the firm has only £5000 to invest then it can invest in only one project. If $r = 0.04$, it will select the second since $PV_1 < PV_2$. However, if $r = 0.08$, it will select the first project since $PV_1 > PV_2$.

Example R6.6

A firm is considering two projects, both of which involve an immediate investment of £6000. The first project provides net returns of £4000, £4000 and £6000 during the first, third and fifth years following the investment, while the second project provides net returns of £3000, £3000 and £10 000 during the same years. Find for each project:

(a) the rate of interest which would make the present value of the stream of returns equal to the original investment;
(b) the rate of interest at which the firm would be indifferent between the two projects.

(You need not apply any discounting procedures to net returns during the first year. Interest is paid annually.)

Consider the following rates of interest: 20, 35, 60, 75 per cent. Can you tell, without making further calculations, what, for the above rates of interest, the firm's actions should be:

(i) if it has only £6000 available for investment;
(ii) if it has unlimited funds available for investment?

(The firm may invest in one project, two projects or no projects at all.)

Notes

1. We are assuming, for simplicity, that interest is paid once a year and always at the end of the year. We could, if necessary, use a time unit of, for example, six months instead.
2. If, alternatively, we assume that net returns in any year become available to the firm only at the end of that year, we obtain an expression for present value of

$$PV = \frac{800}{1.05} + \frac{1200}{(1.05)^2} + \frac{700}{(1.05)^3} + \frac{500}{(1.05)^4} + \frac{300}{(1.05)^5}$$

This is $1/1.05$ times the value given by eqn [6.25].
3. We are assuming throughout this section that the firm always has the option of investing as much of its available funds as it wishes in some outside 'money market' at the stated rate of interest.
4. We are assuming here that the firm is not so desperate for immediate cash that it prefers early returns under any circumstances. In technical terms this is sometimes referred to as an absence of 'time preference proper'.

7 The differentiation of functions of one variable

7.1 The gradients of non-linear functions

In section 1.4 we defined the gradient of the straight line $y = mx + c$ as the increase in y per unit change in x. For a straight line the gradient was a constant given by the coefficient m in eqn [1.17]. For non-linear functions the gradient is a less straightforward concept and we define it as follows. Suppose the graph of our non-linear function is that shown in Fig. 7.1. We define the gradient of the function at point A *as the gradient of the tangent to the graph of the function at point A*. The tangent at point A is simply the straight line that 'just touches' the graph at this point. The gradient of the function at A is therefore the gradient of this straight line. Similarly, the gradient of the function at point B is the gradient of the tangent at point B. Since the graphs of non-linear functions are curves rather than straight lines it is obvious that the gradient of a non-linear function will not be constant but will vary from point to point. For example, the gradient of the function in Fig. 7.1 is positive at point A but negative at point B.

The gradient of a function at a point measures the responsiveness of y to very small or *infinitesimal* changes in x about that point. For example, in Fig. 7.1 the gradient at C is greater than that at A, implying that the responsiveness of y to infinitesimal changes in x is greater at the former point.

The concept of gradients is much used in economics. For example, consider the *total cost* function given by eqn [1.15] and graphed in Fig. 1.4. *Marginal cost* is defined simply as the gradient of the total cost function. It therefore measures the responsiveness of total cost to infinitesimal changes in output at various points on the function. Readers may be more familiar with a definition of marginal cost as the increase in total cost incurred when one extra unit of output is produced. The mathematical definition given here is slightly different since we are considering tiny or infinitesimal changes in output rather than whole unit changes.

Notice that the mathematical definition also measures changes in cost *per unit* increase in output. It is still possible to measure such rates of change even when output changes of less than one whole unit are considered. If, for example, output increases by 0.01 units and as a result total cost rises by 0.03p, then the change in costs is $0.03/0.01 = 3$p per unit increase in output. The mathematical definition simply measures changes in cost per unit output change over *infinitesimally small* increases in output. Notice that the mathematical definition presupposes that output *can* be changed by infinitesimal amounts. This may be a reasonable approximation for many goods but is obviously unrealistic for durable goods such as automobiles or washing machines. One cannot increase output by one-thousandth of a washing machine! In

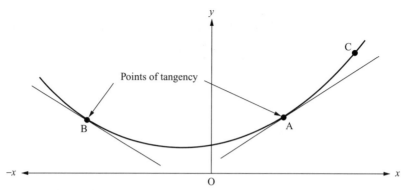

Fig. 7.1 The gradient of a non-linear function

such cases the 'whole unit' definition of marginal cost is preferable. Notice that if we specify the firm's total costs as given by equations such as [1.15], then we are implicitly assuming that infinitesimal changes in output are possible. Once we accept [1.15] then obviously there is no reason why we should not substitute in values of output q equal to, for example, 5.1486 and 5.1487. When a cost function is valid for all positive values of q in this way it is said to be *continuous*. Continuous functions are much used in economics and it is well to be aware of the implicit assumption about the possibility of infinitesimal changes that is involved in their use.

Clearly, if we knew that a firm's total cost function was given by eqn [1.15] then we could find the firm's marginal cost at various output levels by drawing tangents to the curve in Fig. 1.4 and measuring their gradients. However, this procedure would be tedious and also almost certainly inaccurate. Fortunately, there is a mathematical way of calculating the gradient of a curve at a point, but before we introduce this method we need to consider at greater length the concept of a limit.

7.2 More about limits

We have already encountered the concept of a *limit* in our discussion of geometric progressions. We saw in section 6.1 that provided the common ratio of a GP lay between 1 and −1, then the sum of the first n terms in the GP tended to a finite quantity $a/(1 - c)$ as the number of terms became larger and larger. We referred to this finite quantity as the limit of S_n as n tended to infinity and wrote (see eqn [6.15])

$$\underset{n \to \infty}{\text{Limit}} \, S_n = \frac{a}{1 - c}$$

To appreciate more fully the concept of a limit it is best to consider a series of examples. To take a simple case first, suppose we require the 'limit' of the quantity $1/(x + 3)$ as x becomes larger and larger, that is as x tends to infinity. We can find this limit simply by successively substituting larger an larger values of x into the expression $1/(x + 3)$. For example,

Table 7.1 The limit of $(2x + 1)/(x + 50)$ as $x \to \infty$

x	2x + 1	x + 50	(2x + 1)/(x + 50)
10	21	60	0.3500
100	201	150	1.3400
1 000	2 001	1 050	1.9057
10 000	20 001	10 050	1.9901
100 000	200 001	100 050	1.9990
1 000 000	2 000 001	1 000 050	1.9999

if $x = 100$ then $1/(x + 3) = 0.009\ 708\ 73 \approx 0.01$

if $x = 1000$ then $1/(x + 3) = 0.000\ 997\ 01 \approx 0.001$

if $x = 10\ 000$ then $1/(x + 3) = 0.000\ 099\ 97 \approx 0.0001$

Clearly the larger is x, the closer to zero becomes $1/(x + 3)$. Hence we can write

$$\operatorname*{Limit}_{x \to \infty}\left(\frac{1}{x + 3}\right) = 0$$

The following example is not quite so obvious. Suppose we require

$$\operatorname*{Limit}_{x \to \infty}\left(\frac{2x + 1}{x + 50}\right)$$

Values of $2x + 1$, $x + 50$ and finally $(2x + 1)/(x + 50)$ are computed in Table 7.1 for successively larger values of x. Clearly as x becomes larger and larger, the values in the last column get closer and closer to 2, so we have

$$\operatorname*{Limit}_{x \to \infty}\left(\frac{2x + 1}{x + 50}\right) = 2$$

What happens in this case is that, as x becomes increasingly large, the 1 in $(2x + 1)$ and the 50 in $(x + 50)$ become increasingly unimportant so that $(2x + 1)/(x + 50)$ approaches $2x/x$ which is, of course, 2.

Example 7.1

Find the limits as $x \to \infty$ of:

(a) $\dfrac{x - 1}{x^2 + 3}$ (b) $\dfrac{x^2 + 2x}{x^3 + 5}$

We next consider a somewhat different type of limit

$$\operatorname*{Limit}_{x \to 1}\left(\frac{x - 1}{x^2 + 3x - 4}\right) \qquad\qquad [7.1]$$

Table 7.2 The limit of $(x - 1)/(x^2 + 3x - 4)$ as $x \to 1$

x	$x - 1$	$x^2 + 3x - 4$	$(x - 1)/(x^2 + 3x - 4)$
2	1	6	0.166 67
1.1	0.1	0.51	0.196 08
1.01	0.01	0.050 1	0.199 60
1.001	0.001	0.005 001	0.199 960
1.0001	0.0001	0.000 500 01	0.199 996

We are now attempting to find what happens to the quantity in brackets in [7.1] as x gets closer and closer to unity, that is *as x tends to unity*. The important point to note here is that we cannot obtain the answer we want simply by substituting $x = 1$ in the bracketed expression since when $x = 1$

$$\frac{x - 1}{x^2 + 3x - 4} = \frac{1 - 1}{1 + 3 - 4} = \frac{0}{0} = ?$$

Since 0/0 is an indeterminate quantity which we cannot compute, what we have to do is to examine what happens to the bracketed quantity in [7.1] as we substitute in values for x becoming closer and closer to 1. We do this in Table 7.2 from which it should be clear that[1]

$$\text{Limit}_{x \to 1} \left(\frac{x - 1}{x^2 + 3x - 4} \right) = \frac{1}{5} \tag{7.2}$$

There is, in fact, a quicker way of determining the limit in [7.1]. Note that

$$\frac{x - 1}{x^2 + 3x - 4} = \frac{x - 1}{(x - 1)(x + 4)} = \frac{1}{x + 4}$$

Since when $x = 1$, obviously $1/(x + 4) = \frac{1}{5}$, we again have

$$\text{Limit}_{x \to 1} \left(\frac{x - 1}{x^2 + 3x - 4} \right) = \text{Limit}_{x \to 1} \left(\frac{1}{x + 4} \right) = \frac{1}{5}$$

The reason we evaluated [7.1] the 'long way round' using Table 7.2 was to illustrate an important point. Although, as x approaches unity, both the numerator $(x - 1)$ and the denominator $(x^2 + 3x - 4)$ in [7.1] approach zero, their ratio $(x - 1)/(x^2 + 3x - 4)$ approaches a determinate non-zero quantity. It in fact approaches one-fifth!

Something similar happens with the following limit:

$$\text{Limit}_{x \to 0} \left[\frac{(2 + x)^2 - 4}{x} \right] \tag{7.3}$$

In this case we seek a limit as x approaches zero. Again we cannot just substitute $x = 0$ in [7.3] since when $x = 0$

Table 7.3 The limit of $[(2 + x)^2 - 4]/x$ as $x \rightarrow 0$

x	$(2 + x)^2 - 4$	$[(2 + x)^2 - 4]/x$
10	140	14
1	5	5
0.1	0.41	4.1
0.01	0.040 1	4.01
0.001	0.004 001	4.001
0.0001	0.000 400 01	4.0001

$$\frac{(2 + x)^2 - 4}{x} = \frac{0}{0} = ?$$

We therefore allow x to approach zero gradually as in Table 7.3, from which it is clear that the limit we require equals 4.[2] There is again a quicker way of finding the limit we require. Note that

$$\frac{(2 + x)^2 - 4}{x} = \frac{4 + x^2 + 4x - 4}{x} = \frac{x^2 + 4x}{x} = x + 4$$

Obviously, when $x = 0$, $x + 4 = 4$, so we have

$$\underset{x \rightarrow 0}{\text{Limit}} \left[\frac{(2 + x)^2 - 4}{x} \right] = \underset{x \rightarrow 0}{\text{Limit}} \, (x + 4) = 4 \qquad [7.4]$$

Again, the reason we also adopted a tabular method of obtaining the above limit was to illustrate that, although numerator and denominator in [7.3] tend to zero as x tends to zero, their ratio, the bracketed term in [7.3], clearly does not. This is, in fact, the case with many 'ratios' or 'quotients' of the form $a(x)/b(x)$ where a and b are functions of x. Even if, as x approaches zero, $a(x)$ and $b(x)$ happen to approach zero, it is still possible for $a(x)/b(x)$ to approach some determinate non-zero number. This is so despite the fact that, when $x = 0$, $a(x)/b(x)$ is indeterminate.

Example 7.2

By letting x approach zero, find:

(a) $\underset{x \rightarrow 0}{\text{Limit}} \left[\dfrac{(x + 5)^2 - 25}{2x} \right]$

(b) $\underset{x \rightarrow 0}{\text{Limit}} \left[\dfrac{x^3 + 2x^2 - 8x}{x^2 - 2x} \right]$

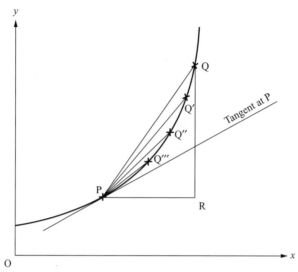

Fig. 7.2 Gradients of chords and tangent

7.3 The derivative of a function

We can now return to the problem of finding the gradient of a non-linear function. Consider the non-linear function graphed in Fig. 7.2 and suppose we require the gradient of this curve at point P. Remember that by this we mean the gradient of the tangent to the curve at point P. We adopt the following approach. Suppose Q is a neighbouring point on the curve. The line PQ is known as a *chord* of the curve. The gradient of the chord PQ is equal to QR/PR. Now suppose we bring the point Q 'closer and closer' along the curve towards P – that is, to Q′, Q″, Q‴, etc. As Q approaches P, the gradient of the chord PQ will have a value that gets closer and closer to the gradient of the tangent at P. That is,

$$\underset{Q \to P}{\text{Limit}} \, (\text{gradient PQ}) = \text{gradient of tangent at P}$$

The gradient of PQ is, of course, QR/PR and as Q approaches P, the distance PR becomes closer and closer to zero. Since the gradient of the tangent at P is the gradient of the curve at P, we therefore have

$$\text{gradient of curve at P} = \underset{PR \to 0}{\text{Limit}} \left(\frac{QR}{PR} \right) \qquad [7.5]$$

Notice that as Q approaches P, not only does PR approach zero but so also does QR. However, we know from our examples in section 7.2 that this does not mean that the *ratio* QR/PR will not approach a non-zero quantity.

We now apply the above technique to a specific non-linear function. As an example we take the functional relationship

$$y = 3x^2 \qquad [7.6]$$

which is graphed in Fig. 7.3.

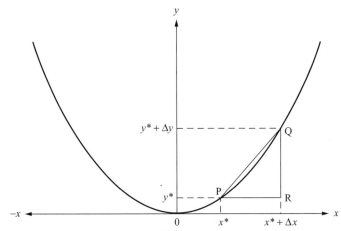

Fig. 7.3 The relationship $y = 3x^2$

What we require at this point is some expression or 'formula' (it might be $8x^3$, $6x + 4$, $5x^2$, etc., or something more complicated) such that to find the gradient of the curve [7.6] at the point where, for example, x is 1, all we have to do is to substitute the value $x = 1$ into the appropriate formula. Given such a formula, this would be a much quicker and more accurate way of finding the gradient at $x = 1$ than actually graphing $y = 3x^2$ by hand and trying to draw the tangent to the curve at the point $x = 1$. Finding the appropriate formula for $y = 3x^2$ is the problem and to solve it we make use of the above technique and particularly eqn [7.5].

Suppose the point P on the curve in Fig. 7.3 has the coordinates (x^*, y^*). If Q is a point 'close' to P on the curve its coordinates will not differ much from those of P and we shall write its coordinates as $(x^* + \Delta x, y^* + \Delta y)$. Δx (pronounced delta x) is simply the 'small difference' between the x-coordinates of the points Q and P, while Δy is the 'small difference' between their y-coordinates. Mathematicians frequently use the shorthand Δx and Δy to refer to small changes or differences in x and y.

The gradient of the chord PQ in Fig. 7.3 is QR/PR where, clearly, QR $= \Delta y$ and PR $= \Delta x$. Hence

$$\text{gradient of chord PQ} = \frac{\Delta y}{\Delta x} \qquad [7.7]$$

It follows, using [7.5], that

$$\text{gradient of curve at P} = \underset{\Delta x \to 0}{\text{Limit}} \left(\frac{\Delta y}{\Delta x} \right) \qquad [7.8]$$

To find the required gradient, then, we need to obtain an expression for $\Delta y/\Delta x$ and then see what happens to this expression as Δx approaches zero. Since point Q lies on the graph of the functional relationship $y = 3x^2$, its coordinates $x^* + \Delta x$ and $y^* + \Delta y$ must satisfy this relationship. That is,

$$y^* + \Delta y = 3(x^* + \Delta x)^2$$

or

$$y^* + \Delta y = 3x^{*2} + 6x^*\Delta x + 3(\Delta x)^2 \qquad [7.9]$$

However, point P also lies on the graph, so its coordinates $x*$ and $y*$ must also satisfy $y = 3x^2$. That is,

$$y* = 3x*^2 \qquad [7.10]$$

Taking [7.10] from [7.9] we have

$$\Delta y = 6x*\Delta x + 3(\Delta x)^2$$

and, dividing throughout by Δx,

$$\frac{\Delta y}{\Delta x} = 6x* + 3\Delta x \qquad [7.11]$$

We now have the expression we wanted for $\Delta y/\Delta x$. Substituting into [7.8] we have

$$\text{gradient of curve at P} = \underset{\Delta x \to 0}{\text{Limit}}\,(6x* + 3\Delta x) = 6x* \qquad [7.12]$$

Thus we can say that if $(x*, y*)$ is any point on the graph of $y = 3x^2$, then the gradient at this point is simply $6x*$. We have therefore found the formula we were searching for earlier, a general expression for the gradient of the curve for $y = 3x^2$. The expression is $6x*$. For example, $(1, 3)$ is a point on the graph which has $x* = 1$. The gradient of the curve at this point must therefore be $6x* = 6$. Similarly the gradients at the points $(4, 48)$ and $(-2, 12)$ will be 24 and -12 respectively. The negative gradient at the point $(-2, 12)$ reflects the fact that, as we can see from Fig. 7.3, the graph slopes downwards when x is negative.

As a second example of this technique for finding gradients, consider the functional relationship $y = 4x^2 + 2x$. Notice that it is not necessary to graph this relationship even roughly to apply the technique. Suppose our two points P and Q on the graph of this relationship again have coordinates $(x*, y*)$ and $(x* + \Delta x, y* + \Delta y)$ respectively. Since Q lies on the graph of $y = 4x^2 + 2x$ we have

$$y* + \Delta y = 4(x* + \Delta x)^2 + 2(x* + \Delta x)$$

or

$$y* + \Delta y = 4x*^2 + 8x*\Delta x + 4(\Delta x)^2 + 2x* + 2\Delta x \qquad [7.13]$$

Similarly, since P also lies on the graph,

$$y* = 4x*^2 + 2x* \qquad [7.14]$$

Subtracting [7.14] from [7.13]

$$\Delta y = 8x*\Delta x + 4(\Delta x)^2 + 2\Delta x$$

Dividing throughout by Δx

$$\frac{\Delta y}{\Delta x} = 8x* + 4\Delta x + 2$$

Hence, using [7.8] we have on this occasion

$$\text{gradient at P} = \underset{\Delta x \to 0}{\text{Limit}}\,(8x* + 4\Delta x + 2) = 8x* + 2 \qquad [7.15]$$

Thus the gradient of this function at the point $(x*, y*)$ is given by $8x* + 2$. For example, the gradient at $(3, 42)$ will be $8(3) + 2 = 26$ and the gradient at $(-1, 2)$ will be $8(-1) + 2 = -6$.

Example 7.3

Use eqn [7.8] to find the gradient of $y = 3x^2 + 8x + 5$ at the points (1, 16), (−2, 1) and (0, 5).

Some terminology and notation

It is a little tiresome to have to keep writing the gradient of a curve or graph as

$$\underset{\Delta x \to 0}{\text{Limit}} (\Delta y / \Delta x)$$

and mathematicians usually replace this complicated expression by the convenient notation or shorthand dy/dx (pronounced dee-y-by-dee-x). That is,

$$\frac{dy}{dx} = \underset{\Delta x \to 0}{\text{Limit}} \left(\frac{\Delta y}{\Delta x} \right) \qquad\qquad [7.16]$$

dy/dx is referred to as *the derivative of y with respect to x*. Notice that it does not mean 'd times y divided by d times x'. It is just convenient notation or shorthand.

It is also convenient to refer to the coordinates of the general point on the graph of a function not as (x^*, y^*) but simply as (x, y). Hence considering again [7.6] and [7.12], we have that if $y = 3x^2$ then

$$\text{gradient at } (x, y) = \frac{dy}{dx} = 6x$$

Similarly for our second example, $y = 4x^2 + 2x$, we have from [7.15]

$$\text{gradient at } (x, y) = \frac{dy}{dx} = 8x + 2$$

Notice that both our examples of functional relationships are of the form $y = f(x)$ where $f(x)$ is a function of x. An alternative shorthand for dy/dx is $f'(x)$ where $f'(x)$ is known as *the derivative of the function f(x)*. Thus

$$\text{if } f(x) = 3x^2 \quad \text{then} \quad f'(x) = 6x$$

and

$$\text{if } f(x) = 4x^2 + 2x \quad \text{then} \quad f'(x) = 8x + 2$$

The process of finding dy/dx or $f'(x)$ is known as *differentiation*. Thus we *differentiate y* to find dy/dx and we *differentiate f(x)* to obtain $f'(x)$. That is, we differentiate to find the derivative.

7.4 General rules of differentiation I

The method used in section 7.3 to differentiate a function of x is fairly tedious and it would be tiresome to have to use it every time we wished to obtain a derivative. Fortunately a whole series of rules exist for differentiation which we will now begin to outline. We shall not prove these rules here but interested readers should consult A. C. Chiang (*Fundamental Methods of Mathematical Economics*).[3] The proofs, in fact, are in all cases based on the method of section 7.3.

The power rule

If $y = ax^n$ where a and n are any two constants then

$$\frac{dy}{dx} = nax^{n-1}$$
[7.17]

Similarly, of course, if $f(x) = ax^n$ then $f'(x) = nax^{n-1}$.

What we have here is actually a generalisation of the differentiation we performed first in section 7.3. There we differentiated $y = 3x^2$ to obtain $dy/dx = 6x$. We see that this is but a special case of [7.17] with $a = 3$ and $n = 2$.

Similarly

if $y = 8x^3$ then $\dfrac{dy}{dx} = 3 \cdot 8x^{3-1} = 24x^2$ ($a = 8$, $n = 3$)

if $y = -4x^7$ then $\dfrac{dy}{dx} = 7(-4)x^{7-1} = -28x^6$ ($a = -4$, $n = 7$)

if $y = 6x^4$ then $\dfrac{dy}{dx} = 4 \cdot 6x^{4-1} = 24x^3$ ($a = 6$, $n = 4$)

and

if $f(x) = -3x^5$ then $f'(x) = 5(-3)x^{5-1} = -15x^4$ ($a = -3$, $n = 5$)

if $f(x) = 12x^2$ then $f'(x) = 2 \cdot 12x^{2-1} = 24x$ ($a = 12$, $n = 2$)

It is worth drawing attention to two special cases of [7.17]. Firstly, if $n = 1$ in eqn [7.17] then $y = ax$ and we are differentiating a linear function. Since $y = ax$ has no intercept term, its graph must be a straight line passing through the origin, with a constant gradient, a. The rule [7.17] does, in fact, yield this expected result since

if $y = ax^1$ then $\dfrac{dy}{dx} = 1 \cdot ax^{1-1} = ax^0 = a$ ($x^0 = 1$)

Thus, *the derivative of a linear function is always a constant.*

If $n = 0$ in eqn [7.17] then, since $x^0 = 1$, we are differentiating $y = a$ where a is some constant. Since the graph of $y = a$ is just a horizontal straight line passing through the point $(0, a)$ on the y-axis, its gradient must always be zero. The rule [7.17] also yields this expected result since

if $y = ax^0 = a$ then $\dfrac{dy}{dx} = 0 \cdot ax^{0-1} = 0$

Thus, *the derivative of a constant will always be zero.*

Example 7.4

Differentiate: (a) $y = -4x^8$; (b) $y = 10x^3$; (c) $y = 6$; (d) $y = 3x^{42}$; (e) $y = -9x$.

Example 7.5

Find $f'(x)$ when: (a) $f(x) = 12x^3$; (b) $f(x) = 12x$; (c) $f(x) = 12$.

The power rule (7.17) can also be applied when n is either negative and/or a fraction. Any readers who are uncertain of the interpretation of fractional and negative powers should consult the introductory section on mathematical prerequisites. Suppose we wish to differentiate

$$y = 3/x^4 \qquad [7.18]$$

We can still use the power rule by reinterpreting $1/x^4$ as x^{-4} and writing [7.18] as

$$y = 3x^{-4} \qquad [7.19]$$

Since [7.19] is of the form $y = ax^n$ with $n = -4$, we can differentiate using the power rule and obtain

$$\frac{dy}{dx} = (-4)3x^{-5} = -12x^{-5} = -12/x^5 \qquad [7.20]$$

Suppose next that we wish to differentiate

$$y = 2\sqrt[5]{x} \qquad [7.21]$$

The trick this time is to remember that $\sqrt[5]{x}$ can be written as $x^{1/5}$ so that we have

$$y = 2x^{1/5} \qquad [7.22]$$

The power rule [7.17] can now be applied with $n = 1/5$, giving

$$\frac{dy}{dx} = (\tfrac{1}{5})2x^{-4/5} = \frac{2}{5x^{4/5}} \qquad [7.23]$$

Note that $x^{4/5}$ can be reinterpreted as $(\sqrt[5]{x})^4$.

Powers of course can be both negative and fractional. For example,

$$y = 3/x^{1/4} \qquad [7.24]$$

Again, to apply the power rule we must rewrite [7.24] as

$$y = 3x^{-1/4} \qquad [7.25]$$

so that

$$\frac{dy}{dx} = -(\tfrac{3}{4})x^{-5/4} = -\frac{3}{4x^{5/4}} \qquad [7.26]$$

Decimal powers can be differentiated in the usual way by using the power rule. For example, if

$$y = 3x^{2.4} \quad \text{then} \quad \frac{dy}{dx} = 7.2x^{1.4} \qquad [7.27]$$

The trick in differentiating all the above relationships is to get the function into the form $y = ax^n$ and then to apply the power rule [17.7]. For example,

if $y = 4\sqrt{x} = 4x^{1/2}$ then $\dfrac{dy}{dx} = 2x^{-1/2} = 2/x^{1/2} = 2/\sqrt{x}$

if $y = 1/x^6 = x^{-6}$ then $\dfrac{dy}{dx} = -6x^{-7} = -6/x^7$

if $y = 4x^{0.4}$ then $\dfrac{dy}{dx} = 1.6x^{-0.6} = 1.6/x^{0.6}$

if $y = 2/\sqrt{x} = 2x^{-1/2}$ then $\dfrac{dy}{dx} = -x^{-3/2} = -1/x^{3/2} = -1/(\sqrt{x})^3$

Example 7.6

Differentiate with respect to x:

(a) $1/x^3$ (b) $2x^{0.8}$ (c) $4/x^2$ (d) $x^{3/2}$ (e) $1/\sqrt[3]{x}$

Addition and subtraction rules

If a function is the sum of, or the difference between, two 'power functions' of the kind ax^n discussed previously, then to differentiate this sum or difference we just differentiate it 'term by term'. For example, if

$$y = 3x^3 + 4x^2 \qquad\qquad [7.28]$$

then

$$\frac{dy}{dx} = 9x^2 + 8x \qquad\qquad [7.29]$$

To obtain [7.29] we have simply applied the rule [7.17], firstly to the term $3x^3$ in [7.28] and then to the term $4x^2$, finally adding them. Similarly

if $y = 8x^5 - 3x^3$ then $\dfrac{dy}{dx} = 40x^4 - 9x^2$

The same procedure is possible when dealing with more than two terms. Thus

if $y = 4x^4 + 2x^3 - 6x^2$ then $\dfrac{dy}{dx} = 16x^3 + 6x^2 - 12x$

if $y = x^3 - 4x^2 + x + 6$ then $\dfrac{dy}{dx} = 3x^2 - 8x + 1$ [7.30]

To differentiate the last term in the last example, remember that the derivative of a constant is zero. We in fact graphed the functional relationship [7.30] in Fig. 1.10. Let us use its derivative to determine the gradient of this graph when $x = -2$, $x = 1$ and $x = 4$:

when $x = -2$ gradient $= 3(-2)^2 - 8(-2) + 1 = 29$

when $x = 1$ gradient $= 3(1)^2 - 8(1) + 1$ $= -4$

when $x = 4$ gradient $= 3(4)^2 - 8(4) + 1$ $= 17$

Inspection of Fig. 1.10 reveals that the graph indeed has largish positive gradients when $x = -2$ and 4 but a smaller negative gradient when $x = 1$.

Obviously, the concept of differentiation can be applied to variables other than x and y. For example,

if $z = 8w^3 - 5w$ then $\dfrac{dz}{dw} = 24w^2 - 5$ (differentiating with respect to w)

if $q = 9p^4 + 3p^2$ then $\dfrac{dq}{dp} = 36p^3 + 6p$ (differentiating with respect to p)

Similarly

if $f(z) = 9z^3 + 8$ then $f'(z) = 27z^2$ (differentiating with respect to z)

if $g(p) = 5p^3 - 4p$ then $g'(p) = 15p^2 - 4$ (differentiating with respect to p)

Example 7.7

Find dy/dx when:

(a) $y = 3x^2 - 12x + 4$;
(b) $y = 5x^3 + 10$;
(c) $y = x^6 - 3x^4 + 8x^2 + 5$.

Example 7.8

What are the derivatives of:

(a) $x^3 - 3x^2 + 10x + 4$;
(b) $x^2 + 1/x^2$?

Example 7.9

By using the power rule and the addition rule, find the gradient of the function $f(x) = 4x^3 + 3x + 7$ at the points where $x = 2$, $x = 4$ and $x = 6$.

Example 7.10

Find the gradient of the curve $y = 3x^2 + 1$ at the points where it is intersected by the straight line $y = 3x + 1$.

Example 7.11

Find the gradient of the curve $y = 1 - x - 2x^2$ at the points where it cuts the x-axis. Find, also, any points on the curve where the gradient is zero.

7.5 Some economic applications

As an economic example of the use of derivatives let us return to the total cost function [1.15], graphed in Fig. 1.4, for the values $a = 1$, $b = 2$ and $c = 8$. That is,

$$TC = q^2 + 2q + 8 \qquad [7.31]$$

Notice that since output, q, is a flow variable and total cost, TC, depends on output, total cost is itself a flow variable – that is, it has to be measured per unit of time.

At the beginning of this chapter we defined *marginal cost* (*MC*) as the gradient of the total cost curve. Readers should again look carefully at the definition of *MC* in section 7.1, in particular the fact that changes in cost do not have to be measured over a single whole unit. Since we are working in terms of infinitesimally small increases in output, to obtain marginal cost we simply have to differentiate the cost function [7.31] with respect to output, q

$$\frac{d(TC)}{dq} = MC = 2q + 2 \qquad [7.32]$$

We can now use [7.32] to determine marginal cost at any level of output. For example,

when $q = 3$ $MC = 8$

when $q = 10$ $MC = 22$

when $q = 30$ $MC = 62$

Thus, for the total cost function [7.31] we see that marginal cost rises as output rises. That is, the higher the level of output, the greater is the sensitivity of total cost to further increases in output (or alternatively, the greater the increase in total cost per unit increase in output).

As any economics student will realise, *average cost* differs from marginal cost. Average cost (*AC*) is simply defined as total cost divided by total output, q, and thus $AC = TC/q$. We can therefore obtain AC directly from the total cost function [7.31]:

$$AC = \frac{TC}{q} = q + 2 + \frac{8}{q} \qquad [7.33]$$

Equation [7.33] can now be used to obtained average cost at any level of output. For example,

when $q = 3$ $AC = 7.67$

when $q = 10$ $AC = 12.8$

when $q = 30$ $AC = 36$

Example 7.12

If a firm's total cost function is given by

$$TC = 3q^2 + 5q + 75$$

where q is output, find the firm's marginal cost when output is: (a) 10; (b) 20. What is average cost at these output levels? At what output level are average and marginal costs equal?

Example 7.13

A firm's total cost function is given by

$$TC = 0.25q^3 - 3q^2 + 20q + 150$$

Graph this function. Find the firm's average cost and marginal cost functions and graph them on the same diagram. Comment on your graphs. The firm's variable costs are given by

$$TVC = 0.25q^3 - 3q^2 + 20q$$

Average variable cost (AVC) is defined as total variable cost divided by total output. That is, $AVC = TVC/q$. Graph the average variable cost function on the same diagram as the average and marginal cost functions. At what output level are average variable cost and marginal cost equal?

Another concept familiar to readers will be that of marginal revenue. Suppose a firm producing a perishable good faces a flow demand function

$$d = 16 - 0.5p$$

Since the good is perishable, flow demand and market demand are identical and hence the output or quantity, q, that the firm is able to sell at a price p is given by

$$q = 16 - 0.5p \qquad\qquad [7.34]$$

We can rearrange [7.34] to express price in terms of quantity

$$p = 32 - 2q \qquad\qquad [7.35]$$

The total revenue earned by the firm (TR) is given by the product of price and the quantity it can sell. That is,

$$TR = pq = 32q - 2q^2 \qquad\qquad [7.36]$$

Equation [7.36] expresses total revenue as a function of output and is normally referred to as the firm's *total revenue function*. Notice that an expression for total revenue could also have been found by multiplying [7.34] throughout by p to give $pq = 16p - 0.5p^2$. This is not incorrect but it turns out, as we shall see later, that eqn [7.36] is a more useful expression for total revenue. Note that the total revenue function [7.36] expresses TR as a function of *output* (not price) and this is what makes it so useful. Notice also that, to find the TR function, we first had to take [7.34] and express p in terms of q in [7.35].[4] This is generally necessary if we have to find the TR function from a demand equation that expresses q in terms of p as in [7.34].

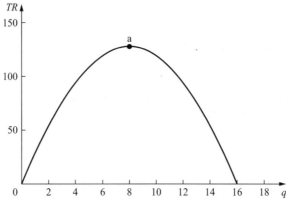

Fig. 7.4 Graph of total revenue function [7.36]

The graph of the function [7.36] is shown in Fig. 7.4. Notice that since output is a flow variable and total revenue is dependent on output, total revenue is itself a flow variable.

Marginal revenue (*MR*) is defined as the gradient or derivative of the total revenue function. It measures the responsiveness of total revenue to increases in output. Like marginal cost, marginal revenue (*MR*) measures increases in revenue per unit increase in output. Again changes do not have to be measured over a single unit of output. When working in terms of infinitesimal changes, we obtain marginal revenue by differentiating the *TR* function [7.36] with respect to *q*:

$$MR = \frac{\mathrm{d}(TR)}{\mathrm{d}q} = 32 - 4q \qquad [7.37]$$

We can use [7.37] to determine marginal revenue at any level of output. For example,

when $q = 3$ $MR = 20$

when $q = 5$ $MR = 12$

when $q = 10$ $MR = -8$

Thus for the total revenue function [7.36] marginal revenue falls as output increases. Alternatively, the increase in total revenue per unit increase in output becomes smaller as output rises. Notice that it is possible for marginal revenue to be negative. This simply means that increases in *q*, output sold, require such a large reduction in price that revenue *pq* falls. This occurs to the right of point a in Fig. 7.4.

Average revenue (*AR*) is defined as the firm's total revenue divided by its output. Since total revenue is *pq*, average revenue is obviously identical to price, so that we can rewrite [7.35] as

$$AR = 32 - 2q \qquad [7.38]$$

Equation [7.38] expresses average revenue as a function of output and is known as the firm's *average revenue function*.

Equation [7.38] can now be used to find average revenue for any level of output *q*. For example,

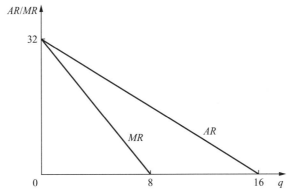

Fig. 7.5 Average and marginal revenue schedules

when $q = 3$ $AR = 26$

when $q = 5$ $AR = 22$

when $q = 10$ $AR = 12$

Graphs of the MR and AR functions [7.37] and [7.38] are both shown in Fig. 7.5. Notice that for linear MR and AR functions, such as those above, the MR curve will always slope more steeply than that of AR and, in fact, the MR curve will always have a gradient twice that of the AR curve. For example, the MR function [7.37] has a gradient of -4 whereas the AR function [7.38] has a gradient of -2.

Elasticities of demand and supply

Consider again the demand function [7.34]. The gradient or derivative of this linear function is obviously -0.5 and tells us that a fall of 1 unit in price always leads to a rise of 0.5 units in quantity demanded. The derivative is therefore a measure of the responsiveness of demand to changes in price but it is a measure the size of which depends on the units of measurement used. It is therefore of little use for comparing the demand responsiveness of different products. For this reason, when measuring the responsiveness of demand to a change in price, economists use the price elasticity of demand which is defined as

$$E_p = -\frac{\text{proportionate change in quantity demanded}}{\text{proportionate change in price}}$$

$$= -\frac{\Delta q/q}{\Delta p/p} = -\frac{\Delta q}{\Delta p}\frac{p}{q} \qquad\qquad [7.39]$$

In [7.39] Δp represents a 'small change' in price and Δq represents the resultant small change in demand. The minus sign attached to the expression means that for a normal downward-sloping demand curve, we measure elasticities as positive.

To measure elasticity at a single point on a demand curve (or, expressing it differently, for infinitesimally small changes), we simply need to determine what happens to [7.39] as the price change Δp approaches zero. Since by definition

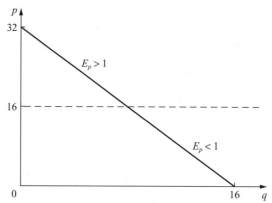

Fig. 7.6 Varying elasticity of demand

$$\text{Limit}_{\Delta p \to 0} \frac{\Delta q}{\Delta p} = \frac{dq}{dp}$$

where dq/dp is simply the derivative of q with respect to p, the elasticity at a point is given by

$$E_p = -\frac{dq}{dp} \frac{p}{q} \qquad [7.40]$$

The demand function [7.34] is graphed in Fig. 7.6. The first point to note is that since the gradient of this demand curve is a constant, the elasticity of demand will vary at different points on it. The gradient is -0.5 so that the elasticity is given by $E_p = 0.5(p/q)$. Hence

when $p = 2$ $q = 16 - 0.5(2) = 15$ and $E_p = 0.5(2/15) = 0.067$

when $p = 10$ $q = 16 - 0.5(10) = 11$ and $E_p = 0.5(10/11) = 0.455$

when $p = 20$ $q = 16 - 0.5(20) = 6$ and $E_p = 0.5(20/6) = 1.667$

In fact, as illustrated in Fig. 7.6, at price levels above $p = 16$, $E_p > 1$ whereas at price levels below $p = 16$, $E_p < 1$. At $p = 16$, E_p equals unity.

For elasticity to vary along a demand curve as in the above case is quite usual. There is, in fact, only one family of demand curves for which price elasticity is a constant at all points. Consider the following demand function:

$$q = Ap^{-\alpha} \qquad [7.41]$$

where $A = $ constant and $\alpha = $ constant. In this case $dq/dp = -A\alpha p^{-\alpha-1}$ (using the power rule), so that

$$E_p = -\frac{dq}{dp} \frac{p}{q} = \frac{A\alpha p^{-\alpha-1} p}{Ap^{-\alpha}} = \frac{\alpha p^{-\alpha}}{p^{-\alpha}} = \alpha = \text{constant}$$

A demand function of the form [7.41] with a constant price elasticity, $\alpha = 2$ and $A = 10$ is graphed in Fig. 7.7. Such a function, as well as having a constant elasticity, has some other useful properties. Since $q = 10p^{-2}$ it follows that, as $p \to 0$, $q \to \infty$. Thus the function never intersects or touches the q-axis no matter how low price becomes. Also, as $p \to \infty$, $q \to 0$, so

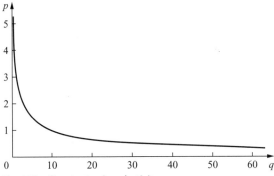

Fig. 7.7 Constant price elasticity

that the function only approaches the p-axis as price becomes infinitely large. That is, demand never becomes zero at finite price levels. Because many products are believed to have demand curves of this general shape, and because of the mathematical convenience of having a constant elasticity, functions of the type [7.41] are very popular among economists.

When $E_p > 1$, we normally refer to demand as being *price elastic* and when $E_p < 1$, *price inelastic*. Whether demand is elastic or inelastic has an important consequence for the behaviour of total revenue when price changes, as we shall see at the end of section 7.6.

Example 7.14

If a firm's market demand function is given by

$$q = 240 - 4p - 2p^2 \quad 0 \leqslant p \leqslant 10$$

find the price elasticity of demand for its product when price $p = 4$ and when $p = 6$.

Elasticity of supply with respect to price is defined similarly to elasticity of demand – that is, in terms of proportionate changes. The supply referred to might be that of a firm or possibly that of an industry. Supply elasticity is defined as

$$E'_p = \frac{\text{proportionate change in quantity supplied}}{\text{proportionate change in price}}$$

$$= \frac{\Delta q/q}{\Delta p/p} = \frac{\Delta q}{\Delta p}\frac{p}{q} \qquad [7.42]$$

where q now refers to quantity *supplied*.

To measure elasticity of supply at a single point on a supply curve we simply have to switch to the derivative dq/dp from the small changes Δq and Δp. That is,

$$E'_p = \frac{dq}{dp}\left(\frac{p}{q}\right) \qquad [7.43]$$

Notice that no negative sign appears in the definition of elasticity of supply unlike that in the demand elasticity. This is because we normally expect supply curves to slope upwards.

Example 7.15

A firm's supply curve is given by

$$q = 5p + 50\sqrt{p}$$

Graph this supply curve and find the elasticity of supply when: (a) $p = 9$; (b) $p = 100$.

7.6 General rules of differentiation II

We saw at the end of section 7.4 that it was possible to differentiate a sum or difference term by term. Differentiating products is slightly more complicated. For example, if

$$y = (4x^3 + 2x)(3x^2 + 6x) \qquad [7.44]$$

it is *not* possible to find dy/dx by first differentiating $4x^3 + 2x$, next differentiating $3x^2 + 6x$ and then multiplying the two derivatives together. One way of differentiating [7.44] is simply to multiply out the bracketed terms and then differentiate. That is,

$$y = 12x^5 + 24x^4 + 6x^3 + 12x^2$$

so that

$$\frac{dy}{dx} = 60x^4 + 96x^3 + 18x^2 + 24x$$

However, as we shall see later, it is convenient to have a rule for differentiating products such as that in [7.44] without actually multiplying the products out. Such a rule exists and we present it now, again without proof.

Differentiation of products

If $u(x)$ and $v(x)$ are both functions of x, and $y = u(x)v(x)$, then

$$\frac{dy}{dx} = v\frac{du}{dx} + u\frac{dv}{dx} \quad \text{product rule} \qquad [7.45]$$

Let us apply rule [7.45] to [7.44]. In this case $u = 4x^3 + 2x$ and $v = 3x^2 + 6x$, so

$$\frac{du}{dx} = 12x^2 + 2 \qquad \frac{dv}{dx} = 6x + 6$$

Hence using [7.45]

$$\frac{dy}{dx} = (3x^2 + 6x)(12x^2 + 2) + (4x^3 + 2x)(6x + 6)$$

$$= 36x^4 + 72x^3 + 6x^2 + 12x + 24x^4 + 24x^3 + 12x^2 + 12x$$

$$= 60x^4 + 96x^3 + 18x^2 + 24x$$

So we indeed obtain the same result as above.

As a further example suppose

$$y = x^2(5x^2 + 3x) \qquad\qquad [7.46]$$

To differentiate [7.46] we may again use the product rule [7.45]. This time we can let $u = x^2$ and $v = 5x^2 + 3x$ so that

$$\frac{du}{dx} = 2x \qquad \frac{dv}{dx} = 10x + 3$$

Hence, using the product rule,

$$\frac{dy}{dx} = (5x^2 + 3x)2x + x^2(10x + 3)$$

$$= 10x^3 + 6x^2 + 10x^3 + 3x^2$$

$$= 20x^3 + 9x^2$$

Notice that we could again perform the differentiation by multiplying out the terms in [7.46] to give

$$y = 5x^4 + 3x^3$$

We therefore again obtain $dy/dx = 20x^3 + 9x^2$.

As we pointed out earlier there may seem little purpose to the product rule if we can obtain derivatives by first multiplying out terms as above. However, as we shall see later in this chapter and in further chapters, many more complicated products cannot be obtained simply by multiplying out terms and then the product rule [7.45] becomes most useful. We have used the above examples simply to illustrate the procedure for using the product rule.

A rule also exists for the differentiation of quotients or ratios.

Differentiation of quotients

If $u(x)$ and $v(x)$ are both functions of x, and $y = u(x)/v(x)$, then

$$\frac{dy}{dx} = \frac{v(du/dx) - u(dv/dx)}{v^2} \qquad \text{quotient rule} \qquad [7.47]$$

As an example of the application of rule [7.47] let us differentiate

$$y = (5x + 6)/(2x^2 + 3x)$$

In this case $u = 5x + 6$ and $v = 2x^2 + 3x$, so we have

$$\frac{du}{dx} = 5 \qquad \frac{dv}{dx} = 4x + 3$$

Hence, using [7.47] we have

$$\frac{dy}{dx} = \frac{(2x^2 + 3x)5 - (5x + 6)(4x + 3)}{(2x^2 + 3x)^2}$$

$$= \frac{-2(5x^2 + 12x + 9)}{(2x^2 + 3x)^2}$$

The derivative of a quotient can sometimes be a fairly complicated expression!

As a further, somewhat easier, example of the use of the quotient rule consider

$$y = \frac{3x - 5}{2x + 4} \tag{7.48}$$

To differentiate [7.48] we let $u = 3x - 5$ and $v = 2x + 4$. Thus

$$\frac{du}{dx} = 3 \quad \frac{dv}{dx} = 2$$

Hence, using [7.47] we have

$$\frac{dy}{dx} = \frac{(2x + 4)3 - (3x - 5)2}{(2x + 4)^2} = \frac{22}{(2x + 4)^2}$$

Example 7.16

Use the product and quotient rules to differentiate the following:

(a) $y = (4x^3 + 6)(5x + 7)$ (b) $3x^2(4x^3 + 5x)$ (c) $\dfrac{5x + 4}{x^2}$

(d) $y = \dfrac{3x^2 + 8x}{x^3 + 2}$ (e) $\dfrac{2x - 5}{2x + 3}$

The chain rule

This rule is very useful for differentiating rather more complicated functions than we have handled so far and we shall make further use of it in later chapters. Suppose

$$y = (3x^2 + 6)^7 \tag{7.49}$$

One way of differentiating [7.49] would be to expand $(3x^2 + 6)^7$ but this would be very tedious. Instead, suppose we let

$$u = 3x^2 + 6 \quad \text{so that} \quad y = u^7 \tag{7.50}$$

Notice that in [7.50], y is now a function of u, which is itself a function of x. For this reason y is said to be a *function of a function*.

Suppose now that Δx is some small change or difference in x and that this leads to the small change Δu in u and hence to the small change Δy in y. Obviously

$$\frac{\Delta y}{\Delta x} = \frac{\Delta y}{\Delta u} \frac{\Delta u}{\Delta x} \tag{7.51}$$

We require dy/dx which is the limit of $\Delta y/\Delta x$ as $\Delta x \to 0$. Since as $\Delta x \to 0$ it is the case that $\Delta u \to 0$ and hence that $\Delta y \to 0$, it follows that

$$\underset{\Delta x \to 0}{\text{Limit}} \frac{\Delta y}{\Delta u} = \frac{dy}{du} \quad \text{and} \quad \underset{\Delta x \to 0}{\text{Limit}} \frac{\Delta u}{\Delta x} = \frac{du}{dx}$$

Hence, we have from eqn [7.51]

$$\frac{dy}{dx} = \frac{dy}{du} \frac{du}{dx} \quad \textbf{chain rule} \qquad [7.52]$$

We can now use the rule [7.52] to differentiate [7.49]. From [7.50] we have

$$\frac{dy}{du} = 7u^6 \quad \text{and} \quad \frac{du}{dx} = 6x$$

so that applying eqn [7.52]

$$\frac{dy}{dx} = 7u^6(6x) = 42xu^6$$

We normally require dy/dx as a function of x alone, so using the first part of [7.50]

$$\frac{dy}{dx} = 42x(3x^2 + 6)^6 \qquad [7.53]$$

Notice that in applying rule [7.52] to differentiate [7.49], what we have to do is first apply the power rule [7.17], treating the term in brackets just as if it was an x, and then multiply by the derivative of the term in brackets. That is,

$$\frac{dy}{dx} = 7(.)^6 \frac{d(.)}{dx}$$

As a further example of the use of the chain rule suppose

$$y = 8(2x^2 + 4x)^5$$

This time we let $u = 2x^2 + 4x$ so that $y = 8u^5$. Hence

$$\frac{dy}{du} = 40u^4 \quad \text{and} \quad \frac{du}{dx} = 4x + 4$$

Applying the chain rule [7.52] gives

$$\frac{dy}{dx} = 40u^4(4x + 4)$$

Again, we require dy/dx in terms of x alone, so substituting for u

$$\frac{dy}{dx} = 40(2x^2 + 4x)^4(4x + 4)$$

Notice that, again, the quick way to obtain the required derivative is to write

$$\frac{dy}{dx} = 40(.)^4 \frac{d(.)}{dx}$$

Similarly

if $y = (4x^3 + 2x)^5$ then $\dfrac{dy}{dx} = 5(.)^4 \dfrac{d(.)}{dx} = 5(4x^3 + 2x)^4(12x^2 + 2)$

if $y = (6x + 8)^{10}$ then $\dfrac{dy}{dx} = 10(6x + 8)^9 6 = 60(6x + 8)^9$

if $f(x) = (3x^2 + 5x + 4)^3$ then $f'(x) = 3(3x^2 + 5x + 4)^2(6x + 5)$

Example 7.17

Use the chain rule to find $f'(x)$ when:

(a) $f(x) = (3x^2 + 5)^7$;
(b) $f(x) = (3x + 4)^{10}$;
(c) $f(x) = (5x^2 + 4x)^{-2}$;
(d) $f(x) = (2x + 4)^{1/2}$.

The product and quotient rules have sometimes to be made use of in combination with the chain rule.

Example 7.18

Differentiate:

(a) $y = (x^2 + 4)^4(x^3 - 3x)^2$ (b) $y = \dfrac{(1 + x)^3}{(2x - 1)^2}$ (c) $y = \dfrac{3x^2 + 4}{(x + 6)^5}$

Example 7.19

If

$$z = \dfrac{3t^4 + 6}{(t + 3)^6} \quad \text{find} \quad \dfrac{dz}{dt}$$

Equation [7.52] is generally referred to as the *chain rule* because it can be extended to as many functions of functions as are necessary. For example, suppose $x = t^2 + 5$ in [7.49]. If we require dy/dt the rule [7.52] can be extended to

$$\dfrac{dy}{dt} = \dfrac{dy}{du}\dfrac{du}{dx}\dfrac{dx}{dt}$$

Hence, since $dx/dt = 2t$, we have

$$\dfrac{dy}{dt} = 42x(3x^2 + 6)^6 2t = 84t(t^2 + 5)[3(t^2 + 5)^2 + 6]^6$$

The inverse function rule

Consider the functional relationship [1.37] reproduced below:

$$y = 2x^3 + 4x \qquad [7.54]$$

This was graphed as Fig. 1.11. We saw in Chapter 1 that, while the graph of the inverse function $x = x(y)$ could be obtained easily enough by the procedure of inverting axes (see Fig. 1.12), it was not possible to write out the exact functional form $x = x(y)$ in any compact way. Finding the derivative dx/dy of this function is therefore not straightforward. However, it may be found by using the following inverse function rule.

Suppose, as in [7.54]

$$y = y(x) \qquad [7.55]$$

Let us differentiate both sides of [7.55] with respect to y. The derivative of y with respect to y is obviously 1, while for the RHS of eqn [7.55]

$$\frac{dy(x)}{dy} = \frac{dy(x)}{dx}\frac{dx}{dy}$$

Hence we have

$$\frac{dy(x)}{dx}\frac{dx}{dy} = 1$$

Thus providing $dy(x)/dx$ is non-zero we have

$$\frac{dx}{dy} = 1 \bigg/ \frac{dy}{dx} \qquad [7.56]$$

Equation [7.56] is the *inverse function rule*. We can use it to find dx/dy for [7.54]. Differentiating [7.54] with respect to x

$$\frac{dy}{dx} = 6x^2 + 4$$

Hence using eqn [7.56]

$$\frac{dx}{dy} = \frac{1}{6x^2 + 4}$$

Notice, however, that dx/dy is expressed in terms of x rather than y.

More about price elasticities

Recall that, at the end of section 7.5, we suggested that whether demand was price elastic or price inelastic had an important consequence for the behaviour of total revenue. We can now use the product rule [7.45] to justify this statement. A firm's total revenue is the product of price and output sold, that is pq, where price itself is a function of output (see e.g. [7.35]). That is,

$$TR = p(q)q \qquad\qquad [7.57]$$

Let us now differentiate [7.57] with respect to q using the product rule:

$$\frac{d(TR)}{dq} = p(q) + q\frac{dp}{dq} \qquad\qquad [7.58]$$

The first term on the RHS of [7.58] is simply $p(q)$ times the derivative of q (which is unity). The second term is just q times the derivative of p. On the LHS, we have the derivative of total revenue which of course is marginal revenue. Hence, rearranging the RHS of [7.58]

$$MR = p\left(1 + \frac{q\,dp}{p\,dq}\right) \qquad\qquad [7.59]$$

where for convenience we have written $p(q)$ as p. Using the definition [7.39] of price elasticity of demand, [7.59] can be written as

$$MR = p\left(1 - \frac{1}{E_p}\right) \qquad\qquad [7.60]$$

Equation [7.60] represents a useful relationship between marginal revenue and the price elasticity of demand. It implies that if demand is elastic at a particular point ($E_p > 1$), then marginal revenue is positive and hence total revenue increases when there is an increase in quantity sold (i.e. when there is a fall in price). On the other hand, if demand is inelastic ($E_p < 1$) then marginal revenue is negative and total revenue falls when there is an increase in quantity sold and a fall in price. Of course, if $E_p = 1$, then marginal revenue is zero and total revenue remains unchanged as quantity rises and price falls.

The above result has important implications for firms considering a price cut in an attempt to increase total revenue received from sales. Provided the firm's demand curve is downward sloping, a cut in price will always increase demand. However, only if $E_p > 1$ will a price cut increase total revenue because only then will the increase in quantity sold be more than sufficient to compensate for the price cut. If $E_p < 1$ then a price cut will reduce total revenue since the increase in q is insufficient to compensate for the fall in p.

Revision examples

Example R7.1

Find both arithmetically and algebraically:

(a) the limits as $x \to \infty$ of

(i) $\dfrac{4x + 3}{2x + 1}$ $\qquad$ (ii) $\dfrac{x^2 + 2x + 3}{x + 5}$

(b) (i) $\underset{x \to 2}{\text{Limit}}\left(\dfrac{x^2 + 2x - 8}{x - 2}\right)$ $\qquad$ (ii) $\underset{x \to -3}{\text{Limit}}\left(\dfrac{x + 3}{x^2 + 4x + 3}\right)$

(c) the limits as $x \to 0$ of

(i) $\dfrac{x^3 + x^2 - 6x}{x^2 + 3x}$ (ii) $\dfrac{(x-3)(x+2) + 6}{x^2 - 3x}$

Example R7.2

It is clear that the graph of $y = 5 + 3x$ is a straight line with gradient 3. However, use the technique of section 7.3 and equation [7.5] to demonstrate that the gradient actually is 3.

Example R7.3

(a) Differentiate $y = 3x^2 + 5x - 3$ and find the gradient of this curve at the points (2, 19) and (−3, 9). At what point is the gradient zero?
(b) Differentiate $y = 0.20x^5 - 2.5x^2 - 4x$ and find the gradient of this curve: (i) when $x = 2$; (ii) at the origin.
(c) Differentiate $p = 2q^3 + 5q^2 - 12q$ and find the gradient of this curve at the points where it intersects the q-axis.

Example R7.4

Differentiate:

(a) $y = 3/x^3$ (b) $y = 1/\sqrt{x}$ (c) $y = \sqrt[3]{x}$ (d) $y = \dfrac{2}{x^2} + 5x + 3$

(e) $y = 3x^{0.25}$ (f) $y = 3x^{-1/4}$ (g) $y = 6x^{2/5}$ (h) $y = 2x^{-2} + 3\sqrt{x}$

Example R7.5

The demand for a firm's product is given by $q = 200 - 4p$. Find the firm's total revenue, average revenue and marginal revenue when $p = 25$. Show that the price elasticity of demand equals unity at this price. Sketch the demand curve and indicate on your sketch the portions of the curve where elasticity is: (a) less than unity; (b) greater than unity.

Example R7.6

A firm's total cost curve is given by

$$TC = 2q^2 + 5q + 98$$

Find the firm's total cost (TC), marginal cost (MC) and average cost (AC) functions. Hence find TC, MC and AC when $q = 5$ and $q = 10$. Find the level of output at which $MC = AC$. Hence, graph the marginal and average cost curves *on the same diagram*. Comment on the curves.

Example R7.7

Find the price elasticity of demand when price $p = 4$ for the following demand functions:

(a) $q = 200 - 2p - p^2$;

(b) $q = 20 + 900p^{-3}$.

Example R7.8

Use the product and quotient rules to differentiate the following:

(a) $y = (2x^2 + 3x)(5x - 2)$;

(b) $y = 8(2x + 5)^3$;

(c) $y = \dfrac{3x - 4}{3x + 3}$;

(d) $y = 3(3x^2 + 2x)^7$;

(e) $y = \dfrac{2x + 4}{3x^2 + 4x}$.

Example R7.9

Differentiate the following functions:

(a) $y = \dfrac{(4x - 3)^2}{2x + 1}$;

(b) $y = \left(5x^3 - 2x^2 + \dfrac{5}{x}\right)^{-2/3}$;

(c) $y = (5x + 3)^2(3x - 4)^4$;

(d) $y = \dfrac{(1 + x)^3}{(2x - 1)^2}$;

(e) $y = (2x - 3)^{3/2}(4x - 1)^{4/3}$.

Example R7.10

(a) Find dx/dy when:

    (i) $y = 8x^4 + 3x^2 + 6$;

    (ii) $y = (3x + 6)^3$.

(b) Find dy/dx when:

    (i) $x = \dfrac{4y - 2}{3y - 1}$;

    (ii) $x = 4(2y^2 + 3)^4$.

Notes

1. We would have obtained exactly the same answer if we had allowed x to approach 1 from 'the other direction', for example $x = 0$, 0.9, 0.99, etc.
2. Again the same result is obtained if we allow x to approach zero from 'the other direction', for example $x = -10, -1, -0.01$, etc.
3. A. C. Chiang (1984) *Fundamental Methods of Mathematical Economics*, 3rd edn, International Student edn. McGraw-Hill, Tokyo.
4. That is, in terms of Chapter 16 we find the inverse function.

8 Higher-order derivatives

Consider, for example, the functional relationship

$$y = x^3 - 6x^2 + 9x + 4 \qquad\qquad [8.1]$$

Differentiating with respect to x

$$\frac{dy}{dx} = 3x^2 - 12x + 9 \qquad\qquad [8.2]$$

Clearly dy/dx, the derivative of y with respect to x, is itself a function of x. It is therefore possible to apply the technique of finding a derivative to a derivative itself. That is, we can differentiate dy/dx – in the above case differentiate [8.2] – to obtain

$$\frac{d(dy/dx)}{dx} = 6x - 12 \qquad\qquad [8.3]$$

To interpret [8.3] remember, firstly, that the derivative of y with respect to x, dy/dx, tells us the gradient of [8.1]. For a reason that will shortly become clear, it is often referred to as a *first-order* derivative. Relationships [8.1] and [8.2] are graphed in Figs 8.1 and 8.2 respectively.

Since in [8.3] we are differentiating the function [8.2], which is graphed in Fig. 8.2, clearly what [8.3] tells us is the gradient of this graph. For example, when $x = 4$, using [8.3] we see that

$$\frac{d(dy/dx)}{dx} = 6(4) - 12 = 12$$

Thus the gradient of the graph in Fig. 8.2 at point C (i.e. when $x = 4$) is 12. We normally write $d(dy/dx)/dx$ as d^2y/dx^2 (pronounced dee-two-y-by-dee-x-two) and it is known as *the second-order derivative of y with respect to x*. That is,

$$\frac{d^2y}{dx^2} = 6x - 12 \qquad\qquad [8.4]$$

Alternatively, since y is a function of x, if we write this function as

$$f(x) = x^3 - 6x^2 + 9x + 4$$

then

$$f'(x) = 3x^2 - 12x + 9$$

and if we differentiate a second time, we obtain the second-order derivative of $f(x)$ which we write as $f''(x)$. That is,

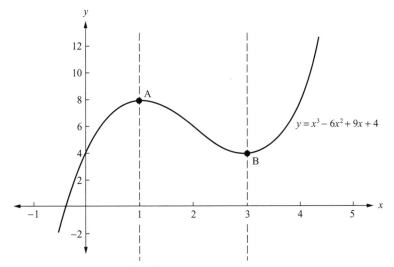

Fig. 8.1 Graph of $y = x^3 - 6x^2 + 9x + 4$

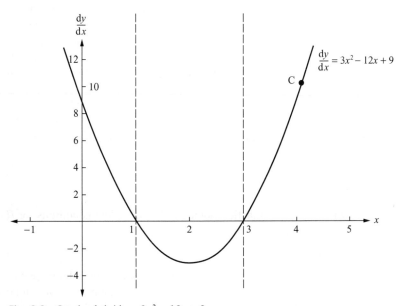

Fig. 8.2 Graph of $dy/dx = 3x^2 - 12x + 9$

$f''(x) = 6x - 12$

Notice that in either notation to obtain the second-order derivative (of y or $f(x)$) we differentiate twice with respect to x. Summarising, d^2y/dx^2 tells us the gradient of dy/dx. Similarly $f'(x)$ tells us the gradient of $f(x)$.

Example 8.1

Find the first- and second-order derivatives of:

(a) $y = 3x^2 + 2x + 5$;

(b) $y = 2x/(x^2 + 3x)$;

(c) $f(x) = (3x - 5)^7$.

8.1 Stationary points

Second-order derivatives are used to find the stationary points and in particular the turning-points of curves. Consider point A in Fig. 8.1. At this point the value of y in [8.1] has reached what is known as a *local maximum*. That is, the value of y is larger at A than at any other point on the graph in that neighbourhood. We call it merely a *local* maximum since obviously higher values of y can be obtained for $x = 10$, 100, etc. Similarly, point B is known as a *local minimum* because here y takes a smaller value than at any neighbouring point.

It is not difficult to see that for a point on a graph or curve to be a local maximum or minimum, the tangent to the curve at this point must be horizontal. That is, the curve must have a zero gradient. *A necessary condition for a point to be either a local maximum or minimum is therefore that dy/dx = 0*. Local maxima and minima are known as *turning-points*.

What condition enables us to distinguish between the two types of turning-point? Consider point A first. As we move along the curve through point A, its gradient is at first positive, then zero at A and then negative. That is, the gradient, dy/dx, is decreasing at point A. Clearly, as is illustrated in Fig. 8.3, this must always be the case for local maxima. But if dy/dx is decreasing as x increases then d^2y/dx^2 (the gradient of dy/dx, where dy/dx is graphed in Fig. 8.2) must be negative. We can therefore say that a point will be a *local maximum* if the following conditions hold at that point:

$$\frac{dy}{dx} = 0 \quad \text{and} \quad \frac{d^2y}{dx^2} < 0 \qquad\qquad [8.5]$$

Alternatively, if we wish to use the function notation, the equivalent conditions for $f(x)$ to have a local maximum at a point are

$$f'(x) = 0 \quad \text{and} \quad f''(x) < 0 \qquad\qquad [8.6]$$

Now consider the local minimum at point B in Fig. 8.1 As we move along the curve through this point its gradient is at first negative, then zero at B and finally positive. Hence dy/dx is increasing at point B. As illustrated in Fig. 8.4, this must always be the case for local minima. Since when dy/dx is increasing, d^2y/dx^2 must be positive, conditions for a *local minimum* are therefore

$$\frac{dy}{dx} = 0 \quad \text{and} \quad \frac{d^2y}{dx^2} > 0 \qquad\qquad [8.7]$$

or alternatively

$$f'(x) = 0 \quad \text{and} \quad f''(x) > 0 \qquad\qquad [8.8]$$

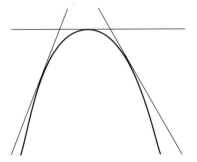

Fig. 8.3 A local maximum

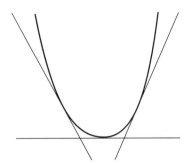

Fig. 8.4 A local minimum

We can use the above conditions to confirm that the functional relationship [8.1] has a local maximum when $x = 1$ and a local minimum when $x = 3$ as sketched in Fig. 8.1. We know that $dy/dx = 0$ for all turning-points.

Hence from [8.2] we have

$$\frac{dy}{dx} = 3x^2 - 12x + 9 = 0$$

Thus dividing throughout by 3, turning-points must occur when

$$x^2 - 4x + 3 = 0 \qquad [8.9]$$

Equation [8.9] is a quadratic equation, most easily solved by factorisation. Hence local maxima and minima can only occur when

$$(x - 3)(x - 1) = 0$$

or when $x = 1$ and $x = 3$. We now check whether d^2y/dx^2 is positive or negative at these values of x. Using [8.4]

when $x = 1$ $\quad \dfrac{d^2y}{dx^2} = 6x - 12 = -6$

when $x = 3$ $\quad \dfrac{d^2y}{dx^2} = 6x - 12 = 6$

Since, when $x = 1$, d^2y/dx^2 is negative, a local maximum is confirmed at this point. Similarly since, when $x = 3$, d^2y/dx^2 is positive, a local minimum is confirmed here.

The usefulness of the conditions [8.5]–[8.8] is that they enable us to find local maxima and minima of functions without actually graphing the functions. For example, suppose

$$f(x) = 3x^2 + 8x + 7 \qquad [8.10]$$

Taking the first derivative

$$f'(x) = 6x + 8$$

The first derivative will be zero when $6x + 8 = 0$, that is when $x = -\frac{4}{3}$. The second derivative is

$$f''(x) = 6$$

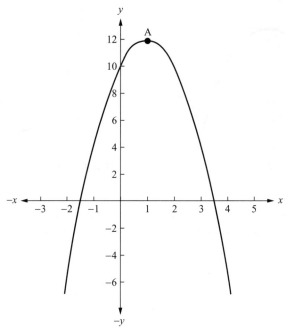

Fig. 8.5 The graph $y = 10 + 4x - 2x^2$

Since the second derivative equals 6 regardless of the value of x, it is obviously positive when $x = -\frac{4}{3}$. Hence this function has a local minimum at the point $x = -\frac{4}{3}$.

As a further example consider

$$y = 10 + 4x - 2x^2 \qquad\qquad\qquad [8.11]$$

Taking the first derivative

$$\frac{dy}{dx} = 4 - 4x$$

In this case the first derivative is zero only when $x = 1$. Since $d^2y/dx^2 = -4$, which is negative, [8.11] must have a local maximum when $x = 1$. The graph of [8.11] is shown in Fig. 8.5. Notice that in this case y not only is larger at point A than at any neighbouring point in the graph, but takes its maximum value for *all* possible values of x at this point. Such a point is not merely a local maximum and is referred to as a *global maximum*. Similarly, if the function [8.10] were graphed it would be seen that $f(x)$ has a *global minimum* when $x = -\frac{4}{3}$ and not merely a local minimum.

As a rather more complicated example of the use of derivatives in finding turning-points consider

$$y = 4x + \frac{9}{x} \qquad\qquad\qquad [8.12]$$

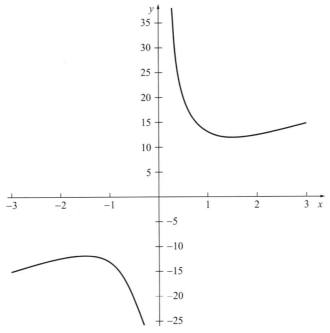

Fig. 8.6   Graph of $y = 4x + 9/x$

Differentiating with respect to x gives

$$\frac{dy}{dx} = 4 - 9x^{-2}$$

Setting the derivative to zero yields

$$4 - 9x^{-2} = 0 \quad \rightarrow \quad 4x^2 = 9 \quad \rightarrow \quad x = 1.5 \quad \text{or} \quad x = -1.5$$

There are therefore two possible turning-points. Differentiating a second time we have

$$\frac{d^2y}{dx^2} = 18x^{-3} = \frac{18}{x^3} \qquad\qquad [8.13]$$

When $x = 1.5$, the second derivative $d^2y/dx^2 = 18/(1.5)^3$ which is positive. Hence y has a local minimum when $x = 1.5$. When $x = -1.5$, however, $d^2y/dx^2 = 18(-1.5)^3$ is negative so that y has a local maximum when $x = -1.5$.

The function [8.12] is graphed in Fig. 8.6. Notice that this function is more unusual than those we have looked at before in that its graph is in two sections. This is not uncommon for more complicated functions.

Example 8.2

Show that $y = 2x^3 + 3x^2 - 12x - 5$ has a local maximum at $x = -2$ and a local minimum at $x = 1$. Hence graph this relationship. Are the local maximum and minimum also global?

Example 8.3

Find the local maxima and minima of the following functions:

(a) $f(x) = 10 + 5x^2 - 2x$;

(b) $f(z) = 3z^2 - 6z + 12$;

(c) $f(x) = 2x/(x + 6)^2$.

Points of inflection

So far we have ignored the possibility that, when dy/dx is zero, d^2y/dx^2 is neither positive nor negative but is also zero. Suppose, however,

$$y = 2x^3 - 24x^2 + 96x + 12 \qquad [8.14]$$

In this case

$$\frac{dy}{dx} = 6x^2 - 48x + 96$$

If we set the first derivative equal to zero we obtain

$$6x^2 - 48x + 96 = 0 \quad \rightarrow \quad x^2 - 8x + 16 = 0$$

$$\rightarrow \quad (x - 4)(x - 4) - 0$$

Hence only at $x = 4$ is dy/dx equal to zero. Differentiating a second time

$$\frac{d^2y}{dx^2} = 12x - 48$$

so that when $x = 4$, $d^2y/dx^2 = 0$ as well as dy/dx. Clearly neither the conditions [8.5] nor [8.7] hold, so apparently we have neither a local maximum nor a local minimum. Yet when $x = 4$, the gradient of [8.14] is zero. The graph of [8.14] is sketched in Fig. 8.7. We see that there is indeed no local maximum or minimum when $x = 4$. In fact, at point P, we have what is known as a *point of inflection*.

We can now see that when $dy/dx = 0$, three possibilities arise. We have either a local maximum as at point A in Fig. 8.1, or a local minimum as at point B in Fig. 8.1, or a point of inflection as in Fig. 8.7. It is convenient to refer to all such points as *stationary points* because in each case y is, momentarily, neither rising nor falling.

We know that provided $dy/dx = 0$, a negative value for d^2y/dx^2 implies a local maximum, while a positive value implies a local minimum. Is it the case that a zero value for d^2y/dx^2 always implies a point of inflection? Unfortunately the matter is not as simple as that. $d^2y/dx^2 = 0$ may signify a point of inflection but this is not necessarily the case. Consider, for example,

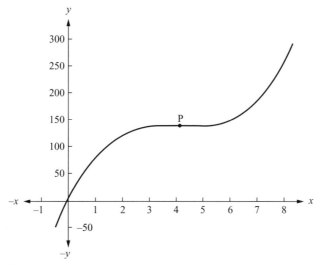

Fig. 8.7 A point of inflection

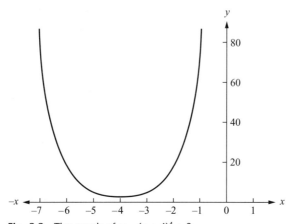

Fig. 8.8 The graph of $y = (x + 4)^4 + 3$

$$y = (x + 4)^4 + 3 \tag{8.15}$$

The graph of this function is sketched in Fig. 8.8 and clearly has a minimum when $x = -4$. The first- and second-order derivatives of [8.15] are

$$\frac{dy}{dx} = 4(x + 4)^3 \qquad \frac{d^2y}{dx^2} = 12(x + 4)^2$$

dy/dx is zero only when $x = -4$, which is consistent with the graph. However, when $x = -4$, d^2y/dx^2 is also zero, but obviously we have a minimum at this point and not a point of inflection. To obtain a foolproof way of distinguishing between the various kinds of stationary points we have to consider higher-order derivatives.

Higher-order derivatives

Just as it is possible to differentiate a first-order derivative to obtain the second-order derivative, so it is possible to differentiate the second-order derivative and obtain the *third-order derivative*. We normally write this as

$$\frac{d(d^2y/dx^2)}{dx} = \frac{d^3y}{dx^3}$$

Hence, if, for example, $y = x^6$ then

$$\frac{dy}{dx} = 6x^5, \quad \frac{d^2y}{dx^2} = 30x^4 \quad \text{and} \quad \frac{d^3y}{dx^3} = 120x^3$$

Although interpretation of higher-order derivatives is not always easy, we can obviously carry this procedure further and find the *fourth-order derivative*, d^4y/dx^4, and the *fifth-order derivative*, d^5y/dx^5, etc. Notice that if y is a function of x alone, then all derivatives will be functions of x alone so further differentiation is always possible.[1]

Let us now return to the functional relationship [8.15] which we know has a stationary point at $x = -4$. If we evaluate all the higher-order derivatives at the point $x = -4$ we obtain

$$\frac{d^2y}{dx^2} = 12(x + 4)^2 = 0$$

$$\frac{d^3y}{dx^3} = 24(x + 4) = 0$$

$$\frac{d^4y}{dx^4} = 24 > 0$$

All derivatives from the fifth order onwards are of course zero. However, the fourth-order derivative is positive and it is this that tells us that in this case, the stationary point at $x = -4$ is a minimum. The general rules (which we shall not prove) for distinguishing between stationary points are as follows:

1. If the first non-zero higher-order derivative (evaluated at the stationary point) occurs after an *odd* number of differentiations, then we have a *point of inflection*.
2. If the first non-zero derivative (evaluated at the stationary point) occurs after an *even* number of differentiations then if that higher-order derivative is *negative* we have *a local maximum*, while if it is *positive* we have *a local minimum*.

The local maxima and minima referred to may, of course, be global maxima and minima but this will not necessarily be the case.

We can now see why [8.15] had a local minimum at $x = -4$. We had to differentiate an even number of times (four) before we found a non-zero derivative at $x = -4$ and this fourth-order derivative was positive.

We now summarise the procedure for finding the local maxima and minima and points of inflection of a function.

1. Equate the first derivative to zero and find all stationary points. That is, let

$$\frac{dy}{dx} = 0 \quad \text{or} \quad f'(x) = 0 \qquad [8.16]$$

Equation [8.16] is known as the *first-order condition*.

2. Evaluate the second-order derivative at each stationary point:

if $\dfrac{d^2y}{dx^2}$ or $f''(x)$ is negative we have a local maximum $\qquad$ [8.17]

if $\dfrac{d^2y}{dx^2}$ or $f''(x)$ is positive we have a local minimum $\qquad$ [8.18]

Equations [8.17] and [8.18] are sometimes referred to as the *second-order conditions* for local maxima and minima respectively.

3. If at any stationary point the second-order derivative is zero, carry on differentiating until a non-zero higher-order derivative is found.

Example 8.4

Find the stationary points of the following. Are they maxima or minima or points of inflection?

(a) $y = (3x + 6)^4$;
(b) $y = x^3 + 6x^2 + 12x + 15$;
(c) $y = (2x - 8)^3$.

8.2 The relationship between average and marginal cost functions

As a first illustration of the use of the techniques introduced in section 8.1 we shall prove a well-known relationship between average and marginal cost functions. A firm's total costs are a function of its output, q

$$TC = TC(q)$$

Average cost is simply total cost divided by output, and is hence also a function of output

$$AC = \frac{TC(q)}{q} \qquad [8.19]$$

We now differentiate eqn [8.19] with respect to output, using the quotient rule [7.47]

$$\frac{d(AC)}{dq} = \frac{q[d(TC)/dq] - (1)TC(q)}{q^2}$$

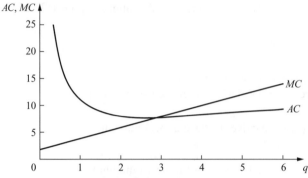

Fig. 8.9 Average and marginal cost functions

Assuming that the average cost function is 'U-shaped' and hence has a minimum value, the above derivative must be zero at that point. That is,

$$\frac{q[\mathrm{d}(TC)/\mathrm{d}q] - TC(q)}{q^2} = 0 \qquad [8.20]$$

Multiplying throughout by q^2 and remembering that $\mathrm{d}(TC)/\mathrm{d}q$ is simply marginal cost, eqn [8.20] becomes

$$qMC = TC(q)$$

or

$$MC = \frac{TC(q)}{q} = AC$$

Thus we have shown that, *when average cost is a minimum, marginal cost equals average cost*. This is simply another way of saying that the marginal cost curve cuts the average cost curve at its minimum point. We can verify this for the total cost function given by [7.31]

$$TC = q^2 + 2q + 8$$

For this function average and marginal costs are

$$AC = \frac{TC}{q} = q + 2 + \frac{8}{q}$$

$$MC = 2q + 2$$

Average cost is a minimum when

$$\frac{\mathrm{d}(AC)}{\mathrm{d}q} = 1 - \frac{8}{q^2} = 0 \quad \text{or} \quad q = \sqrt{8} = 2.83$$

When output $q = \sqrt{8}$, both marginal and average costs equal $2 + 2\sqrt{8} = 7.66$. These marginal and average cost functions are in fact graphed in Fig. 8.9.

Example 8.5

A firm's total cost function is given by

$$TC = 0.25q^3 - 3q^2 + 20q + 15$$

Verify for this firm that the marginal cost curve cuts the average cost curve at its lowest point.

8.3 Profit maximisation

We begin this section with a numerical example. Suppose a firm's total cost function is given by eqn [7.31]

$$TC = q^2 + 2q + 8$$

and that it faces the market demand function [7.34]. Its total revenue function will be eqn [7.36]

$$TR = 32q - 2q^2$$

The firm's profits, Π, are the difference between its total revenue and its total cost, that is $\Pi = TR - TC$. Hence

$$\Pi = -3q^2 + 30q - 8 \qquad [8.21]$$

Equation [8.21] tells us the firm's profit at various levels of output q. We refer to it as the firm's *profit function*.

If we assume that the firm is a profit maximiser, we can use the techniques of section 8.1 to find the firm's optimal level of output, q. Firstly, applying [8.16], we differentiate the profit function [8.21] with respect to output and set this derivative equal to zero:

$$\frac{d\Pi}{dq} = -6q + 30 = 0$$

Clearly only when output $q = 5$ will $d\Pi/dq = 0$. To determine whether this is indeed a profit-maximising output level we have to check that the second-order condition for a local maximum is met. Differentiating a second time

$$\frac{d^2\Pi}{dq^2} = -6 < 0$$

So by [8.17] the profit function has a local maximum at $q = 5$. Since the profit function is quadratic, its graph will have the general shape of quadratic functions described in Chapter 1, so we can safely say that it has a global maximum as well as a local maximum at $q = 5$.

The firm's profit-maximising output is therefore $q = 5$. To find the price it will charge, we use [7.35]. When $q = 5$, $p = 32 - 2q = 22$. Hence the firm maximises profits at a price of 22 units and an output of 5 units.[2] We can also substitute $q = 5$ into the profit function [8.21] to obtain the maximum profit level $\Pi = -3(5)^2 + 30(5) - 8 = 67$. It is clear that the technique of differentiation is of considerable use in determining profit-maximising output levels, so let us examine the conditions for profit maximisation in more detail.

In general, we can express both a firm's total revenue and its total cost in terms of output alone. That is,

$$TR = TR(q) \quad \text{and} \quad TC = TC(q) \tag{8.22}$$

Profit is the difference between total revenue and total cost and hence will also be a function of q alone:

$$\Pi(q) = TR(q) - TC(q)$$

To maximise profit we differentiate with respect to q and set the derivative equal to zero

$$\frac{d\Pi}{dq} = \frac{d(TR)}{dq} - \frac{d(TC)}{dq} = 0 \tag{8.23}$$

Equation [8.23] is the *first-order condition for profit maximisation*. Notice that on the RHS of [8.23] we have $d(TR)/dq$ which we defined in Chapter 7 as *marginal revenue* and $d(TC)/dq$ which we defined as *marginal cost*. We can therefore rewrite the first-order condition as

$$MR = MC \tag{8.24}$$

Hence, for profit maximisation, marginal revenue and marginal cost have to be equal. Many readers will no doubt be familiar with this condition but it is not enough to ensure profit maximisation. From section 8.1 we know that we have also to examine the second-order derivative $d^2\Pi/dq^2$. For a point of maximum profit it is sufficient that this second-order derivative be negative. That is,

$$\frac{d^2\Pi}{dq^2} = \frac{d^2(TR)}{dq^2} - \frac{d^2(TC)}{dq^2} < 0 \tag{8.25}$$

Equation [8.25] is known as the *second-order condition for profit maximisation* and it is just as important as the first-order condition [8.24]. Without it [8.24] could be defining a point of minimum profit or even a point of inflection.

The economic interpretation of the second-order condition is less straightforward than that of the first-order condition. Since the first derivative of total revenue with respect to output is marginal revenue, the second derivative of total revenue is simply the first derivative of marginal revenue. That is,

$$\frac{d^2(TR)}{dq^2} = \frac{d(MR)}{dq} \tag{8.26}$$

Similarly, the second derivative of total cost is the first derivative of marginal cost

$$\frac{d^2(TC)}{dq^2} = \frac{d(MC)}{dq} \tag{8.27}$$

Using [8.26] and [8.27] we can rewrite the second-order condition [8.25] as

$$\frac{d(MR)}{dq} < \frac{d(MC)}{dq} \tag{8.28}$$

Since the derivative of a function is simply its gradient, we see that the second-order condition states that, for an output level at which $MR = MC$ to be a point of maximum profit, we require

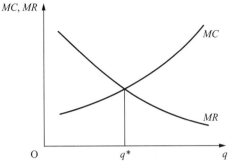

Fig. 8.10 Profit maximisation

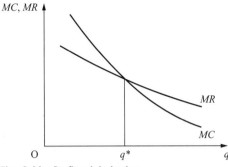

Fig. 8.11 Profit minimisation

that the gradient of the *MR* function be less than the gradient of the *MC* function at that output level. That is, the marginal cost curve should intersect the marginal revenue curve 'from below' as illustrated in Fig. 8.10, rather than 'from above' as in Fig. 8.11.[3] If an output level is to be one of maximum profit, then it must be the case that neither increases nor decreases in output result in a rise in profit. In Fig. 8.10 if output is raised above q^*, $MC > MR$, that is the additional cost incurred is greater than the additional revenue received. Hence profit will fall. On the other hand, if output falls below q^*, then $MC < MR$ and the resultant fall in revenue exceeds the fall in cost so that profit will again fall. Thus q^* in Fig. 8.10 is a profit-maximising output level. In contrast, in Fig. 8.11 either a rise or a fall in output from q^* will lead to a rise in profits so in this case we have a profit-*minimising* output level which is of little interest to the firm.

We can easily check this interpretation of the second-order conditions for the numerical example at the beginning of this section. In this case the marginal revenue and marginal cost functions are

$$MR = 32 - 4q \quad MC = 2q + 2$$

so that $MR = MC$ when $q = 5$ as expected. Both functions are linear so that the *MR* function has a constant negative gradient of -4 while the *MC* function has a constant positive gradient of 2. Their intersection is therefore as depicted in Fig. 8.10 rather than Fig. 8.11, confirming that we have a point of maximum profit.

Example 8.6

A firm's total cost function is that given in Example 8.5. The firm faces a market demand curve

$$q = 100/3 - (4/3)p$$

At what output level will the firm maximise profits? What will its price and profit level be at this level of output?

There may be occasions when a firm does not necessarily wish to maximise profits. A firm could instead wish to maximise its revenue (e.g. it might simply wish to grow more rapidly in the short term, by increasing its sales). We can use the technique of differentiation to maximise the total revenue function [7.36] for the firm above. That is,

$$TR = 32q - 2q^2$$

Differentiating TR with respect to output and setting the derivative to zero gives

$$\frac{d(TR)}{dq} = 32 - 4q = 0 \quad \rightarrow \quad q = 8$$

The second derivative $d^2(TR)/dq^2 = -4$, indicating a local maximum. Thus total revenue is maximised when output is 8 (a larger output than the above profit-maximising output). At $q = 8$, price $p = 32 - 2q = 16$ so that the revenue-maximising price is lower than the profit-maximising price. Maximum total revenue is given by $TR = 32(8) - 2(8)^2 = 128$. Notice that at the revenue-maximising output the firm's profit comes to, using [8.19], $-3(8)^2 + 30(8) - 8 = 40$. This is, not surprisingly, lower than the profit-maximising output.

Example 8.7

The demand function facing a monopolist is given by

$$p = 60 - 0.75q$$

and its average cost function takes the form

$$AC = 10 + 0.5q + \frac{50}{q}$$

Find the value of q which gives:

(i) maximum total revenue;
(ii) minimum average costs;
(iii) maximum profits.

In each case verify your results using the second-order test. Calculate:

(a) the value of maximum total revenue;
(b) the revenue-maximising price;
(c) the value of profits at the profit-maximising output level;
(d) the profit-maximising price.

8.4 Taxation and the profit-maximisation model

There are basically three ways in which a government may tax a firm. It can tax profits, it can tax sales and it can tax revenues. We shall consider the effect of each of these methods of taxation in turn.

Profit taxes are most easily dealt with. Suppose firstly that the government simply imposes a 'lump sum' tax on profits – that is, it demands a fixed sum A, regardless of the level of profits. A firm's *net profits* will now be

$$\Pi^* = TR - TC - A \tag{8.29}$$

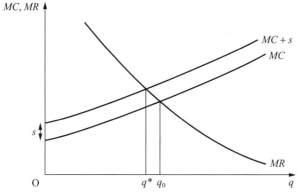

Fig. 8.12 Effect of a sales tax

Since the firm will now seek to maximise net profits, we obtain the first-order condition in this case by differentiating eqn [8.29]. Since A is a constant this simply yields $MR = MC$, the same condition as when no tax was imposed. The second-order condition is also unchanged, so we can conclude that the firm's output and price will be unchanged by the imposition of a lump sum tax, although of course its profits will be smaller.

An alternative form of profit taxation is for the government to claim a fixed proportion t of the firm's profits. Net profits are then

$$\Pi^* = (1 - t)(TR - TC) \tag{8.30}$$

However, on differentiating [8.30] and dividing throughout by $(1 - t)$, we see that again the first- and second-order conditions are unchanged so that this form of profit tax also has no effect on the firm's price and output.

In contrast, sales and revenue taxes will affect price and output. Considering a sales or output tax first, suppose the government imposes a tax of s per unit of output sold. Net profits will now be

$$\Pi^* = TR - TC - sq \tag{8.31}$$

Differentiating [8.31] with respect to q, we now obtain a first-order condition $MR = MC + s$, the second-order condition remaining unchanged. The determination of the profit-maximising output level q^* is illustrated in Fig. 8.12. Since marginal revenue now has to be equated to marginal cost *plus* the tax rate s, we see that q^* is less than q_0, the output that would be produced in the absence of taxation. Since the firm's demand curve is downward sloping, price will be correspondingly higher. Thus the imposition of sales tax will reduce output and increase price.

A revenue tax involves a fixed proportion, r, of total revenue (or equivalently of the price paid) being surrendered to the government. Net profits in this situation are

$$\Pi^* = (1 - r)TR - TC \tag{8.32}$$

The first-order condition is now $(1 - r)MR = MC$ and the determination of optimal output, q^*, is illustrated in Fig. 8.13. Since $(1 - r)$ lies between zero and unity, we again see that q^* is lower than q_0, the output level in the absence of taxation. Thus a revenue tax, like a sales tax, leads to a fall in output with a corresponding rise in price.

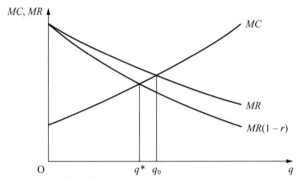

Fig. 8.13 Effect of a revenue tax

It is instructive to introduce sales and revenue taxes into the numerical example used at the beginning of section 8.3. Firstly, we introduce a revenue tax $r = 0.25$. That is, the government takes 25 per cent of total revenue in tax. Using [8.32], and the same TR and TC functions, net profits become

$$\Pi^* = 0.75(32q - 2q^2) - (q^2 + 2q + 8)$$

$$= -2.5q^2 + 22q - 8 \qquad \qquad [8.33]$$

To maximise net profit we differentiate [8.33] with respect to output q, and equate the derivative to zero:

$$\frac{d\Pi^*}{dq} = -5q + 22 = 0 \quad \rightarrow \quad q = 4.4$$

Differentiating a second time gives $d^2(\Pi^*)/dq^2 = -5$ which indicates a local maximum. Thus net profits are maximised when output is 4.4. With $q = 4.4$, price $p = 32 - 2q = 23.2$. Maximum net profit can be found from [8.33] as $\Pi^* = -2.5(4.4)^2 + 22(4.4) - 8 = 40.4$.

Note that the imposition of a revenue tax has resulted in the firm reducing its output from the original $q = 5$ before the tax to only $q = 4.4$. In addition the tax has caused the firm to increase its price from the original 22, obtained earlier, to 23.2. The firm's profits have been cut from 67 (see earlier) to 40.4 because of the tax. The government gains the quantity $0.25TR$ from its revenue tax, that is 25 per cent of total revenue. Government revenue therefore equals $0.25(32q - 2q^2)$ which, with $q = 4.4$, gives a value of 25.52.

Secondly let us introduce a sales tax $s = 6$ into the model. The net profit function is now, using [8.31] and the same TR and TC functions,

$$\Pi^* = 32q - 2q^2 - (q^2 + 2q + 8) - 6q$$

$$= -3q^2 + 24q - 8 \qquad \qquad [8.34]$$

In this case, to maximise net profit we differentiate [8.34] with respect to q and set the derivative to zero:

$$\frac{d\Pi^*}{dq} = -6q + 24 = 0 \quad \rightarrow \quad q = 4$$

The second derivative $d^2(\Pi^*)/dq^2 = -6$, indicating a local maximum. Thus in this case net profit is maximised when output $q = 4$. When $q = 4$, price $p = 32 - 2q = 24$. Net profit can now be found by substituting $q = 4$ into [8.34], this time giving $\Pi^* = 40$.

Notice that the imposition of a tax (this time a sales tax) has resulted in a reduction in output to 4 from the original profit-maximising output of 5 obtained earlier. Also the firm has been forced to increase price to 24 from the original 22 obtained earlier. The firm's profits have been cut to 40 from the original 67 because of the sales tax. The government, however, has benefited by collecting tax, this time, by the amount $sq = 6 \times 4 = 24$. The tax is simply the tax per unit multiplied by the number of units produced.

We now consider a more general case where both a revenue tax and a sales tax are imposed on a firm. Using s and r for the respective tax rates, net profits become

$$\Pi^* = (1 - r)TR - TC - sq \tag{8.35}$$

or, using eqns [7.32] and [7.36],

$$\Pi^* = (1 - r)(32q - 2q^2) - q^2 - 2q - 8 - sq \tag{8.36}$$

Differentiating [8.36] with respect to q (remember r and s are constants) yields

$$\frac{d\Pi^*}{dq} = (1 - r)(32 - 4q) - 2q - 2 - s$$

Setting this derivative to zero we obtain as the first-order condition for profit maximisation

$$q(6 - 4r) = 32(1 - r) - 2 - s \tag{8.37}$$

Differentiating the net profit function a second time

$$\frac{d^2\Pi^*}{dq^2} = -4(1 - r) - 2$$

Since $(1 - r)$ lies between zero and unity, $d^2\Pi^*/dq^2 < 0$, so the second-order condition for a maximum is met. Hence we can solve [8.37] to find the profit-maximising output level

$$q = \frac{30 - 32r - s}{6 - 4r} \tag{8.38}$$

Since the firm faces the market demand function [7.34], the profit-maximising price level is

$$p = 32 - 2q = \frac{192 - 128r - 60 + 64r + 2s}{6 - 4r}$$

or

$$p = \frac{66 - 32r + s}{3 - 2r} \tag{8.39}$$

We can now use eqns [8.38] and [8.39] to examine the precise effect of changes in the tax rates on price and output levels. Considering a sales tax first, if $r = 0$ eqns [8.38] and [8.39] become

$$q = \frac{30 - s}{6} \quad \text{and} \quad p = \frac{66 + s}{3}$$

Hence

$$\frac{dq}{ds} = -\frac{1}{6} \quad \text{and} \quad \frac{dp}{ds} = \frac{1}{3} \tag{8.40}$$

Thus we can say that output will fall by one-sixth of a unit for every unit rise in the output tax rate s. Similarly a unit rise in s always increases price by one-third of a unit.

Next, considering a revenue tax, if $s = 0$ then [8.38] and [8.39] become

$$q = \frac{15 - 16r}{3 - 2r} \quad \text{and} \quad p = \frac{66 - 32r}{3 - 2r}$$

Differentiating, using the quotient rule,

$$\frac{dq}{dr} = \frac{-18}{(3 - 2r)^2} \quad \text{and} \quad \frac{dp}{dr} = \frac{36}{(3 - 2r)^2} \tag{8.41}$$

Since $(3 - 2r)^2 > 0$, we see that a rise in r, the proportion of total revenue claimed in tax, always reduces output and increases price. The precise output and price changes, however, depend on the value of r which lies between 0 and 1. For example, if $r = 0.2$ then

$$\frac{dq}{dr} = -2.66 \quad \text{and} \quad \frac{dp}{dr} = 5.33 \tag{8.42}$$

The derivatives [8.42] measure changes in output and price per unit change in r. However, as r lies between 0 and 1 we do not normally expect unit changes in this tax rate! What we can say, however, is that, if $r = 0.2$, then a rise in this tax rate by one-hundredth of a unit to 0.21 will result in a fall in output of about 0.027 units and a rise in price of about 0.053 units.

Example 8.8

Consider the firm of Example 8.6. How would its profit, price and output be affected by:

(a) a sales tax of $s = 2$ per unit of output sold;
(b) a revenue tax equal to 10 per cent of total revenue?

8.5 Reduced and structural forms of the profit-maximisation model

The reader should have recognised the type of analysis carried out at the end of section 8.4. We considered the effect of changes in variables (the tax rates) determined outside our model, on variables (price and output) determined by, or inside, our model. We discussed this form of analysis at length in Chapter 4 when we considered the reduced and structural forms of models.

The profit-maximisation model in the absence of taxation can be viewed as a three-equation model determining the equilibrium values of three variables – profit, price and output. The three equations are, firstly, a profit equation expressing profit, Π, as a function of output q

$$\Pi = \Pi(q) \tag{8.43}$$

Secondly, we have a condition for profit maximisation (it is assumed that the second-order condition holds)

$$\frac{d\Pi}{dq} = \Pi'(q) = 0 \tag{8.44}$$

Thirdly, we have the firm's demand curve, expressing output as a function of price,

$$q = q(p) \tag{8.45}$$

Equation [8.44] determines the profit-maximising level of output, q, and once q is determined, eqns [8.43] and [8.45] determine the levels of profit and price respectively.

If sales and revenue taxes are imposed, net profits become a function of output and the tax rates r and s, as in eqn [8.36]

$$\Pi^* = \Pi^*(q, r, s) \tag{8.43a}$$

The condition for net profit maximisation is

$$\frac{d\Pi^*}{dq} = \Pi^{*\prime}(q, r, s) = 0 \tag{8.44a}$$

The firm's demand curve is unchanged:

$$q = q(p) \tag{8.45a}$$

Equations [8.43a]–[8.45a] constitute a three-equation system in three endogenous variables, Π^*, p and q, and two exogenous variables, r and s. For given values of its exogenous variables it can be solved to yield profit-maximising or equilibrium values of Π^*, p and q.

The best way to handle a system such as this is, of course, to derive its reduced form, expressing the endogenous Π^*, p and q in terms of the exogenous variables alone. We in fact derived the reduced form equations for p and q for the numerical example of section 8.4. These were eqns [8.38] and [8.39]. A reduced form equation for Π^* can be obtained by using eqn [8.38] to substitute for q into the net profit eqn [8.36].

Example 8.9

A firm employs one variable factor of production, labour. The labour required to produce an output, Q, is given by

$$L = 5Q + 0.5Q^2$$

The firm's total costs are

$$TC = 10 + WL$$

where W is the wage rate, and it faces a market demand curve

$$Q = 20 - 2P$$

where P is the price of its product.

If the firm seeks to maximise profits it can be represented by a three-equation system in four variables – profit, price, output and wage rate. If the wage rate is exogenous, find the reduced form of this system and hence analyse the effect of a rise in the wage rate on the firm's price and output.

Revision examples

Example R8.1

Find any local maxima and minima of the following functions:

(a) $y = 3x^2 + 12x + 5$;

(b) $y = x^3 + 4.5x^2 - 30x + 7$;

(c) $y = 2x^3 - 54x$;

(d) $y = x^2/(x - 4)$.

Graph the function (b) and confirm the positions of any local maxima and minima.

Example R8.2

Find any local maxima, local minima or points of inflection for the following functions:

(a) $y = 2(4x - 8)^5$;

(b) $y = x^3 + 9x^2 + 27x + 4$.

Graph the function (b).

Example R8.3

A firm's total costs (TC) are the sum of its total fixed costs (TFC) and its total variable costs (TVC). Its total variable costs are given by

$$TVC = 4q^2 + 10q$$

where q is output. If, when $q = 10$, $TC = 700$, what are the firm's fixed costs?

Verify that the firm's marginal cost curve cuts its average cost curve at the point of minimum average cost.

Example R8.4

The demand curve for a firm's product is given by $q = 52 - 4p$ and its average cost curve has the equation

$$AC = 3 + q + \frac{5}{q}$$

Derive the firm's profit function and hence find the profit-maximising output and price levels. Find also the output at which total revenue is maximised. Find the profit levels: (a) at the profit-maximising output level; (b) at the revenue-maximising output level. Interpret your answer to (b).

Example R8.5

A profit-maximising firm faces a market demand curve of the form $p = 600 - 5q$ where p and q are price and output. The firm's total costs are given by

$$TC = 4q^2 + 150q + 30$$

What levels of price and output will the firm choose? What is the level of maximum profit?

If the government imposes a tax equal to 25 per cent of total revenue, how will this affect the firm's price, output and profits? How much revenue will the government get in tax?

Example R8.6

The demand function facing a profit-maximising monopolist is $q = 100 - 2p$ and its average cost curve is

$$AC = 10 + 1.5q + \frac{60}{q}$$

At what levels of price p and output q will profits be maximised? If the government imposes a sales tax of 5 per unit of output sold, how much will the firm now produce and what price will it charge? What will be the government's revenue?

Notes

1. Many of these derivatives may equal zero. For example, if $y = x^6$ then $d^6y/dx^6 = 720$ and all further higher-order derivatives are zero.
2. Remember that we have not specified the units in which price and output are measured. An output of 5 units is not necessarily 'low'. Output might be measured in millions of tonnes!
3. In Fig. 8.11 both the MR and MC curves are downward sloping and hence have negative gradients. However, the gradient of the MR curve is 'less negative' than that of the MC curve. In mathematical terms this means that the gradient of the MR curve is greater than that of the MC curve. That is, $d(MR)/dq > d(MC)/dq$ and hence the second-order condition for profit maximisation [8.28] does not hold.

9 Integration

Integration is simply the reverse of differentiation. For example, given a functional relationship

$$y = x^2 + 3 \tag{9.1}$$

we can differentiate to find its gradient or derivative

$$\frac{dy}{dx} = 2x \tag{9.2}$$

Integration involves 'finding y given dy/dx'. That is, we know the derivative and have to find the relationship that gives rise to it. There is one minor complication. Since the derivative of a constant is zero, any relationship of the form

$$y = x^2 + c \tag{9.3}$$

where c is constant, will have the gradient or derivative [9.2]. Hence, if all we are given is [9.2] we cannot say that [9.1] is true but only that a relationship of the general form [9.3] must hold. The situation is illustrated in Fig. 9.1. If we know that the gradient of the curve is given by $dy/dx = 2x$, this tells us nothing about the *position* of the curve. For example, the curves graphed in Fig. 9.1 all have the same gradient of 4 when $x - 2$ and in general all have $dy/dx = 2x$. Obviously, there will be an infinite number of such curves. The constant c in [9.3] is known as a *constant of integration*. Integration of functions always gives rise to such constants.

9.1 Notation and terminology

If [9.2] holds then y is said to be the integral of $2x$ with respect to x and we write this statement as

$$y = \int 2x \, dx = x^2 + c \tag{9.4}$$

'$\int$' is an elongated 's' and is known as the integral sign.

In general, if $dy/dx = f'(x)$ where $f'(x)$ is any function of x then we write

$$y = \int f'(x) \, dx \tag{9.5}$$

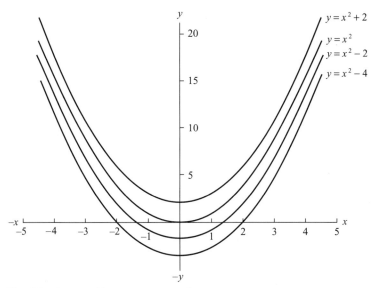

Fig. 9.1 Curves with a common gradient

Alternatively, just as the derivative of $f(x)$ is written $f'(x)$, we write $f(x)$ as the integral of $f'(x)$ with respect to x:

$$f(x) = \int f'(x)\,dx \qquad\qquad [9.6]$$

9.2 Rules for integration I

Integration is frequently a trial and error process where we differentiate various functions in an attempt to obtain the derivative we started with. However, just as there are set rules for differentiation, so there are several useful rules for integration.

The power rule

This is simply the reverse of the power rule for differentiation. That is,

if $\dfrac{dy}{dx} = bx^m$ then $y = \dfrac{b}{m+1}x^{m+1} + c$ $m \neq -1$

where c is the constant of integration (check that differentiating y in this case does yield $dy/dx = bx^m$).

Alternatively, using the notation just introduced

$$\int bx^m\,dx = \dfrac{b}{m+1}x^{m+1} + c \quad m \neq -1 \quad \textbf{power rule} \qquad [9.7]$$

Notice that the rule does not apply when $m = -1$, that is when $dy/dx = b/x$. Applying the rule in this case would involve dividing by zero. We shall consider the integration of functions of the form b/x in Chapter 15.

As examples of the use of the power rule for integration note that

$$\text{if } \frac{dy}{dx} = 4x^3 \quad \text{then} \quad y = x^4 + c; \quad \text{if } \frac{dy}{dx} = 6x \quad \text{then} \quad y = 3x^2 + c$$

$$\text{if } \frac{dy}{dx} = 5 \quad \text{then} \quad y = 5x + c; \quad \text{if } \frac{dy}{dx} = 3x^{10} \quad \text{then} \quad y = \frac{3}{11}x^{11} + c$$

Similarly

$$\int 6x^4\, dx = \frac{6}{5}x^5 + c \quad \int 4x^2\, dx + \frac{4}{3}x^3 + c$$

In all the above cases c is some undetermined constant of integration.

Example 9.1

Evaluate:

(a) $\int 5x^4\, dx$; (b) $\int 6x^3\, dx$; (c) $\int 10\, dx$; (d) $\int 3x^8\, dx$.

Addition and subtraction rules

Just as sums and differences can be differentiated 'term by term' so they can be integrated 'term by term'. For example,

$$\text{if } \frac{dy}{dx} = 3x^2 + 8x \quad \text{then} \quad y = x^3 + 4x^2 + c$$

Similarly

$$\int (x^4 - 6x)\, dx = \frac{1}{5}x^5 - 3x^2 + c$$

The rule can of course be extended to more than two terms. For example,

$$\text{if } \frac{dy}{dx} = 8x^2 - 3x + 5 \quad \text{then} \quad y = \frac{8}{3}x^3 - \frac{3}{2}x^2 + 5x + c$$

and

$$\int (3x^5 + 8x^3 - 3x^2 + 5x - 4)\, dx = \frac{1}{2}x^6 + 2x^4 - x^3 + \frac{5}{2}x^2 - 4x + c$$

The reader should verify that in each of the above cases differentiation reverses the integration process.

Example 9.2

Integrate the following with respect to x:

(a) $4x^2 + 10x + 3$;
(b) $8x^2 - 5x$;
(c) $9x^4 + 5x^2 - 3$.

The rules for integration can also be applied to negative and fractional powers. For example,

$$\int \frac{4}{x^3}\, dx = \int 4x^{-3}\, dx = -2x^{-2} + c = -\frac{2}{x^2} + c$$

Also, for example,

$$\int \sqrt{x}\, dx = \int x^{1/2}\, dx = \tfrac{2}{3} x^{3/2} + c$$

Example 9.3

Evaluate:

(a) $\displaystyle\int \frac{3}{x^2}\, dx$ (b) $\displaystyle 3\int x^{0.6}\, dx$ (c) $\displaystyle\int (x^{0.25} + 3x^{-4})\, dx$

9.3 Total and marginal functions

Perhaps the most obvious use of integration in economics is to obtain a total cost function from a known marginal cost function and a total revenue function from a known marginal revenue function. For example, suppose we know that a firm's marginal cost function is given by

$$MC = 6q^2 - 6q + 5 \qquad\qquad [9.8]$$

Since marginal cost is the derivative of total cost, we obtain the total cost function by integrating [9.8] with respect to output, q. That is,

$$TC = \int (6q^2 - 6q + 5)\, dq$$

or

$$TC = 2q^3 - 3q^2 + 5q + c \qquad\qquad [9.9]$$

Notice that [9.9] contains an unknown constant of integration, c. Since when $q = 0$, $TC = c$, the constant c in this case measures the firm's fixed costs that have to be met regardless of the level of output. Note that we cannot determine the level of fixed cost simply from knowledge of the marginal cost function. However, if we had the additional information that, for example, when output $q = 5$, total costs were 230, then by substituting these values in [9.9] we obtain

$$230 = 2(5)^3 - 3(5)^2 + 5(5) + c$$

We can then deduce that fixed costs must be 30. That is,

$$TC = 2q^3 - 3q^2 + 5q + 30$$

Integration can similarly be used to derive a total revenue function from a marginal revenue function. For example, if

$$MR = 8 - 0.2q$$

then the total revenue function will be

$$TR = \int (8 - 0.2q)\, dq$$

or

$$TR = 8q - 0.1q^2 + c \qquad\qquad [9.10]$$

Notice that [9.10] also contains a constant of integration. However, since it is reasonable to assume that a firm's total revenue will be zero when output $q = 0$, we normally expect the constant of integration to be zero in this case.

Example 9.4

A firm's marginal cost function is given by

$$MC = 0.75q^2 - 6q + 20$$

If, when output is $q = 10$, total costs are 200, what is the firm's total cost function?

9.4 Rules for integration II

Integration by parts

The product rule for differentiation [7.32] stated that if $y = u(x)v(x)$ and both u and v were functions of x then

$$\frac{dy}{dx} = v\frac{du}{dx} + u\frac{dv}{dx}$$

Integrating with respect to x we have

$$y = \int v\frac{du}{dx}\, dx + \int u\frac{dv}{dx}\, dx \qquad\qquad [9.11]$$

Replacing y by uv and rearranging [9.11] gives us the so-called *integration by parts* rule:

$$\int u \frac{dv}{dx} dx = uv - \int v \frac{du}{dx} dx \qquad [9.12]$$

The use of rule [9.12] is best illustrated by examples. Suppose we require

$$12 \int x(x + 1)^2 dx \qquad [9.13]$$

One way of integrating [9.13] is to multiply out and integrate term by term. That is,

$$12 \int x(x + 1)^2 dx = \int (12x^3 + 24x^2 + 12x) dx$$

$$= 3x^4 + 8x^3 + 6x^2 + c \qquad [9.14]$$

where c is a constant of integration.

To verify that the integral [9.13] is equal to [9.14] we use the rule [9.12]. In [9.13] let

$$u = 12x \quad \text{and} \quad \frac{dv}{dx} = (x + 1)^2$$

so that

$$\frac{du}{dx} = 12 \quad \text{and} \quad v = (1/3)(x + 1)^3$$

Hence applying [9.12]

$$\int 12x(x + 1)^2 dx = 4x(x + 1)^3 - 4 \int (x + 1)^3 dx$$

$$= 4x(x + 1)^3 - (x + 1)^4 + d$$

$$= (x + 1)^3(4x - x - 1) + d$$

$$= (x + 1)^3(3x - 1) + d \qquad [9.15]$$

where d is a constant of integration.

Multiplying out [9.15] gives the same answer as for [9.14] except that the constant of integration turns out to be different. In fact c in [9.14] equals $d - 1$. This is the result of our having firstly to integrate dv/dx above to obtain v and secondly to integrate again when using rule [9.12].

Consider next the integral

$$4 \int x(x + 4)^9 dx \qquad [9.16]$$

One way of evaluating [9.16] would again be to expand $(x + 4)^9$. This time, however, expansion would be very tedious so it is preferable to use rule [9.12]. Letting

$$u = 4x \quad \text{and} \quad \frac{dv}{dx} = (x + 4)^9 \qquad [9.17]$$

we can apply rule [9.12]. From [9.17]

$$\frac{du}{dx} = 4 \quad \text{and} \quad v = \frac{1}{10}(x + 4)^{10}$$

Hence, applying eqn [9.12],

$$\int 4x(x+4)^9\,dx = \frac{2}{5}x(x+4)^{10} - \int \frac{2}{5}(x+4)^{10}\,dx$$

$$= \frac{2}{5}x(x+4)^{10} - \frac{2}{55}(x+4)^{11} + c \qquad [9.18]$$

where c is a constant of integration. The reader should verify that differentiating [9.18] leads back to the $4x(x+4)^9$ in [9.16].

Notice that the integration by parts rule does not actually evaluate the integral [9.16]. It merely replaces integral [9.16] by another integral that is more easily evaluated. The rule will not always help because sometimes the second integral is more complicated than the first! For example, if we had assigned u and dv/dx in the reverse way in integral [9.16] and let

$$\frac{dv}{dx} = 4x \quad \text{and} \quad u = (x+4)^9$$

we would have had

$$v = 2x^2 \quad \text{and} \quad \frac{du}{dx} = 9(x+4)^8$$

Applying rule [9.12] would then have given

$$\int 4x(x+4)^9\,dx = 2x^2(x+4)^9 - \int 18x^2(x+4)^8\,dx \qquad [9.19]$$

The final integral in eqn [9.19] is more difficult to work out than the original integral. Unfortunately it is often the case that however we assign u and dv/dx we get a more awkward integral. The use of the rule is not always helpful.

Example 9.5

Integrate by parts:

(a) $\int 8x(2x+3)^5\,dx$;
(b) $\int 6x(x+10)^7\,dx$;
(c) $\int x^2(x+5)^8\,dx$;
(d) $\int 3x(x+5)^{1/2}\,dx$.

(In (c) you will have to use the integration by parts rule twice to obtain the required answer.)

Integration by substitution

This rule is in fact the reverse of the chain rule [7.52] for differentiation. It is best stated as

$$\int f(u)\frac{du}{dx}\,dx = \int f(u)\,du \qquad [9.20]$$

This rule is also best understood by the use of examples. Suppose we require

$$6\int x^2(x^3 + 4)\,dx \qquad\qquad [9.21]$$

The simplest way of evaluating [9.21] is simply to multiply out, so that

$$6\int x^2(x^3 + 4)\,dx = \int (6x^5 + 24x^2)\,dx = x^6 + 8x^3 + c \qquad\qquad [9.22]$$

where c is a constant of integration. Alternatively we can use rule [9.20].
If we let $u = x^3 + 4$ in [9.21] and then $du/dx = 3x^2$. Thus we can write [9.21] as

$$2\int u\frac{du}{dx}\,dx$$

Hence using rule [9.21] we have

$$2\int u\,du = u^2 + d \qquad\qquad [9.23]$$

where d is another constant of integration. Substituting for u gives

$$6\int x^2(x^3 + 4)\,dx = (x^3 + 4)^2 + d = x^6 + 8x^3 + 16 + d \qquad\qquad [9.24]$$

The expressions [9.22] and [9.24] are the same except that the constant c in [9.22] equals $d + 16$ in [9.24].
As a further example consider the integral

$$6\int x^2(3x^3 + 5)^4\,dx \qquad\qquad [9.25]$$

Evaluating [9.25] by multipying out is tedious so we make use of rule [9.20]. If we let $u = 3x^3 + 5$ then $du/dx = 9x^2$. We can now express [9.25] as

$$1.5\int u^4\frac{du}{dx}\,dx$$

Hence, using [9.20], we have

$$1.5\int u^4\,du = 0.3u^5 + c = 0.3(3x^3 + 5)^5 + c \qquad\qquad [9.26]$$

where c is a constant of integration.
For rule [9.20] to work it must be possible to express an integral in the required form. For example, we could not use the rule to evaluate

$$\int 6x^2(3x^2 + 5)^4\,dx$$

because although it is possible to let $u = 3x^2 + 5$, it is not the case that $du/dx = 6x^2$. Similarly we could use the rule to evaluate the first of the following integrals but not the second:

$$\int 3x^2(x^3 + 4)^5\,dx \quad \int 8x(x^3 + 4)^5\,dx$$

Example 9.6

Integrate by substitution:

(a) $\int 6x^3(x^4 + 3)^5 \, dx$ (b) $\int x^2(x^3 + 5)^7 \, dx$ (c) $\int 4x(2x^2 + 4)^{-3} \, dx$ (d) $\int \dfrac{5x^2}{(x^3 + 5)^6} \, dx$

Example 9.7

Integrate the following with respect to x:

(a) x^{-3};

(b) $\sqrt{x}$;

(c) $8x^2 + 5/x^2$;

(d) $5x(x + 4)^{3/2}$;

(e) $3x/\sqrt{(x^2 + 2)}$.

9.5 Definite integrals

The integrals we have handled in previous sections are known as *indefinite integrals*. They are functions. For example, the integral in [9.25] is clearly a function of x. In contrast *definite integrals* are, as we shall see, numbers that refer to areas beneath curves. Consider

$$f(x) = \int (5x^2 + 3x) \, dx = \frac{5}{3}x^3 + \frac{3}{2}x^2 + c \qquad [9.27]$$

The indefinite integral [9.27] is obviously a function of x. An example of a definite integral would be

$$\int_3^6 (5x^2 + 3x) \, dx \qquad [9.28]$$

by which we mean *the value of the integral when $x = 6$ minus the value of the integral when $x = 3$*. $x = 6$ is known as the upper limit of the integral and $x = 3$ the lower limit. Since

when $x = 6$ $f(x) = \dfrac{5}{3}(6)^3 + \dfrac{3}{2}(6)^2 + c = 414 + c$

when $x = 3$ $f(x) = \dfrac{5}{3}(3)^3 + \dfrac{3}{2}(3)^2 + c = 58.5 + c$

the value of the definite integral [9.28] is

$414 + c - (58.5 + c) = 355.5$

Notice that the constant of integration cancels out when evaluating a definite integral. This will always be the case, so in future we shall omit them when dealing with definite integrals. We normally use the following notation when evaluating definite integrals such as [9.28]:

$$\int_3^6 (5x^2 + 3x)\,dx = \left[\frac{5}{3}x^3 + \frac{3}{2}x^2\right]_3^6 = (360 + 54) - (45 + 27/2) = 355.5 \qquad [9.29]$$

The term in square brackets in [9.29] is simply the indefinite integral, with constant of integration suppressed. This is then evaluated within the ordinary brackets first for $x = 6$ and then for $x = 3$. Similarly

$$\int_1^3 (3x^2 + 5x - 4)\,dx = \left[x^3 + \frac{5}{2}x^2 - 4x\right]_1^3$$

$$= \left(27 + \frac{45}{2} - 12\right) - \left(1 + \frac{5}{2} - 4\right) = 38$$

and

$$\int_{-4}^2 (2x^2 + 8x + 1)\,dx = \left[\frac{2}{3}x^3 + 4x^2 + x\right]_{-4}^2$$

$$= \left(\frac{16}{3} + 16 + 2\right) - \left(-\frac{128}{3} + 64 - 4\right) = 6$$

Example 9.8

Evaluate:

(a) $\int_1^4 (2x^3 + 3x + 5)\,dx$;
(b) $\int_2^5 (x^2 - 5x + 3)\,dx$;
(c) $\int_1^3 2x^2(x^3 - 2)\,dx$;
(d) $\int_1^\infty x^{-2}\,dx$.

Integration and the area under curves

Consider the definite integral of the linear function $3x + 2$

$$\int_2^5 (3x + 2)\,dx = \left[\frac{3}{2}x^2 + 2x\right]_2^5 = \left(\frac{75}{2} + 10\right) - (6 + 4) = 37.5 \qquad [9.30]$$

Now consider Figs 9.2 and 9.3 where in each case we have graphed the straight line $y = 3x + 2$. In Fig. 9.2 we consider the area between line and x-axis from the origin to the point $x = 5$, the upper limit of the integral [9.30]. This is the sum of the area of the triangle A, which is 75/2, and the area of the rectangle B, which is 10. Notice that these areas are exactly the same as the

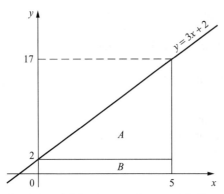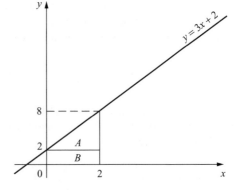

Figs 9.2 and 9.3 Areas under a straight line

numbers obtained when we substituted $x = 5$ into the square-bracketed term in [9.30]. In Fig. 9.3 we consider the area under the line from the origin to the point $x = 2$, the lower limit of the integral [9.30]. The areas of triangle A and rectangle B are this time 6 and 4 respectively. So the sum of these areas is exactly equal to the number obtained when we substituted the lower limit $x = 2$ into the square-bracketed term in [9.30]. Clearly in evaluating the definite integral [9.30] we are in fact *calculating the area between the line $y = 3x + 2$ and the x-axis from the point $x = 2$ to the point $x = 5$.*

A similar exact relationship holds between definite integrals of non-linear functions and their graphs. It can be shown that if $f'(x)$ is any function of x then

$$\int_b^a f'(x)\, dx = \left[f(x) \right]_b^a = f(a) - f(b) \tag{9.31}$$

measures the area between the graph of $f'(x)$ and the x-axis from $x = b$ to $x = a$. For example, consider the functional relationship

$$y = 2x^2 - 12x + 10 \tag{9.32}$$

which is graphed in Fig. 9.4. For example, suppose we wished to find the area A in Fig. 9.4 between this graph and the x-axis. That is, the area from $x = 5$ to $x = 6$. Using [9.31]

$$\text{area } A = \int_5^6 (2x^2 - 12x + 10)\, dx = \left[\frac{2}{3}x^3 - 6x^2 + 10x \right]_5^6$$

$$= (144 - 216 + 60) - \left(\frac{250}{3} - 150 + 50 \right) = \frac{14}{3}$$

Thus the required area is 14/3 square units.

Now consider the area B in Fig. 9.4. This lies between $x = 3$ and $x = 4$. Applying [9.31]

$$\text{area } B = \int_3^4 (2x^2 - 12x + 10)\, dx = \left[\frac{2}{3}x^3 - 6x^2 + 10x \right]_3^4$$

$$= \left(\frac{128}{3} - 96 + 40 \right) - (18 - 54 + 30) = -\frac{22}{3}$$

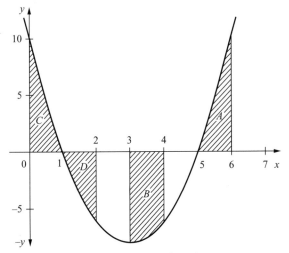

Fig. 9.4 Areas between curve and x-axis

Notice that we have obtained a negative value for area B. This is because the area lies below the x-axis (i.e. where y is negative). *Areas beneath the x-axis are always measured as negative if we use the method of definite integrals.* This leads to one minor complication. Suppose we required the sum of the areas C and D, that is the area between the graph and the x-axis from x = 0 to x = 2. Because areas below the x-axis, such as D, are counted as negative if we evaluated the integral

$$\int_0^2 (2x^2 - 12x + 10)\, dx$$

we would have calculated the area C − D not C + D. To calculate C + D we have to calculate each of the areas C and D separately. The graph intersects the x-axis where x = 1 and where x = 5 (check this). Hence

$$\text{area } C = \int_0^1 (2x^2 - 12x + 10)\, dx = \left[\frac{2}{3}x^3 - 6x^2 + 10x \right]_0^1 = \frac{14}{3} - 0 = \frac{14}{3}$$

$$\text{area } D = \int_1^2 (2x^2 - 12x + 10)\, dx = \left[\frac{2}{3}x^3 - 6x^2 + 10x \right]_1^2 = \frac{4}{3} - \frac{14}{3} = -\frac{10}{3}$$

The total or 'absolute' area C + D is therefore the sum of 14/3 and 10/3 (ignoring the negative sign). That is, the combined area C + D is 8 square units.

Example 9.9

Find the area between $y = x^2 - 7x + 10$ and the x-axis from x = 1 to x = 4. (*Hint*: graph the curve.)

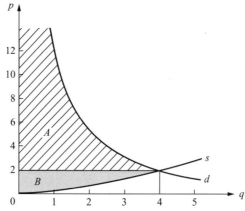

Fig. 9.5 Consumer surplus

9.6 Consumer and producer surplus

Integration is rather less used in economics than differentiation but one task it is useful for is that of calculating consumer surplus and producer surplus. Suppose, for example, a market demand curve is given by

$$p = \frac{50}{(q+1)^2} \qquad\qquad [9.33]$$

and the corresponding market supply curve by

$$p = 0.08q^2 + 0.16q + 0.08 \qquad\qquad [9.34]$$

These curves are graphed in Fig. 9.5 and intersect at a price $p = 2$ and quantity $q = 4$.

Consumer surplus is the extra satisfaction received by consumers over and above what they actually pay for. It is the difference between what consumers as a whole would have been prepared to pay if they had no other choice and what they actually pay. If suppliers were able to extract from each consumer the maximum he/she was prepared to pay, total revenue obtained would be equal to the area under the demand curve in Fig. 9.5 between $q = 0$ and $q = 4$. Total revenue actually obtained is, however, equal to price times quantity at the equilibrium point. Consumer surplus is therefore equal to the shaded area A and actual total revenue equal to the area of the rectangle beneath. Hence

$$\text{consumer surplus} = \int_0^4 \frac{50}{(q+1)^2}\, dq - 8$$

Since

$$\int_0^4 \frac{50}{(q+1)^2}\, dq = \left[\frac{-50}{(q+1)}\right]_0^4 = \left(-\frac{50}{5}\right) - (-50) = 40$$

we obtain a value for consumer surplus of 32.

Producer surplus may be defined as the difference between the revenue producers must receive if they are to produce a given output and the revenue they actually receive. It is given by the dotted region B in Fig. 9.5. Since total revenue is again given by 8, we have

$$\text{producer surplus} = 8 - \int_0^4 (0.08q^2 + 0.16q + 0.08) \, dq$$

$$= 8 - \left[\left(\frac{0.08}{3} \right) q^3 + 0.08q^2 + 0.08q \right]_0^4$$

$$= 8 - [3.31 - 0] = 4.69$$

Example 9.10

An individual's demand, q, for a commodity is given by

$$q = \frac{64\,000}{(p-5)^3}$$

where p is the price of the commodity. Find the consumer surplus for this individual when demand is 125 units.

If the supply function for the commodity is $q = 8 + 9p$, verify that market equilibrium occurs when $q = 125$. Hence calculate the producer surplus.

Revision examples

Example R9.1

Evaluate the following integrals:

(a) $12 \int x^4 dx$ (b) $\int (8x^3 + 3x^2) \, dx$ (c) $3 \int (4x + 5) \, dx$ (d) $3 \int \frac{1}{x^2} \, dx$ (e) $4 \int \sqrt{x} \, dx$

Example R9.2

A firm's marginal cost and marginal revenue functions are

$$MC = 6q^2 + 8q + 10$$
$$MR = 50 - q$$

If the firm's total costs are 3360 when output $q = 10$ and its total revenue is zero when $q = 0$, find the firm's total cost and total revenue functions. What are the firm's fixed costs?

Example R9.3

(a) Integrate by parts

(i) $\int 5x(3x + 4)^5 \, dx$ (ii) $4 \int \dfrac{x}{(x + 3)^2} \, dx$

(b) Integrate by substitution

(i) $3 \int x^3(2x^4 + 3)^6 \, dx$ (ii) $\int \dfrac{4x}{(4x^2 + 3)^5} \, dx$

Example R9.4

Evaluate the following definite integrals:

(a) $\int_{-3}^{3} (5x^4 + 3) \, dx$ (b) $\int_{-\infty}^{1} x^{-3} \, dx$ (c) $2 \int_{1}^{2} x(x^2 + 3)^3 \, dx$

Example R9.5

Consider the curve $y = x^3 - 4x^2 + x + 6$ sketched in Fig. 1.10.

(a) Find the total area between the curve and the x-axis.
(b) Find the area between the curve and the y-axis between the points $y = 6$ and $y = 0$.

Example R9.6

A consumer faces the following demand curve:

$$p = \frac{81\,000}{(q - 2)^2}$$

Find the consumer surplus when $q = 92$ and $p = 10$.

10 Differentiations of functions of more than one variable

10.1 Functions of more than one variable

Many functional relationships in economics involve more than one independent or 'right-hand side' variable. For example, in Chapters 3–5 we frequently referred to demand functions where flow demand depended not only on the own-price of a good but also on the prices of substitute goods and on the income of consumers. We begin this chapter by explaining a little more rigorously what we mean by a function of more than one variable. Suppose, for example,

$$z = 3w^2 + 2x^2y + 4wy^2 \tag{10.1}$$

Equation [10.1] obviously tells us the value of z corresponding to any given set of values for the variables w, x and y. For example, when $w = 1$, $x = 2$ and $y = -1$, z takes the value -1. Moreover z *always* takes the value -1 when w, x and y take the above values. Similarly, for any given set of values of w, x and y there will be a corresponding unique value for z. For example, when $w = 0$, $x = 1$ and $y = 1$, z always takes the value 2.

Since given values of w, x and y always result in the same value for z, z is said to be a function of w, x and y and [10.1] is referred to as a functional relationship. Notice, however, that it is possible to have an equation or relationship expressing z in terms of w, x and y which is not a functional relationship in the sense just defined. For example, suppose

$$z = \sqrt{(wxy)} \tag{10.2}$$

Then if $w = 2$, $x = 2$ and $y = 1$, $wxy = 4$ and the value of z is not unique but could be either $+2$ or -2. Equation [10.2] is therefore not a functional relationship under our definition.

Graphical representation

The graphical representation of functions of a single variable was a relatively easy matter since, as we saw in Chapter 1, we were able to use a vertical axis to measure the dependent variable and a horizontal axis to measure the independent variable. With two or more independent variables graphical representation is a little more complicated. Suppose, for example,

$$z = x^2y - 4y \tag{10.3}$$

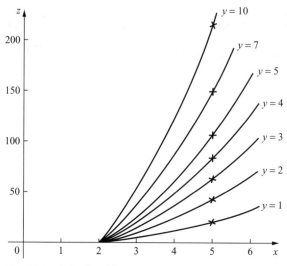

Fig. 10.1 A family of iso-y curves

In this case z is a function of two variables x and y. One way of graphically representing [10.3] would be to extend our coordinate system in Fig. 1.1 into three dimensions by introducing a third 'z-axis' rising vertically out of the page, at right angles to the y- and x-axes. Any set of values for x, y and z can then be represented by a point in this three-dimensional coordinate system. For example, $x = 2$, $y = 1$ and $z = 3$ would represent a point 3 z-units directly above the point on the page where $x = 2$ and $y = 1$. The relationship [10.3] can be used to generate a series of such points, simply by selecting arbitrary values for x and y and calculating the corresponding value for z. These points will form a three-dimensional surface which is the graphical representation of the relationship [10.3]. Unfortunately most students find difficulty in handling three-dimensional constructions and of course such an approach cannot be used if we have more than two independent variables. We shall therefore, as far as possible, eschew the use of three-dimensional diagrams in this book and instead make much use of what we shall call *iso-value curves*.

Referring back to eqn [10.3], let us arbitrarily set $y = 3$. Equation [10.3] then becomes

$$z = 3x^2 - 12 \tag{10.4}$$

In eqn [10.4], z is expressed simply as a function of a single variable and hence we can graph this relationship in two dimensions in the usual manner. This is done in Fig. 10.1 and is the curve labelled $y = 3$. For convenience we have only graphed that part of [10.4] where both z and x are positive. This curve describes the relationship between z and x when y is held constant at the value 3. We shall refer to it as an *iso-y curve*.

Clearly, we can construct other iso-y curves. If instead we set $y = 5$ in [10.3] we obtain $z = 5x^2 - 20$ which is the curve graphed and labelled $y = 5$ in Fig. 10.1. In general the iso-y curve corresponding to $y = y_0$, where y_0 is any number, can be obtained by graphing the relationship

$$z = y_0x^2 - 4y_0 \tag{10.5}$$

A family of such curves is in fact drawn in Fig. 10.1 for varying positive values of y. Each curve describes the relationship between z and x for a given fixed y-value. They are non-linear with a common intersection point on the x-axis when $z = 0$ and $x = 2$.

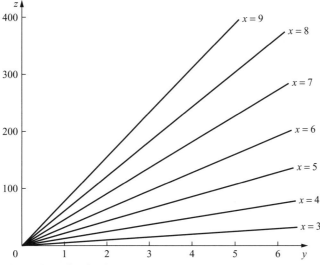

Fig. 10.2 A family of iso-x curves

Just as it is possible to hold y constant and graph the relationship between z and x, so we can hold x constant and graph the relationship between z and y. For example, if we set $x = 4$ in eqn [10.3] we obtain

$$z = 12y \qquad\qquad [10.6]$$

Equation [10.6] describes the relationship between z and y when x is fixed at the value 4. We refer to it as an iso-x curve and it is graphed and labelled $x = 4$ in Fig. 10.2. Clearly we can construct other iso-x curves. In general the iso-x curve corresponding to $x = x_0$, where x is any constant, can be obtained by graphing

$$z = x_0^2 y - 4y$$

or

$$z = (x_0^2 - 4)y \qquad\qquad [10.7]$$

A family of iso-x curves is graphed in Fig. 10.2. Again for convenience we have only graphed them for positive z and y. Although these curves happen to be linear, this will not necessarily be the case. These iso-value curves also have a common intersection point – they all pass through the origin.

Example 10.1

Consider the following functional relationships:

(a) $z = 5x^2y^2 + 4xy + 5$;

(b) $z = 6xy^3 - 3x^2y$.

In each case graph iso-x curves for $x = 2, 4, 6$ and iso-y curves for $y = 1, 2, 3$.

Example 10.2

For eqn [10.1], graph the iso-*x*–*y* curves obtained when:

(a) $x = 1$ and $y = 1$;
(b) $x = 2$ and $y = 1$;
(c) $x = 1$ and $y = 2$.

10.2 Partial differentiation

Consider again the iso-*y* curves graphed in Fig. 10.1. Suppose we wished to find the gradients of these curves at the point where for example $x = 5$; that is, at the points on the curves marked with crosses.

We know that the iso-*y* curve corresponding to $y = y_0$ where y_0 is any constant is obtained by substituting $y = y_0$ into the original eqn [10.3] to obtain eqn [10.5]:

$$z = y_0 x^2 - 4y_0 \qquad [10.5]$$

To obtain its gradient we simply differentiate in the usual manner. If y_0 is treated as a constant, then differentiating the first term in eqn [10.5] is no different from differentiating $6x^2$ or $-20x^2$. Applying the power rule gives the derivative of $x^2 y_0 = y_0 x^2$ simply as $2y_0 x$ or $2xy_0$. Again treating y_0 as constant, the derivative of the $-4y_0$ term in eqn [10.5] is of course zero. We obtain, therefore, the derivative of eqn [10.5] as

$$\frac{dz}{dx} = 2y_0 x \qquad [10.8]$$

Hence, for example, the gradients of the iso-*y* curves corresponding to $y_0 = 2$, $y_0 = 3$, $y_0 = 4$ and $y_0 = 5$ are, substituting in eqn [10.8],

$$\frac{dz}{dx} = 4x, \quad \frac{dz}{dx} = 6x, \quad \frac{dz}{dx} = 8x \quad \text{and} \quad \frac{dz}{dx} = 10x$$

respectively. So, when $x = 5$, the gradients of the iso-*y* curves are 20, 30, 40 and 50 respectively. That is, as y_0 increases the gradient at $x = 5$ increases, as indicated by Fig. 10.1.

The process of fixing *y* at y_0 in [10.5] and then differentiating with respect to *x* is known as *partial differentiation* and the expression obtained for dz/dx in [10.8] is known as a *partial derivative*. That is, we partially differentiate to obtain the partial derivative. To distinguish the partial derivative in [10.8] from an 'ordinary' derivative we normally write it as $\partial z/\partial x$ not dz/dx. That is,

$$\frac{\partial z}{\partial x} = \text{partial derivative of } z \text{ with respect to } x$$

It is also customary to dispense with the zero subscript on y_0 in eqn [10.8], write $2y_0 x$ as $2yx$ and simply remember to treat *y* as a constant when we differentiate. We shall therefore rewrite eqn [10.8] as

$$\frac{\partial z}{\partial x} = 2yx \qquad\qquad [10.9]$$

and refer to [10.9] as the partial derivative of the original eqn [10.3].

The 'curly d's' in [10.9] act as an important signal. In particular the ∂x in $\partial y/\partial x$ indicates that, when performing the partial differentiation with respect to x, we hold constant any or all other variables (apart from x) on the RHS of [10.9]. By any or all variables in this case we mean, of course, y.

Given the general expression [10.9] for the gradient of the iso-y curves in Fig. 10.1, we can use this expression to obtain the gradient of any of the iso-y curves at any point. For example, to find the gradient of the $y = 3$ curve when $x = 8$, we can substitute these values into [10.9] to obtain a gradient of 48. This implies that when y is held constant at $y = 3$, z increases at a rate of 48 per unit increase in x.

When a variable z is a function of two further variables x and y, as in eqn [10.3], the partial derivative with respect to x (i.e. [10.9]) tells us the effect on z per unit increase in x when y is held constant. Notice that since $\partial z/\partial x$ depends on *both* x and y, the effect on z of a unit *change* in x will always depend on the actual values of x and y. This, of course, is simply another way of saying that the gradient of an iso-y curve in Fig. 10.1 depends both on which iso-y curve we are considering and on the point on this iso-y curve where we measure its gradient.

It is possible to differentiate [10.3] partially with respect to y as well as with respect to x. To do this we just differentiate [10.3] in the normal way but this time treat the symbol x as a constant. We then obtain

$$\frac{\partial z}{\partial y} = x^2 - 4 \qquad\qquad [10.10]$$

Note that, in this case, the curly ∂y in $\partial z/\partial y$ indicates that when partially differentiating with respect to y we must hold constant any variables other than y. That is, on this occasion, we hold x constant.

What eqn [10.10] tells us is the effect on z of a unit change in y when x is held constant. That is, just as [10.9] gives information on the gradients of the iso-y curves in Fig. 10.1, eqn [10.10] gives information on the gradients of the iso-x curves in Fig. 10.2. For example, when $x = 4$, $\partial z/\partial y = 12 = $ constant. This simply means that the gradient of the $x = 4$ curve in Fig. 10.2 is constant and equal to 12. Since all the curves in Fig. 10.2 happen to be straight lines, this is what we should expect.

As a further example suppose

$$z = 8xy^2 - 6x^2 + 3y \qquad\qquad [10.11]$$

and we wish to find:

(a) the gradient of the iso-$x = 1$ curve at the point where $y = 2$;
(b) the gradient of the iso-$y = 2$ curve at the point where $x = 3$.

We can use the technique of partial differentiation to answer (a) and (b) above without actually having to graph the curves. Firstly, an iso-x curve involves holding x constant so that we need to differentiate partially with respect to y. Using [10.11],

$$\frac{\partial z}{\partial y} = 16xy + 3 \qquad\qquad [10.12]$$

In [10.12] since we are differentiating with respect to y we hold everything but y constant. Equation [10.12] gives us a general expression for the gradient of an iso-x curve. To find the gradient of the iso-$x = 1$ curve we simply substitute $x = 1$ into [10.12]:

$$\text{when } x = 1 \quad \frac{\partial z}{\partial y} = 16y + 3 \qquad\qquad [10.13]$$

Finally, to obtain the gradient of the iso-$x = 1$ curve at the point $y = 2$ we just need to substitute $y = 2$ into [10.13], giving a value of 35.

The interpretation of the value of 35 obtained for the gradient is quite logical. If x is held constant at the value $x = 1$, then, when y reaches the value 2, z is increasing at a rate of 35 per unit increase in y.

To answer (b) above we have to hold y constant – that is, we have to differentiate [10.11] partially with respect to x. Hence

$$\frac{\partial z}{\partial x} = 8y^2 - 12x \qquad\qquad [10.14]$$

Note that in [10.14] the curly ∂x implies that we are differentiating with respect to x and hence have to hold everything but x constant. Equation [10.14] gives a general expression for the gradient of an iso-y curve.

To find the gradient of the iso-$y = 2$ curve at $x = 3$, we can simply substitute $x = 3$ and $y = 2$ into [10.14] to give a gradient of -4. The negative value implies that, if y is held constant at the value 2, then, when x has reached a value of 3, z is falling at a rate of 4 per unit increase in x.

Readers should make rough sketches of both the iso-x curves and iso-y curves in this example and, from the sketches, interpret the gradients just obtained.

Example 10.3

For the functional relationships in Example 10.1 find by partial differentiation:

(a) the gradient of the iso-x curve for $x = 6$ at the point where $y = 3$;
(b) the gradient of the iso-y curve for $y = 3$ at the point where $x = 10$.

Example 10.4

Partially differentiate the following both with respect to x and with respect to y:

(a) $z = 8x^5y^2 + 5x^2y^2 + 6x^2 + 3xy + 7$;
(b) $z = 12x^{-4}y^{-2}$;
(c) $z = (3x + y)^2(x^2 + 2y^2x)^3$ (use the product rule);
(d) $z = (3x^2y^2 + 5x)^7$ (use the chain rule);
(e) $z = \dfrac{4x^2 + 5}{x^2 + y^2 + 3xy}$ (use the quotient rule).

The notion of partial derivatives can be extended to functions of more than two variables with little difficulty. For example, if

$$z = v^2 + 2wx + 3y^2 + 4vw^2x^2 \qquad [10.15]$$

then z can be partially differentiated with respect to, in turn, v, w, x and y. For example, to find the partial derivative with respect to w, we differentiate z, treating v, x and y all as constants. Hence

$$\frac{\partial z}{\partial w} = 2x + 8vwx^2 \qquad [10.16]$$

Notice that the curly ∂w in $\partial z/\partial w$ signals that, when we differentiate with respect to w, we keep all variables other than w constant. That is, we keep v, x and y constant. $\partial z/\partial w$ gives us information on the gradient of the curve obtained when constant values of v, x and y are substituted into [10.15].[1] Notice that this gradient depends not only on the value w but also on the values of v, x and y.

Similarly, to differentiate [10.15] partially with respect to v, we treat all variables but v as constant. That is, we treat w, x and y as constant and obtain

$$\frac{\partial z}{\partial v} = 2v + 4w^2x^2 \qquad [10.17]$$

$\partial z/\partial v$ describes the change in z per unit change in v when w, x and y are all held constant. Partial derivatives with respect to x and y may also of course be formed.

Example 10.5

If $k = 3abcd + 2ba^2 + 4c^2d + 3a^3c^3$ find

$$\frac{\partial k}{\partial a}, \ \frac{\partial k}{\partial b}, \ \frac{\partial k}{\partial c} \quad \text{and} \quad \frac{\partial k}{\partial d}$$

10.3 Partial differentiation and the *ceteris paribus* assumption

We have stressed the fact that partial differentiation involves considering the effect on one variable of changes in another *when all other variables remain constant*. This idea of treating 'all other factors' as constant is a very familiar one to the economist – it corresponds to the famous *ceteris paribus* assumption of which we made considerable use in Chapters 3–5. For example, in Fig. 4.1 we illustrated a market situation where flow demand and flow supply depended both on the price, p_1, of the good in question and on the price, p_2, of a close substitute (see eqns [4.4] and [4.5]). It proved possible to graph the usual flow demand and flow supply curves in Fig. 4.1 only under the *ceteris paribus* assumption that the price of the substitute took on some fixed value, for example $p_2 = 4$ or $p_2 = 11$. All the curves drawn in Fig. 4.1 are in fact iso-value curves in the sense described in section 10.1. The solid lines are iso-p_2 curves (one for demand and one for supply), corresponding to the fixed value $p_2 = 4$, while the dashed lines are iso-p_2 curves for $p_2 = 11$.

Elasticities of demand reconsidered

At the end of section 7.5 we defined price elasticity of demand as

$$E_p = -\frac{dq}{dp}\frac{p}{q} \qquad\qquad [7.40]$$

that is, as the proportionate change in quantity demanded, q, divided by the proportionate change in price. Implicit in this definition is the *ceteris paribus* assumption that when price changes all other factors that might influence demand remain constant. Other factors in this case would be the prices of substitutes and complements and the incomes and tastes of consumers.

Given the meaning of a partial derivative, it should now be clear that a more appropriate expression for the price elasticity of demand for a good is

$$E_p = -\frac{\partial q}{\partial p}\frac{p}{q} \qquad\qquad [10.18]$$

where $\partial q/\partial p$ is the *partial* derivative of demand with respect to the own-price of the good. For example, consider again eqn [4.38] in section 4.3. Here we had a flow demand function where demand for a good depended on its price p_1, the price of a substitute good, p_2, and on consumer income, Y. Writing flow demand as q_1 rather than d_1,

$$q_1 = -2600 + 7Y - 200p_1 + 300p_2 \qquad\qquad [4.38]$$

Partially differentiating with respect to the own-price of the good, treating p_2 and Y as constants, we obtain

$$\frac{\partial q_1}{\partial p_1} = -200$$

It is important to note that $\partial q_1/\partial p_1$ is the gradient of an iso-p_2–Y. Such a curve is akin to the demand curve found in introductory economics. As noted earlier, the traditional demand curve is drawn up under the *ceteris paribus* assumption that all other factors apart from price p_1 are held constant. For example, if p_2 is held constant at 6 and Y at 500, then [4.38] becomes

$$q_1 = 2700 - 200p_1$$

which is a typical linear demand curve as illustrated in Fig. 10.3.[2]

Given that $\partial q_1/\partial p_1 = -200$, [10.18] gives the price elasticity of demand for the good as

$$E_{p_1} = -\frac{\partial q_1}{\partial p_1}\frac{p_1}{q_1} = 200\left(\frac{p_1}{q_1}\right) \qquad\qquad [10.19]$$

Notice that the price elasticity given by [10.18] is not a constant but depends on the levels of p_1, p_2 and Y. For example, when $p_1 = 5$, $p_2 = 6$ and $Y = 500$, $q_1 = 1700$ and hence price elasticity of demand is 0.59. In other words, at these levels of prices and income, a 1 per cent rise in p_1 will cause a fall in demand of 0.59 per cent. However, when, for example, $p_1 = 4$, $p_2 = 5$ and $Y = 400$, $q_1 = 900$ and hence price elasticity is 0.89 – considerably larger.

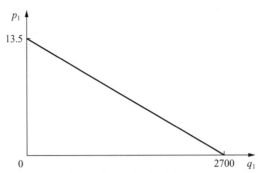

Fig. 10.3 A linear demand schedule

We have already noted at the end of section 7.5 that price elasticity of demand for a good normally varies with the price of that good. In Fig. 7.6 we illustrated how price elasticity varied at different points on a demand curve. We now see that price elasticity also varies with the prices of substitutes (and complements) and also with the level of consumer income. This is because variation in such variables shifts demand curves such as that drawn in Fig. 7.6.

Income and cross-price elasticities

Demand for a good will also be influenced by changes in consumer income. The income elasticity of demand for a good is generally defined as

$$E_Y = \frac{\text{proportionate change in quantity demanded}}{\text{proportionate change in income}}$$

$$= \frac{\Delta q_1/q_1}{\Delta Y/Y} = \frac{\Delta q_1}{\Delta Y}\frac{Y}{q_1} \qquad [10.20]$$

where the *ceteris paribus* assumption now is that, when income changes, price and any other factors that might influence demand remain unchanged. It should be clear from what has gone before that the mathematical definition for income elasticity must be

$$E_Y = \frac{\partial q_1}{\partial Y}\frac{Y}{q_1} \qquad [10.21]$$

where $\partial q_1/\partial Y$ is the partial derivative of quantity demanded with respect to income. For example, given the demand function [4.38]

$$E_Y = 7\left(\frac{Y}{q_1}\right) \qquad [10.22]$$

Notice that income elasticity, like price elasticity, is not a constant but depends on the levels of p_1, p_2 and Y. For example, when $p_1 = 5$, $p_2 = 11$ and $Y = 500$, $q_1 = 3200$ so that income elasticity is 1.09. That is, at these levels of prices and income, a 1 per cent rise in income results in a rise in demand of 1.09 per cent.

The responsiveness of demand for a good to a change in the price of some other good (maybe a close substitute or complement) is measured by what are known as *cross-elasticities*. The cross-price elasticity of demand for good 1 with respect to the price of good 2 is defined as

$$E_{p_2} = \frac{\text{proportionate change in quantity demand of good 1}}{\text{proportionate change in price of good 2}} \qquad [10.23]$$

$$= \frac{\Delta q_1/q_1}{\Delta p_2/p_2} = \frac{\Delta q_1}{\Delta p_2}\frac{p_2}{q_1} \qquad [10.24]$$

Since [10.24] is always calculated under the *ceteris paribus* assumption that own-price, income, etc., remain constant, it is again clear that we are dealing with a partial derivative.

$$E_{p_2} = \frac{\partial q_1}{\partial p_2}\frac{p_2}{q_1} \qquad [10.25]$$

If two goods are substitutes then the cross-price elasticity [10.25] will be positive, whereas if two goods are complements the cross-price elasticity will be negative. Considering the demand function [4.38] for example

$$E_{p_2} = 300\frac{p_2}{q_1} > 0 \quad \text{since } p_2 > 0 \quad \text{and} \quad q_1 > 0 \qquad [10.26]$$

so that the two goods in this case are substitutes.

Example 10.6

The demand function for a good is

$$q = 300 - 20p_1p_2 + 3p_2Y$$

where p_1 is the price of the good, p_2 is the price of another good and Y is income. If $p_1 = 10$, $p_2 = 5$ and $Y = 500$ find the own-price, income and cross-price elasticities of demand. Are the two goods substitutes or complements?

Example 10.7

If a good's demand function is $q = Ap_1^\alpha p_2^\beta Y^\gamma$ where p_1, p_2 and Y are as defined in Example 10.6, show that the own-price, cross-price and income elasticities are all constants and equal to α, β and γ respectively.

10.4 Production functions and utility functions

A firm's *production function* expresses its output, q, as a function of its inputs, typically assumed to be capital, k, and labour, l:

$$q = q(k, l) \qquad [10.27]$$

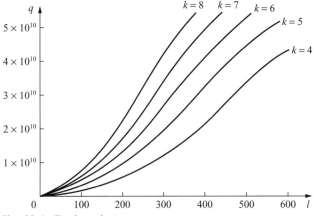

Fig. 10.4 Total product curves

It is assumed that [10.27] tells us the maximum possible output obtainable for given inputs. The purely *technical* problem of how this maximum output is obtained does not concern us.

The output variable, q, is clearly a flow variable and the input variables k and l are also normally measured as flows per unit of time. They might for example be measured in machine-hours and person-hours per week. It might seem that an alternative would be to measure labour and particularly capital in stock terms. However, it has to be remembered that we are concerned here with inputs into the productive process. For example, a given labour force will provide a greater input when it is working overtime than when it is only employed for a normal working week. Similarly, a firm may have considerable excess capacity during a downturn in the business cycle. 'Machines' may be idle at such times so that capital inputs from a given stock will be far lower than during times of full capacity working.

Measuring inputs in flow terms has a further advantage. All the variables in [10.27] are normally assumed to be continuously variable and infinitely divisible so that it is possible to apply the techniques of differential calculus to the production function. This is a far more reasonable assumption if we are dealing with, for example, machine-hours rather than machines. It is easier to visualise a firm varying capital input by one-hundredth of a machine-hour rather than one-hundredth of a machine.

Suppose the production function [10.27] takes the form

$$q = 12\,000k^2l^2 - 2k^3l^3 \tag{10.28}$$

A *total product of labour curve* describes the relationship between output and labour input when capital input has been fixed at some given level. For example, if $k = 5$ then [10.28] becomes

$$q = 300\,000l^2 - 250l^3 \tag{10.29}$$

The total product curve [10.29] is graphed in Fig. 10.4 and labelled $k = 5$. In the terminology used earlier in this chapter a total product of labour curve is clearly an iso-k curve. A family of such curves is in fact presented in Fig. 10.4.

Clearly, it is also possible to construct total product of capital or iso-l curves.

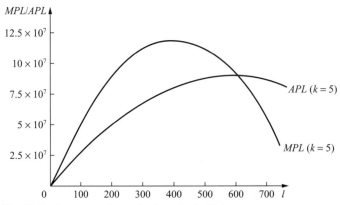

Fig. 10.5 Average and marginal product of labour curves

The *marginal product of labour* is defined as the increase in output per unit increase in labour input *when capital inputs are held constant*. It should be clear, from what has gone before in this chapter, that to obtain the marginal product of labour (*MPL*) we need to differentiate the production function [10.27] partially with respect to labour, *l*. For the production function [10.28]

$$MPL = \frac{\partial q}{\partial l} = 24\,000k^2l - 6k^3l^2 \qquad [10.30]$$

A marginal product of labour curve describes the relationship between the *MPL* and labour input, *l*, for a fixed level of capital input. For example, if $k = 5$ then [10.30] becomes

$$MPL = 600\,000l - 750l^2 \qquad [10.31]$$

The marginal product of labour curve [10.31] is graphed in Fig. 10.5 and is clearly another iso-*k* curve. Notice that an alternative way of obtaining eqn [10.31] is to differentiate [10.29] with respect to *l*.

Figure 10.5 demonstrates that the *MPL* function [10.31] obeys what is often referred to in economics as the *law of diminishing marginal productivity*. That is, if increasing amounts of a variable factor (in this case labour) are applied to a fixed amount of another factor (in this case capital), the marginal product of the variable factor will eventually decline.

The *marginal product of capital* (*MPK*) is defined as the increase in output per unit increase in capital input *when labour inputs are held constant*. Clearly to obtain it we have to differentiate the production function partially with respect to capital *k*. For the production function [10.28]

$$MPK = \frac{\partial q}{\partial k} = 24\,000kl^2 - 6k^2l^3 \qquad [10.32]$$

A marginal product of capital curve describes the relationship between the *MPK* and capital inputs at a fixed level of labour input. Such curves are clearly iso-*l* curves and can be obtained by substituting fixed values for *l* in eqn [10.32].

We can also define the average products of labour and capital. The *average product of labour* (*APL*) is simply defined as *total* output per unit of *total* labour input. For the production function [10.28]

$$APL = \frac{q}{l} = 12\,000k^2l - 2k^3l^2 \qquad\qquad [10.33]$$

An average product of labour curve describes the relationship between the *APL* and labour input for a fixed level of capital input. For example, when $k = 5$, eqn [10.33] becomes

$$APL = 300\,000l - 250l^2 \qquad\qquad [10.34]$$

The *APL* curve [10.34] is also graphed in Fig. 10.5. Notice that as labour input increases, the *APL* first rises, then reaches a maximum value when $l = 600$, and finally declines. Notice that the *MPL* curve for $k = 5$ intersects the corresponding *APL* curve at its maximum point.

The *average product of capital* (*APK*) is defined as *total* output per unit of *total* capital input. For the production function [10.28]

$$APK = \frac{q}{k} = 12\,000kl^2 - 2k^2l^3 \qquad\qquad [10.35]$$

An average product of capital curve describes the relationship between the *APK* and capital inputs when labour inputs are held constant. Such curves are iso-*l* curves and are obtained by substituting fixed value for *l* in eqn [10.35].

Example 10.8

For the production function given by eqn [10.28]:

(a) Sketch total product of capital curves for labour inputs $l = 400$, 500 and 600.
(b) Sketch, on the same diagram, average and marginal product of capital curves for $l = 400$.

Utility functions

A consumer's *utility function* expresses the total utility or 'satisfaction' obtained by the consumer as a function of the quantities of the goods he/she consumes. If *n* goods are consumed in all, we therefore write the utility function as

$$u = u(q_1, q_2, q_3, \ldots, q_n) \qquad\qquad [10.36]$$

where *u* is utility and $q_1, q_2, \ldots, q_n$ represent the quantities of the goods consumed. Utility, of course, is not a measurable concept but, as we shall see, it is still an extremely useful one. The reader may also be aware that utility, being non-measurable, is regarded by economists as an *ordinal* rather than a *cardinal* concept. However, in this book, we shall not be concerned with this distinction.

Utilities and quantities consumed are flow variables and hence have to be measured per unit of time. The quantities consumed are assumed to be continuously variable and infinitely divisible so we can apply the techniques of calculus to eqn [10.36].

The consumer's *marginal utility* obtained from the consumption of any good is defined as the increase in utility per unit increase in the consumption of that good *when consumption of all other goods remains unchanged*. To obtain it we have to differentiate the utility function [10.36] partially with respect to the relevant good. For example, in a two-good world, if the utility function is

$$u = 10q_1^2 q_2^3 \qquad\qquad [10.37]$$

then the marginal utility from good 1 will be

$$MU_1 = \frac{\partial u}{\partial q_1} = 20q_1 q_2^3 \qquad\qquad [10.38]$$

Similarly, the marginal utility obtained from an extra unit of the consumption of good 2 will be

$$MU_2 = \frac{\partial u}{\partial q_2} = 30q_1^2 q_2^2 \qquad\qquad [10.39]$$

Example 10.9

If a consumer has a utility function $u = 2q_1^2 q_2^3 q_3 - 4q_1 q_2^2$, find the marginal utility obtained from consuming an extra unit of the second good when $q_1 = 2$, $q_2 = 4$ and $q_3 = 3$.

The last two sections have consisted of no more than a series of definitions together with their interpretation in terms of partial derivatives. Definitions may often seem tedious but we shall make considerable use of the concepts just introduced in the next few chapters.

10.5 Higher-order partial derivatives

In Chapter 8 we saw that it was possible to differentiate functions of a single variable more than once to form second-order and third-order derivatives, etc. Similarly for functions of more than one variable it is possible to form higher-order partial derivatives. For example, consider the relationship [10.3]

$$x = x^2 y - 4y \qquad\qquad [10.3]$$

We saw that partially differentiating [10.3] with respect to x yielded

$$\frac{\partial z}{\partial x} = 2xy \qquad\qquad [10.40]$$

and that this partial derivative gave us a general expression for the gradients of the iso-y curves in Fig. 10.1. Clearly we can partially differentiate [10.3] with respect to x a second time and obtain *the second-order partial derivative with respect to x*. This is normally written $\partial^2 z/\partial x^2$ so that from [10.40]

$$\frac{\partial^2 z}{\partial x^2} = 2y \qquad\qquad [10.41]$$

The second-order partial derivative [10.41] tells us the rate at which the gradients of the iso-y curves in Fig. 10.1 change as x increases. For example, when $y = 3$, $\partial^2 z/\partial x^2 = 6$ which is a positive number. This reflects the fact that the gradient of the $y = 3$ curve increases as x increases. Notice, also, that the larger is y the larger is $\partial^2 z/\partial x^2$. Thus the gradients of the iso-y curves increase more rapidly the higher is the fixed y-value.

We can also obtain from [10.3] *the second-order partial derivative with respect to y.* Partially differentiating [10.3] a first time with respect to y yields as we have seen

$$\frac{\partial z}{\partial y} = x^2 - 4 \qquad\qquad [10.42]$$

The partial derivative [10.42] gave us a general expression for the gradients of the iso-x curves graphed in Fig. 10.2. Partially differentiating a second time with respect to y yields

$$\frac{\partial^2 z}{\partial y^2} = 0 \qquad\qquad [10.43]$$

The fact that this second-order partial derivative is zero reflects the fact that the gradients of the linear iso-x curves in Fig. 10.2 are constant and hence do not change as y increases.

There remains another possibility. It is possible to take a function of two variables such as that in [10.3] and partially differentiate it, first with respect to x to form $\partial z/\partial x$, and then to differentiate $\partial z/\partial x$ partially *with respect to y.* When we do this we obtain what is known as a cross-partial derivative and we write it as $\partial^2 z/\partial x\partial y$. That is, for [10.40]

$$\frac{\partial(\partial z/\partial x)}{\partial y} = \frac{\partial^2 z}{\partial x\partial y} = 2x \qquad\qquad [10.44]$$

It is also possible to take a function such as [10.3] and first partially differentiate it with respect to y to form $\partial z/\partial y$ and then partially differentiate *with respect to x.* This gives us another cross-partial derivative which we write as $\partial^2 z/\partial y\partial x$. That is, for [10.42]

$$\frac{\partial(\partial z/\partial y)}{\partial x} = \frac{\partial^2 z}{\partial y\partial x} = 2x \qquad\qquad [10.45]$$

Notice that for the function in [10.3] we are dealing with

$$\frac{\partial^2 z}{\partial x\partial y} = \frac{\partial^2 z}{\partial y\partial x} \qquad\qquad [10.46]$$

Thus *the order in which we performed the partial differentiation* (i.e. first with respect to x and then with respect to y or vice versa) made no difference to the end result. This in fact will always be the case for the functions we deal with in this book.[3] As a further example, suppose

$$z = 3wxy - 2x^2wy^2 \qquad\qquad [10.47]$$

In [10.47], z is a function of three variables w, x and y, so we can form three first-order partial derivatives:

$$\frac{\partial z}{\partial w} = 3xy - 2x^2y^2 \qquad \frac{\partial z}{\partial x} = 3wy - 4xwy^2 \qquad \frac{\partial z}{\partial y} = 3wx - 4x^2wy$$

We can form second-order partial derivatives with respect to w, x and y. That is,

$$\frac{\partial^2 z}{\partial w^2} = 0 \quad \frac{\partial^2 z}{\partial x^2} = -4wy^2 \quad \frac{\partial^2 z}{\partial y^2} = -4x^2 w$$

There are in fact six cross-partial derivatives:

$$\frac{\partial^2 z}{\partial w \partial x} = 3y - 4xy^2 \quad \frac{\partial^2 z}{\partial w \partial y} = 3x - 4x^2 y \quad \frac{\partial^2 z}{\partial x \partial w} = 3y - 4xy^2$$

$$\frac{\partial^2 z}{\partial x \partial y} = 3w - 8xwy \quad \frac{\partial^2 z}{\partial y \partial w} = 3x - 4x^2 y \quad \frac{\partial^2 z}{\partial y \partial x} = 3w - 8xwy$$

Notice, again, that the order in which we perform the partial differentiation does not matter. That is,

$$\frac{\partial^2 z}{\partial w \partial x} = \frac{\partial^2 z}{\partial x \partial w} \quad \frac{\partial^2 z}{\partial w \partial y} = \frac{\partial^2 z}{\partial y \partial w} \quad \frac{\partial^2 z}{\partial x \partial y} = \frac{\partial^2 z}{\partial y \partial x}$$

The usefulness of cross-partial derivatives will become apparent in the next few chapters.

Example 10.10

For the function given in Example 10.5 show that

$$\frac{\partial^2 k}{\partial a \partial b} = \frac{\partial^2 k}{\partial b \partial a}, \quad \frac{\partial^2 k}{\partial a \partial c} = \frac{\partial^2 k}{\partial c \partial a} \quad \text{and} \quad \frac{\partial^2 k}{\partial c \partial d} = \frac{\partial^2 k}{\partial d \partial c}$$

An alternative notation

Consider, again, eqn [10.47] where z is a function of w, x and y. That is,

$$z = f(w, x, y)$$

An alternative shorthand or notation for the first-order partial derivatives is to write them as

$$\frac{\partial z}{\partial w} = f_w \quad \frac{\partial z}{\partial x} = f_x \quad \frac{\partial z}{\partial y} = f_y$$

That is, f_w is the partial derivative of the function f with respect to w etc. The second-order and cross-partial derivatives can be written in the same way. For example,

$$\frac{\partial^2 z}{\partial x^2} = f_{xx} \quad \frac{\partial^2 z}{\partial w \partial x} = f_{wx} \quad \frac{\partial^2 z}{\partial y \partial w} = f_{yw}$$

and so on. Thus f_{xx} is the second-order partial derivative of the function f with respect to x. Similarly f_{yw} is the cross-partial derivative obtained when f is differentiated first with respect to y and then with respect to w.

We shall not be making use of this alternative notation in this book but it is commonly in use and it is as well to be familiar with it.

Example 10.11

For the function $f(u, v, w) = u^2v^2 + u^2w^2 - 2vw + w^2$ find $f_u, f_v, f_w, f_{vu}, f_{wu}$ and f_{vw}.

Revision examples

Example R10.1

For each of the following, find the gradient of the iso-$x = 6$ curve at the point where $y = 3$ and the gradient of the iso-$y = 3$ curve where $x = -1$:

(a) $z = 3x^2y + 4xy^2 + 2x$;
(b) $z = 6x^2y^2 - 2y^2x$.

Example R10.2

Partially differentiate the following with respect to x and with respect to y:

(a) $z = 4x^2y - 3xy + 4$ (b) $z = 4x^4y^3$
(c) $z = 3x + 8y$ (d) $z = 2x^2 + 4y^2 + 2xy + 4$
(e) $z = 7y^2$ (f) $z = 4y/x^2$

Example R10.3

Find all the first-order partial derivatives of

$$z = 4abc^2 + d^2c^3 + 5cb^2 + 2c^3a^4$$

Hence show that

$$\frac{\partial^2 z}{\partial a \partial b} = \frac{\partial^2 z}{\partial b \partial a} \quad \text{and} \quad \frac{\partial^2 z}{\partial b \partial d} = \frac{\partial^2 z}{\partial d \partial b}$$

Example R10.4

Find $\partial z/\partial x$ and $\partial z/\partial y$ when:

(a) $z = (3x^2 + 2y)^5$ (use chain rule);
(b) $z = (2x + 4)(5x + 3y)^8$ (use product rule).

Example R10.5

The demand for a good q_1 is given by

$$q_1 = 200 + 20y - 3yp_1 + 2yp_2 - 40p_1p_2$$

If consumer income $y = 30$, own-price $p_1 = 2$ and the price of a second good $p_2 = 3$, find the own-price, income and cross-price elasticities of demand. Are the goods substitutes or complements at the given configuration of prices and income?

Example R10.6

A firm's production function is given by

$$Q = 800L^{0.6}K^{0.4}$$

(a) Find equations for the average and marginal products of labour.
(b) Find the marginal products of labour and capital when $K = 4$ and $L = 10$.

Notes

1. If [10.15] is to be represented graphically then three of its independent variables have to be held constant arbitrarily. For example, if we set $v = 1$, $w = 1$ and $x = 1$ then we obtain an 'iso-v–w–x curve' $z = 7 + 3y^2$ that can be graphed in two dimensions. Similarly if $v = 0$, $w = -1$ and $y = 1$ we obtain an iso-v–w–y curve $z = 3 - 2x$.

2. Since economists, when drawing demand curves, place the price p_1 on the vertical axis and the quantity demanded q_1 on the horizontal axis, the slope of the conventional demand curve is *not* equal to $\partial q_1/\partial p_1$. However, for *linear* demand curves such as that in Fig. 10.3, the slope of a demand curve can be obtained by taking the inverse of $\partial q_1/\partial p_1$.

3. It will in fact always be the case, provided the first-order derivatives $\partial z/\partial x$ and $\partial z/\partial y$ are *continuous*. That is, the graphs of $\partial z/\partial x$ and $\partial z/\partial y$ must not contain any 'discontinuities' – it must be possible to sketch them 'without lifting pen from paper'.

11 Total differentials and total derivatives

11.1 Differentials

Suppose y is some function of a single variable x, $y = f(x)$. In section 7.3 we defined the first-order derivative of y with respect to x by considering a small change in x, Δx, and the resulting small change in y, Δy. We obtained the first-order derivative dy/dx by finding the limit of $\Delta y / \Delta x$ as $\Delta x \to 0$. Clearly for small changes, that is Δx not actually zero but very close to it, it must be the case that

$$\frac{\Delta y}{\Delta x} \approx \frac{dy}{dx} \quad \text{or} \quad \Delta y \approx \frac{dy}{dx} \Delta x \qquad [11.1]$$

where the sign $\approx$ means 'approximately equal to'.

The closer Δx and Δy are to zero, the closer the approximation [11.1] becomes. In fact for 'infinitesimal' changes in x and y the approximation is so close that we can write [11.1] as an equality:

$$\Delta y = \frac{dy}{dx} \Delta x \qquad [11.2]$$

Infinitesimal changes in x and y such as those in [11.2] are known as *differentials*. That is, Δx is the differential in x and Δy is the differential in y that results. Equation [11.2] enables us to find the change in y that results from any given differential or infinitesimal change in x, provided we know the derivative dy/dx. Since dy/dx measures the change in y *per unit* change in x, the validity of eqn [11.2] should be obvious – to find the change in y we have simply to multiply the change in x by the derivative dy/dx.

Now suppose we have a variable z that is a function of two variables x and y, $z = z(x, y)$. Suppose y remains constant but there is an infinitesimal change in x of Δx. By an argument identical to that above, the resultant change in z must be

$$\Delta z = \frac{\partial z}{\partial x} \Delta x \qquad [11.3]$$

where $\partial z / \partial x$ is the partial derivative of z with respect to x. Note that we make use of the partial derivative because we are considering a situation where y is held constant.

Next consider the effect of an infinitesimal change in y when x is held constant. The resultant change in z must now be

$$\Delta z = \frac{\partial z}{\partial y}\Delta y \qquad \qquad [11.4]$$

where $\partial z/\partial y$ is the partial derivative of z with respect to y.

Finally, suppose we have infinitesimal changes Δx and Δy in both x and y simultaneously. Provided the changes are sufficiently small, we see from [11.3] and [11.4] that the resultant change in z must now be

$$\Delta z = \frac{\partial z}{\partial x}\Delta x + \frac{\partial z}{\partial y}\Delta y \qquad \qquad [11.5]$$

In eqn [11.5], the infinitesimal changes Δx and Δy are again referred to as differentials in x and y. The resultant change in z, Δz, is known as the *total differential* of the function $z = z(x, y)$. This distinguishes it from the Δz's in eqns [11.3] and [11.4].

For convenience, differentials such as Δx, Δy and Δz are often written as dx, dy and dz, etc., in which case [11.5] is rewritten as

$$dz = \frac{\partial z}{\partial x}\,dx + \frac{\partial z}{\partial y}\,dy \qquad \qquad [11.6]$$

Equation [11.6] can be extended to cover the case where z is a function of more than two variables. For example, if $z = z(x_1, x_2, x_3, \dots)$ then

$$dz = \frac{\partial z}{\partial x_1}\,dx_1 + \frac{\partial z}{\partial x_2}\,dx_2 + \frac{\partial z}{\partial x_3}\,dx_3 \dots \qquad \qquad [11.7]$$

For example, if

$$z = 3x^2y + 2xyw^2 \qquad \qquad [11.8]$$

and dx, dy and dw are differentials in x, y and w, then the total differential or resultant change in z is given by

$$dz = \frac{\partial z}{\partial x}\,dx + \frac{\partial z}{\partial y}\,dy + \frac{\partial z}{\partial w}\,dw$$

$$= (6xy + 2yw^2)\,dx + (3x^2 + 2xw^2)\,dy + 4xyw\,dw$$

Notice that dz depends not only on dx, dy and dw but also on the actual values of x, y and w.

Example 11.1

Find the total differential of:

(a) $z = 5x^2yw^3$;

(b) $z = 5x^3y + 4xy^3$;

(c) $z = (u + 4)^2(v + 3)^3$.

Example 11.2

If $z = 6x^2y^2$ use the technique of total differentials to find approximately the change in z when x changes from 100 to 101 and y changes from 300 to 302.

11.2 The reduced form of a non-linear system

We explained the advantages and uses of reduced forms in Chapter 4. However, when some or all of the equations in a system are non-linear, deriving the reduced form may be difficult or even impossible. When this is the case the total differentials of section 11.1 can be of considerable help.

Consider, for example, the simultaneous system given by eqns [4.38]–[4.40]. This was a three-equation system with three endogenous variables d_1, s_1 and p_1, and two variables, Y and p_2, which we treated as exogenous. The reduced form equation for, for example, the endogenous p_1 was given by eqn [4.43]

$$p_1 = 3.43 + 0.01Y + 0.571p_2$$

We noted that the coefficients on Y and p_2 in such an equation told us the final effect of unit changes in these exogenous variables on the endogenous p_1. For example, a rise of 1 unit in the price p_2 of the substitute good 2 leads eventually to a rise of 0.571 units in the price of good 1. The figure 0.571 is in fact the partial derivative of the endogenous p_1 with respect to the exogenous p_2, that is $\partial p_1/\partial p_2$. Although it tells us the *total* effect of a change in p_2, it is the total effect of the p_2 change when the other exogenous variable, Y, is held constant that is being measured. We therefore write it as $\partial p_1/\partial p_2$ rather than dp_1/dp_2. The coefficient on Y in the above equation is, similarly, the partial derivative $\partial p_1/\partial Y$. Such derivatives are often referred to by economists as *multipliers*.

From our discussion of reduced forms in Chapter 4, it should be clear that multipliers such as $\partial p_1/\partial p_2$ and $\partial p_1/\partial Y$ are of considerable interest. However, when a system involves non-linear equations finding them may not be so easy. For example, consider the system

$$d_1 = 500 - 2p_1 + 3p_2 + 2Y \qquad [11.9]$$

$$s_1 = 300 + 5p_1^2 p_2 - 3p_2^2 \qquad [11.10]$$

$$d_1 = s_1 \qquad [11.11]$$

The variables in [11.9]–[11.11] are identical to those in [4.38]–[4.40]. However, eqn [11.10] is now clearly a non-linear equation. Let us attempt to find the reduced form of this system in the manner of Chapter 4. Substituting for d_1 and s_1 in [11.11] yields

$$500 - 2p_1 + 3p_2 + 2Y = 300 + 5p_1^2 p_2 - 3p_2^2 \qquad [11.12]$$

The only endogenous variable in [11.12] is p_1, so if we could solve this equation for p_1 in terms of the exogenous p_2 and Y we would have a reduced form equation for p_1. Unfortunately [11.12] is a quadratic equation in p_1 with two roots. We could obtain solutions but would then have problems substituting back into [11.9] and [11.10] to find the reduced form equations for d_1 and s_1. We shall adopt another approach.

Applying the rule [11.7] for finding total differentials to eqn [11.10], which has the form $s_1 = s_1(p_1, p_2)$, we have

$$ds_1 = \frac{\partial s_1}{\partial p_1} dp_1 + \frac{\partial s_1}{\partial p_2} dp_2$$

or

$$ds_1 = 10p_1p_2 dp_1 + (5p_1^2 - 6p_2) dp_2 \qquad [11.13]$$

In eqn [11.13] $\partial s_1/\partial p_1$ and $\partial s_1/\partial p_2$ are obtained by partially differentiating [11.10] in the usual way. Similarly, applying rule [11.7] to eqn [11.9], which is of the form $d_1 = d_1(p_1, p_2, Y)$, we have

$$dd_1 = \frac{\partial d_1}{\partial p_1} dp_1 + \frac{\partial d_1}{\partial p_2} dp_2 + \frac{\partial d_1}{\partial Y} dY$$

or

$$dd_1 = -2dp_1 + 3dp_2 + 2dY \qquad [11.14]$$

Finally, if d_1 always equals s_1, then any change in d_1 must equal the change in s_1. That is,

$$dd_1 = ds_1 \qquad [11.15]$$

We can treat [11.13]–[11.15] as a three-equation system in the variables dd_1, ds_1, dp_1, dp_2 and dY. Moreover, it is a linear system in these variables. That is, it does not involve terms such as $(dY)^2$ or $(dp_2)(dp_1)$. Since it is a linear system we can solve it for the changes, dd_1, ds_1 and dp_1, in the endogenous variables, expressing these changes in terms of dp_2 and dY, the changes in the exogenous variables. To do this we solve the system in the usual way treating everything but dd_1, ds_1 and dp_1 just as if they were 'constants'. Substituting [11.13] and [11.14] into eqn [11.15] yields

$$-2dp_1 + 3dp_2 + 2dY = 10p_1p_2dp_1 + (5p_1^2 - 6p_2) dp_2$$

or

$$(2 + 10p_1p_2) dp_1 = (3 - 5p_1^2 + 6p_2) dp_2 + 2dY$$

Hence

$$dp_1 = \left(\frac{3 - 5p_1^2 + 6p_2}{2 + 10p_1p_2}\right) dp_2 + \left(\frac{1}{1 + 5p_1p_2}\right) dY \qquad [11.16]$$

Equation [11.16] tells us the change in the endogenous p_1 that results from given changes in the exogenous p_2 and Y. By substituting for dp_1 in eqn [11.14] and using [11.15] we can, after collecting terms, obtain similar equations for changes in the other endogenous variables d_1 and s_1:

$$dd_1 = ds_1 = \left(\frac{5p_1^2 - 6p_2 + 15p_1p_2}{1 + 5p_1p_2}\right) dp_2 + \left(\frac{10p_1p_2}{1 + 5p_1p_2}\right) dY \qquad [11.17]$$

Equations [11.16] and [11.17] are clearly reduced-form-type equations since they express changes in endogenous variables purely in terms of exogenous changes. Moreover, we know that the full reduced form of the system involves equations of the form

$$p_1 = p_1(p_2, Y) \qquad\qquad [11.18]$$

$$d_1 = d_1(p_2, Y) \qquad\qquad [11.19]$$

$$s_1 = s_1(p_2, Y) \qquad\qquad [11.20]$$

Applying the rule [11.7] for finding total differentials to eqns [11.18]–[11.20] we obtain

$$dp_1 = \frac{\partial p_1}{\partial p_2} dp_2 + \frac{\partial p_1}{\partial Y} dY \qquad\qquad [11.21]$$

$$dd_1 = \frac{\partial d_1}{\partial p_2} dp_2 + \frac{\partial d_1}{\partial Y} dY \qquad\qquad [11.22]$$

$$ds_1 = \frac{\partial s_1}{\partial p_2} dp_2 + \frac{\partial s_1}{\partial Y} dY \qquad\qquad [11.23]$$

If, for example, we compare the coefficients of dp_2 and dY in [11.21] with those in [11.16] we see that

$$\frac{\partial p_1}{\partial p_2} = \frac{3 - 5p_1^2 + 6p_2}{2 + 10p_1 p_2} \qquad \frac{\partial p_1}{\partial Y} = \frac{1}{1 + 5p_1 p_2} \qquad\qquad [11.24]$$

We have therefore obtained the partial derivatives of the endogenous p_1 with respect to the exogenous p_2 and Y. The expressions [11.24] are in fact akin to the numbers 0.571 and 0.01 in eqn [4.43]. That is, they are the required multipliers.

Similarly, comparing [11.22] and [11.23] with [11.17] we obtain

$$\frac{\partial d_1}{\partial p_2} = \frac{\partial s_1}{\partial p_2} = \frac{5p_1^2 - 6p_2 + 15p_1 p_2}{1 + 5p_1 p_2}$$

$$\frac{\partial d_1}{\partial Y} = \frac{\partial s_1}{\partial Y} = \frac{10p_1 p_2}{1 + 5p_1 p_2} \qquad\qquad [11.25]$$

Summarising, the most useful information obtainable from reduced form equations is often the partial derivatives of the endogenous variables with respect to the exogenous variables, that is the so-called multipliers. Non-linear systems are often difficult to solve for the endogenous variables, so we are unable to obtain the reduced form in the usual way. However, it is possible to obtain the required multipliers by making use of the concept of total differentials.

One point should be stressed. In a linear system partial derivatives such as the $\partial p_1/\partial p_2$ and the $\partial p_1/\partial Y$ in [11.24] are constants. For example, in eqn [4.43] they took the values 0.571 and 0.01 respectively. In non-linear systems, however, such partial derivatives or multipliers are not constant – their value will vary with the values of the endogenous and exogenous variables in the model. This means that the effect of exogenous changes on the endogenous variables within the model will not always be the same. For example, in [11.24] $\partial p_1/\partial p_2$ depends on p_1 and p_2. If the values of these variables are such that $3 + 6p_2 > 5p_1^2$ then $\partial p_1/\partial p_2$ will be positive so that the final effect of a rise in p_2 will be a rise in the endogenous p_1. However, if the levels of p_1 and p_2 are such that $3 + 6p_2 < 5p_1^2$ then a rise in p_2 leads to fall in p_1.

Example 11.3

Suppose the demand function [11.9] had been instead

$$d_1 = 500 + 2Y^2 p_2 - Y p_1$$

By following the same procedure as above obtain the multipliers $\partial p_1 / \partial p_2$ and $\partial p_1 / \partial Y$ for this case.

It is sometimes possible to derive useful results about the influence of exogenous variables without knowing the precise functional forms of equations within a system. For example, the system we have just considered has the general form

$$d_1 = d_1(p_1, p_2, Y) \tag{11.26}$$

$$s_1 = s_1(p_1, p_2) \tag{11.27}$$

$$d_1 = s_1 \tag{11.28}$$

Taking the total differential of eqn [11.26] leads to the equation above [11.14] which can be rewritten as

$$dd_1 = \left(\frac{\partial d_1}{\partial p_1}\frac{p_1}{d_1}\right)\left(\frac{dp_1}{p_1}\right)d_1 + \left(\frac{\partial d_1}{\partial p_2}\frac{p_2}{d_1}\right)\left(\frac{dp_2}{p_2}\right)d_1 + \left(\frac{\partial d_1}{\partial Y}\frac{Y}{d_1}\right)\left(\frac{dY}{Y}\right)d_1 \tag{11.29}$$

Dividing eqn [11.29] throughout by d_1 yields

$$\frac{dd_1}{d_1} = -E_1^d\left(\frac{dp_1}{p_1}\right) + E_2^d\left(\frac{dp_2}{p_2}\right) + E_Y^d\left(\frac{dY}{Y}\right) \tag{11.30}$$

where E_1^d, E_2^d and E_Y^d are the elasticities of demand for good 1, with respect to p_1, p_2 and Y respectively, and dd_1/d_1, dp_1/p_1, dp_2/p_2 and dY/Y are the *proportionate* changes in d_1, p_1, p_2 and Y.

Similarly, taking the total differential of eqn [11.27] leads eventually to

$$\frac{ds_1}{s_1} = E_1^s\left(\frac{dp_1}{p_1}\right) + E_2^s\left(\frac{dp_2}{p_2}\right) \tag{11.31}$$

where E_1^s and E_2^s are the elasticities of supply with respect to p_1 and p_2 respectively and ds_1/s_1 is the proportionate change in the supply of good 1.

Since $d_1 = s_1$, proportionate changes in demand must always equal proportionate changes in supply

$$\frac{dd_1}{d_1} = \frac{ds_1}{s_1} \tag{11.32}$$

Substituting eqns [11.30] and [11.31] into eqn [11.32] yields

$$-E_1^d\left(\frac{dp_1}{p_1}\right) + E_2^d\left(\frac{dp_2}{p_2}\right) + E_Y^d\left(\frac{dY}{Y}\right) = E_1^s\left(\frac{dp_1}{p_1}\right) + E_2^s\left(\frac{dp_2}{p_2}\right) \tag{11.33}$$

Equation [11.33] can be solved to express the proportionate change in the endogenous p_1 in terms of proportionate changes in the exogenous Y and p_2.

$$\frac{dp_1}{p_1} = \left(\frac{E_2^d - E_2^s}{E_1^d + E_1^s}\right)\left(\frac{dp_2}{p_2}\right) + \left(\frac{E_Y^d}{E_1^d + E_1^s}\right)\left(\frac{dY}{Y}\right) \tag{11.34}$$

If good 1 is a normal good, then $E_Y^d > 0$ in [11.34] and almost certainly $E_1^d + E_1^s > 0$. That is, the income elasticity of demand for the good is positive and so is the sum of the 'own-price' elasticities of demand and supply. Hence we can say immediately from eqn [11.34] that a proportionate increase in income will lead to a proportionate *increase* in the price of good 1. We can also say that whenever $E_2^d > E_2^s$ an increase in the price of the substitute good p_2 will lead to an *increase* in the price of good 1 but when $E_2^d < E_2^s$ such an increase in p_2 will lead to a *fall* in p_1. Thus, the effect of a change in the exogenous p_2 on the endogenous p_1 will depend on the relative size of the cross-price elasticities of supply and demand for good 1 with respect to p_2. Moreover, these results are independent of the precise functional forms of the demand and supply equations. They must hold whatever the form of these equations.

A macro-economic example

In section 4.5 we obtained the reduced form for the simple linear Keynesian system given by eqns [4.48]–[4.50]. From eqn [4.51], the reduced form equation for Y, we deduced that a rise of 1 unit in government expenditure led to a rise of 5 units in the equilibrium level of income. The coefficient on G in eqn [4.51] was in fact the famous Keynesian multiplier and we demonstrated that for the linear model of section 4.5 it was equal to the reciprocal of the marginal propensity to save. We shall now use the technique of total differentials to show that this Keynesian multiplier will equal the reciprocal of the *MPS* regardless of the form of eqns [4.48] and [4.49] and *whether these equations are linear or non-linear.*

We replace eqn [4.48] by the general form

$$C = f(Y, R) \tag{11.35}$$

which may be non-linear. Similarly, eqn [4.49] becomes

$$I = g(R) \tag{11.36}$$

Equation [4.50] is an equilibrium condition which remains unchanged regardless of the form of the other equations in the system.

$$Y = C + G + I \tag{11.37}$$

Applying the rule [11.7] to eqns [11.35] and [11.36] we obtain the total differentials

$$dC = \frac{\partial C}{\partial Y} dY + \frac{\partial C}{\partial R} dR \tag{11.38}$$

$$dI = \frac{\partial I}{\partial R} dR \tag{11.39}$$

In terms of changes the equilibrium condition [11.37] is

$$dY = dC + dG + dI \tag{11.40}$$

We can treat [11.38]–[11.40] as a three-equation linear system in the endogenous changes dY, dC and dI. We can therefore solve it, expressing these endogenous changes in terms of the exogenous changes dG and dR. Substituting [11.38] and [11.39] into [11.40] we obtain

$$dY = \frac{\partial C}{\partial Y}dY + \frac{\partial C}{\partial R}dR + dG + \frac{\partial I}{\partial R}dR$$

or

$$dY\left(1 - \frac{\partial C}{\partial Y}\right) = dR\left(\frac{\partial C}{\partial R} + \frac{\partial I}{\partial R}\right) + dG$$

Hence

$$dY = dR\left(\frac{\partial C}{\partial R} + \frac{\partial I}{\partial R}\right)\bigg/\left(1 - \frac{\partial C}{\partial Y}\right) + dG\bigg/\left(1 - \frac{\partial C}{\partial Y}\right) \qquad [11.41]$$

Equation [11.41] expresses the endogenous change in income dY in terms of the exogenous changes in the interest rate, dR, and in government expenditure dG. If necessary we could obtain similar equations for the endogenous changes in consumption dC and in investment dI. However, the point is that, since the reduced form equation for Y is $Y = Y(R, G)$, we also have (taking the total differential of this reduced form equation)

$$dY = \frac{\partial Y}{\partial R}dR + \frac{\partial Y}{\partial G}dG \qquad [11.42]$$

Comparing the coefficients of dG in eqns [11.41] and [11.42] we obtain

$$\frac{\partial Y}{\partial G} = \frac{1}{1 - \partial C/\partial Y} \qquad [11.43]$$

$\partial C/\partial Y$ in eqn [11.43] is the marginal propensity to consume so that $1 - \partial C/\partial Y$ is the marginal propensity to save. Hence eqn [11.43] tells us that the change in income per unit change in government expenditure (the multiplier) is equal to the reciprocal of the marginal propensity to save. This is the general result we were seeking.

Example 11.4

Consider the simple Keynesian model

$$C = C(Y^d) \quad Y^d = Y - T \quad Y = C + I + G$$

where C = consumption, Y = income, Y^d = disposable income, I = investment, G = government expenditure and T = total direct taxation. I, G and T are exogenous.

Determine $\partial Y/\partial G$ and $\partial Y/\partial T$. How are these multipliers affected if government expenditure is always exactly equal to total direct taxation?

Example 11.5

Consider the *IS–LM* model

$$C = C(Y, R) \quad I = I(R) \quad E = C + I \quad Y = E + G$$

$$L = L(Y, R) \quad L = M$$

where C = consumption, I = private investment, E = total private expenditure, G = government expenditure, Y = income, R = interest rate, L = demand for money and M = supply of money; M and G are exogenous.

Show that

$$\frac{\partial Y}{\partial G} = \frac{\dfrac{\partial L}{\partial R}}{\dfrac{\partial L}{\partial R}\left(1 - \dfrac{\partial C}{\partial Y}\right) + \dfrac{\partial L}{\partial Y}\dfrac{\partial E}{\partial R}} \quad \text{and} \quad \frac{\partial Y}{\partial M} = \frac{\dfrac{\partial E}{\partial R}}{\dfrac{\partial L}{\partial R}\left(1 - \dfrac{\partial C}{\partial Y}\right) + \dfrac{\partial L}{\partial Y}\dfrac{\partial E}{\partial R}}$$

What happens to the fiscal multiplier $\partial Y/\partial G$ and the money multiplier $\partial Y/\partial M$:

(a) if the interest elasticity of the demand for money is zero?
(b) if the interest elasticity of private expenditure is zero?

Example 11.6

Consider the model

$$z = z(x, y) \quad x = x(u, v) \quad y = y(u, v)$$

where u and v are exogenous. By taking total differentials show that

$$\frac{\partial z}{\partial u} = \frac{\partial z}{\partial x}\frac{\partial x}{\partial u} + \frac{\partial z}{\partial y}\frac{\partial y}{\partial u} \quad \text{and} \quad \frac{\partial z}{\partial v} = \frac{\partial z}{\partial x}\frac{\partial x}{\partial v} + \frac{\partial z}{\partial y}\frac{\partial y}{\partial v}$$

(This is sometimes referred to as the composite function rule.)

11.3 Total derivatives and implicit differentiation

Suppose that $z = (x, y)$ but that y is also itself a function of x, $y = y(x)$. The variable x now influences z both directly and also indirectly via its influence on y. This is illustrated in Fig. 11.1. Taking the total differential of z we have

$$\Delta z = \frac{\partial z}{\partial x}\Delta x + \frac{\partial z}{\partial y}\Delta y$$

where we have written the differentials as in [11.5] to remind ourselves that they are in fact small changes. Dividing throughout by Δx we then have

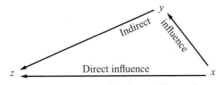

Fig. 11.1 Direct and indirect effects of x on z

$$\frac{\Delta z}{\Delta x} = \frac{\partial z}{\partial x} + \frac{\partial z}{\partial y}\frac{\Delta y}{\Delta x}$$ [11.44]

If we let $\Delta x \to 0$ on either side of eqn [11.44], then remembering our original definition of a derivative in section 7.3 we can write eqn [11.44] as

$$\frac{dz}{dx} = \frac{\partial z}{\partial x} + \frac{\partial z}{\partial y}\frac{dy}{dx}$$ [11.45]

In [11.45] dz/dx is known as the *total derivative* of z with respect to x and must be clearly distinguished from the partial derivative $\partial z/\partial x$. The partial derivative measures the direct effect on z of a change in x, that is the change that occurs 'before the indirect effect via y is felt'. The total derivative, however, measures the total effect of a change in x, both direct and indirect. For example, if $z = 3x^2y^2$ and $y = x^3$, then

$$\frac{\partial z}{\partial x} = 6xy^2 = 6x^7 \quad \text{but} \quad \frac{dz}{dx} = 6xy^2 + 6x^2y(3x^2) = 6x^7 + 18x^7 = 24x^7$$

Thus the direct effect on z of a change in x is given by $6x^7$ but the total effect is $24x^7$. Notice that both the direct and total effect of the change in x depend on the actual value of x itself. Of course we could also have found the total derivative by first substituting for y in $z = 3x^2y^2$ and then differentiating with respect to x in the usual way. However, the advantage of the formulation [11.45] is that it splits the total effect of a change in x into its direct and indirect components.

Example 11.7

Find $\partial z/\partial y$ and dz/dy when:

(a) $z = 3x^2y^5$ with $x = 4y + 6$;
(b) $z = 4x + 3y$ with $x = 4y^4$.

Example 11.8

If $u = 5w^2$ but v does not depend on w, find the total derivative with respect to w of:

(a) $x = 6u^2w$;
(b) $x = 5uvw$;
(c) $x = 4u^3w + 7vw^2$;
(d) $x = w^2 + u^2v^2$.

Implicit differentiation

Suppose again that $z = z(x, y)$ but assume now that the value of z has been arbitrarily set equal to some constant $z = z_0$. Hence

$$z(x, y) = z_0$$ [11.46]

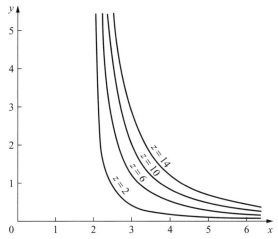

Fig. 11.2 A family of iso-z curves

Equation [11.46] can be thought of as implicitly defining y as a function of x. For example, if $z = x^2y - 4y$ and we set $z = 10$ then this implies that

$$y = \frac{10}{x^2 - 4}$$ [11.47]

We can use the technique of total differentiation outlined in the previous subsection to obtain dy/dx for the *implicit function* [11.46]. If z is a constant then obviously any change in z, dz, must be zero. Hence

$$dz = \frac{\partial z}{\partial x} dx + \frac{\partial z}{\partial y} dy = 0$$ [11.48]

Dividing [11.48] by dx we have

$$\frac{\partial z}{\partial x} + \frac{\partial z}{\partial y} \frac{dy}{dx} = 0 \quad \rightarrow \quad \frac{dy}{dx} = -\frac{\partial z/\partial x}{\partial z/\partial y}$$ [11.49]

For example, for $z = x^2y - 4y$, performing the required partial differentiations we obtain

$$\frac{dy}{dx} = \frac{2xy}{4 - x^2}$$ [11.50]

Notice that an identical result to [11.50] can be obtained by differentiating [11.47] directly. However, as we shall see, the general result [11.49] has some useful economic applications. For now we note that, in the terminology of Chapter 10, equations such as [11.47] define an *iso-z curve*. A family of such curves is illustrated in Fig. 11.2 for the function $z = x^2y - 4y$. That corresponding to eqn [11.47] is labelled $z = 10$, and represents pairs of values for x and y which assign the same constant value of 10 to z. For example, $x = 3$ and $y = 2$ is a point on the iso-$z = 10$ curve, since these values satisfy eqn [11.47] and also, via $z = x^2y - 4y$, assign a value of 10 to z. Similarly, the curve labelled $z = 6$ in Fig. 11.2 is obtained by replacing the 10 in eqn [11.47] by a 6. In general the iso-z curve corresponding to $z = z_0$, where z_0 is any number, can be obtained by graphing the relationship

$$y = \frac{z_0}{x^2 - 4}$$ [11.51]

It should now be clear that dy/dx of eqn [11.49] is to be interpreted in this context as yielding the slope of an iso-z curve.

Example 11.9

Find dy/dx when:

(a) $3x^2 + y^2 = 8$;

(b) $x^3 y^2 = 4$;

(c) $x^2/(y^2 + 7) = 1$;

(d) $y^2 = 6x$.

Example 11.10

If $z = z(u, v, w, t)$ and u, v and w are all functions of t show that

$$\frac{dz}{dt} = \frac{\partial z}{\partial t} + \frac{\partial z}{\partial u}\frac{\partial u}{\partial t} + \frac{\partial z}{\partial v}\frac{\partial v}{\partial t} + \frac{\partial z}{\partial w}\frac{\partial w}{\partial t}$$

11.4 Homogeneous functions and Euler's theorem

Consider the function in

$$z = f(x, y) = 3x^2 y + 2y^3$$ [11.52]

This function has the rather special property that if each of its variables is multiplied by some constant λ then the value of the function itself is multiplied by λ^3. That is, replacing x and y in eqn [11.52] by λx and λy we obtain

$$f(\lambda x, \lambda y) = 3(\lambda x)^2 \lambda y + 2(\lambda y)^3 = \lambda^3(3x^2 y + 2y^3) = \lambda^3 f(x, y) = \lambda^3 z$$

The function [11.52] is said to be homogeneous of degree 3.

Simple numerical examples should make clearer the meaning of homogeneity. In particular, homogeneity of degree 3 implies that, for example, if x and y are both doubled (i.e. if they are both multiplied by a factor of $\lambda = 2$), then z is increased by a factor of $\lambda^3 = 2^3$. That is, z will be multiplied by 8. Similarly, if x and y are both increased by 20 per cent (i.e. x and y are each multiplied by a factor of $\lambda = 1.2$), then z will be increased by a factor $\lambda^3 = (1.2)^3 = 1.728$. That is, z is increased by 72.8 per cent.

Similarly the function in $w = f(x, y, z) = 5x^{0.2}y^{0.5}z^{0.3}$ is said to be homogeneous of degree 1 since if each of the variables in this function is multiplied by a constant λ we obtain

$$f(\lambda x, \lambda y, \lambda z) = 5(\lambda x)^{0.2}(\lambda y)^{0.5}(\lambda z)^{0.3} = \lambda(5x^{0.2}y^{0.5}z^{0.3}) = \lambda w$$

That is, the value of the function is itself multiplied by λ. Notice that if a function is homogeneous of degree 1 then this implies that equiproportionate changes in its variables will lead to the same proportionate change in the value of the function itself. That is, if x, y and z all increase by for example 10 per cent (i.e. by $\lambda = 1.1$), then w will also increase by 10 per cent (i.e. by $\lambda^1 = (1.1)^1$). Similarly if x, y and z are all doubled ($\lambda = 2$), then w will also double ($\lambda^1 = 2$).

In general, a function $f(x, y, z)$ is said to be *homogeneous of degree v* if and only if

$$f(\lambda x, \lambda y, \lambda z) = \lambda^v f(x, y, z) \qquad [11.53]$$

That is, if each of its variables is multiplied by λ, then the function itself is multiplied by λ^v. The definition extends to functions of any number of variables.

The degree of homogeneity v can also lie between zero and unity. For example, $f(x, y) = x^{0.4} y^{0.3}$ is homogeneous of degree 0.7 since

$$f(\lambda x, \lambda y) = (\lambda x)^{0.4} (\lambda y)^{0.3} = \lambda^{0.7} x^{0.4} y^{0.3} = \lambda^{0.7} f(x, y)$$

This implies that, if both x and y increase by for example 40 per cent (i.e. by a factor of $\lambda = 1.4$), then z will be increased by a factor $(1.4)^{0.7} = 1.266$. That is, z will increase by just 26.6 per cent – less than the common increase in x and y.

Consider a further example. Suppose

$$w = f(x, y, z) = \frac{x^2 + y^2}{z^2} \qquad [11.54]$$

Such a function is homogeneous of degree 0 since (remember $\lambda^0 = 1$)

$$f(\lambda x, \lambda y, \lambda z) = \frac{(\lambda x)^2 + (\lambda y)^2}{(\lambda z)^2} = \frac{\lambda^2 (x^2 + y^2)}{\lambda^2 z^2} = \lambda^0 f(x, y, z) = w$$

Hence, for this function, $v = 0$ in the definition [11.53]. Notice that if a function is homogeneous of degree 0 then equiproportionate changes in its variables leave the value of the function itself unchanged.

Homogeneity of degree 0 means that *a function can be expressed in terms of the ratios of its independent variables*. For example, we can write [11.54] as

$$w = \frac{x^2 + y^2}{z^2} = \left(\frac{x}{z}\right)^2 + \left(\frac{y}{z}\right)^2$$

That is, it can be written as a function of the ratios x/z and y/z. Since equiproportionate changes in x, y and z leave the ratios x/z and y/z unchanged, we can see why such equiproportionate changes leave w unchanged.[1]

Example 11.11

(a) Suppose $z = 3x^2 + 4y^2 + 3xy$. Find the effect on z if:

    (i) x and y are both doubled;
    (ii) x and y are both increased by 6 per cent;
    (iii) x and y are both halved;
    (iv) x and y both fall by 30 per cent.

(b) Suppose $z = 1/x + 1/y$. Find the effect on z if:

    (i) x and y are both doubled;
    (ii) x and y are both increased by 10 per cent.

It should perhaps be made clear that most functions are not homogeneous. For example, the function $f(x, y) = x^3y + y^2$ is not homogeneous since in this case

$$f(\lambda x, \lambda y) = (\lambda x)^3\lambda y + (\lambda y)^2 = \lambda^4 x^3 y + \lambda^2 y^2$$

That is, we cannot find any value for v that enables us to write the function in the form [11.53]. As we noted at the outset, homogeneity is a rather special property.

    There are a number of useful economic analogies of homogeneity. For example, in Chapter 10 we introduced the notion of a production function. If a production function is homogeneous then the degree of homogeneity determines the *returns to scale* properties of that production function. Suppose the production function [10.27] is homogeneous of degree v. Then from the definition of homogeneity

$$q(\lambda k, \lambda l) = \lambda^v q \qquad\qquad\qquad [11.55]$$

If $v = 1$ in eqn [11.55] then this implies that equiproportionate increases in labour and capital inputs result in the same proportionate increase in output. Thus the production function is exhibiting *constant returns to scale*. However, if $v > 1$ then equiproportionate increases in inputs result in more than proportionate increases in output and we have *increasing returns to scale*. Finally, if $v < 1$ we have *decreasing returns to scale*.

    Before leaving the definition of homogeneity we should note that it is possible for a function to be homogeneous in some but not all of its variables. For example, suppose

$$w = f(x, y, z) = x^2yz + xy^2z^2 \qquad\qquad\qquad [11.56]$$

It is easily verified that the function in eqn [11.56] is not homogeneous in all of its variables. However, if just the variables x and y are increased by a factor of λ then

$$f(\lambda x, \lambda y, z) = (\lambda x)^2(\lambda y)z + (\lambda x)(\lambda y)^2z^2 = \lambda^3(x^2yz + xy^2z^2) = \lambda^3 w$$

so that the function increases in value by a factor of λ^3. This function is therefore said to be homogeneous of degree 3 in the variables x and y.

Example 11.12

Which of the following functions are homogeneous and to what degree?

(a) $z = 3x^2y$;
(b) $z = \sqrt{(x/3y)}$;
(c) $z = 7x^2 + 4y$;
(d) $z = 8xy^2 + 5x^2y + 3$;
(e) $z = Ax^\alpha y^\beta$;
(f) $z = (x^2y + y^3)/x^3$.

Example 11.13

Show that the following function is homogeneous of degree 0. Express the function in terms of the ratios of variables.

$$w = \frac{3xyz + 4xy^2}{2z^2y + 3x^2y}$$

Example 11.14

In what variables are the following functions homogeneous?

(a) $f(x, y, z) = x^3yz + 4x^2y^2$

(b) $f(x, y, z) = \dfrac{x^2yz + y^2xz}{x^3 + y^3z^2}$

(c) $f(u, v, w) = \sqrt{(3u/v)} + 6w$

Euler's theorem

Consider again eqn [11.53] where the function is homogeneous of degree v. Euler's theorem states that for such a function

$$x\frac{\partial f}{\partial x} + y\frac{\partial f}{\partial y} + z\frac{\partial f}{\partial z} = vf(x, y, z) \qquad [11.57]$$

A proof is provided in the appendix to this chapter. The theorem extends to any number of variables.

Euler's theorem has an interesting interpretation when applied to production functions. If the production function $q = q(k, l)$ is homogeneous of degree v, then applying [11.57] we have

$$k\frac{\partial q}{\partial k} + l\frac{\partial q}{\partial l} = vq \qquad [11.58]$$

Suppose p is the price of output and m and w are the prices of capital and labour inputs respectively. $\partial q/\partial k$ and $\partial q/\partial l$ are, of course, the marginal products of capital and labour. If factors are paid the value of their marginal products (as would be the case under perfect competition) then

$$m = p\frac{\partial q}{\partial k} \quad \text{and} \quad w = p\frac{\partial q}{\partial l} \qquad [11.59]$$

Substituting into [11.58] and rearranging we then have

$$km + lw = v(qp) \qquad [11.60]$$

qp in eqn [11.60] is the firm's total revenue. km and lw are the total payments the firm makes to the factors' capital and labour. Thus if $v = 1$ and constant returns to scale exist, then payments to factors are exactly equal to total revenue and profit must be zero. If $v < 1$ then payments to factors are less than total revenue and the firm makes a profit. However, if $v > 1$, payments exceed revenue and the firm makes a loss.

Revision examples

Example R11.1

(a) If $z = 0.001x^3 + 0.05y^2 + 0.03xy$, find the total differential of z. Hence, find the approximate increase in z when x increases from 400 to 401 and y increases from 200 to 201.
(b) Find the total differential of:

  (i) $z = 3x^2 + 4xy + 5y^2$;

  (ii) $z = 2w^{0.3}x^{0.2}y^{0.5}$;

  (iii) $z = 1/(x + y)^2$.

Example R11.2

Consider the following non-linear market model:

$$d_1 = 300 - 3p_1 - p_2 + 4Y$$
$$s_1 = 200 + 2p_1 - p_2 + 2p_2p_1$$
$$d_1 = s_1$$

The variables are as defined as in Chapter 4, with Y and p_2 being exogenous. Use the technique of total differentials to find $\partial p_1/\partial Y$ and $\partial p_1/\partial p_2$ (i.e. the own-price 'multipliers' for the exogenous variables). Are the goods substitutes or complements? Is good (1) an inferior good?

Example R11.3

Consider the following simple macro-model:

$$C = C(Y, W) \quad I(Y, R) \quad C + I = Y \quad L = L(Y, R) \quad L = M$$

where income Y, consumption C, investment I, the rate of interest R and the demand for money L are endogenous. The supply of money M and the stock of wealth W are exogenous. Find the money and wealth multipliers $\partial Y/\partial M$ and $\partial Y/\partial W$.

Example R11.4

(a) Find $\partial z/\partial x$ and dz/dx when $z = 3x^2y^2$ with $yx^2 = 5$.
(b) Find the total derivative dz/dw if $z = wu/v$ with $u = 4w^2$ and $v = 3/w^2$.
(c) Find dy/dx when: (i) $y^2 = 3x + 2y$; (ii) $y^4 = (1 + x)^2$.

Example R11.5

(a) Which of the following functions are homogeneous and to what degree?

    (i) $z = 8x^3 + 2x^2y + 4xy^2 + 5$;

    (ii) $z = 3/x^2 + 5/y^2$;

    (iii) $z = \dfrac{x^3y^2}{w^5} + \dfrac{w^3y^2}{x^5} + \dfrac{x^3w^2}{y^5}$.

    If (iii) is homogeneous of degree 0, show that z can be expressed in terms of the ratios of variables only.

(b) In what variables are the following functions homogeneous?

    (i) $f(x, y, z) = x^2y^2z^3 + x^3y^3z^2 + x^4y^4z$;

    (ii) $f(x, y, z) = (3x/y)^4 + (zy/3x)^4$.

Example R11.6

Show that the production function $Q = AK^\alpha L^\beta$ obeys Euler's theorem.

Appendix: proof of Euler's theorem

Suppose $w = f(x, y, z)$ is homogeneous of degree v. Then

$$f(\lambda x, \lambda y, \lambda z) = \lambda^v f(x, y, z)$$

Let $u = \lambda x$, $t = \lambda y$ and $w = \lambda z$. Hence

$$f(u, t, w) = \lambda^v f(x, y, z) \tag{11A.1}$$

Partially differentiating both sides of eqn [11A.1] with respect to λ, we have

$$\frac{\partial f}{\partial u}\frac{\partial u}{\partial \lambda} + \frac{\partial f}{\partial t}\frac{\partial t}{\partial \lambda} + \frac{\partial f}{\partial w}\frac{\partial w}{\partial \lambda} = v\lambda^{v-1}f(x, y, z) \tag{11A.2}$$

where the LHS of eqn [11A.1] has been differentiated using the composite function rule (see Example 11.6). However, $\partial u/\partial \lambda = x$, $\partial t/\partial \lambda = y$ and $\partial w/\partial \lambda = z$. Hence eqn [11A.2] becomes

$$x\frac{\partial f}{\partial u} + y\frac{\partial f}{\partial t} + z\frac{\partial f}{\partial w} = v\lambda^{v-1}f(x, y, z) \tag{11A.3}$$

Equation [11A.3] must hold for all values of λ. If we let $\lambda = 1$, then $u = x$, $t = y$ and $w = z$ so that eqn [11A.3] becomes

$$x\frac{\partial f}{\partial x} + y\frac{\partial f}{\partial y} + z\frac{\partial f}{\partial z} = vf(x, y, z) \tag{11A.4}$$

Equation [11A.4] is Euler's theorem.

Note

1. If $f(x, y, z)$ is homogeneous of degree 0 then if we set $\lambda = 1/z$ in eqn [11.53], we have, since $v = 0$,

   $$f(x/z, y/z, 1) = f(x, y, z)$$

   Thus such a function can always be expressed in terms of the ratios x/z and y/z.

12 Unconstrained and constrained optimisation

12.1 The unconstrained optimisation of functions of more than one variable

In section 8.1 we considered the notion of stationary points and in particular the conditions for local maxima and minima when dealing with functions of a single variable. We saw that if $y = f(x)$, then any point for which $dy/dx = 0$ and $d^2y/dx^2 > 0$ was a local minimum. Similarly any point for which $dy/dx = 0$ and $d^2y/dx^2 < 0$ will be a local maximum.[1]

Suppose, now, that we have some function of two variables

$$z = f(x, y) \tag{12.1}$$

For [12.1] z is said to have a local minimum when $x = a$ and $y = b$, if it is not possible to obtain a smaller value of z by making slight changes in the values of x and y. That is, z takes a smaller value at $x = a$ and $y = b$ than for any 'neighbouring' paris of values for x and y. Notice that we speak only of 'neighbouring' paris of values for x and y. There might still be some pair of values 'far away' from $x = a$ and $y = b$ that yields a smaller value for z. For this reason we refer to the minimum value of z as a local minimum rather than a global minimum.[2]

There are in fact, three ways in which we can make small changes in x and y:

(a) we can keep $x = a$ and vary y;
(b) we can keep $y = b$ and vary x;
(c) we can vary both x and y at the same time.

If z has a local minimum at $x = a$ and $y = b$ then it must be impossible to reduce z by any of the methods (a), (b) or (c). Considering case (a) first, if we fix the value x and examine the effect on z of varying y, then we are dealing with what we called in Chapter 10 an iso-x curve. If [12.1] does indeed have a local minimum when $x = a$ and $y = b$, then this iso-$x = a$ curve must look something like that in Fig. 12.1, with its minimum at the point P. For such an iso-x curve it is impossible to obtain a smaller value for z by changing y from $y = b$.

It should be clear from our discussion of functions of one variable that, at the point P in Fig. 12.1, the following conditions must hold:

$$\frac{\partial z}{\partial y} = 0 \quad \text{and} \quad \frac{\partial^2 z}{\partial y^2} > 0 \tag{12.2}$$

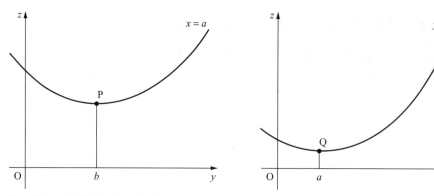

Figs 12.1 and 12.2 A local minimum

where we deal now with partial derivatives since the value of x is being held constant. If the conditions [12.2] hold (i.e. we are at point P in Fig. 12.1), then we cannot obtain a smaller z by varying y alone.

Similarly, considering case (b) above, if we fix $y = b$ and vary x then we obtain an iso-$y = b$ curve. If z has a local minimum at $x = a$ and $y = b$ then the iso-y curve must have a form similar to that in Fig. 12.2 with a local minimum at the point Q. Hence we see that it is impossible to obtain a smaller z by keeping y fixed and varying x from $x = a$.

It is clear that at the point Q in Fig. 12.2, the following conditions must hold:

$$\frac{\partial z}{\partial x} = 0 \quad \text{and} \quad \frac{\partial^2 z}{\partial x^2} > 0 \qquad\qquad [12.3]$$

The derivatives are again partial because we are now holding y constant. If the conditions [12.3] hold (i.e. we are at point Q in Fig. 12.2), then we cannot obtain a smaller z by varying x alone.

Clearly, both the conditions [12.2] and [12.3] must hold if $z = f(x, y)$ is to have a local *minimum*. Suppose, however, that z has a local *maximum* at $x = a$ and $y = b$. By this we mean that z takes a larger value at $x = a$ and $y = b$ than for any 'neighbouring' pair of values for x and y. The iso-x and iso-y curves of Figs 12.1 and 12.2 would now both exhibit local maxima, so that for $z = f(x, y)$ to have a local maximum it is necessary that

$$\frac{\partial z}{\partial y} = 0 \quad \text{and} \quad \frac{\partial^2 z}{\partial y^2} < 0 \qquad\qquad [12.4]$$

$$\frac{\partial z}{\partial x} = 0 \quad \text{and} \quad \frac{\partial^2 z}{\partial x^2} < 0 \qquad\qquad [12.5]$$

Although we have not yet considered case (c) above, where we attempt to decrease (or increase) z by varying x and y at the same time, let us see how far we can get by applying the conditions [12.2]–[12.5] to an actual function. Suppose, for example,

$$z = 3x^2 + 4y^2 - 12x - 8y + 4xy \qquad\qquad [12.6]$$

We seek *turning-points* for [12.6], that is local minima and/or local maxima. We know that for a local maximum *or* a local minimum it must be the case that $\partial z/\partial y$ and $\partial z/\partial x$ equal zero. That is, for [12.6]

$$\frac{\partial z}{\partial y} = 8y - 8 + 4x = 0 \qquad\qquad [12.7]$$

$$\frac{\partial z}{\partial x} = 6x - 12 + 4y = 0 \qquad\qquad [12.8]$$

Equations [12.7] and [12.8] represent two linear simultaneous equations in x and y which we can easily solve to obtain $x = 2$ and $y = 0$. We next obtain the second-order partial derivatives

$$\frac{\partial^2 z}{\partial y^2} = 8 \quad \text{and} \quad \frac{\partial^2 z}{\partial x^2} = 6 \qquad\qquad [12.9]$$

The second-order partial derivatives obviously obey conditions [12.2] and [12.3] rather than [12.4] and [12.5]. Clearly we do not have a local maximum, but do we have a local minimum? To be sure of this we need to consider (c) above. When $x = 2$ and $y = 0$ it is not possible to make z smaller by varying y alone or by varying x alone. For it also to be impossible to make z smaller by varying y and x together it must be the case that

$$\frac{\partial^2 z}{\partial y^2} \frac{\partial^2 z}{\partial x^2} > \left(\frac{\partial^2 z}{\partial y \partial x}\right)^2 \qquad\qquad [12.10]$$

It is difficult to provide an intuitive explanation of the condition [12.10] but a proof is provided in the appendix to this chapter. Here we shall simply check whether it holds for the function in [12.6]. We have from [12.7] and [12.8]

$$\left(\frac{\partial^2 z}{\partial y \partial x}\right)^2 = (4)^2 = 16 \quad \text{whereas} \quad \frac{\partial^2 z}{\partial y^2} \frac{\partial^2 z}{\partial x^2} = (8)(6) = 48$$

Clearly the condition [12.10] is met, so we can be certain that z in [12.6] has a local minimum when $x = 2$ and $y = 0$.

Let us summarise the conditions that must hold if we are to have a local minimum or local maximum.

Firstly, it must be the case that

$$\frac{\partial z}{\partial y} = 0 \quad \text{and} \quad \frac{\partial z}{\partial x} = 0 \qquad\qquad [12.11]$$

These are the *first-order conditions* that must hold for both a local minimum and a local maximum. For a local minimum we must also have

$$\frac{\partial^2 z}{\partial y^2} > 0, \quad \frac{\partial^2 z}{\partial x^2} > 0 \quad \text{and} \quad \frac{\partial^2 z}{\partial y^2} \frac{\partial^2 z}{\partial x^2} > \left(\frac{\partial^2 z}{\partial y \partial x}\right)^2 \qquad\qquad [12.12]$$

For a local maximum we must have, as well as [12.11],

$$\frac{\partial^2 z}{\partial y^2} < 0, \quad \frac{\partial^2 z}{\partial x^2} < 0 \quad \text{and} \quad \frac{\partial^2 z}{\partial y^2} \frac{\partial^2 z}{\partial x^2} > \left(\frac{\partial^2 z}{\partial y \partial x}\right)^2 \qquad\qquad [12.13]$$

Relations [12.12] and [12.13] are known as *second-order conditions*.

Notice that the third conditions in [12.12] and [12.13] are identical. In fact if

$$\frac{\partial^2 z}{\partial y^2}\frac{\partial^2 z}{\partial x^2} < \left(\frac{\partial^2 z}{\partial y \partial x}\right)^2 \tag{12.14}$$

then we have *neither a local minimum nor a local maximum* even if all the other conditions hold.[3] One of the types of point implied by condition [12.14] is described in the appendix to this chapter.

As a further illustration of the use of conditions [12.11]–[12.13] let us find any local maxima and minima for

$$z = 4x^2 + y^2 - xy - x^3 \tag{12.15}$$

The first- and second-order partial derivatives of [12.15] are

$$\frac{\partial z}{\partial y} = 2y - x \quad \frac{\partial z}{\partial x} = 8x - y - 3x^2$$

$$\frac{\partial^2 z}{\partial y^2} = 2 \quad \frac{\partial^2 z}{\partial y \partial x} = -1 \quad \frac{\partial^2 z}{\partial x^2} = 8 - 6x$$

Applying the condition [12.11] we set the first-order derivatives equal to zero. That is,

$$2y - x = 0 \quad \text{and} \quad 8x - y - 3x^2 = 0 \tag{12.16}$$

There are two solutions to the pair of eqns [12.16]. We can obtain them by substituting $x = 2y$ into the second equation. This yields the quadratic equation

$$15y - 12y^2 = 0 \quad \rightarrow \quad 5y - 4y^2 = 0 \quad \rightarrow \quad y(5 - 4y) = 0$$

Hence either $y = 0$ or $y = \frac{5}{4}$. Using $x = 2y$, the corresponding values of x are $x = 0$ and $x = \frac{5}{2}$. Thus there are two paris of values which could conceivably be local maxima or local minima: $x = 0$ and $y = 0$; and $x = \frac{5}{2}$ and $y = \frac{5}{4}$.

We now check to see which, if either, of the conditions [12.12] and [12.13] are satisfied by these pairs of values. For $x = 0$ and $y = 0$ we have

$$\frac{\partial^2 z}{\partial y^2} = 2 \quad \frac{\partial^2 z}{\partial y \partial x} = -1 \quad \frac{\partial^2 z}{\partial x^2} = 8 - 6x = 8$$

Clearly the conditions [12.12] are satisfied since $(8)(2) > (-1)^2$. Hence [12.15] has a local minimum when $x = 0$ and $y = 0$.

For $x = \frac{5}{2}$ and $y = \frac{5}{4}$ we have

$$\frac{\partial^2 z}{\partial y^2} = 2 \quad \frac{\partial^2 z}{\partial y \partial x} = -1 \quad \frac{\partial^2 z}{\partial x^2} = 8 - 6x = -7$$

In this case neither [12.12] nor [12.13] is satisfied since $\partial^2 z/\partial y^2$ and $\partial^2 z/\partial x^2$ are of opposite sign. Also [12.14] holds in this case since $(-7)(2) < (-1)^2$. Hence [12.15] has neither a local maximum nor a local minimum at this point. The function [12.15] hence has a local minimum when $x = 0$ and $y = 0$ but no local maximum. The local minimum value of z can be found by substituting $x = 0$ and $y = 0$ into [12.15]. This yields $z = 0$ as the local minimum value.[4]

Example 12.1

Find any local maxima or minima for the following functions:

(a) $z = 8xy + 2x^2 - 3y^2 + 4x - y$;

(b) $y = 3u^2 + 4v^2 - 12u - 8v$;

(c) $z = 4x^2 - 5xy + 3y^2 + x^3$.

12.2 Profit maximisation again

In section 8.3 we defined a firm's profits as the difference between its total revenue and its total cost

$$\Pi = TR - TC \qquad [12.17]$$

By expressing total revenue and total costs as a function of output alone, we were then able to obtain the profit-maximising output level. Profits were maximised when output was such that marginal revenue equalled marginal cost, the second-order condition being that the marginal cost curve should intersect the marginal revenue curve 'from below'.

In this chapter we express the firm's profit-maximisation problem in slightly different terms. We introduced the idea of a production function as eqn [10.27]

$$q = q(k, l)$$

where q was the firm's output while k and l were its inputs of capital and labour respectively. Suppose p is the price of output, with m and w being the prices of capital and labour inputs. Total cost in eqn [12.17] is the sum of the firm's expenditure on capital and labour. That is,

$$TC = mk + wl \qquad [12.18]$$

Since total revenue is simply the product of p and q we can therefore rewrite eqn [12.17] as

$$\Pi = pq - mk - wl$$

or, using the production function to express q in terms of k and l,

$$\Pi = pq(k, l) - mk - wl \qquad [12.19]$$

Suppose that the firm operates under conditions of perfect competition so that we can regard the price it obtains for its output and the prices it pays for its inputs as given constants.[5] Equation [12.19] then expresses profit as a function of capital and labour inputs. We can now re-express the firm's problem as that of choosing not the level of output but the levels of inputs that maximise profits. To obtain profit-maximising conditions for this problem we simply apply conditions [12.11] and [12.13].

Applying [12.11] we take the partial derivatives of [12.19] and equate them to zero

$$\frac{\partial \Pi}{\partial k} = p\frac{\partial q}{\partial k} - m = 0 \quad \rightarrow \quad \frac{\partial q}{\partial k} = \frac{m}{p} \qquad [12.20]$$

$$\frac{\partial \Pi}{\partial l} = p\frac{\partial q}{\partial l} - w = 0 \quad \rightarrow \quad \frac{\partial q}{\partial l} = \frac{w}{p} \tag{12.21}$$

The first-order conditions [12.20] and [12.21] state that the level of inputs must be such that the real price paid for each factor (i.e. the price expressed in terms of the amount of output it would buy) must equal its marginal product. For example, the marginal product of labour must be set equal to the real wage rate. Applying [12.13] we obtain the second-order conditions

$$\frac{\partial^2 \Pi}{\partial k^2} = p\frac{\partial^2 q}{\partial k^2} < 0 \quad \rightarrow \quad \frac{\partial^2 q}{\partial k^2} < 0 \tag{12.22}$$

$$\frac{\partial^2 \Pi}{\partial l^2} = p\frac{\partial^2 q}{\partial l^2} < 0 \quad \rightarrow \quad \frac{\partial^2 q}{\partial l^2} < 0 \tag{12.23}$$

$$p^2 \frac{\partial^2 q}{\partial k^2}\frac{\partial^2 q}{\partial l^2} > p^2 \left(\frac{\partial^2 q}{\partial k \partial l}\right)^2 \quad \rightarrow \quad \frac{\partial^2 q}{\partial k^2}\frac{\partial^2 q}{\partial l^2} > \left(\frac{\partial^2 q}{\partial k \partial l}\right)^2 \tag{12.24}$$

The second derivatives $\partial^2 q/\partial k^2$ and $\partial^2 q/\partial l^2$ measure the slopes of the marginal product of capital curve and the marginal product of labour curve respectively. The conditions [12.22] and [12.23] thus imply that *diminishing marginal products for both labour and capital are a necessary condition for profit maximisation*. For example, if [12.23] holds, an input of one extra unit of labour will then lead to an increase in output smaller than that provided by the previous unit of labour. Since by [12.21], the marginal product of the previous unit was equal to the real wage rate w/p, the marginal product of the extra unit of labour will be less than the real wage rate. Hence input of the extra labour unit will result in a fall in profit.

Example 12.2

A firm's production function is $q = 20k^{0.5}l^{0.25}$. If $p = 5$, $m = 10$ and $w = 20$ can be taken as given, find the levels of q, k and l at which the firm's profits are maximised.

The optimising techniques developed in section 12.1 enable us to tackle economic problems a little more complicated than those in Chapter 8. Suppose, for example, a firm sells a single product in two completely different markets. The firm's demand curves are given by

$$p_1 = 262 - 4q_1 \quad p_2 = 222 - 2q_2 \tag{12.25}$$

where p_1 and p_2 are the (different) prices in the two markets and q_1 and q_2 are the outputs.

The output is produced in a single plant with a total cost function

$$TC = q^2 + 2q + 300 \tag{12.26}$$

where total output $q = q_1 + q_2$.

If the firm wishes to maximise profit, what price should it set in each market and how much output will be sold in each market?

The firm's profit Π is given as the difference between its total revenue and its total cost. That is, as usual,

$$\Pi = TR - TC \tag{12.27}$$

The key decision variables in this problem are the outputs q_1 and q_2. We therefore require that profit should be expressed in terms of q_1 and q_2.

The firm receives revenue from both markets and, using [12.25], we have

$$TR_1 = p_1 q_1 = 262 q_1 - 4 q_1^2 \qquad [12.28]$$

and

$$TR_2 = p_2 q_2 = 222 q_2 - 2 q_2^2 \qquad [12.29]$$

where TR_1 and TR_2 are the total revenues from the respective markets. The firm's overall revenue is clearly $TR = TR_1 + TR_2$. TR is now expressed in terms of the decision variables q_1 and q_2.

Total cost is given by [12.26]. Substituting in for $q = q_1 + q_2$ gives

$$TC = (q_1 + q_2)^2 + 2(q_1 + q_2) + 300$$
$$= q_1^2 + q_2^2 + 2 q_1 q_2 + 2 q_1 + 2 q_2 + 300 \qquad [12.30]$$

Equation [12.30] expresses total cost as a function of q_1 and q_2.

We can now express profit in terms of the two decision variables q_1 and q_2. From [12.27],

$$\Pi = TR_1 + TR_2 - TC$$

Thus, using [12.28], [12.29] and [12.30], we have

$$\Pi = 262 q_1 - 4 q_1^2 + 222 q_2 - 2 q_2^2 - (q_1^2 + q_2^2 + 2 q_1 q_2 + 2 q_1 + 2 q_2 + 300)$$

Grouping terms gives

$$\Pi = 260 q_1 + 220 q_2 - 2 q_1 q_2 - 5 q_1^2 - 3 q_2^2 - 300 \qquad [12.31]$$

Equation [12.31] is the firm's profit function, expressing Π in terms of q_1 and q_2. We can now use our partial differentiation techniques to maximise profits. Firstly we differentiate Π with respect to q_1 and q_2:

$$\frac{\partial \Pi}{\partial q_1} = 260 - 2 q_2 - 10 q_1$$

$$\frac{\partial \Pi}{\partial q_2} = 220 - 2 q_1 - 6 q_2$$

Setting the two partial derivatives to zero gives

$$260 - 2 q_2 - 10 q_1 = 0 \quad \rightarrow \quad 5 q_1 + q_2 = 130 \qquad [12.32]$$
$$220 - 2 q_1 - 6 q_2 = 0 \quad \rightarrow \quad q_1 + 3 q_2 = 110 \qquad [12.33]$$

Multiplying [12.32] by 3 and subtracting the result from [12.33] yields $-14 q_1 = -280$ and hence $q_1 = 20$. Substitution of q_1 into either [12.32] or [12.33] then gives $q_2 = 30$.

We have a potential turning-point at $q_1 = 20$ and $q_2 = 30$. To confirm that this turning-point is a local maximum, we must check the second-order conditions. The second-order derivatives are

$$\frac{\partial^2 \Pi}{\partial q_1^2} = -10 \qquad \frac{\partial^2 \Pi}{\partial q_2^2} = -6 \qquad \frac{\partial^2 \Pi}{\partial q_1 \partial q_2} = -2$$

We see that

$$\frac{\partial^2 \Pi}{\partial q_1^2} < 0, \quad \frac{\partial^2 \Pi}{\partial q_2^2} < 0 \quad \text{and} \quad \left(\frac{\partial^2 \Pi}{\partial q_1^2}\right)\left(\frac{\partial^2 \Pi}{\partial q_2^2}\right) > \left(\frac{\partial^2 \Pi}{\partial q_1 \partial q_2}\right)^2$$

Thus the second-order conditions for a local maximum are satisfied.

The firm's profits are maximised when $q_1 = 20$ and $q_2 = 30$. We can now use the two demand functions to find the prices in the two markets. From [12.25], we obtain $p_1 = 182$, $p_2 = 162$. Also, if we substitute for q_1 and q_2 in [12.30], we obtain the firm's maximum profit.

Example 12.3

A firm sells its single product in two distinct markets. Its average revenue functions in the two markets are

$$AR_1 = 315 - 6q_1 \quad AR_2 = 103 - 2q_2$$

where q_1 and q_2 are its outputs in the respective markets. Its total cost function is

$$TC = 15q_1 + 600$$

where $q = q_1 + q_2$. Find the profit-maximising output and price in each market and the firm's total profit.

Example 12.4

A firm's total cost functions for its two plants (both producing the same single product) are

$$C_1 = 3q_1^2 + 2q_1 + 6 \quad C_2 = 2q_2^2 + 2q_2 + 4$$

where q_1 and q_2 are the outputs at the respective plants. The firm's average revenue function is

$$AR = 74 - 6q$$

where $q = q_1 + q_2$ and p is the price of the product. If profits are to be maximised, how much should be produced at each plant and what should be the price of the product? Suppose that, instead of facing the above AR curve, the firm can sell as much as it wishes at a fixed price of 40. How much will the firm produce at each plant now?

12.3 Constrained optimisation

Although maximisation and minimisation problems are common in economics, the ability to maximise or minimise is often restricted by other factors. For example, a consumer is assumed to maximise utility but the utility level he/she can achieve is constrained by the total amount available to be spent. Similarly a firm may wish to minimise its total costs but may be restricted in its objective by the need to produce a certain minimum level of output. Consider the functional relationship

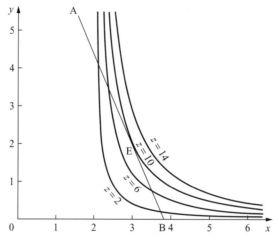

Fig. 12.3 Tangency between iso-*z* line and constraint

$$z = x^2 y - 4y \qquad\qquad [12.34]$$

If we wish to find the *unconstrained* maximum value of z we seek, out of all possible pairs of values for x and y, that pair which when substituted into [12.34] yields the largest value for z. We can consider any pair of values for x and y that we like – we are not constrained in any way in our choice. In fact, it is not difficult to see that we can make z as large as we wish. For example, if we set y equal to any positive constant, then the larger we make x the larger z becomes. Hence the unconstrained maximum value of z is infinite.

Suppose now that we wish to maximise [12.34] *subject to the constraint*

$$5y + 12x = 46 \qquad\qquad [12.35]$$

We now have a *constrained maximisation problem* as opposed to an unconstrained one. By this we mean that out of all pairs of values for x and y *that satisfy the constraint* [12.35] we seek that pair which, when substituted into [12.34], yields the largest value for z. Unlike in the unconstrained problem we now restrict or constrain our choice to pairs of values for x and y that satisfy [12.35].

We can illustrate the constrained maximisation problem graphically by considering the iso-z curves for [12.34]. These were graphed in Fig. 11.2 and are reproduced in Fig. 12.3. The constraint [12.35] is graphed as the line AB in the figure. As usual, for convenience we have only graphed that part of [12.34] where both x and y are positive.

Notice that the further an iso-z curve is from the origin the higher the fixed value of z to which it corresponds. In our constrained maximisation problem, since we consider only pairs of values for x and y which satisfy the constraint, in terms of Fig. 12.3 this implies considering only points which are on the line AB. To solve our problem we need to ascertain the 'highest' iso-z line that can be reached while we remain on the line AB. We will have then maximised z subject to the constraint.

It should be clear that the highest obtainable iso-z line is that labelled $z = 10$, which 'just touches' or is tangential to the constraint line AB. The solution to our problem is therefore represented by point E in Fig. 12.3. The coordinates of this point ($x = 3$ and $y = 2$) represent the pair of values for x and y which, while satisfying the constraint, yield the largest value of z. This maximum value of z is of course $z = 10$.

Obtaining graphical solutions to constrained maximisation and minimisation problems in the above manner is tedious and often impossible. An awful lot of iso-z curves have to be graphed before we find one that happens to be tangential to the constraint line! Obviously we require an analytical or non-graphical method and the calculus techniques described in Chapters 10 and 11 provide us with one.

The crucial property of point E in Fig. 12.3 is that the iso-z curve passing through this point has, at E, a gradient equal to the constant gradient of the constraint line AB. From [12.35] we see that the gradient of the constraint line is $-12/5$, whereas we can obtain an expression for the gradient of an iso-z curve by using the implicit differentiation technique of section 11.3. Using eqn [11.49]

$$\frac{dy}{dx} = -\frac{\partial z/\partial x}{\partial z/\partial y} = -\frac{2xy}{x^2 - 4} \qquad [12.36]$$

Equating this expression for the gradient of an iso-z curve to $-12/5$ we obtain

$$-12/5 = -2xy/(x^2 - 4) \quad \rightarrow \quad 12(x^2 - 4) = 10xy$$

$$\rightarrow \quad 6x^2 - 5xy = 24 \qquad [12.37]$$

Equation [12.37] is a relationship between x and y that the coordinates of point E must satisfy. We shall refer to it as an *optimality condition* since only if the coordinates of E satisfy it can E be optimal in the sense of representing a solution to our constrained maximisation problem.

The coordinates of E must also satisfy [12.35], the equation of the constraint line on which E lies. We therefore have two eqns, [12.35] and [12.37], which we can solve to obtain these coordinates. From eqn [12.35] $y = 46/5 - (12/5)x$. Substituting into eqn [12.37] we have

$$6x^2 - 5x[46/5 - (12/5)x] = 24 \quad \rightarrow \quad 9x^2 - 23x - 12 = 0 \qquad [12.38]$$

Equation [12.38] is a quadratic equation in x that can be solved either by formula or factorisation. Factorising yields

$$(x - 3)(9x + 4) = 0 \quad \rightarrow \quad x = 3 \quad \text{and} \quad x = -4/9$$

We thus obtain *two* solution values for x. The corresponding y-values can be obtained using $y = 46/5 - (12/5)x$. The two solutions to eqns [12.35] and [12.37] are therefore $x = 3$, $y = 2$ and $x = -4/9$, $y = 154/15$. The first of these solutions obviously corresponds to point E in Fig. 12.3 Substituting $x = 3$ and $y = 2$ into equation [12.34] we obtain the maximum possible value of z as $z = (3)^2(2) - 4(2) = 10$.

But what of the solution $x = -4/9$, $y = 154/15$? To interpret this solution it is necessary to realise that the iso-z curves of Fig. 12.3 are drawn only for positive values of x, y and z. The reader should graph the complete iso-z curve for, for example, $z = 10$. It will be found to have two further portions which are not 'joined up' with the portion graphed in Fig. 12.3. One such portion lies below the x-axis and the other is a 'mirror image' of that shown in Fig. 12.3, lying to the left of the y-axis. Next graph iso-z curves for negative values of z, for example $z = -39$ and $z = -40$. It will now become clear that the constraint line [12.35] is also tangential to an iso-z curve between $z = -39$ and $z = -40$. This point, however, represents a *minimum* value for z. It in fact lies on the 'lowest' iso-z curve that can be reached while remaining on the constraint line.

Example 12.5

Without attempting to graph the iso-z curves, find the local minimum of the function $z = x^2 + y^2 + 8y$ subject to the constraint $x + y = 2$. Can you verify that the optimal point is a local minimum?

The Lagrange method

In this section we introduce a second method, known as the Lagrange method, of solving constrained optimisation problems. Students initially find this method somewhat bewildering but it is a technique frequently used by economists. We shall approach it by way of a series of systematic steps. Consider again the problem of the previous subsection where we wish to maximise the *objective function* [12.34]

$$z = x^2y - 4y$$

subject to the constraint [12.35]

$$5y + 12x = 46$$

The first step in the Lagrange method is to rearrange the constraint in such a way that the RHS equals zero and then form a new function of the kind

$$F = \text{objective function} - \lambda(\text{LHS of constraint}) \tag{12.39}$$

where λ is a new variable and is referred to as a *Lagrange multiplier*. The new function in [12.39] is known as a *Lagrangian*. In the present example the constraint is rearranged as $5y + 12x - 46$ and we form the Lagrangian

$$F = x^2y - 4y - \lambda(5y + 12x - 46) \tag{12.40}$$

The crucial point to accept now is that if we find the values of x, y *and* λ that maximise or minimise a Lagrangian of the form [12.39] then *the same x- and y-values will be the pair that maximise or minimise the objective function subject to the constraint*. A rigorous proof of this will not be provided but it is possible to see intuitively why it should be so. In solving the above constrained optimisation problem we are concerned solely with x- and y-values that satisfy the constraint – that is, that make $5y + 12x - 46 = 0$. However, from [12.40], if $5y + 12x - 46 = 0$, then $F = z$. But when F and z are identical, the values of x and y which maximise or minimise F must also maximise of minimise z. Hence maximising or minimising F is equivalent to maximising or minimising z subject to [12.35] since it is *only* when [12.35] is satisfied that $F = z$.

The second step in the Lagrange method is therefore to find maximum or minimum values of F in the usual way. That is, we partially differentiate F with respect to x, y and λ in turn and set each of these derivatives to zero. In the above example this yields

$$\frac{\partial F}{\partial x} = 2xy - 12\lambda = 0 \tag{12.41}$$

$$\frac{\partial F}{\partial y} = x^2 - 4 - 5\lambda = 0 \tag{12.42}$$

$$\frac{\partial F}{\partial \lambda} = -(5y + 12x - 46) = 0 \qquad\qquad [12.43]$$

Equations [12.41]–[12.43] represent three equations which have to be solved for the optimal values of x, y and λ. Notice that the third equation is simply another way of writing the original constraint [12.35]. Equations [12.41] and [12.42] can be used to eliminate the Lagrangian multiplier λ. That is, from eqn [12.41]

$$\lambda = \frac{xy}{6} \quad\text{and from eqn [12.42]}\quad \lambda = \frac{x^2 - 4}{5} \qquad\qquad [12.44]$$

Hence

$$\frac{xy}{6} = \frac{x^2 - 4}{5} \quad\rightarrow\quad 6x^2 - 5xy = 24 \qquad\qquad [12.45]$$

Notice that eqn [12.45] is exactly the same as the optimality condition [12.37] of the previous subsection. The optimal values of x and y have to satisfy this relationship. In constrained optimisation problems elimination of the Lagrangian multiplier will always yield such optimality conditions.

We are now left with solving eqns [12.43] and [12.45] for the optimal values of x and y. Since eqn [12.43] is the original constraint and eqn [12.45] is the optimality condition, it is obvious that we will obtain the same solutions as in the previous subsection – $(x = 3, y = 2)$ and $(x = -4/9, y = 154/15)$. We leave, for the moment, the question of how, when using the Lagrange method, we distinguish between local maxima and local minima.

Example 12.6

Solve the optimisation problem of Example 12.5 using the Lagrange multiplier method.

Example 12.7

Use the Lagrangian multiplier method to find any local maxima and/or minima for the following functions subject to the given constraint:

(a) $z = 3x + 5y$ subject to $x^3 y = 10$;

(b) $w = 4uv$ subject to $u^2 + v^2 = 1$;

(c) $z = x^2 + y^2$ subject to $x^2 + y^2 - 4x + 2y = 0$.

For each of these functions see if you can deduce whether the optimal points are local maxima or minima.

Interpretation of the Lagrange multiplier

On first acquaintance with the Lagrange method the sudden appearance of a new variable, λ, invariably results in some bafflement. However, it is possible to give a clear meaning to the

Lagrange multiplier and this meaning often has a useful economic interpretation. Consider the general constrained maximisation problem: maximise

$$z = z(x, y) \tag{12.46}$$

subject to

$$f(x, y) = c \tag{12.47}$$

A change in c in the constraint [12.47] will normally result in a different maximum value for z. For example, in the problem of the last two subsections, an increase in the RHS of the constraint [12.35] from 46 to 47 would push the constraint line in Fig. 12.3 out from the origin and enable a higher iso-z line to be reached. The Lagrange multiplier of the last subsection in fact tells us the *change in maximum z per unit change in the constraint constant c*. That is, it is the partial derivative of z with respect to c:

$$\lambda = \frac{\partial z}{\partial c} \tag{12.48}$$

We write λ as a partial derivative since the constraint function $f(x, y)$ generally involves other constants (e.g. the constraint [12.35] contains a 5 and a 12) which we are assuming remain unchanged. Similarly, in a constrained minimisation problem, the Lagrange multiplier tells us the change in *minimum z* per unit change in the constraint constant c.

It is not difficult to prove [12.48]. Forming the Lagrangian in the usual manner

$$F = z(x, y) - \lambda[f(x, y) - c] \tag{12.49}$$

Partially differentiating with respect to x and y and setting the derivatives to zero

$$\frac{\partial F}{\partial x} = \frac{\partial z}{\partial x} - \lambda \frac{\partial f}{\partial x} = 0 \qquad \frac{\partial F}{\partial y} = \frac{\partial z}{\partial y} - \lambda \frac{\partial f}{\partial y} = 0 \tag{12.50}$$

Eliminating λ from eqns [12.50] we obtain the optimality condition

$$\frac{\partial z/\partial x}{\partial f/\partial x} = \frac{\partial z/\partial y}{\partial f/\partial y} \tag{12.51}$$

Noting that since all the partial derivatives in [12.51] are functions of x and y, we can treat the three equations [12.46], [12.47] and [12.51] as a three-equation system determining optimal values of the endogenous x, y and z for given values of the exogenous c. One of the reduced form equations of this system is of course of the form

$$z = g(c) \tag{12.52}$$

Since the system will normally be a non-linear one, we have to use the total differential method of section 11.2 to determine its reduced form coefficients or multipliers. Taking the total differentials of [12.46] and [12.47] we have

$$dz = \frac{\partial z}{\partial x} dx + \frac{\partial z}{\partial y} dy \tag{12.53}$$

$$dc = \frac{\partial f}{\partial x} dx + \frac{\partial f}{\partial y} dy \tag{12.54}$$

We do not in fact need to take the differential of [12.51] since we can obtain the result we want by multiplying [12.54] throughout by the LHS of [12.51]

$$\left(\frac{\partial z/\partial x}{\partial f/\partial x}\right) dc = \left(\frac{\partial z/\partial x}{\partial f/\partial x}\right)\frac{\partial f}{\partial x} dx + \left(\frac{\partial z/\partial x}{\partial f/\partial x}\right)\frac{\partial f}{\partial y} dy$$

$$= \frac{\partial z}{\partial x} dx + \frac{\partial z}{\partial y} dy \quad \text{(using eqn [12.51])}$$

Hence, using [12.53] and the first equation [12.50]

$$dz = \left(\frac{\partial z/\partial x}{\partial f/\partial x}\right) dc \quad \rightarrow \quad dz = \lambda\, dc \tag{12.55}$$

Since taking the total differential of [12.52] gives $dz = (\partial z/\partial c)dc$, comparing coefficients with eqn [12.55] yields the result we require, $\lambda = \partial z/\partial c$.

As an economic example of the use and interpretation of a Lagrangian multiplier, consider the following example. Suppose a firm has a production function

$$Q = 100L^{0.6}K^{0.4} \tag{12.56}$$

and the firm can take the prices of labour L and capital K as constant at the values \$12 and \$6 per unit respectively. If the firm wishes to minimise the cost of producing 20 000 units of output, the question is how much of each factor of production should the firm employ?

The firm's total costs are given by

$$C = 12L + 6K \tag{12.57}$$

The firm wishes to minimise costs, so [12.57] is clearly the firm's objective function. Costs have to be minimised subject to the constraint that output produced has to be 20 000 units. Since output is determined via the production function [12.56], the constraint can be written as

$$100L^{0.6}K^{0.4} = 20\,000 \tag{12.58}$$

The constrained optimisation problem can therefore be expressed as minimising [12.57] subject to the constraint [12.58]. We form the Lagrangian function in the usual way, giving

$$F = 12L + 6K - \lambda(100L^{0.6}K^{0.4} - 20\,000) \tag{12.59}$$

We now choose L, K and λ so as to minimise F. Partially differentiating with respect to L, K and λ and setting all derivatives to zero yields

$$\frac{\partial F}{\partial L} = 12 - 60\lambda L^{-0.4}K^{0.4} = 0 \tag{12.60}$$

$$\frac{\partial F}{\partial K} = 6 - 40\lambda L^{0.6}K^{-0.6} = 0 \tag{12.61}$$

$$\frac{\partial F}{\partial \lambda} = -(100L^{0.6}K^{0.4} - 20\,000) = 0 \tag{12.62}$$

We can use [12.60] and [12.61] to eliminate λ for the moment. From [12.60] we have

$$\lambda = 0.20L^{0.4}K^{-0.4} \quad \text{and from [12.61]} \quad \lambda = 0.15L^{-0.6}K^{0.6} \tag{12.63}$$

Hence

$$0.20L^{0.4}K^{-0.4} = 0.15L^{-0.6}K^{0.6} \qquad [12.64]$$

or, multiplying both sides of [12.64] by $L^{0.6}K^{0.4}$

$$0.20L = 0.15K \quad \rightarrow \quad L = 0.75K \qquad [12.65]$$

If we now substitute for L in [12.62] we obtain

$$100(0.75K)^{0.6}K^{0.4} = 20\,000$$

Hence

$$84.1K^{0.6}K^{0.4} = 20\,000 \quad \rightarrow \quad 84.1K = 20\,000$$

So that $K = 237.81$ and using [12.65] $L = 178.36$.

When L and K take these values, we can use [12.57] to obtain the minimum value of total cost as

$$C = 12(178.36) + 6(237.81) = \$3567.2$$

Finally we can find and then interpret the value of the Lagrangian multiplier λ. We can obtain λ by substituting in the values for L and K, using either of the expressions in [12.63]. Using the first we obtain

$$\lambda = 0.20(178.36)^{0.4}(237.81)^{-0.4}$$

$$= 0.20(7.953)(0.112) = \$0.178 \qquad [12.66]$$

As we saw earlier in this subsection, the Lagrangian multiplier tells us the change in the maximand or minimand when we make a small change in the constraint. In our current example λ therefore tells us the effect on minimum cost of an increase in required output from 20 000 to 20 001 units. Clearly any increase in output must result in an increase in total cost. But the increase of 1 unit in output results, using [12.66], in an increase in cost of \$0.18.

This may seem a small value for marginal cost but note that the firm's average cost can be found by dividing the total cost, obtained above as \$3567.2, by the total output of 20 000. This gives an average cost of \$0.178 virtually equal to marginal cost. Clearly, at outputs around 20 000, marginal cost is no higher than average cost.

12.4 Distinguishing between constrained maxima and constrained minima

The reader will have noticed that we have not introduced any second-order conditions for distinguishing between local maxima and local minima when tackling constrained optimisation problems. The reason for this is that such conditions are complicated and beyond our scope. However, it is often the case that a little 'trial and error' will give us the information we need.

As an example let us go back to the first constrained optimisation problem we tackled in this chapter. Suppose the Lagrange method is used to maximise/minimise

$$z = x^2y - 4y \quad \text{subject to} \quad 5y + 12x = 46$$

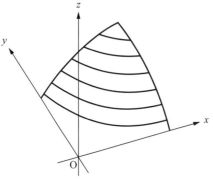

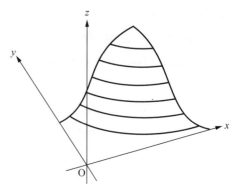

Fig. 12.4 A strictly concave surface   **Fig. 12.5** A strictly quasi-concave surface

and, as we saw earlier, one of the possible optimal points is $x = 3$ and $y = 2$ giving a value of $z = 10$.

An obvious way of demonstrating whether $z = 10$ is a local maximum or local minimum is to try making slight changes in the values $x = 3$ and $y = 2$. However, remember that, if we make a change in x, the corresponding change in y must be such that the constraint $5y + 12x = 46$ is still satisfied.

Suppose we increase x from the original 3 to 3.1. The required y-value can be obtained by substituting $x = 3.1$ into the constraint. That is, y must change to $y = 1.76$, rather less than the original $y = 2$. Substituting $x = 3.1$ and $y = 1.76$ into the objective function gives a value $z = 9.87$. This is *less* than the z-value at $x = 3$ and $y = 2$.

If instead we decrease x from 3 to 2.9, the constraint implies that we have to change y from 2 to 2.24. The resultant value for z is just 9.88. Again we obtain a z-value *less* than that obtained at $x = 3$ and $y = 2$. Given that the z-value at $x = 3$, $y = 2$ is greater than that at any neighbouring values for x, we can therefore say that z has a local maximum at these values.

Although 'trial and error' methods are often very useful in optimisation problems, a more general approach is sometimes necessary. Fortunately, such an approach is often possible in economics for two reasons. Firstly, in economics, we are often only concerned with positive solution values for x and y – that is, those which lie in the positive quadrant to the 'north-east' of the origin. Secondly, as we shall see in Chapters 13 and 14, it is often the case in economics that the objective function and the constraints we deal with can be assumed to have certain clearly defined properties. When this is the case, any solution point in the positive quadrant can be deemed either a maximum or a minimum without having to resort to complicated second-order conditions.[6]

In constrained maximisation problems in economics, it is often the case that the constraint is *linear* while the objective function may be assumed to be *strictly quasi-concave* with positive first-order partial derivatives. The precise definition of strict quasi-concavity need not concern us but an intuitive interpretation is possible for the case of functions of two variables. If $z = z(x, y)$ is strictly concave then, if the function is graphed in a three-dimensional coordinate system with a vertical z-axis, its surface appears dome-like when viewed from below. Such a surface is illustrated in Fig. 12.4. However, if $z = z(x, y)$ is strictly quasi-concave its surface need not necessarily be dome-like but could be bell-shaped as illustrated in Fig. 12.5.

Provided $z = z(x, y)$ has partial derivatives that are always positive that is $\partial z/\partial x > 0$ and $\partial z/\partial y > 0$, then either strict concavity or strict quasi-concavity ensures that all iso-z curves in the x–y plane will be everywhere convex to the origin. That is, they will have the shape

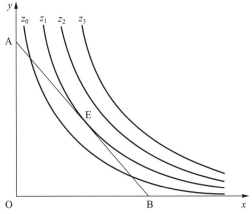

Fig. 12.6 Constrained maximisation

illustrated in Fig. 12.6. Moreover, the further an iso-z curve is from the origin in the positive quadrant, the larger will be the z-value associated with it. That is, $z_3 > z_2 > z_1 > z_0$ in Fig. 12.6. The requirement of positive partial derivatives ensures this.[7] Either strict concavity or strict quasi-concavity implies convex iso-z curves like those in Fig. 12.6 but since strict quasi-concavity is a less strong assumption than strict concavity, the former assumption is all that economists normally need to make.

Suppose now that the constraint takes the form

$$ax + by = c \quad a > 0, b > 0, c > 0 \tag{12.67}$$

Since a, b and c are positive, the constraint line will have a *negative* slope equal to $-a/b$ and will intersect the y-axis in Fig. 12.6 at a point *above* the origin where $y = c/b$. It will in fact look like the constraint line AB drawn in Fig. 12.6. Given such iso-z curves and such a constraint it is clear that any point of tangency in the positive quadrant, such as E in Fig. 12.6, must represent a constained *maximum* for z. The point E cannot be a minimum since it is possible to reach the iso-z curve corresponding to $z_0 < z_1$ while remaining on the constraint line. It is also clear that E represents a global maximum as well as a local maximum.

Summarising, we can say that any positive solutions yielded by the Lagrange method will be local maxima if:[8]

1. The objective function is strictly quasi-concave with positive first-order partial derivatives.
2. The constraint is linear and of the form implied by eqn [12.67].

Moreover, any such local maximum will also be a global maximum.

In economics it is also often possible to make similar assumptions about the problems involved in constrained minimisation problems. For example, a typical minimisation problem in economics is: minimise

$$z = ax + by \quad a > 0, b > 0 \tag{12.68}$$

subject to

$$f(x, y) = c \tag{12.69}$$

The objective function [12.68] is obviously linear. Consequently the iso-z curves will be straight lines which are negatively sloped since a and b are both positive. Moreover, the

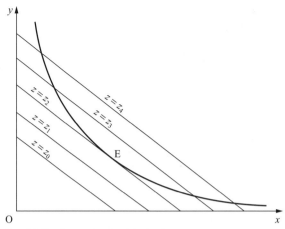

Fig. 12.7 Constrained minimisation

positiveness of a and b implies that the further an iso-z line is from the origin in the positive quadrant, the larger is the corresponding z-value. The iso-z lines are therefore as illustrated in Fig. 12.7 with $z_4 > z_3 > z_2 > z_1 > z_0$.

Suppose it is reasonable to assume that the constraint function $f(x, y)$ in [12.69] is strictly quasi-concave with $\partial f/\partial x$ and $\partial f/\partial y$ both positive. This implies that the graph of the constraint is everywhere convex to the origin in Fig. 12.7. The point of tangency E in Fig. 12.7 is clearly a local minimum rather than a local maximum and, moreover, it is obviously also a global minimum. Hence we can say that any positive solutions yielded by the Lagrange method will be a local minima if:

1. The objective function is linear and of the form implied by [12.68].
2. The constraint [12.69] is strictly quasi-concave with $\partial f/\partial x$ and $\partial f/\partial y$ both positive.

Moreover, of course, any such local minimum is also a global minimum.

The idea of strict quasi-concavity can be extended to functions of more than two variables. It is not then possible to interpret the property geometrically and an algebraic definition is necessary. While the algebraic definition is beyond the scope of this book, we note, however, that, even for functions of more than two variables, it is still possible to deduce the nature of any positive solutions yielded by the Lagrange method provided the objective function and the constraint have the appropriate properties.

Revision examples

Example R12.1

Find any local maxima/minima for the following functions:

(a) $z = 5x^2 + 4y^2 - 2xy - 22x + 12y + 7$;

(b) $z = 48x - 4x^3 - 5y^2$;

(c) $z = y^2/x + 3x + 5y$;

(d) $w = 2uv + 3u^2 + 6v^2$.

Example R12.2

A firm produces its single-good outputs at two factories whose average cost functions are given by

$$AC_1 = 3q_1 - 4 + 9/q_1 \quad AC_2 = 5q_2 - 4 + 13/q_2$$

where q_1 and q_2 are the outputs at the respective factories.

The firm sells in a single market and faces a demand curve given by $q = 664 - 4p$ where p is the price of the good and $q = q_1 + q_2$. If prices are to be maximised, how much should be produced at each plant and what price will be charged? What is the maximum profit obtained?

Example R12.3

A firm sells a single product in two separate markets. Its average revenue functions in the two markets are

$$AR_1 = 156 - 3Q_1 \quad AR_2 = 108 - 2Q_2$$

where Q_1 and Q_2 are outputs in the respective markets. Its total cost function in its single plant is

$$TC = Q^2 + 4Q + 500$$

where total output $Q = Q_1 + Q_2$.

Find the profit-maximising price and output in each market. At what total cost is this output produced?

If the firm's fixed costs remain unchanged but average variable cost becomes constant at 50 per unit of output, how will this affect the firm's outputs in the two markets?

Example R12.4

Use the Lagrange method to find any turning-points for the following functions:

(a) $z = x + 2y$ where $8xy = 30$;
(b) $z = 2y + 3x - x^2 - y^2$ where $3x + y = 5$.

Determine whether any turning-points are local minima or local maxima.

Example R12.5

A firm operating under perfect competition employs two factors of production both of which are variable. Its production function is

$$q = 4x^{0.5} + 8y^{0.5}$$

where x and y are factor inputs and the prices of the factors are 6 and 4 respectively. If the total cost outlay cannot exceed 378, show that the maximum output that can be produced is 84.

If the firm's output is fixed at 84, find the minimum cost at which it can produce this output. Hence find average cost and marginal cost at this output level.

Example R12.6

A consumer has a utility function $U = 5q_1^4q_2^2$ where q_1 and q_2 are the quantities consumed of two goods. If the prices of the two goods are 6 and 9 respectively and can be regarded as constant, use the Lagrange method to find the quantities consumed that will maximise consumer utility when total expenditure is 54.

Find the value of the Lagrangian multiplier and interpret it.

Suppose total expenditure is increased to 540. What quantities of the two goods will now be consumed?

Appendix: the second-order conditions for maxima and minima in functions of two variables

Recall that if $y = f(x)$ then if $dy/dx = 0$ and $d^2y/dx^2 \neq 0$ then we can be sure we have either a local maximum or a local minimum. If z is a function of two variables

$$z = f(x, y) \tag{12A.1}$$

then the equivalent conditions that ensure a local maximum or minimum are $dz = 0$ and $d^2z \neq 0$ where d^2z is the change in dz. Since

$$dz = \frac{\partial z}{\partial x} dx + \frac{\partial z}{\partial y} dy \tag{12A.2}$$

then if we are to have $dz = 0$ for any possible values of dx and dy obviously we require $\partial z/\partial x = 0$ and $\partial z/\partial y = 0$. These are the first-order conditions. Since $\partial z/\partial x$ and $\partial z/\partial y$ are both functions of x and y, if we let $dz = h$ then

$$dz = h = h(x, y) \tag{12A.3}$$

Taking the total differential of h

$$d^2z = dh = \frac{\partial h}{\partial x} dx + \frac{\partial h}{\partial y} dy \tag{12A.4}$$

But from eqn [12A.2]

$$\frac{\partial h}{\partial x} = \frac{\partial^2 z}{\partial x^2} dx + \frac{\partial^2 z}{\partial y \partial x} dy \quad \text{and} \quad \frac{\partial h}{\partial y} = \frac{\partial^2 z}{\partial x \partial y} dx + \frac{\partial^2 z}{\partial y^2} dy \tag{12A.5}$$

Hence substituting in eqn [12A.4] and recalling that $\partial^2 z/\partial y \partial x = \partial^2 z/\partial x \partial y$ we have

$$d^2z = \frac{\partial^2 z}{\partial x^2}(dx)^2 + 2\frac{\partial^2 z}{\partial y \partial x}(dx)(dy) + \frac{\partial^2 z}{\partial y^2}(dy)^2 \tag{12A.6}$$

We can rewrite eqn [12A.6] as

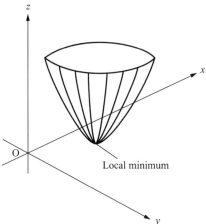

Fig. 12A.1 Local minimum

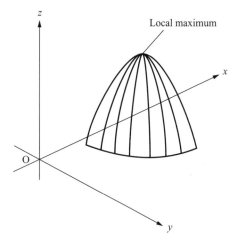

Fig. 12A.2 Local maximum

$$d^2z = (dy)^2 \left[\frac{\partial^2 z}{\partial x^2} \left(\frac{dx}{dy} \right)^2 + 2 \frac{\partial^2 z}{\partial y \partial x} \left(\frac{dx}{dy} \right) + \frac{\partial^2 z}{\partial y^2} \right] \qquad [12A.7]$$

For a local maximum or minimum we require $d^2z \neq 0$. Hence in eqn [12A.7] we require the term in square brackets to be non-zero. However, this is equivalent to requiring the quadratic equation in dx/dy

$$\frac{\partial^2 z}{\partial x^2} \left(\frac{dx}{dy} \right)^2 + 2 \frac{\partial^2 z}{\partial y \partial x} \left(\frac{dx}{dy} \right) + \frac{\partial^2 z}{\partial y^2} = 0 \qquad [12A.8]$$

to have no real solutions. Since $ax^2 + bx + c = 0$ has no real solutions when $b^2 < 4ac$, the condition for d^2z to be non-zero is

$$\frac{\partial^2 z}{\partial y^2} \frac{\partial^2 z}{\partial x^2} > \left(\frac{\partial^2 z}{\partial y \partial x} \right)^2 \qquad [12A.9]$$

Equation [12A.9] ensures that we have either a local maximum or a local minimum. We already know that if $\partial^2 z / \partial y^2$ and $\partial^2 z / \partial x^2$ are both positive then we have a local minimum, whereas if they are both negative then we have a local maximum.

If [12A.1] is graphed using a three-dimensional coordinate system, then local maxima and local minima appear as illustrated in Figs 12A.1 and 12A.2 respectively. If the first-order conditions $\partial z / \partial x = 0$ and $\partial z / \partial y = 0$ hold, but instead of [12A.9] we have

$$\frac{\partial^2 z}{\partial y^2} \frac{\partial^2 z}{\partial x^2} < \left(\frac{\partial^2 z}{\partial y \partial x} \right)^2 \qquad [12A.10]$$

then we have what is known as a *saddle point*.[9] This is because the three-dimensional graph of [12A.1] takes on the shape of a 'saddle' in the neighbourhood of such a point. A saddle point is illustrated in Fig. 12A.3.

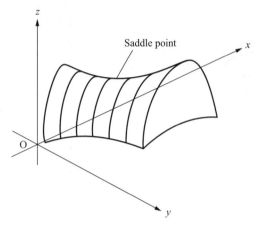

Fig. 12A.3 Saddle point

Notes

1. While these conditions are sufficient to ensure a local maximum/minimum they are not absolutely necessary. A re-examination of the general rules at the end of section 8.1 for distinguishing between stationary points should make this clear.
2. The difference between local and global minima is of course analogous to that discussed in section 8.1 in the context of functions of one variable.
3. If $\partial^2 z/\mathrm{d}y^2$ and $\partial^2 z/\mathrm{d}x^2$ are of opposite sign, then it is bound to be the case that

$$\frac{\partial^2 z}{\partial y^2}\frac{\partial^2 z}{\partial x^2} < \left(\frac{\partial^2 z}{\partial y \partial x}\right)^2$$

So as expected we have neither a local maximum nor a local minimum.
4. This is not, however, a global minimum. Graph the iso-$x = 0$ and iso-$y = 0$ curves if you are not convinced of this.
5. Under perfect competition the firm is too small relative to the markets it operates in either to influence the price of its product by its own sales or to influence factor prices by its own purchases of factors.
6. The Lagrangian [12.31], for example, is a function of three variables $F = F(x, y, \lambda)$. Conditions for local maxima and minima for such functions exist just as they do for functions of two variables. However, we shall not deal with them in this book.
7. For example, the iso-z curves could not be circular if $\partial z/\partial x > 0$ and $\partial z/\partial y > 0$.
8. The economist also often finds it necessary to assume that the iso-z curves never intersect the x- and y-axes. Without such an assumption there can be no *guarantee* that the Lagrange method will yield a positive solution. The constrained maximum tangency point could lie outside the positive quadrant if this extra assumption is not made.
9. If an equality sign holds in [12A.10] then it is necessary to examine the signs of higher-order differentials – that is, $\mathrm{d}^3 z$, $\mathrm{d}^4 z$, etc. – to determine whether we have a local maximum or minimum. The situation is similar to that for functions of one variable where the second-order derivative is zero.

13 Calculus in economics I: the firm

13.1 Isoquants and iso-cost lines

Consider a firm with a production function of the kind introduced in section 10.4

$$q = q(k, l) \tag{13.1}$$

Suppose the firm produces an output q_0. Since capital, k, and labour, l, are assumed to be continuously variable and infinitely divisible, there are an infinite number of possible combinations of k and l which could produce this given output. In the terminology of the last few chapters, such combinations trace out the iso-q curve corresponding to $q = q_0$. A family of such curves is shown in Fig. 13.1. In economics they are referred to as *isoquants*.

For example, the output q_0 could be produced either with very little capital and much labour (point B) or by a totally different technique involving little labour and much capital input (point A). It is generally assumed that production functions such as [13.1] are strictly quasi-concave, with positive marginal products $\partial q / \partial k$ and $\partial q / \partial l$. All isoquants are therefore convex to the origin. Also the further an isoquant is from the origin the larger the level of output to which it corresponds. That is, $q_3 > q_2 > q_1 > q_0$ in Fig. 13.1 The convexity of the isoquants can be justified by the argument that the more labour intensive the productive process in use, the harder it becomes to substitute even more labour for capital while leaving output unchanged. That is, when l is large relative to k, the greater the quantity of labour required to replace 1 unit of capital without changing output. Similarly the more capital intensive the process the greater the quantity of capital necessary to replace 1 unit of labour while leaving output unchanged.

Example 13.1

Consider the production function $q = 10\sqrt{(kl)}$. Show that the isoquant corresponding to an output $q = 100$ has an equation $l = 100/k$. Sketch this isoquant and verify that the isoquant corresponding to $q = 120$ lies further from the origin than the isoquant for $q = 100$.

We can obtain the slope of an isoquant by implicitly differentiating [13.1] in the manner of section 11.3

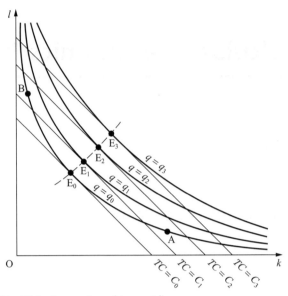

Fig. 13.1 Isoquants and iso-cost lines

$$\frac{\partial l}{\partial k} = -\frac{\partial q/\partial k}{\partial q/\partial l} \tag{13.2}$$

The negative of this slope is defined as the *marginal rate of technical substitution* of labour for capital (*MRTS*). It measures the rate at which the firm can substitute capital for labour while leaving output unchanged:

$$MRTS = -\frac{\partial l}{\partial k} = \frac{\partial q/\partial k}{\partial q/\partial l} \tag{13.3}$$

That is, the *MRTS* is the ratio of the marginal product of capital to the marginal product of labour. Notice that convexity of the isoquants implies a *diminishing marginal rate of substitution* as more and more capital is substituted for labour.

Example 13.2

Find the *MRTS* for the production function in Example 13.1.

The total cost of production is given by

$$TC = mk + wl \tag{13.4}$$

Assuming that the firm operates under conditions of perfect competition, m and w, the prices of capital and labour, can be taken as given. For such given m and w there will be an infinite number of possible combinations of capital and labour which will result in a same given total cost. Such combinations trace out the iso-cost curve corresponding to that level of total cost. A family of such curves is also graphed in Fig. 13.1. Because of the linear form of [13.4], they are all straight lines and are therefore referred to as *iso-cost lines*. For example, any point on the iso-cost line $TC = C_0$ represents a combination of k and l which, when substituted into

[13.4], results in a total cost of C_0. The equation of the iso-cost line corresponding to a total cost of C_0 can be obtained by rearranging [13.4]. That is,

$$wl = C_0 - mk \quad \rightarrow \quad l = \frac{C_0}{w} - \left(\frac{m}{w}\right)k$$

Since $m > 0$ and $w > 0$, an iso-cost line is negatively sloped and the further it is from the origin, the larger the total cost to which it corresponds. Hence in Fig. 13.1

$$C_3 > C_2 > C_1 > C_0 \tag{13.5}$$

Example 13.3

If $m = 4$ and $w = 16$ in [13.4], sketch the iso-cost lines corresponding to $TC = 110$ and $TC = 120$ and verify that the second iso-cost lies further from the origin than the first.

Although the economist typically assumes that a firm's ultimate aim is the maximisation of profits we shall begin our analysis of the firm by considering two subsidiary aims which can be formulated as constrained optimisation problems.

13.2 Constrained optimisation and the firm

Output maximisation subject to a cost constraint

A firm will obviously wish to maximise the output it can produce for a given total cost outlay. We can formulate this problem as that of choosing factor inputs k and l so as to maximise [13.1] subject to

$$mk + wl = C_0 \tag{13.6}$$

where C_0 is the given total cost. We therefore have a constrained minimisation problem. This problem satisfies all the conditions outlined at the end of Chapter 12 that are necessary to ensure that the Lagrange method will yield a local maximum as desired and that this local maximum will be a global maximum. The production function is strictly quasi-concave with positive marginal products, while the constraint is linear with m, w and C_0 all positive. Forming the Lagrangian in the usual way we have

$$F = q(k, l) - \lambda(mk + wl - C_0) \tag{13.7}$$

Partially differentiating with respect to k, l, and the Lagrangian multiplier λ and setting the derivatives to zero

$$\frac{\partial F}{\partial k} = \frac{\partial q}{\partial k} - \lambda m = 0 \tag{13.8}$$

$$\frac{\partial F}{\partial l} = \frac{\partial q}{\partial l} - \lambda w = 0 \tag{13.9}$$

$$\frac{\partial F}{\partial \lambda} = -mk - wl + C_0 = 0 \qquad [13.10]$$

Eliminating λ from eqns [13.8] and [13.9] we obtain what we referred to in section 12.3 as an optimality condition, which in this case takes the form

$$\frac{\partial q/\partial k}{\partial q/\partial l} = \frac{m}{w} \qquad [13.11]$$

Equation [13.10] is identical to the original constraint [13.6]. What [13.11] tells us is that if the firm is to maximise output then it must choose k and l so that *the ratio of the marginal products of capital and labour is made equal to the ratio of their prices*. Using [13.3], another way of stating this optimality condition is to say that the marginal rate of substitution of labour for capital should be made equal to the factor price ratio.

Since the *MRTS* is the negative of the slope of an isoquant whereas m/w is the negative of the slope of an iso-cost line, [13.11] implies that output maximisation occurs at a point of tangency between an isoquant and an iso-cost line. E_0, E_1, E_2 and E_3 are such points in Fig. 13.1. To determine which point of tangency, we of course refer to the constraint [13.6] which is the iso-cost line corresponding to C_0. Therefore E_0 is the point of output maximisation.

Equations [13.8] and [13.9] also yield the value of the Lagrangian multiplier as

$$\lambda = \frac{\partial q/\partial k}{m} = \frac{\partial q/\partial l}{w} \qquad [13.12]$$

From our discussion in Chapter 12 we know that λ tells us the increase in maximum possible output that results from a unit increase in the total outlay on factor inputs when factor prices are constant. That is, $\lambda = \partial q/\partial C_0$. Equation [13.12] in fact indicates that this increase will be the same regardless of whether the extra unit is spent on capital or labour.[1]

Example 13.4

If a firm's production is $q = 10\sqrt{(kl)}$ as in Example 13.1, find the maximum output that can be produced for a total cost of 160 if the iso-cost lines take the form $TC = 4k + 16l$ as in Example 13.3. Find the optimality condition and illustrate the optimal point graphically. Find and interpret the value of the Lagrange multiplier.

Cost minimisation subject to an output constraint

Suppose the firm's output is predetermined and it wishes to minimise the total cost of producing this given output. The firm now has to choose k and l so as to minimise

$$C = mk + wl \qquad [13.13]$$

subject to

$$q(k, l) = q_0 \qquad [13.14]$$

where q_0 is the given output level. The constraint implies that the firm is restricted (by the form of its production function) in the ways it can combine capital and labour to produce the given q_0.

The constrained minimisation problem we have formulated satisfies all the conditions of Chapter 12 that guarantee that the Lagrange method will yield the required global minimum. The objective function [13.13] is linear with factor prices m and w both positive, while the constraint [13.14] is the isoquant corresponding to $q = q_0$ and is derived from a quasi-concave production function with positive marginal products. We form the Lagrangian

$$G = mk + wl - \mu[q(k, l) - q_0] \qquad [13.15]$$

where we write the Lagrangian multiplier as μ to distinguish it form that in [13.7]. Setting the partial derivatives of G to zero

$$\frac{\partial G}{\partial k} = m - \mu \frac{\partial q}{\partial k} = 0 \qquad [13.16]$$

$$\frac{\partial G}{\partial l} = w - \mu \frac{\partial q}{\partial l} = 0 \qquad [13.17]$$

$$\frac{\partial G}{\partial \mu} = -q(k, l) + q_0 = 0 \qquad [13.18]$$

Eliminating μ from eqns [13.16] and [13.17] we obtain the optimality condition

$$\frac{\partial q / \partial k}{\partial q / \partial l} = \frac{m}{w} \qquad [13.19]$$

Notice that [13.19] is identical to the optimality condition [13.11]. If a firm wishes to minimise cost, then, just as when maximising output, it must choose k and l so that the ratio of marginal products is equal to the ratio of factor prices. Alternatively, the marginal rate of substitution must be set equal to the factor price ratio. The optimality condition [13.19] implies that, like constrained output maximisation, constrained cost minimisation occurs at a point of tangency between an isoquant and an iso-cost line. In this case, however, the firm while remaining on the given isoquant has to reach the lowest iso-cost line possible. Since the given isoquant is that corresponding to $q = q_0$ the point of cost minimisation is E_0 in Fig. 13.1.

Equations [13.16] and [13.17] also yield the value of the Lagrangian multiplier as

$$\mu = \frac{m}{\partial q / \partial k} = \frac{w}{\partial q / \partial l} \qquad [13.20]$$

In this case $\mu = \partial C / \partial q_0$. That is, the Lagrangian multiplier tells us the increase in minimum cost that results per unit increase in the output that has to be produced. Hence it tells us the *marginal cost* of producing an extra unit of output.[2] Equation [13.20] in fact tells us that this marginal cost will be the same whether the extra output is produced entirely by employing more capital or entirely by employing more labour.[3]

Notice that the point E_0 in Fig. 13.1 is both the solution to a constrained output-maximisation problem and a constrained cost-minimisation problem. This will in fact be so for all such points of tangency between isoquant and iso-cost curve. For example, the point E_3 represents the solution both to the problem of minimising the cost of producing an output q_3 and also to the problem of maximising the output that can be produced for a given total cost outlay of C_3.

Example 13.5

If a firm's production function is $q = 10\sqrt{(kl)}$ and $TC = 4k + 16l$ as in Example 13.4, find the minimum cost of producing an output $q = 100$. Find the optimality condition and illustrate the optimal point graphically. What is the marginal cost of producing an extra unit of output?

The dashed line through all such points of tangency in Fig. 13.1 is known as the firm's *expansion path*. The cost-minimising/output-maximising firm will select only those combinations of labour and capital which lie on its expansion path. The equation of the expansion path is given by the common optimality condition [13.19] since this is the condition for tangency between isoquants and iso-cost curves.

Example 13.6

What is the expansion path for the firm in Examples 13.4 and 13.5?

Example 13.7

A firm's production function is $q = 12\,000k^2l^2 - 2k^3l^3$. Find the expansion path. Find the maximum output that can be produced for a total cost of 300, if $m = 4$ and $w = 15$.

13.3 Profit-maximisation and cost-minimisation models

A firm is usually free to vary both its output and its total cost, unlike in the models of section 13.2. The economist normally assumes that both outputs and inputs will be varied so as to maximise profit. We considered the case of profit maximisation in section 12.2 where total profits

$$\Pi = pq(k, l) - mk - wl \qquad [13.21]$$

were maximised for given values of the output price, p, and the factor prices, m and w. The first-order conditions for profit maximisation were given by eqns [12.20] and [12.21]:

$$\frac{\partial q}{\partial k} = \frac{m}{p} \quad \text{and} \quad \frac{\partial q}{\partial l} = \frac{w}{p} \qquad [13.22]$$

That is, dividing the first of the conditions [13.22] by the second,

$$\frac{\partial q/\partial k}{\partial q/\partial l} = \frac{m/p}{w/p} = \frac{m}{w}$$

Thus a profit-maximising firm will choose a combination of capital and labour which lies on its expansion path. In other words, a profit-maximising firm is economically efficient in the sense that its output is produced at the minimum possible cost. Moreover, that output is the maximum that can be produced for that total cost outlay.

Under conditions of perfect competition in both product and factor markets the firm takes all prices as given. The profit-maximisation model consists effectively of three equations – the production function $q = q(k, l)$ and the two optimality conditions [13.22]. For given values of the exogenous real factor prices m/p and w/p, these three equations determine the values of the endogenous variables, q, k and l. The reduced form of the model therefore consists of three equations of the form

$$q = q* \left(\frac{m}{p}, \frac{w}{p} \right) \qquad\qquad [13.23]$$

$$k = k* \left(\frac{m}{p}, \frac{w}{p} \right) \qquad\qquad [13.24]$$

$$l = l* \left(\frac{m}{p}, \frac{w}{p} \right) \qquad\qquad [13.25]$$

For example, if the production function is

$$q = 0.6k^{0.5} + 0.4l^{0.5} \qquad\qquad [13.26]$$

then the conditions [13.22] yield

$$\partial q/\partial k = 0.3k^{-0.5} = m/p \quad \text{and} \quad \partial q/\partial l = 0.2l^{0.5} = w/p \qquad\qquad [13.27]$$

Thus the reduced form equations [13.24] and [13.25] become

$$k = \frac{0.09}{(m/p)^2} \qquad\qquad [13.24a]$$

$$l = \frac{0.04}{(w/p)^2} \qquad\qquad [13.25a]$$

We can now find the reduced form equation for output by substituting for k and l in the production function [13.26]:

$$q = 0.6 \left(\frac{0.09}{(m/p)^2} \right)^{0.5} + 0.4 \left(\frac{0.04}{(w/p)^2} \right)^{0.5}$$

or

$$q = \frac{0.18}{m/p} + \frac{0.08}{w/p} \qquad\qquad [13.23a]$$

Thus k, l and q have been expressed in terms of m/p and w/p alone.

In general, the first of the reduced form equations [13.23] tells us the output a firm is prepared to supply at given product and factor prices. Notice that the reduced form equation [13.23] *is homogeneous of degree 0 in the three prices p, m and w*. That is, equiproportionate changes in output price p and factor prices m and w will leave profit-maximising output unchanged. This is because in eqn [13.23], q depends on only the *ratios m/p and w/p* (i.e. relative or real factor prices) and not on the absolute values of p, m and w. Equiproportionate changes in these absolute values of course leave the ratios m/p and w/p unchanged. The homogeneity arises because the optimality conditions [13.22] involve merely the price ratios m/p and w/p and not the absolute prices p, w and m.

For given factor prices m and w, eqn [13.23] expresses output q as a function of output price p. If we graphed this relationship we would obtain the firm's *supply curve* – that is, it would tell us the outputs the firm was prepared to supply at different output prices. For example, if the factor prices are $m = 6$ and $w = 8$ in eqn [13.23a], then we obtain the firm's supply curve as $q = 0.04p$. This is a linear supply curve passing through the origin.

The last two reduced form equations [13.24] and [13.25] express the firm's demands for capital and labour in terms of the real factor prices m/p and w/p. Notice that these equations are also homogeneous of degree 0 in the absolute prices p, m and w. Thus equiproportionate changes in all prices leave the firm's factor demands unchanged.

Example 13.8

A firm has the production function $q = 10(kl)^{0.4}$ and faces the constant factor prices $m = 4$ and $w = 16$. If the firm is a profit maximiser and takes product price p as given, find its supply curve. If product price is 10, find the profit-maximising values of k, l and q. Demonstrate that a doubling of m, w and p leaves supply and the factor demands unchanged.

Obtain the reduced form equations [13.23], [13.24] and [13.25] when the production function takes the above form.

Once the optimal values of q, k and l are determined by the reduced form equations [13.23]–[13.25] we can find the firm's maximised profit by substituting these values for q, k and l into the profit equation [13.21].

While constrained output maximisation is rarely the ultimate objective of the firm, there are conditions under which the cost-minimisation model may be more appropriate than that of profit maximisation. When output is predetermined or outside the control of the firm, the aim must then be to minimise the cost of producing that output. Such a situation can arise in the provision of certain public utilities, for example gas, water or electricity. Under these conditions the second of the two models of the last subsection is applicable.

The constrained cost-minimisation model is essentially a two-equation model involving the production constraint [13.14] and the optimality condition [13.19]. These two equations determine the values of the two endogenous variables k and l, for given values of the exogenous factor price ratio m/w and q_0. Notice that since output is predetermined in this model, we treat q_0 as an exogenous variable. The reduced form of the cost-minimisation model has two equations of the form

$$k = k(m/w, q_0) \qquad\qquad [13.28]$$

$$l = l(m/w, q_0) \qquad\qquad [13.29]$$

The reduced form equations [13.28] and [13.29] tell us the firm's factor demands in the cost-minimising case. Notice that the cost-minimising factor demands are homogeneous of degree 0 in the factor prices m and w. That is, equiproportionate changes in m and w leave factor demands unchanged. This is because it is only the factor price *ratio* that appears in the optimality condition [13.19].

As an example of the cost-minimising model, consider again the production function [13.26]. The marginal products $\partial q/\partial k$ and $\partial q/\partial l$ in [13.27] are unchanged. The optimal condition [13.19] becomes

$$\frac{\partial q/\partial k}{\partial q/\partial l} = \frac{0.3k^{-0.5}}{0.2l^{-0.5}} = 1.5\frac{l^{0.5}}{k^{0.5}} = \frac{m}{w} \qquad [13.30]$$

From [13.30] we can obtain

$$l^{0.5} = \frac{2m}{3w}k^{0.5}$$

The output constraint [13.14] in this case is

$$0.6k^{0.5} + 0.4l^{0.5} = q_0 \qquad [13.31]$$

Substituting for $l^{0.5}$, rearranging and squaring gives the reduced form equation for l:

$$l = \frac{q_0^2}{\left[0.4 + 0.9(w/m)\right]^2} \qquad [13.27a]$$

Similarly for k

$$k = \frac{q_0^2}{\left[0.6 + 0.27(m/w)\right]^2} \qquad [13.26a]$$

As expected these factor demand equations are homogeneous of degree 0 in the factor prices m and w.

Once the firm's factor demands k and l are determined by the reduced form equations its minimum total cost can be obtained by substituting for k and l in the cost eqn [13.13]:

$$C = mk + wl = mk(m/w, q_0) + wl(m/w, q_0) \qquad [13.32]$$

Notice that for given factor prices, eqn [13.32] expresses the firm's total cost as a function of the predetermined output q_0. For example, if $m = 6$ and $w = 8$ in [13.26a] and [13.27a] then we obtain $k = 0.148q_0^2$ and $l = 0.391q_0^2$. Equation [13.32] then becomes

$$C = 4.01q_0^2 \qquad [13.33]$$

We shall have reason to refer back to equations such as [13.32] later in this chapter.

Example 13.9

A firm operating under conditions of perfect competition employs two factors of production both of which are variable. Its production function is $q = 4000x_1^{0.5} + 6000x_2^{0.75}$ where x_1 and x_2 are the factor inputs. If the product price is 2 units and the prices of the two factors are 6000 and 4000 respectively, find:

(a) the maximum output that can be produced for a total cost outlay of 200 000;
(b) the profit-maximising output and inputs.

13.4 The Cobb–Douglas production function

The Cobb–Douglas production function is given by

$$q = Ak^\alpha l^\beta \quad 0 < \alpha < 1, \, 0 < \beta < 1 \tag{13.34}$$

We have already come across functions of the type [13.34] on a number of occasions in this book (see Example 13.1, for instance, where $A = 10$, $\alpha = 0.5$ and $\beta = 0.5$). In fact the Cobb–Douglas production function has been much used in applied economics, because it has a number of convenient properties. The implied isoquants are convex to the origin and the marginal products of capital and labour are given by

$$\frac{\partial q}{\partial k} = \alpha A k^{\alpha-1} l^\beta = \alpha \frac{q}{k} \quad \text{and} \quad \frac{\partial q}{\partial l} = \beta A k^\alpha l^{\beta-1} = \beta \frac{q}{l} \tag{13.35}$$

Hence since α and β lie between 0 and 1 both marginal products are always positive. Also

$$\frac{\partial^2 q}{\partial k^2} = \alpha(\alpha - 1)Ak^{\alpha-2}l^\beta < 0 \quad \text{and} \quad \frac{\partial^2 q}{\partial l^2} = \beta(1 - \beta)Ak^\alpha l^{\beta-2} < 0 \tag{13.36}$$

since $\alpha - 1$ and $\beta - 1$ are both negative quantities, so that marginal products 'diminish' as input is increased.

Using [13.35]

$$\frac{\partial q}{\partial k}\frac{k}{q} = \alpha \quad \text{and} \quad \frac{\partial q}{\partial l}\frac{l}{q} = \beta$$

Thus α and β represent the *elasticities* of output with respect to capital and labour respectively. The Cobb–Douglas production function is homogeneous of degree $\alpha + \beta$ since

$$q(\lambda k, \lambda l) = A(\lambda k)^\alpha(\lambda l)^\beta = \lambda^{\alpha+\beta}Ak^\alpha l^\beta = \lambda^{\alpha+\beta}q$$

Hence if $\alpha + \beta = 1$ we have constant returns to scale, if $\alpha + \beta < 1$ we have decreasing returns to scale and if $\alpha + \beta > 1$ we have increasing returns to scale.[4]

We now consider the profit-maximisation and cost-minimisation models for the Cobb–Douglas function with $A = 2$, $\alpha = 0.3$ and $\beta = 0.6$ in eqn [13.34]. For profit maximisation, the optimality conditions [13.22] become, using [13.35],[5]

$$mk = 0.3pq \quad wl = 0.6pq \tag{13.37}$$

The three equations in the profit-maximisation model are therefore the optimality conditions [13.37] and the production function [13.34] which in this case becomes

$$q = 2k^{0.3}l^{0.6} \tag{13.38}$$

We can obtain the reduced form equation for q by substituting for k and l in [13.38] using [13.37]. This gives

$$q = 2\left(\frac{0.3pq}{m}\right)^{0.3}\left(\frac{0.6pq}{w}\right)^{0.6} \quad \rightarrow \quad q^{0.1} = 2(0.3)^{0.3}(0.6)^{0.6}\left(\frac{p}{m}\right)^{0.3}\left(\frac{p}{w}\right)^{0.6}$$

Hence

$$q = 1.29\left(\frac{p}{m}\right)^3\left(\frac{p}{w}\right)^6 \tag{13.39}$$

Substituting for q into eqns [13.37] yields the reduced form equations for k and l:

$$k = 0.387\left(\frac{p}{m}\right)^4\left(\frac{p}{w}\right)^6 \tag{13.40}$$

$$l = 0.774\left(\frac{p}{m}\right)^3\left(\frac{p}{w}\right)^7 \tag{13.41}$$

The three reduced form equations [13.39]–[13.41] are the present case equivalent to eqns [13.23]–[13.25]. Equation [13.39] is the firm's supply of output equation. Equations [13.40] and [13.41] are its factor demand equations. As expected, all the reduced form equations are homogeneous of degree 0 in the prices p, m and w.

In the cost-minimisation model, if the production function has the form [13.38] then the production constraint [13.14] becomes

$$2k^{0.3}l^{0.6} = q_0 \tag{13.42}$$

while the optimality condition [13.19] becomes, using [13.35],

$$mk = 0.5wl \tag{13.43}$$

Equations [13.42] and [13.43] are the two equations in the cost-minimisation model.

From eqn [13.43], $l = 2(m/w)k$. We can obtain the reduced form equation for k by substituting for l in eqn [13.42]:

$$2k^{0.3}2^{0.6}(m/w)^{0.6}k^{0.6} = q_0 \quad \rightarrow \quad 2^{1.6}k^{0.9}(m/w)^{0.6} = q_0$$

Solving for k we obtain

$$k = 0.292\left(\frac{w}{m}\right)^{2/3}q_0^{10/9} \tag{13.44}$$

since $2^{16/9} = 3.429$. Since $l = 2(m/w)k$, the reduced form equation for l is

$$l = 0.583\left(\frac{m}{w}\right)^{1/3}q_0^{10/9} \tag{13.45}$$

The two reduced form equations [13.44] and [13.45] are the present case equivalent to eqns [13.28] and [13.29]. As expected, they are homogeneous of degree 0 in the factor prices m and w.

The firm's minimised total cost is given by

$$C = mk + wl = 1.5wl \quad \text{(using eqn [1.43])}$$

Hence, using eqn [13.45] to substitute for l, we obtain

$$C = 0.875m^{1/3}w^{2/3}q_0^{10/9} \tag{13.46}$$

This is the Cobb–Douglas version of eqn [13.32]. For given m and w it expresses the firm's total costs as a function of its output. We shall return to eqn [13.46] shortly.

Example 13.10

If a firm operates under constant returns and has a Cobb–Douglas production function of the general form $q = Ak^{\alpha}l^{1-\alpha}$ find general versions of the three reduced form equations [13.39], [13.40] and [13.41]. Find also the general version of eqn [13.46].

13.5 Cost and revenue functions in the profit-maximisation model

Students of economics are normally introduced to the profit-maximising firm via cost and revenue functions or curves in the manner of section 8.3. How does this approach tie in with the profit-maximising model of the last few sections? The first point to note is that in section 8.3 the firm was assumed to face a downward-sloping market demand curve – that is, increased output could only be sold at a lower price. In the model of this chapter we have assumed perfect competition in the product market, so that, no matter what the firm's output, price is unaffected. Since price is taken as given, average revenue and marginal revenue are identical and both equal to price. Hence the condition for profit maximisation, introduced in section 8.3, that marginal revenue should equal marginal cost becomes under perfect competition

$$\text{price } p = MC \tag{13.47}$$

We can now show that the conditions for profit maximisation utilised in this chapter, that is eqns [13.22], do in fact imply the condition [13.47]. Firstly, remember that the profit-maximising firm is also a cost minimiser. The results of the cost-minimisation model apply to such a firm because its profit-maximising output has been produced at the minimum possible cost. We know from eqn [13.20] that if cost is minimised then marginal cost is given by

$$MC = \frac{m}{\partial q/\partial k} = \frac{w}{\partial q/\partial l} \tag{13.48}$$

However, from the optimality conditions [13.22], $\partial q/\partial k = m/p$ and $\partial q/\partial l = w/p$. Hence, substituting in [13.48] we see that both these equations reduce to $p = MC$. A firm which chooses its inputs so as to set marginal products equal to relative factor prices, as required by [13.22], is therefore automatically choosing its output so as to set price equal to marginal cost. The two conditions for profit maximisation are equivalent.

Although, in the profit-maximisation model of this chapter, we have assumed perfect competition, this does not mean that this approach is any less general than that based on revenue and cost curves. It is possible to relax the assumption of given product and factor prices although this leads to more complicated conditions for profit maximisation than those of [13.22].

Long- and short-run cost functions

The firm's total revenue curve can always be derived from its market demand curve in the manner of section 7.5. The derivation of a firm's total cost curve (from which its marginal cost is derived), however, requires rather more explanation. Firstly, remember again that the profit-maximising firm is also a cost minimiser, so that we can apply the results of the cost-minimising model. Secondly, a firm's total cost curve tells us *the minimum total cost at which different levels of output can be produced*. The cost-minimisation model in fact provides us with exactly such a relationship. Substitution of the reduced form equations [13.28] and [13.29] into the firm's cost equation [13.13] yielded eqn [13.30], which, for given factor prices m and w, tells us the minimum total cost of producing the output q_0. Equation [13.30] then, for varying levels of q_0, is the firm's total cost curve. For example, for the Cobb–Douglas production function [13.38] the equivalent of eqn [13.30] is eqn [13.46]:

$$C = 0.875m^{1/3}w^{2/3}q_0^{10/9}$$

Hence if, for example, $m = 64$ and $w = 27$ then the firm's total cost function is

$$C = 31.5q^{10/9} \tag{13.49}$$

Graphing [13.49] would yield the firm's total cost curve.

In the terminology normally used by economists the cost functions we have dealt with in this section are *long-run cost functions* since they are derived under the assumption that both the factors employed by the firm – capital and labour – are variable. In economics the *short run* for a firm is defined as a period of time over which inputs of one of the factors employed, for example capital, is fixed. Under such conditions it is possible to derive a short-run total curve for the firm. In the short run, total costs are given by

$$C = m\bar{k} + wl = \alpha + wl \quad (\alpha = \text{constant}) \tag{13.50}$$

Here $\bar{k}$ is the fixed level of capital input. The production function now becomes

$$q = q(\bar{k}l) = q^1(l) \tag{13.51}$$

That is, with capital input fixed, output becomes a function of labour input only. We can therefore rearrange [13.51] to express the labour input required to produce any given output. That is,

$$l = g(q) \tag{13.52}$$

Since there is only one possible way to produce a given output, there is no problem of cost minimisation when only one input is variable. The total cost of producing the given input is obtained simply by substituting for l from [13.52] into eqn [13.50]:

$$C = \alpha + wg(q) \tag{13.53}$$

Equation [13.53] is the firm's short-run total cost function.[6] For given w, it tells us the total cost of producing output q.

For the Cobb–Douglas function [13.38] the short-run production function is $q = 2\bar{k}^{0.3}l^{0.6}$ so that [13.52] becomes

$$l = (\tfrac{1}{2})^{5/3}\bar{k}^{-1/2}q^{5/3} = 0.315\bar{k}^{-1/2}q^{5/3} \tag{13.54}$$

The short-run total cost function [13.50] then becomes

$$C = m\bar{k} + 0.315\bar{k}^{-1/2}wq^{5/3} \tag{13.55}$$

For example, if $\bar{k} = 4$, $m = 64$ and $w = 27$, we have

$$C = 256 + 4.25q^{5/3}$$ [13.56]

The graph of [13.56] is the firm's short-run total cost curve. Fixed costs are 256 and variable costs are given by $4.25q^{5/3}$.

Example 13.11

A firm has the production function

$$q = 100\left(\frac{0.6}{k} + \frac{0.4}{l}\right)^{-1/2}$$

The prices of capital and labour can be regarded as fixed and equal to 27 and 8 respectively. Obtain expressions for:

(a) total cost as a function of output (i.e. the firm's total cost curve);
(b) profit-maximising output as a function of product price (i.e. the firm's supply curve). Perfect competition may be assumed in the product market.

What is the relationship between the expressions obtained in (a) and (b) above?

Example 13.12

A firm operating under perfect competition has the production function $q = (x_1x_2x_3)^{1/3}$ where q is output and x_1, x_2 and x_3 are input levels. In the short run the firm's input of the first factor is fixed at a level $x_1 = \bar{x}_1$. In the long run all the factors are variable. If input prices are 2, 4 and 8 respectively find:

(a) the firm's short-run cost function;
(b) the firm's long-run cost function.

Revision examples

Example R13.1

A firm's production function takes the Cobb–Douglas form $Q = 20K^{0.6}L^{0.7}$. Q is output and the prices of capital K and labour L are fixed and equal to $p_1 = 5$ and $p_2 = 6$ respectively.

(a) Write down expressions for: (i) the firm's *MRTS* of labour for capital; (ii) the firm's total cost.
(b) Determine the maximum output that the firm can produce for a total cost of $C_0 = 500$. What input levels are required to produce this output? Find and interpret the value of the Lagrangian multiplier.
(c) Solve the output-maximisation problem for the general case of factor prices p_1 and p_2 and given total cost C_0, obtaining functions for K and L in terms of p_1, p_2 and C_0. What do these functions represent?

Example R13.2

A firm's production function is $q = 8000(0.4k^{-2} + 0.6l^{-2})^{-0.5}$ where q is output and k and l are factor inputs. The prices of k and l are fixed and equal to 5 and 10 respectively. Find the firm's expansion path. Find the minimum cost of producing an output of 2000.

Example R13.3

A firm's cost function is $C = p_1 x + p_2 y$ where x, y are variable inputs with fixed prices p_1, p_2 respectively. The firm's production function is $q = 10x^{0.6}y^{0.5}$ where q is output.

(a) If $p_1 = 4$, $p_2 = 6$, find the cost-minimising values of x and y if output equals 600. Find the firm's marginal cost at its optimal point. Compare this with the firm's average cost.
(b) Find general expressions for: (i) the cost-minimising inputs and (ii) the cost-minimising output, as functions of q, p_1 and p_2. Interpret the minimum cost function.

Example R13.4

A firm's production function is $q = Ak^{\alpha}l^{\beta}$ and it faces constant factor prices w and m for labour and capital respectively. The firm maximises profit and also faces a fixed product price p.

(a) If $A = 10$, $\alpha = 0.3$, $\beta = 0.6$ and $m = 10$, $w = 20$, $p = 50$, find the profit-maximising levels of q, k and l.
(b) Derive, in terms of A, α, β, m, w and p: (i) the firm's supply of output equation; (ii) the profit-maximising factor demand equations.

Example R13.5

A firm employs three factors, x, y and z, at constant prices p_1, p_2 and p_3 and has a production function $Q = 10x^{0.2}y^{0.6}z^{0.2}$. If output Q is predetermined, find the cost-minimising values for x, y and z in terms of Q and the factor prices. If $p_1 = 3$, $p_2 = 6$ and $p_3 = 12$, find the firm's long-run cost curve.

In the short run inputs of the third factor are fixed at $z = 32$. If output Q is again predetermined, find (in terms of p_1, p_2 and Q) the values of x and y which minimise cost in the short run. If p_1, p_2 and p_3 again take the above values, find the firm's short-run cost curve.

Notes

1. If 1 unit of capital costs m units of money, an extra 1 unit of money will purchase $1/m$ units of capital and hence lead to an increase in output of $(\partial q/\partial k)/m$. Similarly an extra unit of money spent on labour will result in an increase in output of $(\partial q/\partial l)/w$. Equation [13.12] states that these output increases will be the same.

2. Marginal cost was defined at the beginning of Chapter 7.

3. If the increased output is obtained entirely by employing more capital then the increased capital input required will be $1/(\partial q/\partial k)$ and it will cost $m/(\partial q/\partial k)$. Similarly if increased output is the result of employing more labour it will cost $w/(\partial q/\partial l)$. Equation [13.20] states that these increases in cost will be the same.

4. See section 11.4.

5. Profit maximisation requires that both the first-order conditions [12.20] and [12.21] and the second-order conditions [12.22]–[12.24] hold. The optimality conditions [13.22] represent the first-order conditions while from [13.36] we see that the second-order conditions [12.22] and [12.23] are satisfied. It is not difficult to show that if the final second-order condition [12.24] is also to hold it is necessary that $\alpha + \beta < 1$, that is the production function [13.29] must exhibit decreasing returns to scale. For $\alpha = 0.3$ and $\beta = 0.6$, this condition is therefore met.

6. A long-run total cost curve can be shown to be the 'envelope' of the various short-run cost curves obtained by setting different values for k in eqns [13.50] and [13.51]. That is, the long-run curve touches each short-run curve but intersects none (see e.g. R. G. Lipsey (1989) *An Introduction to Positive Economics*, 7th edn, p. 198).

14 Calculus in economics II: the consumer

14.1 Utility maximisation

We introduced the concept of a utility function in section 10.4. In a very simple two-good world we can write a consumer's utility function as

$$u = u(q_1, q_2) \tag{14.1}$$

where u is utility and q_1 and q_2 are the quantities consumed of good 1 and good 2. The graph of all possible combinations of q_1 and q_2 which result in the consumer gaining the same utility level $u = u_0$ is known as an *indifference curve*. The consumer is indifferent between all points on such a curve since they yield the same utility. In the terminology of this book such a curve is the iso-u curve corresponding to $u = u_0$. A family of such curves is shown in Fig. 14.1.

The economist normally assumes that utility functions such as [14.1] are strictly quasi-concave with positive marginal products $\partial u/\partial q_1$ and $\partial u/\partial q_2$. Indifference curves are then convex to the origin and the further they lie from the origin the higher the utility level to which they correspond. That is, $u_3 > u_2 > u_1 > u_0$ in Fig. 14.1. The convexity of the indifference curves is justified by arguing that the greater is consumption of one good relative to the other, the more of this good is required to compensate the consumer for the loss of yet another unit of the other good, if utility is to remain unchanged.

The slope of an indifference curve is obtained by implicitly differentiating [14.1] in the manner of section 11.3:

$$\frac{dq_1}{dq_2} = -\frac{\partial u/\partial q_2}{\partial u/\partial q_1} \tag{14.2}$$

The negative of this slope is known as the marginal rate of substitution of one good for the other (*MRS*). That is,

$$MRS = -\frac{dq_1}{dq_2} = \frac{\partial u/\partial q_2}{\partial u/\partial q_1} \tag{14.3}$$

The *MRS* measures the rate at which the consumer can substitute good 1 for good 2 while maintaining utility unchanged. It is obviously analogous to the *MRS* of labour for capital defined as eqn [13.3]. The *MRS* of one good for another is, from [14.3], equal to the ratio of their marginal products. Convexity of indifference curves implies a *diminishing marginal rate of substitution* as more and more of one good is consumed relative to the other.

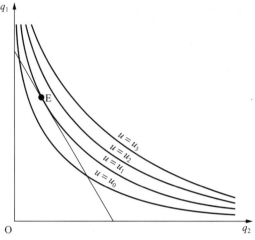

Fig. 14.1 Constrained utility maximisation

Example 14.1

A consumer has a utility function $U = (q_1^{-2} + q_2^{-2})^{-0.5}$. Show that the indifference curve corresponding to a utility level $U = 5$ has the equation

$$q_1 = \frac{5q_2}{\sqrt{(q_2^2 - 25)}}$$

Roughly sketch this indifference curve and confirm that the indifference curve corresponding to $U = 10$ lies further from the origin.

For the above utility function find: (a) the marginal rate of substitution of good 1 for good 2; (b) the marginal utility functions for each good. Do the marginal utilities decrease as consumption increases?

The quantity of goods 1 and 2 the consumer can purchase is limited by his/her income. Assuming that all income is spent on one or other of the goods, expenditure must equal income. That is,

$$p_1q_1 + q_2q_2 = Y \qquad\qquad [14.4]$$

where p_1 and p_2 are the prices of the two goods and Y is the consumer's money income. Equation [14.4] is known as the consumer's *budget constraint* since the quantities consumed, q_1 and q_2, must satisfy this equation. The budget constraint is obviously linear and a typical such line is graphed in Fig. 14.1. Since p_1, p_2 and Y are all positive, the constraint line is negatively sloped and intersects the q_1-axis above the origin.

The economist assumes that the consumer always seeks to maximise the utility derived from the consumption of goods. The consumer therefore aims to reach the 'highest' indifference curve possible, given that he/she must remain on the budget line. The consumer therefore has to solve a constrained maximisation problem – the maximisation of the utility function [14.1] subject to the budget constraint [14.4].

The consumer's constrained maximisation problem satisfies all the conditions given in Chapter 12 that guarantee that any solution in the positive quandrant yielded by the Lagrange method will be a global maximum. The utility function has been assumed strictly quasi-concave with positive marginal utilities, and the budget constraint [14.4] is linear with p_1, p_2 and Y all positive. The Lagrangian in this case is

$$F = u(q_1, q_2) - \lambda(p_1q_1 + p_2q_2 - Y) \qquad [14.5]$$

Setting partial derivatives to zero, we have

$$\frac{\partial F}{\partial q_1} = \frac{\partial u}{\partial q_1} - \lambda p_1 = 0 \qquad [14.6]$$

$$\frac{\partial F}{\partial q_2} = \frac{\partial u}{\partial q_2} - \lambda p_2 = 0 \qquad [14.7]$$

$$\frac{\partial F}{\partial \lambda} = -p_1q_1 - p_2q_2 + Y = 0 \qquad [14.8]$$

Eliminating the Lagrangian multiplier from [14.6] and [14.7] we obtain the optimality condition

$$\frac{\partial u/\partial q_2}{\partial u/\partial q_1} = \frac{p_2}{p_1} \qquad [14.9]$$

Equation [14.8] is of course another way of writing the budget constraint [14.4]. Thus, to maximise utility, the consumer must set the ratio of the marginal utilities of the two goods equal to the ratio of their prices. Alternatively, using [14.3], the marginal rate of substitution of one good for the other must be set equal to their price ratio. Since the *MRS* is the negative of the slope of an indifference curve while p_2/p_1 is the negative of the slope of the budget constraint, the optimality condition [14.9] simply states that the point of utility maximisation in Fig. 14.1 is a point of tangency between an indifference curve and a line with a slope equal to that of the budget constraint line. However, the point of utility maximisation must also be on the budget line. Hence we see that the optimal point is in fact at E in Fig. 14.1 where the budget line is tangential to the indifference curve corresponding to the utility level u_1.

Example 14.2

Suppose the consumer in Example 14.1 wishes to maximise utility and faces prices 8 and 4 respectively for the two goods. If total expenditure is to be 500, what is the consumer's budget constraint? How much of each good should be consumed? Illustrate the consumer's optimal point graphically.

Equations [14.6] and [14.7] also tell us the value of the Lagrangian multiplier. That is,

$$\lambda = \frac{\partial u/\partial q_1}{p_1} = \frac{\partial u/\partial q_2}{p_2} \qquad [14.10]$$

From our discussion of Lagrangian multipliers in Chapter 12, we know that λ, in this case, tells us the resultant increase in maximum utility per unit increase in consumer income Y. That is, $\lambda = \partial u/\partial Y$. Economists refer to $\partial u/\partial Y$ as the *marginal utility of income*.[1]

Example 14.3

Find the marginal utility of income for the consumer in Example 14.1.

There is an obvious analogy between the consumer's maximisation of utility subject to a constraint on his/her income and the problem we considered in section 13.2 – a firm's maximisation of output subject to a constraint on its total costs. In section 13.2 we examined another problem for the firm – that of cost minimisation subject to an output constraint. Can you formulate an analogous problem for the consumer?

14.2 Demand functions

Since the individual consumer is unlikely to be able to influence the price of goods that he/she purchases, we can regard p_1 and p_2 as exogenously determined in the utility-maximisation model. For a given level of consumer income, the model therefore consists of two equations, the optimality condition [14.9] and the budget constraint [14.4], which together determine the values of the endogenous q_1 and q_2 – the consumer's demands for the two goods. The two reduced form equations of the model will therefore be of the form

$$q_1 = q_1(p_1, p_2, Y) \qquad\qquad [14.11]$$

$$q_2 = q_2(p_1, p_2, Y) \qquad\qquad [14.12]$$

Equations [14.11] and [14.12] are known as the consumer's *demand functions* for goods 1 and 2.

   An important property of the demand functions [14.11] and [14.12] is that they are homogeneous of degree 0 in prices and the consumer's money income. That is, equiproportionate changes in the exogenous p_1, p_2 and Y leave the demands q_1 and q_2 unchanged. This property is most easily understood by considering the budget constraint [14.4]. Suppose p_1, p_2 and Y are all increased by the same factor k. The budget constraint then becomes

$$kp_1q_1 + kp_2q_2 = kY$$

   However, dividing throughout by k reduces the budget equation to its original form [14.4]. Thus the position of the budget constraint line in Fig. 14.1 is unchanged so that the point of utility maximisation remains at E. Equiproportionate changes in p_1, p_2 and Y have left q_1 and q_2 unchanged.

   Notice that the property of homogeneity of degree 0 implies that demand for each good depends not on absolute prices and money income but on *relative* prices and *real* income. That is, the demand functions [14.11] and [14.12] can be written in the form

$$q_1 = q_1^*\left(\frac{p_2}{p_1}, \frac{Y}{p_1}\right) \quad \text{and} \quad q_2 = q_2^*\left(\frac{p_2}{p_1}, \frac{Y}{p_1}\right) \qquad [14.13]$$

where p_2/p_1 is the *relative* price ratio for the two goods and Y/p_1 represents the maximum quantity of good 1 the consumer can purchase with his/her given money income – that is, it is a measure of *real* income. Since equiproportionate changes in p_1, p_2 and Y leave the ratios p_2/p_1 and Y/p_1 unchanged, eqns [14.13] imply that such changes leave demands unchanged. Hence they imply homogeneity of degree 0. It must be possible to write the demand function in this form if the homogeneity property is to hold.[2]

The student of economics will also be aware that demand functions such as [14.11] and [14.12] have the property that *own-price substitution effects are always negative*. This is the famous 'law of demand' that states that if, for example, the price p_1 in eqn [14.11] rises but the consumer is compensated for the loss of real income resulting from the price rise, then the consumer's demand q_1 for the first good will fall. In fact the the result of the price change can be decomposed into an *income change* and a *substitution effect*. We shall demonstrate this decomposition in a heuristic manner.

Consider eqn [14.11] again and suppose that p_1 rises by dp_1. The purchasing power of the consumer is reduced and suppose he/she is given compensation dY that just makes up for this loss of purchasing power. That is, the consumer receives just sufficient compensation to be able to buy the same bundle of goods (q_1 and q_2) as he/she purchased before the price change. Thus the compensation must be

$$dY = q_1 \, dp_1 \qquad [14.14]$$

That is, the price change dp_1 has been *compensated*.[3]

The consumer has now experienced two changes, the compensated dp_1 and dY. Supposing that the price of the second good remains unchanged, so that $dp_2 = 0$, we then have, taking the total differential of [14.11],

$$dq_1 = \frac{\partial q_1}{\partial p_1} dp_1 + \frac{\partial q_1}{\partial Y} dY \qquad [14.15]$$

Dividing [14.15] by the compensating price change dp_1 gives

$$\left(\frac{dq_1}{dp_1}\right)_{comp} = \frac{\partial q_1}{\partial p_1} + \frac{\partial q_1}{\partial Y}\frac{dY}{dp_1}$$

where $(dq_1/dp_1)_{comp}$ is the response of q_1 to a compensated price change. That is, the term in brackets represents the substitution effect.

From [14.14] we have $dY/dp_1 = q_1$, so that rearranging [14.15] gives

$$\frac{\partial q_1}{\partial p_1} = \left(\frac{dq_1}{dp_1}\right)_{comp} - q_1\frac{\partial q_1}{\partial Y} \qquad [14.16]$$

$\partial q_1/\partial p_1$, on the LHS of [14.16] is the total effect of a price change in p_1. Since $(dq_1/dp_1)_{comp}$ is the substitution effect, it follows from [14.16] that the income effect must be $q_1(\partial q_1/\partial Y)$.

Since own-price substitution effects are always negative (see e.g. J. E. Rowcroft (1994) *Mathematical Economics. An integrated approach*. Prentice Hall, Hemel Hempstead, p. 255), it follows from [14.16] that

$$\left(\frac{dq_1}{dp_1}\right)_{comp} = \frac{\partial q_1}{\partial p_1} + q_1\frac{\partial q_1}{\partial Y} < \phi \qquad [14.17]$$

Clearly a similar analysis is possible for a change in p_2. In fact for eqn [14.12] we have

$$\left(\frac{dq_2}{dp_2}\right)_{comp} = \frac{\partial q_2}{\partial p_2} + q_2\frac{\partial q_2}{\partial Y} < \phi \qquad [14.18]$$

where $(dq_2/dp_2)_{comp}$ is the own-price substitution effect for good 2.

Worked example

Suppose the consumer's utility function is given by

$$u = 2q_1^2 q_2^3 \tag{14.19}$$

The marginal utilities of the two goods are then given by

$$\frac{\partial u}{\partial q_1} = 4q_1 q_2^3 \quad \text{and} \quad \frac{\partial u}{\partial q_2} = 6q_1^2 q_2^2$$

The optimality condition [14.9] then becomes

$$\frac{6q_1^2 q_2^2}{4q_1 q_2^3} = \frac{p_2}{p_1} \quad \rightarrow \quad p_1 q_1 = \frac{2}{3} p_2 q_2 \tag{14.20}$$

Substituting for $p_1 q_1$ in the budget constraint [14.4] we have

$$\tfrac{2}{3} p_2 q_2 + p_2 q_2 = Y \quad \rightarrow \quad q_2 = 3Y/5p_2 \tag{14.21}$$

and using eqn [14.20]

$$q_1 = 2p_2 q_2/3p_1 \quad \rightarrow \quad q_1 = 2Y/5p_1 \tag{14.22}$$

Equations [14.21] and [14.22] are the consumer's demand functions. Notice that, as expected, equiproportionate changes in p_1, p_2 and Y leave q_1 and q_2 unchanged.[4]

Example 14.4

In the above example the utility function $U = q_1^2 q_2^3$ was shown to result in the demand equations [14.21] and [14.22]. Show that the following utility functions also lead to these same demand equations:

(a) $U = 2q_1^4 q_2^6$ (b) $U = 10q_1^2 q_2^3$ (c) $U = 50 + 10q_1^2 q_2^3$ (d) $U = 10q_1^4 q_2^6$

We can use eqns [14.21] and [14.22] to find the own-price substitution effects. For good 1, we have

$$\partial q_1/\partial p_1 = -0.4Yp_1^{-2} \quad \text{and} \quad \partial q_1/\partial Y = 0.4p_1^{-1}$$

For good 2 we have

$$\partial q_2/\partial p_2 = -0.6Yp_2^{-2} \quad \text{and} \quad \partial q_2/\partial Y = 0.6p_2^{-1}$$

Hence substituting in [14.17] and [14.18] we obtain

$$(dq_1/dp_1)_{\text{comp}} = -0.4Yp_1^{-2} + 0.4Yp_1^{-1}(0.4p_1^{-1}) = -0.24Yp_1^{-2} < 0$$

Similarly,

$$(dq_2/dp_2)_{\text{comp}} = -0.6Yp_2^{-2} + 0.6Yp_2^{-1}(0.6p_2^{-1}) = -0.24Yp_2^{-2} < 0$$

Thus both substitution effects are negative as expected.

Example 14.5

A consumer has the utility function $U = (q_1^{-2} + q_2^{-2})^{-0.5}$ as in Example 14.2. If the prices of the two goods are p_1 and p_2 respectively, and total expenditure is Y, find the consumer's demand equations for the two goods.

Generalisation to many goods

A typical consumer purchases many goods, not just two, and can be regarded as having a utility function of the kind [10.36], reproduced here

$$u = u(q_1, q_2, q_3, \ldots, q_n)$$ [14.23]

Assuming again that all income is spent the budget constraint now becomes

$$p_1q_1 + p_2q_2 + p_3q_3 + \ldots + p_nq_n = Y$$ [14.24]

where p_i is the price of good i and there are n goods in all.

Provided the utility function [14.23] is strictly quasi-concave and all n marginal utilities are always positive we can still apply the Lagrange method to solve the consumer's problem of minimising [14.23] subject to [14.24]. We now form the Lagrangian

$$F = u(q_1, q_2, q_3, \ldots, q_n) - \lambda(p_1q_1 + p_2q_2 + p_3q_3 + \ldots + p_nq_n - Y)$$ [14.25]

Partially differentiating with respect to $q_1, q_2, q_3, \ldots, q_n$ and λ and setting these derivatives to zero, we obtain n equations (one for each good) of the form

$$\frac{\partial F}{\partial q_1} = \frac{\partial u}{\partial q_1} - \lambda p_1 = 0$$

$$\frac{\partial F}{\partial q_2} = \frac{\partial u}{\partial q_2} - \lambda p_2 = 0$$

$$\frac{\partial F}{\partial q_3} = \frac{\partial u}{\partial q_3} - \lambda p_3 = 0$$ [14.26]

$$\vdots \qquad \vdots \qquad \vdots$$

$$\frac{\partial F}{\partial q_n} = \frac{\partial u}{\partial q_n} - \lambda p_n = 0$$

and

$$\frac{\partial F}{\partial \lambda} = -p_1q_1 - p_2q_2 - p_3q_3 \ldots - p_nq_n + Y = 0$$ [14.27]

We can take any pair of the equations [14.26] and eliminate the Lagrangian multiplier, λ, in the usual manner. For example, taking the third and fourth such equations we obtain an optimality condition

$$\frac{\partial u/\partial q_3}{\partial u/\partial q_4} = \frac{p_3}{p_4}$$

In all we obtain $n - 1$ such optimality conditions:

$$\frac{\partial u / \partial q_i}{\partial u / \partial q_j} = \frac{p_i}{p_j} \qquad\qquad [14.28]$$

Equations [14.28] imply that if the consumer is to maximise utility then the ratio of the marginal utilities for *any* two goods (e.g. good i and good j) must be set equal to the ratio of their prices. Equation [14.27] is, as usual, simply another way of writing the budget constraint [14.24].

The optimality conditions [14.28] together with the budget constraint [14.24] represent an n-equation system that determines the values of the endogenous quantities consumed, $q_1, q_2, \ldots, q_n$, in terms of the prices $p_1, p_2, \ldots, p_n$ and consumer income, Y. The reduced form of this system consists therefore of n equations of the form

$$q_1 = q_1(p_1, p_2, p_3, \ldots, p_n, Y)$$

$$q_2 = q_2(p_1, p_2, p_3, \ldots, p_n, Y)$$

$$q_3 = q_3(p_1, p_2, p_3, \ldots, p_n, Y) \qquad\qquad [14.29]$$

$$\vdots \qquad\qquad \vdots$$

$$q_n = q_n(p_1, p_2, p_3, \ldots, p_n, Y)$$

The n equations [14.29] represent the consumer's demand functions for the n goods. Each such equation expresses demand for a particular good in terms of all prices and consumer income, Y. As in the two-good case, the demand functions are homogeneous of degree 0 in prices and the consumer's money income. This is because equiproportionate changes in $p_1, p_2, \ldots, p_n$ and Y leave the budget constraint [14.24] unchanged.

Example 14.6

A household consumes three goods and has a utility function $U = q_1^2 q_2^3 q_3^4$. The household wishes to make a total expenditure of Y and faces given prices p_1, p_2 and p_3, respectively, for the three goods. If utility is to be maximised how much of each good should be consumed? What is the marginal utility of expenditure for such a household?

Market demands

We have made the implicit assumption throughout this chapter that, as far as the consumer is concerned, quantities purchased are the same as quantities consumed. For example, no distinction has been made between the q's appearing in the utility function [14.23] and the q's appearing in the budget constraint [14.24]. We have in fact ruled out the possibility that goods might be in any way durable and hence that stocks of a good might be held. Equations such as [14.29] hence yield not merely the consumer's desired consumption but also the consumer's desired purchases of goods. These are obviously flow demand equations but we now see that in the terminology of section 3.2 they are also market demand equations. The derivation of such equations under conditions where stocks of a good are held is more complicated and is beyond the scope of this book.

The flow demand equations we made use of in Chapters 3 and 4 referred to the total demand for a good, not merely that of an individual consumer. The flow demand, d_1, for a good in these chapters must therefore be regarded as the aggregate of all individual consumer's demands. That is,

$$d_1 = q_{11} + q_{12} + q_{13} + \ldots + q_{1N} \tag{14.30}$$

where q_{1i} is the demand for good 1 by the ith consumer and there are N consumers in all.

Since all the individual consumer demands are homogeneous of degree 0 in prices and money income, it follows that aggregate demand d_1 will have the same property. That is, equiproportionate changes in all prices and in each consumer's income should leave d_1 unchanged. Notice, however, that d_1 depends on *each* consumer's income, not just on aggregate income as we assumed in Chapters 3 and 4. Consumers are unlikely to have identical demand functions. This means that the market demand functions of earlier chapters are likely to shift if there is any change in the *distribution of income*. For example, suppose one consumer's income increases but another consumer's income falls by the same amount, leaving aggregate income unchanged. Since consumers are different, any increase in demand by the first consumer is unlikely to be exactly matched by a fall in demand by the second consumer. Hence, although aggregate income is unchanged, aggregate demand changes because of the alteration in the distribution of income.

14.3 Maximising utility over time

When we first formulated the budget constraint [14.4] we assumed that all income was spent. All the analysis that followed was based on this assumption. However, it is obvious that the normal consumer does not spend all his/her income – some of it is saved. We cannot therefore write the budget constraint as [14.4]. Also, once saving and its counterpart, borrowing, are permitted, it becomes clear that the total resources available to the consumer for the purchase of goods are no longer limited to his/her current income. Income may be supplemented by borrowing and by the spending of income saved from previous periods.

A consumer saves because he/she wishes to postpone consumption until some future period. Hence if we are to introduce saving into our analysis we have to consider the problem of maximising utility over an interval of time that is greater than the current 'period'. As an introduction to such *intertemporal utility maximisation* we shall consider a simple model in which the consumer aims to maximise utility over just two periods – the 'current period' and a next or 'future period' of equal length.

To simplify the analysis further we assume that the consumer consumes just one non-durable good. Total utility over the two periods is given by the function

$$u = u(c_1, c_2) \tag{14.31}$$

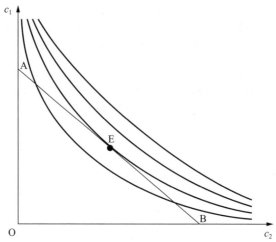

Fig. 14.2 Utility maximisation over time

where c_1 and c_2 are the quantities consumed in current and future periods respectively. If the utility function [14.31] is strictly quasi-concave with marginal utilities $\partial u/\partial c_1$ and $\partial u/\partial c_2$ which are always positive, then we can represent [14.31] by a system of convex indifference curves of the usual type. Such a system is illustrated in Fig. 14.2.

Suppose the consumer's income in the current period is Y_1 and that he/she expects an income of Y_2 in the future period. Assume the consumer has no resources 'carried over' from periods before the current period and wishes to have none 'left over' at the end of the future period. Suppose the price of the single good is p_1 in the current period and is expected to be p_2 in the future. Let r be the rate of interest per period at which it is assumed that the consumer can borrow or lend without limit. The maximum amount the consumer can spend during the current period is therefore $Y_1 + Y_2/(1 + r)$, that is current income plus the maximum amount he/she can borrow on the strength of expected income in the future. Notice that the consumer can borrow no more than $Y_2/(1 + r)$ because if he/she borrows more than this he/she would have to pay back more than Y_2 in the future period – an amount in excess of the consumer's income in that period. If spending is $Y_1 + Y_2/(1 + r)$ in the current period then future period spending must be zero since all income is used to repay the borrowing of the previous period. Total current consumption will then be

$$\text{OA} = \frac{Y_1 + Y_2/(1 + r)}{p_1} \qquad [14.32]$$

units of the good. Future consumption will of course be zero. Such a spending pattern is represented by point A in Fig. 14.2.

Consider next the opposite extreme where the consumer spends nothing in the current period. All income is saved and earns interest $Y_1 r$. Total resources available in the future period are therefore $Y_1(1 + r) + Y_2$, that is current-period income, plus interest earned on it, plus future-period income. If all these resources are spent in the future period then consumption in that period will be

$$OB = \frac{Y_1(1+r)+Y_2}{p_2} = \frac{Y_1 + Y_2/(1+r)}{p_2/(1+r)} \qquad [14.33]$$

units of the good, while current consumption will now of course be zero. This spending pattern is represented by point B in Fig. 14.2.

The line joining A and B in Fig. 14.2 represents the consumer's budget constraint. That is, it defines all possible combinations of c_1 and c_2 the consumer can choose, assuming there are no resources remaining at the end of the two periods. We can easily derive the equation of this budget constraint. Its slope is $-OA/OB$ and hence using [14.32] and [14.33] equals $-p_2/p_1(1+r)$. Since its intercept on the c_1-axis is given by [14.32] its equation is

$$c_1 = \frac{Y_1 + Y_2/(1+r)}{p_1} - \frac{p_2}{p_1(1+r)}c_2 \qquad [14.34]$$

or, rearranging,

$$p_1c_1 = Y_1 + \frac{Y_2}{1+r} - \frac{p_2c_2}{1+r} \quad \rightarrow \quad p_1c_1 + \frac{p_2c_2}{1+r} = Y_1 + \frac{Y_2}{1+r} \qquad [14.35]$$

The consumer therefore faces the problem of choosing c_1 and c_2 so as to maximise the utility function [14.31] subject to the budget constraint [14.35]. We therefore form the Lagrangian

$$F = u(c_1, c_2) - \lambda\left(p_1c_1 + \frac{p_2c_2}{1+r} - Y_1 - \frac{Y_2}{1+r}\right)$$

Setting partial derivatives to zero we obtain

$$\frac{\partial F}{\partial c_1} = \frac{\partial u}{\partial c_1} - \lambda p_1 = 0 \qquad [14.36]$$

$$\frac{\partial F}{\partial c_2} = \frac{\partial u}{\partial c_2} - \lambda \frac{p_2}{1+r} = 0 \qquad [14.37]$$

$$\frac{\partial F}{\partial \lambda} = -p_1c_1 - \frac{p_2c_2}{1+r} + Y_1 + \frac{Y_2}{1+r} = 0 \qquad [14.38]$$

Eliminating the Lagrangian multiplier from eqns [14.36] and [14.37] we obtain the optimality condition

$$\frac{\partial u/\partial c_2}{\partial u/\partial c_1} = \frac{p_2/(1+r)}{p_1} \qquad [14.39]$$

The LHS of [14.39] is obviously the ratio of the marginal utilities of c_2 and c_1. The quantity $p_2/(1+r)$ on the RHS of [14.39] can be interpreted as the present value (i.e. the value in period 1) of the price, p_2, that has to be paid for a unit of consumption in period 2. If this is not clear the reader should consult the section on present values in Chapter 6. We shall therefore refer to $p_2/(1+r)$ as a *discounted price*. The optimality condition [14.39] therefore states that, for the consumer to maximise utility over the two periods, then the ratio of the marginal utility of future consumption to the marginal utility of current consumption must be set equal to the ratio of the discounted prices of future and current consumption.[5]

Another way of interpreting [14.39] is to note that the LHS of this equation equals the negative of the slope of the indifference curves in Fig. 14.2. Implicitly differentiating [14.31]

$$\frac{dc_1}{dc_2} = -\frac{\partial u/\partial c_2}{\partial u/\partial c_1} \tag{14.40}$$

The negative of the slope of an indifference curve is the *marginal rate of substitution of current consumption for future consumption*. That is, it measures the rate at which a consumer can substitute current consumption for future consumption while maintaining total utility unchanged. Thus the condition [14.39] states that, if utility is to be maximised, the marginal rate of substitution of current for future consumption must be set equal to the ratio of their discounted prices.

Since the RHS of [14.39] is the negative of the slope of the budget constraint [14.34], while we have seen that the LHS equals the negative of the slope of an indifference curve, it is clear than the point of utility maximisation must be one of tangency between an indifference curve and the budget constraint – in fact point E in Fig. 14.2.

It is now possible to say something about the effect of price and rate of interest changes on consumption. Firstly, consider the effect of a change in the price ration p_2/p_1. Suppose, for example, current price p_1 rises relative to future price p_2. This has the effect of reducing the slope of the budget constraint line (see eqn [14.34]). The budget line in Fig. 14.2 in fact tilts in an anticlockwise direction. Suppose, however, the consumer is compensated with sufficient extra income in the current and/or future period so as to enable him/her to remain on the same indifference curve. Since the budget line tilts in an anticlockwise direction it is clear that the relative rise in current price, p_1, will lead to a decline in current consumption, c_1, and an increase in future consumption, c_2. That is, *the consumer responds by substituting future consumption for current consumption*.

Now consider the effect of a rise in the rate of interest r. From [14.34] we see that this also has the effect of tilting the budget line in an anticlockwise direction. Hence, provided consumer income is adjusted so as to leave the consumer on the same indifference curve, *the effect of an interest rate increase is for the consumer to substitute future consumption for current consumption* just as he/she does in response to a rise in current price relative to future price. In fact the interest rate rise can be regarded as a fall in the discounted future price, $p_2/(1 + r)$, and hence as making future consumption cheaper relative to current consumption.

Example 14.7

A consumer aims to maximise utility over two periods. The consumer's utility function is $U = c_1^3 c_2^2$ where c_1 is consumption in period 1 and c_2 is consumption in period 2. Prices are 30 and 22 respectively in the two periods and the rate of interest is 10 per cent. If the consumer's money income is 80 and 110 in the two periods respectively, and no income is saved, what will be the consumption levels in each period? How will the consumer react if the interest rate increases to 20 per cent? Comment on the changes in consumption levels.

Example 14.8

An intertemporal utility function is $U = c_1^\alpha + c_2^\alpha$ where α lies between zero and unity. c_1 and y_1 are consumption and income in the first period and c_2 and y_2 respectively refer to the second period. The price level p remains constant over the two periods and the rate of interest is zero. If utility is to be maximised show that

$$c_1 = c_2 = \frac{Y_1 + Y_2}{2p}$$

There are three reasons why c_1 and c_2 turn out to be equal in this question. What are these reasons?

For given values of r, p_1, p_2, Y_1 and Y_2 the above model is a two-equation system determining the values of the endogenous c_1 and c_2. The two equations are, of course, the optimality condition [14.39] and the budget constraint [14.35]. Notice, however, that since Y_1, Y_2 and r are taken as exogenous, the whole of the RHS of [14.35] is exogenously determined and we shall write it as W. That is,

$$W = Y_1 + \frac{Y_2}{1 + r} \qquad\qquad [14.41]$$

W is in fact the *present value of the consumer's two-period income stream*. We can also write the discounted price of consumption in period 2 as

$$p_2^* = \frac{p_2}{1 + r}$$

The budget line [14.31] can now be rewritten as

$$p_1 c_1 + p_2^* c_2 = W \qquad\qquad [14.42]$$

The optimality condition [14.39] and the rewritten budget constraint [14.42] can now be regarded as determining c_1 and c_2 for given values of the exogenous p_1, p_2^* and W. The reduced form of the model therefore consists of two equations of the form

$$c_1 = c_1(p_1,\ p_2^*,\ W) \qquad\qquad [14.43]$$
$$c_2 = c_2(p_1,\ p_2^*,\ W) \qquad\qquad [14.44]$$

Notice that eqn [14.43] states that current-period consumption depends not just on current prices and current income. It depends also on the discounted future price and on the present value of the consumer's current *and* future income. This result would be equally valid if we had included more than a single good in our model. If utility is maximised intertemporally, *the demand for any good will depend not merely on current prices and income but on current and future prices and on the present value of current and future income.*

It should be clear from the above that there is no theoretical justification for formulating demand equations expressing current demand for a good as a function of current prices and current income alone. Yet that is just what we have done in Chapters 3 and 4 of this book! Economists in fact frequently formulate demand equations in this way. Luckily it is possible to make sense of this approach, provided it is possible to assume that the consumer approaches problems of intertemporal utility maximisation in a certain way. Suppose the consumer solves these problems in two stages. Firstly, the consumer decides how much of the total resources at his/her disposal to spend in each of the periods (including the current period) over which he/she aims to maximise utility. The consumer does this by solving a problem similar to that discussed earlier in this section except that c_1, for example, now refers to total current expenditure rather than current demand for a single good. Secondly, having decided on total current expenditure, the consumer next decides on its allocation between various goods according to their relative current prices. Current demand for any good can then be expressed as a function of *current* prices and total *current* expenditure only.

Provided it is reasonable to regard the consumer as behaving in this way it is possible to make theoretical sense out of the demand equations of the first part of this chapter and of those of Chapters 3 and 4. The consumer income variable, Y, has to be reinterpreted as total expenditure. We can then regard the equations as being merely the consumer's solution to the second stage of his problem.

It is obviously somewhat implausible to regard the consumer as maximising utility over just two periods. However, the analysis of sections 14.1 and 14.2 can be extended to cover more than two periods without difficulty. Consider the two-period budget constraint [14.35]. We have already noted that the RHS of this constraint equals the present value of the consumer's current and future income. Notice now that the LHS of the constraint equals the present value of the consumer's current and future expenditure. It can be shown that the budget constraint in the multi-period case can be built up in the same way. For example, if there are T periods in all, then the present value of current and future income becomes

$$Y_1 + \frac{Y_2}{1+r} + \frac{Y_3}{(1+r)^2} + \frac{Y_4}{(1+r)^3} + \ldots + \frac{Y_T}{(1+r)^{T-1}} \qquad [14.45]$$

Similarly the present value of current and future expenditure is

$$p_1c_1 + \frac{p_2c_2}{1+r} + \frac{p_3c_3}{(1+r)^2} + \frac{p_4c_4}{(1+r)^3} + \ldots + \frac{p_Tc_T}{(1+r)^{T-1}} \qquad [14.46]$$

Provided that at the beginning of the current period the consumer has no resources carried over from the past and plans to have no resources left at the end of the final period, the multi-period budget constraint can be obtained by equating eqns [14.45] and [14.46]. The consumer then has to minimise a utility function, $u(c_1, c_2, c_3, \ldots, c_T)$, subject to this constraint. The application of the Lagrange method to this problem is left to the reader.

Example 14.9

A household plans to consume c_1, c_2 and c_3 over three successive periods. The price level p and the interest rate r are expected to remain constant over the three periods and the household expects to receive money incomes Y_1, Y_2 and Y_3 respectively. The household has an intertemporal utility function $U = c_1^3 c_2^2 c_3$. Let 'total money resources' W be defined as

$$W = Y_1 + \frac{Y_2}{1+r} + \frac{Y_3}{(1+r)^2}$$

If utility is to be maximised, show that c_1, c_2 and c_3 should all be proportional to 'total real resources' W/p, where the proportions depend on the rate of interest.

Revision examples

Example R14.1

A household has a utility function $U = x^{0.5} + y^{0.5}$, where x and y are the quantities consumed of two goods. Find the equation of the indifference curve corresponding to the utility level $U = 15$. Sketch this indifference curve.

Obtain an expression for the marginal rate of substitution of good 1 for good 2. If the household faces prices 3 and 6 respectively for the two goods and decides that total expenditure on the good is to be 450, how much of each good should be consumed?

Example R14.2

A consumer has a utility function $U = q_1^a q_2^b$, where q_1 and q_2 are the quantities consumed of two goods. The consumer faces a budget constraint $p_1 q_1 + p_2 q_2 = m$, where p_1 and p_2 are the respective prices of the two goods and m is total expenditure.

(a) If $a = 5$, $b = 3$, $m = 5000$, $p_1 = 4$ and $p_2 = 6$, what levels of demand, q_1 and q_2, will maximise utility? Find and interpret the value of the Lagrangian multiplier.
(b) Find general expressions for the utility-maximising demands in terms of a, b, p_1, p_2 and m. Comment on the properties of these demand functions.

Example R14.3

A household consumes quantities q_1 and q_2 of two goods and has a utility function

$$U = (q_1 - 3)^2 (q_2 - 5)^4 \quad \text{where } q_1 > 3 \text{ and } q_2 > 5$$

Prices p_1 and p_2 of the two goods are fixed and the household intends to make a total expenditure m. If utility is to be maximised find the demand functions for the two goods. (*Hint*: rewrite the budget constraint as $3p_1 + 5p_2 + p_1(q_1 - 3) + p_2(q_2 - 5) = m$.)

Example R14.4

A consumer's utility function is $U = q_1^3 q_2^4$ where q_1 and q_2 are the quantities consumed. If the prices of the goods are $p_1 = 3$ and $p_2 = 5$, write down an expression for the consumer's total expenditure Y.

(a) Suppose the consumer desires a utility level $U_0 = 5000$. If the consumer wishes to minimise expenditure on the two goods, what quantities of each good should he/she consume? What is the minimum expenditure required?
(b) Solve the above expenditure-minimising problem for the general case where the prices are p_1 and p_2 and where the given utility level is U_0; q_1 and q_2 will be functions of p_1, p_2 and U_0. What do these functions represent?

Example R14.5

Consider the quadratic utility function

$$U = 30x_1 + 20x_2 - 3x_1^2 - 6x_2^2$$

where x_1 and x_2 are the quantities consumed of two goods. If the prices of the goods are p_1 and p_2 respectively and total expenditure is Y, derive the demand equations for the goods, assuming utility maximisation. Verify that the demand equations are homogeneous of degree 0 in p_1, p_2 and Y.

Notes

1. It is sometimes referred to as the marginal utility of money. However, a more appropriate name would be the marginal utility of total expenditure. If some part of consumer income is saved, then Y cannot be regarded as income but is merely the consumer's total expenditure.
2. Alternatively, they could be written in the form $q_1 = q_1(p_1/p_2, Y/p_2)$ and $q_2 = q_2(p_1/p_2, Y/p_2)$.
3. In fact two approaches are possible. We can compensate the consumer sufficiently to maintain his/her level of utility constant or we can compensate the consumer sufficiently to enable him/her to purchase the same bundle of goods. In the main text we have adopted the second approach, but, for very small changes in price, the result is identical.
4. The demand functions [14.17] and [14.18] also have the special property that q_1 is not dependent on p_2 and q_2 is not dependent on p_1, that is, there are no 'cross-price' effects. However, this property is not a general one and is a consequence of the form [14.15] given to the utility function in this example.
5. The discounted price of current consumption is simply the current price p_1.

15 Exponential and logarithmic functions

In this chapter we introduce two special types of function which are frequently useful when dealing with the economics of growth. However, before dealing with these functions the reader should thoroughly revise the section on the powers of numbers on pages xix–xxiv of the material on mathematical prerequisites at the beginning of this text.

15.1 Exponential functions

Consider the functional relationship

$$y = 3^x \tag{15.1}$$

Since the independent variable x appears as a power or exponent in the function in [15.1], we refer to the function as an *exponential function*. The corresponding values for y for varying values of x between -3 and 2 and the graph of the relationship [15.1] are shown in Fig. 15.1.

In general, the function in any relationship of the form

$$y = a^x \quad \text{where} \quad a > 1 \tag{15.2}$$

is known as an exponential function. Since it is always the case that $a^0 = 1$, all exponential functions will therefore have an intercept on the y-axis equal to unity. Also, since for $a > 1$ it is the case that

$$\text{as } x \to -\infty, \quad y \to 0 \quad \text{and} \quad \text{as } x \to \infty, y \to \infty \tag{15.3}$$

all exponential functions will have graphs similar to that in Fig. 15.1. That is, as x becomes more and more negative, y gets closer to zero so that the graph approaches the x-axis. However, as x becomes more and more positive, the value of y increases without limit.

A more general type of exponential function is

$$y = ca^{bx} \quad \text{where} \quad a > 1, b > 0, c > 0 \tag{15.4}$$

The graph of [15.4] has a similar shape to that of [15.1] in Fig. 15.1, but, since $y = ca^0 = c$ when $x = 0$, the function in [15.4] cuts the y-axis at the point where $y = c$.

x	-3	-2	-1	0	1	2
$y = 3^x$	$^1/_{27}$	$^1/_9$	$^1/_3$	1	3	9

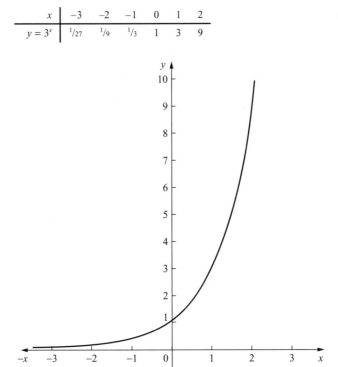

Fig. 15.1 An exponential function

Example 15.1

Graph the exponential functions $f(x) = 5^x$ and $g(x) = 2(5)^{2x}$ on the same diagram.

Example 15.2

The exponential function in eqn [15.3] can also have a b-value that is negative. For example, graph the exponential relationship $y = 4(2)^{-3x}$.

15.2 Logarithmic functions

We discussed inverse functions in section 1.6. Recall that, if a function expresses y in terms of x, then to find the inverse function we simply have to express x in terms of y. For example, [1.35] became [1.36].

Suppose we now require the inverse function of [15.1], $y = 3^x$. That is, *for any given y, the value of x we require is that power to which 3 has to be raised to obtain the original value of y.* For example, if y is 9 then the required value of x is 2 because the 3 in [15.1] has to be raised

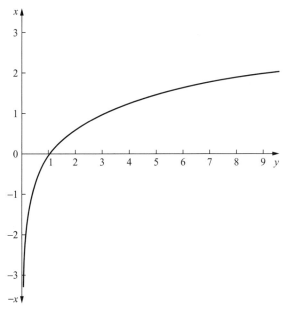

Fig. 15.2 A logarithmic function

to the power of 2 to give 9. That is, $3^2 = 9$. Similarly, if $y = 81$ then $x = 4$ because 3^4 is 81. Moreover, if $y = 1/27$ then the required value of x is -3 because the 3 in [15.1] has to be raised to the power of *minus 3* to give 1/27. That is, $3^{-3} = 1/27$.

The graph of this inverse function is shown in Fig. 15.2. It is obtained in the manner of section 6.1. That is, we invert the axis in Fig. 15.1, replotting the graph with the x-variable on the vertical axis and the y-variable on the horizontal. As usual, to obtain the graph of the inverse function, we rotate the axis anticlockwise through 90° and take the mirror image of the result.

However, how should we write the equation of the graph in Fig. 15.2? We can hardly keep writing 'the power to which 3 must be raised to yield y'. Mathematicians in fact use shorthand for these words, writing them simply as $\log_3 y$. That is, given eqn [15.1], we have

$$x = \log_3 y \qquad [15.5]$$

The function in [15.5], $f(y) = \log_3 y$, is an example of a *logarithmic function* or log function as it is often abbreviated to. The subscript 3 in [15.5] is known as the *base* of the logarithmic function.

Clearly any exponential function of the kind [15.2] will have an inverse function which will be a logarithmic function. For example, if $y = 8^x$ then $x = \log_8 y$. That is, x equals the power to which 8 has to be raised to yield y.

In general we write the inverse function of [15.2] as

$$x = \log_a y \quad (a > 1) \qquad [15.6]$$

where a is the base of the logarithmic function [15.6]. Logarithmic functions should provide readers with no difficulty if they just remember that [15.6] *is implied by and is in fact just another way of writing* [15.2].

Since the graphs of all logarithmic functions can be obtained by inverting axes for the corresponding exponential function, it should be clear that these graphs will all be similar to that in Fig. 15.2. All such graphs will intersect the y-axis when $y = 1$. Also, for all such functions

$$\text{as } y \to 0, \quad x \to -\infty \quad \text{and} \quad \text{as } y \to \infty, \quad x \to \infty \qquad [15.7]$$

Example 15.3

Graph the logarithmic function $f(x) = \log_6 4x$.

Example 15.4

The more general exponential function $y = ca^{bx}$ in [15.3] can also be inverted. Can you puzzle out the inverse function in this case?

Logarithms and their properties

The expression $\log_a y$ is spoken as 'the logarithm of y to the base a'. Since $x = \log_a y$ implies $y = a^x$ the logarithm of any number y is simply the power to which the base a must be raised to yield that number. For example,

$\log_{10} 100 = 2$	because $10^2 = 100$
$\log_6 216 = 3$	because $6^3 = 216$
$\log_3 3 = 1$	because $3^1 = 3$
$\log_8 \sqrt{8} = 1/2$	because $8^{1/2} = \sqrt{8}$
$\log_2(1/16) = -4$	because $2^{-4} = 1/16$
$\log_4(1/64) = -3$	because $4^{-3} = 1/64$

Notice that since the base a always exceeds unity *it is impossible to obtain the logarithm of a negative number.* For example, $\log_4(-3)$ does not exist since there is no value of x for which $4^x = -3$. For this reason the graphs of logarithmic functions always lie to the right of the y-axis as does that in Fig. 15.2.

You should have been able to work out the above logarithms without resorting to a calculator. The numbers have been carefully selected! To calculate the following, you should also manage without a calculator. However, if necessary, resort to the x^y button.

Example 15.5

Find: (a) $\log_4 64$; (b) $\log_7 343$; (c) $\log_{55} 1$; (d) $\log_3(1/27)$;
  (e) $\log_5 \sqrt[3]{5}$; (f) $\log_9 1$; (g) $\log_2(1/64)$; (h) $\log_3(1/81)$.

Logarithms have a number of useful properties which we shall now consider. All these properties in fact follow directly from the rules concerning exponents outlined at the beginning of this chapter. They hold for any value of the base $a > 1$.

Rule

$$\log_a xy = \log_a x + \log_a y \qquad [15.8]$$

The rule [15.8] may be easily proved. If we let $M = \log_a x$ and $N = \log_a y$ then from the definition of a logarithm we have $x = a^M$ and $y = a^N$. Hence

$$xy = a^M a^N = a^{M+N}$$

Again using the definition of a logarithm we therefore have

$$\log_a xy = M + N = \log_a x + \log_a y$$

Thus to obtain the logarithm of the product of two numbers we add the logarithms of those numbers.

Note that rule [15.8] can be extended to any number of variables. For example,

$$\log_a wxyz = \log_a w + \log_a x + \log_a y + \log_a z$$

The following rules for handling logarithms can also be easily derived using the rules for handling exponents. They also hold for any base $a > 1$.

Rule

$$\log_a(x/y) = \log_a x - \log_a y \qquad [15.9]$$

Rule

$$\log_a x^n = n \log_a x \qquad [15.10]$$

Rule

$$\log_a x = \frac{1}{\log_x a} \quad (x > 1) \qquad [15.11]$$

Notice that the rule [15.10] holds for any value of n. In particular it holds for $n = 0$. Hence since $x^0 = 1$ it follows that $\log_a 1 = 0$ – that is, *the logarithm of unity is zero* no matter what the base.

Worked example

Show that if

$$z = Kw^b x^c y^d \qquad\qquad [15.12]$$

then, for any base of logarithm,

$$\log z = \log K + b \log w + c \log x + d \log y \qquad\qquad [15.13]$$

To show this, firstly we take logs of both sides of [15.12]:

$$\log z = \log(Kw^b x^c y^d) \qquad\qquad [15.14]$$

$$= \log K + \log w^b + \log x^c + \log y^d \qquad\qquad \text{(using rule [15.8])}$$

$$= \log K + b \log w + c \log x + d \log y \qquad\qquad \text{(using rule [15.10])}$$

Example 15.6

(a) If $A = 5d^2 e^4 / b^3 c^4$, find $\log A$.
(b) If $K = 3w^{-3} x^3 y^6 z^{-4}$, find $\log K$.

The logarithms in Example 15.4 and earlier could be computed without the use of a calculator. But how do we calculate, for example, $\log_6(31.23)$ or $\log_4(231.4)$? Most calculators do not have a facility for working out logs to the base 6 or 4. Normally, however, calculators do have a button for calculating 10^x and its inverse function $\log_{10} x$. We can use this button to calculate, for example, $\log_6(31.23)$. We let $x = \log_6(31.23)$ so that

$$6^x = 31.23 \qquad\qquad [15.15]$$

Taking logs to the base 10 on both sides of [15.15] (using rule [15.10]) gives

$$x \log_{10} 6 = \log_{10}(31.23)$$

Hence using the $\log_{10}$ button on a calculator we have

$$0.7782x = 1.4946 \quad \rightarrow \quad x = 1.9206$$

Thus $\log_6(31.23)$ is 1.92. We can check this by using the x^y button and noting that $6^{1.92} = 31.23$.
Similarly if we let $x = \log_4(231.4)$ then $4^x = 231.4$. Taking logs to the base 10 gives $x\log_{10} 4 = \log_{10}(231.4)$. Hence, using a calculator

$$0.6021x = 2.3644 \quad \rightarrow \quad x = 3.9269$$

Example 15.7

Use the $\log_{10}$ facility on your calculator to find:

(a) $\log_8(65.3)$;　(b) $\log_3(1324)$;　(c) $\log_5(0.003\,45)$;　(d) $\log_7(728)$.

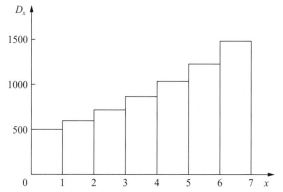

Fig. 15.3 Compound growth with interest paid once a year

15.3 The natural exponential function

The exponential functions which are of most interest to economists are those for which the constant, a, in eqns [15.2] and [15.4] takes a value approximately equal to 2.718 28. We shall see why this apparently strange constant is selected shortly. It is usually given the symbol 'e' so that [15.2] becomes

$$y = e^x \quad e \simeq 2.718\,28 \tag{15.16}$$

and [15.4] takes the more general form

$$y = ce^{bx} \tag{15.17}$$

The function in [15.16] is known as the *natural exponential function* and is often referred to as *the* exponential function. As we shall now see, its importance stems from the implications of such a function for the rate of growth in the dependent y-variable.

Recall from the beginning of Chapter 6 that a deposit of A invested at $100r$ per cent per annum 'grows' to $A(1 + r)$ after one year and in general to $A(1 + r)^x$ after x years. In deriving these expressions the assumption was made that interest was paid just once a year – in fact at the end of the year. That is, the value of the investment, D_x, grows in stepwise fashion. For example, if $A = 500$ and $r = 0.2$ or 20 per cent, then D_x would grow over time in the manner illustrated in Fig. 15.3. Notice that in Fig. 15.3 each step is 20 per cent 'higher' than the previous step so that the size of the steps increases over time. Since each step is $100r = 20$ per cent higher than that previous, *the rate of interest r can be interpreted as the annual proportionate growth rate in D_x over time*. That is, the growth rate is $r = 0.2$ or 20 per cent per annum.

Figure 15.3 could in fact refer to any economic variable whose growth rate is a constant 20 per cent per annum, provided of course that growth occurs only in sudden steps at the end of each year. Unfortunately many economic variables vary continuously rather than in a stepwise manner so we need to refine our analysis to allow for this.[1]

Referring back to the investment deposit example, suppose that interest, instead of being paid once a year at a rate r every year, is paid twice a year at a rate $r/2$ every six months. The value

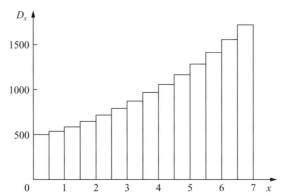

Fig. 15.4 Compound growth with interest paid twice a year

of the investment after six months is now $A(1 + r/2)$, after one year $A(1 + r/2)^2$, after 18 months $A(1 + r/2)^3$, etc. In general after x years it will be worth

$$D_x = A(1 + r/2)^{2x} \qquad\qquad [15.18]$$

Clearly the value of the investment will now grow over time in a manner similar to Fig. 15.3 except that the steps will occur every six months – that is, twice as frequently. Also, the steps will be only half as steep. For example, if $r = 0.2$ then each step will be just 10 per cent higher than the previous step. Such a time path is illustrated in Fig. 15.4.

Now suppose that interest is paid three times a year at a rate $r/3$, every four months. The value of the investment after four months will be $A(1 + r/3)$, after eight months $A(1 + r/3)^2$ and after one year $A(1 + r/3)^3$. In general after x years it will have grown to

$$D_x = A(1 + r/3)^{3x} \qquad\qquad [15.19]$$

Similarly if interest is paid four times a year at a rate $r/4$ then in x years' time the value of the investment will have grown to

$$D_x = A(1 + r/4)^{4x} \qquad\qquad [15.20]$$

A study of the sequence formed by eqns [15.18]–[15.20] makes it clear that if interest is paid m times a year at a rate equal to r/m then after x years the investment will have grown to

$$D_x = A(1 + r/m)^{mx} \qquad\qquad [15.21]$$

Obviously, the larger is m in [15.21], that is the more frequently interest is paid, the more frequent will be the steps in figures such as 15.3 and 15.4 and the smaller will be each individual step. It is now of interest to consider what happens, firstly to the figures and secondly to eqn [15.21], when m becomes very large indeed – that is, as m tends to infinity. Clearly the time path in the figures will eventually become a smooth curve, with the value of the investment increasing *continuously* over time.

The reader may object that no investment account pays interest continuously throughout the year. However, many economic variables, for example population, technological knowledge and the educational level of the work-force, can be regarded as varying continuously and it is often useful to consider the consequences of their growing at a constant rate. It is, then, of interest to discover what happens to eqn [15.21] as m becomes larger and larger. Since A is a constant we require

$$\underset{m\to\infty}{\text{Limit }} D_x = \underset{m\to\infty}{\text{Limit }} A(1 + r/m)^{mx} = A \underset{m\to\infty}{\text{Limit }} (1 + r/m)^{mx} \qquad [15.22]$$

Mathematicians have shown that in fact

$$\underset{m\to\infty}{\text{Limit }} (1 + r/m)^{mx} = e^{rx} \qquad [15.23]$$

where e is the rather mysterious number, approximately equal to 2.718 28, introduced at the beginning of this section.

We shall not attempt to prove the general result [15.23] but we can verify it for particular cases. For example, if $r = 1$ and $x = 1$ then [15.23] becomes

$$\underset{m\to\infty}{\text{Limit }} \left(1 + \frac{1}{m}\right)^{m} = e \qquad [15.24]$$

We can see that [15.24] is correct by actually examining what happens to $(1 + 1/m)^m$ as m becomes very large. The results of increasing m are shown below:

m	10	100	1000	10 000	100 000
$(1 + 1/m)^m$	2.5937	2.7048	2.7169	2.7181	2.7183

It can be seen that as $m \to \infty$, $(1 + 1/m)^m$ converges but it does not converge to any number that can be expressed as a fraction, however complicated. That is why we either write this number as 2.718 28 ... or give it the convenient symbol e. Equation [15.24] is in fact the mathematicians' definition of e. It is probably best thought of simply as a number similar to $\pi = 3.14159\ldots$, the ratio of the circumference of a circle to its diameter. Often, e is referred to as the *exponential constant*. Combining [15.22] and [15.23] and writing Limit $D_x = y$ we have

$$y = Ae^{rx} \qquad [15.25]$$

Equation [15.25] has the form [15.17] with $c = A = 500$ and with $b = r = 0.2$. But what [15.24] also tells us is that if a variable has a 'starting value' of A and grows *continuously* at a constant proportionate rate of r per annum then its value after x years of such growth will be Ae^{rx}. For example, if $A = 500$ and $r = 0.2$, then its value after $x = 10$ years will be

$$y = 500e^2 = 500(2.718\,28)^2 = 3694.5 \qquad [15.26]$$

Since eqn [15.25] refers to a variable that grows continuously over time it may be used to calculate the value of y for non-integer or fractional values of x. For example, if $A = 200$ and $r = 0.1$, then the value of the variable after 8.37 years is

$$y = 200e^{0.837} = 200(2.718\,28)^{0.837} = 200(2.309) = 461.8$$

The natural exponential function [15.16] has a similar shape to that shown in Fig. 15.1, intersecting the y-axis when $y = 1$, and is graphed in Fig. 15.5. The exponential function [15.25] is graphed in Fig. 15.6, for the case $A = 500$, $r = 0.2$. This curve cuts the y-axis at the point where $y = A = 500$. In the limit, that is as m becomes larger and larger, the step functions in Figs 15.3 and 15.4 gradually approach the smooth curve of Fig. 15.6.

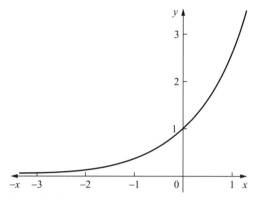

Fig. 15.5 The natural exponential function

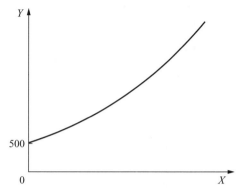

Fig. 15.6 The exponential function $Y = 500e^{0.2x}$

Example 15.8

A price index has a value of 20 at time $t = 0$ and grows exponentially at a constant rate of 0.2 per time period. What value will the price index take: (a) at time $t = 10$; (b) at time $t = 42.6$; (c) at time $t = 83.4$? Calculate the value of the price index when $t = -5.6$. How would you interpret this value?

Example 15.9

Real GNP in £ billions takes the value 114 in 1975 and the value 210 in 1985. The GNP series is an annual series increasing in stepwise fashion although the variable is a continuous variable.

(a) Use the relationship $D_x = D_0(1 + r)^x$ to calculate the average growth rate r per annum (i.e. per step) in the GNP series (D_0 = value at $x = 0$, D_x = value at $x = 1, 2, 3, 4, \ldots$).
(b) Use the relationship $D_x = D_0 e^{gx}$ to determine the average continuous exponential growth rate, g.

Compare the values obtained for r and g. Comment on any difference.

Example 15.10

Graph the function $f(x) = 10e^{-2x}$.

Example 15.11

An expenditure series has the value 50 at $t = 0$ but *declines* exponentially at a constant rate of 0.04 per time period (i.e. it has a *negative* growth rate). Find the value of the variable at times $t = 10$, $t = 12.4$ and $t = -6$.

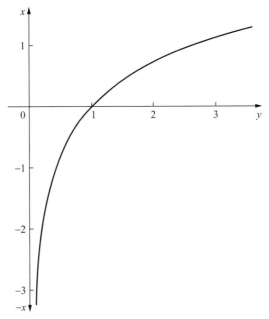

Fig. 15.7 The natural logarithmic function

Natural logarithms

Since [15.16] is the exponential function $y = e^x$, its inverse function is the logarithmic function

$$x = \log_e y \qquad\qquad [15.27]$$

The base of this logarithmic function is of course the exponential constant e. Thus in [15.27] x is the power to which e must be raised to yield y. This function is referred to as the *natural logarithmic function* and [15.27] is often written as

$$x = \ln y \qquad\qquad [15.28]$$

The natural logarithmic function is graphed in Fig. 15.7. It can of course be obtained by inverting the axes for the natural exponential function in Fig. 15.5.

The logarithm of a number or variable to the base e is known as a natural logarithm. These are the logarithms most commonly used by mathematicians for a reason that will become clear in section 15.5. Most calculators have a facility for calculating the natural log of a number. Thus

$$\log_e 26.4 = \ln 26.4 = 3.273$$

$$\log_e 2174 = \ln 2174 = 7.684$$

$$\log_e 0.05 = \ln 0.05 = -2.996$$

Example 15.12

Find the inverse function if: (a) $x = 4 \ln(3y)$; (b) $y = 3 \ln(6x)$; (c) $y = \ln(x^2)$.

15.4 The differentiation of exponential and logarithmic functions

We have seen that eqn [15.25]

$$y = Ae^{rx}$$

implies that if x represents time in, for example, years then y grows at a constant proportionate rate of r per year regardless of the value of A. We can therefore set $A = 1$ without altering this property. If we also set $r = 1$ we obtain the natural exponential function [15.16] reproduced here:

$$y = e^x \qquad\qquad [15.29]$$

Equation [15.29] therefore implies that y grows continuously at a constant proportionate rate of unity (i.e. 100 per cent) per year. The rate of change in y per year is dy/dx so that the proportionate change in y is $(1/y)dy/dx$. Hence [15.29] implies that

$$\frac{1}{y}\frac{dy}{dx} = 1$$

Hence

$$\frac{dy}{dx} = y \quad \text{so that} \quad \frac{dy}{dx} = e^x \qquad\qquad [15.30]$$

Differentiating the natural exponential function simply leaves that function unchanged! The exponential function is in fact the only function that has as its derivative that same function. It follows that

$$\frac{dy}{dx} = \frac{d^2y}{dx^2} = \frac{d^3y}{dx^3} = \frac{d^4y}{dx^4} = \ldots = e^x \qquad\qquad [15.31]$$

All higher-order derivatives of e^x are also equal to e^x.

We can obtain the derivative of the natural logarithmic function by using the inverse rule [7.56]. If

$$y = \ln x \qquad\qquad [15.32]$$

then since this implies $x = e^y$ and hence $dx/dy = e^y$, we have for [15.32]

$$\frac{dy}{dx} = \frac{1}{dx/dy} = \frac{1}{e^y} = \frac{1}{x} \qquad\qquad [15.33]$$

That is, the derivative of $\ln x$ is $1/x$. Recall that when discussing the power rule of integration in Chapter 9 we observed that eqn [9.7] did not apply when $m = -1$. We can now supply the missing case. From [15.33], obviously the integral of x^{-1} must be $\ln x + c$ where c is a constant of integration. Hence

$$\int bx^{-1}\,dx = b \ln x + c \qquad\qquad\qquad\qquad [15.34]$$

where b is any constant.

We cannot apply the rule [15.30] to differentiate more general functions such as [15.25]. We have to apply the chain rule [7.52] as well. For example, if $y = e^{2x^2}$, then letting $u = 2x^2$ we have $y = e^u$ and

$$\frac{dy}{dx} = \frac{dy}{du}\frac{du}{dx} = e^u 4x = 4xe^{2x^2}$$

Similarly

if $y = 8e^{3x}$ then $\dfrac{dy}{dx} = 8e^{3x} \times$ derivative $(3x) = 24e^{3x}$

if $y = e^{4x^2+3x}$ then $\dfrac{dy}{dx} = e^{4x^2+3x} \times$ derivative $(4x^2 + 3x)$

$$= (8x + 3)e^{4x^2+3x}$$

The chain rule must also be used to differentiate relationships of the kind $y = \ln f(x)$ where $f(x)$ is any function of x. For example,

if $y = \ln 6x$ then $\dfrac{dy}{dx} = \dfrac{1}{6x} \times$ derivative $(6x) = \dfrac{1}{x}$

if $y = 3 \ln (4x^2 + 3)$ then $\dfrac{dy}{dx} = \dfrac{3}{4x^2 + 3} \times$ derivative $(4x^2 + 3)$

$$= \frac{24x}{4x^2 + 3}$$

Example 15.13

Differentiate the following, if necessary using the chain and product rules:

(a) $5e^x$;

(b) $\ln (5x^2 + 6)$;

(c) $x^2 e^x$;

(d) $3xe^{-5x}$;

(e) $8e^{4x} \ln 3x^2$;

(f) $e^{3x}(2x^2 + 6x)$;

(g) $\ln (3x + 4)^{-0.5}$.

Example 15.14

In the last chapter we showed that, if the utility function $U = q_1^2 q_2^3$ is maximised subject to a budget constraint, then the demand equations [14.21] and [14.22] result. Show that identical demand equations arise if the utility function is

(a) $u = 2 \log q_1 + 3 \log q_2$ (b) $u = 10 e^{q_1^2 q_2^2}$

15.5 The natural exponential function in economics

As we noted earlier, it is sometimes convenient to assume that an economic variable grows continuously at a constant proportionate rate. If t is time and

$$z = z_0 e^{gt} \quad (g = \text{constant}) \tag{15.35}$$

then since, when $t = 0$, $e^{gt} = 1$, z_0 is the value of z when $t = 0$. Also since $dz/dt = z_0 g e^{gt}$ the proportionate rate of change in z is

$$\frac{1}{z}\frac{dz}{dt} = \frac{1}{z} z_0 g e^{gt} = g \tag{15.36}$$

Thus [15.35] implies that z has a 'starting value' of z_0 and grows at a constant proportionate rate of g per period of time. In such a case the variable z is said to 'grow exponentially' or to have an *exponential growth rate*.

The above interpretation of [15.35] no more than summarises in a slightly different notation what we deduced about eqn [15.25] earlier. The point is, however, that variables that grow exponentially have some convenient properties. For example, suppose $z = z(x, y)$ where x and y are functions of time. Then using [11.6] $dz = (\partial z/\partial x)\,dx + (\partial z/\partial y)\,dy$ and dividing throughout by dt we have

$$\frac{dz}{dt} = \frac{\partial z}{\partial x}\frac{dx}{dt} + \frac{\partial z}{\partial y}\frac{dy}{dt} \tag{15.37}$$

where dz/dt, dx/dt and dy/dt are the derivatives of z, x and y with respect to time.

If x and y grow exponentially at rates λ and μ respectively, then $x = x_0 e^{\lambda t}$ and $y = y_0 e^{\mu t}$. Hence

$$\frac{1}{x}\frac{dx}{dt} = \lambda \quad \text{and} \quad \frac{1}{y}\frac{dy}{dt} = \mu \tag{15.38}$$

From [15.37] it follows that the proportionate rate of growth in z is g where

$$g = \frac{1}{z}\frac{dz}{dt} = \frac{1}{z}\frac{\partial z}{\partial x}(x\lambda) + \frac{1}{z}\frac{\partial z}{\partial y}(y\mu)$$

Hence

$$g = E_x \lambda + E_y \mu \tag{15.39}$$

where E_x and E_y are the elasticities of z with respect to x and y respectively.

Equation [15.39] implies that if x and y have constant exponential growth rates λ and μ, then provided the elasticities E_x and E_y remain constant over time, z will grow exponentially at a rate $g = E_x\lambda + E_y\mu$. For example, suppose output is determined by the Cobb–Douglas production function [13.29]

$$q = Ak^\alpha l^\beta$$

Recall from section 13.4 that α and β in the Cobb–Douglas production function represent the elasticities of output with respect to capital and labour respectively. If capital input, k, and labour input, l, grow exponentially at rates λ and μ, then, applying [15.39], output q will grow at a rate

$$g = \alpha\lambda + \beta\mu \qquad [15.40]$$

Clearly if capital and labour were to grow at the *same* rate, λ, then output would grow at a rate $g = (\alpha + \beta)\lambda$. Hence if the production function exhibited constant returns to scale, that is $\alpha + \beta = 1$, output would *grow exponentially at the same rate as labour and capital*.

As a further example of the use of [15.39] consider the national income equation

$$Y = C + Z \qquad [15.41]$$

Suppose consumption, C, and non-consumption expenditure, Z, grow exponentially at rates λ and μ respectively. In this case since, from [15.41], both $\partial Y/\partial C$ and $\partial Y/\partial Z$ equal unity, we have

$$E_C = \frac{\partial Y}{\partial C}\frac{C}{Y} = \frac{C}{Y} \quad \text{and} \quad E_z = \frac{\partial Y}{\partial Z}\frac{Z}{Y} = \frac{Z}{Y} \qquad [15.42]$$

Hence [15.39] indicates that national income, Y, grows exponentially at a constant rate

$$g = \frac{C}{Y}\lambda + \frac{Z}{Y}\mu \qquad [15.43]$$

provided C/Y, the 'share' of consumption in national income, and Z/Y, the 'share' of non-consumption expenditure in national income, remain constant over time. If C and Z grow at the *same* constant rate, λ, then [15.43] becomes $g = (C/Y + Z/Y)\lambda = \lambda$. Hence national income will *grow at the same exponential rate as its components*.

As we have demonstrated, it is mathematically feasible for many economic variables to grow exponentially at exactly the same rate. This convenient property makes it possible to envisage a more general type of economic equilibrium than that considered in Chapter 3 where all variables remain constant over time. Equilibrium can also be thought of as a situation where all variables grow at the same rate over time. Such a notion of equilibrium is much used by economists in their discussion and theories of economic growth.

Example 15.15

Demand for a good is given by

$$q = Ap^{-0.4}s^{0.2}y^{0.4}$$

where p is own-price, s is the price of a substitute good and y is consumer income. p grows at an exponential rate 0.02, s remains constant and y grows at an exponential rate 0.05. Show that q grows exponentially and find its growth rate.

Example 15.16

In a market for a single good, the flow demand and supply functions are

$$d = ApY^2 \quad \text{and} \quad s = Bp^2$$

where A and B are constants, p is the price of the good and Y is an index of income. Y is exogenous and $d = s$ always. Find the reduced form for the system. If Y grows exponentially at a rate g, show that p, d and s must also grow exponentially and find their growth rates.

Revision examples

Example R15.1

Find the inverse functions of:

(a) $y = 4e^{6x}$ (b) $y = 3 \log_e(5x)$

Example R15.2

(a) Find, without using a calculator:

(i) $\log_5(125)$ (ii) $\log_3(243)$ (iii) $\log_{43}(1)$ (iv) $\log_8(64)$
(v) $\log_2(1/128)$ (vi) $\log_4(256)$ (vii) $\log_6(1/216)$ (viii) $\log_6\sqrt{6}$

(b) Use a calculator to find if possible:

(i) $\log_{10}(26.4)$ (ii) $\log_5(213.2)$ (iii) $\log_3(19)$
(iv) $\log_9(6)$ (v) $\ln(248)$ (vi) $\log_{10}(-5.3)$

Example R15.3

An index of population takes the value 105 in 1975 and grows exponentially at a constant rate of 5 per cent per annum. What value will the index take in 1985? What value did the index take in 1965?

Population growth slowed after 1985 and in 1995 the index had only reached 223. What was the growth rate between 1985 and 1995? If population growth continues at its 1985–95 rate, in which year will the index be 300?

Example R15.4

Differentiate the following:

(a) $5e^{2x}$ (b) $\ln(2x)$ (c) $5x^3 \ln(3x)$ (d) $2x^2 e^{3x}$

(e) x^2/e^{3x} (f) $\ln(2x + 4)^2$ (g) $\ln(3x)$ (h) $e^{-3x}\log(1 + x)^5$

Example R15.5

An aggregate wage index, W, is constructed as a weighted average of two sub-indexes, W_1 for the service sector and W_2 for the manufacturing sector. That is,

$$W = \alpha W_1 + (1 - \alpha)W_2 \qquad 0 < \alpha < 1$$

If W_1 and W_2 grow exponentially at constant rates g_1 and g_2 respectively, under what conditions will W also grow at a constant exponential rate? What will be the growth rate?

Note

1. Although many economic variables vary continuously, actual data on them may change in stepwise fashion. For example, data on national income might be collected for each year. Such a data series would then exhibit annual stepwise changes despite the fact that national income varies continuously.

16 Introduction to dynamics

16.1 Difference equations

In section 3.4 we made the important distinction between static and dynamic analysis in economics. We noted that, whereas static analysis of a model enabled us to determine the equilibrium values of the variables, a dynamic analysis involves the study of how a model or economic system behaves when it is in a state of disequilibrium. In particular, whereas a comparative static analysis tells us, following a disturbance, where a new equilibrium position is, a dynamic analysis enables us to determine whether such an equilibrium is ever actually reached.

We shall begin our introduction to dynamics by considering again the flow model given by eqns [3.10], [3.12] and [3.13]. This had an equilibrium point, depicted in Fig. 3.3, at which price $p = 11$ and both flow demand, d, and flow supply, s, equalled 2600. In section 3.4 we examined the consequences of a shift in the demand curve from eqn [3.12] to eqn [3.16]. The market could then be described by the equations reproduced below as

$$s_t = -700 + 300p_t \qquad\qquad [16.1]$$

$$d_t = 8400 - 400p_t \qquad\qquad [16.2]$$

$$d_t = s_t \qquad\qquad [16.3]$$

Notice that t subscripts have been added to the variables in eqns [16.1]–[16.3]; d_t, s_t, and p_t now refer to flow demand, flow supply and price in period t. If we regard the period in which the demand shift occurred as period $t = 0$ then, provided there are no further shifts in demand or supply, the above equations can be regarded as holding for all succeeding periods – that is, periods $t = 1$, $t = 2$, $t = 3$, $t = 4$, etc. The notation is such that p_8 refers to price in period $t = 8$, d_6 refers to flow demand in period $t = 6$, etc. This market had an equilibrium point, depicted in Fig. 3.4, with $p = 13$ and $d = s = 3200$. We shall now consider in some detail the problem of whether, following the demand shift, this new equilibrium is reached and, if so, by what path through time it is reached.

If we are to consider the behaviour of this market when it is in disequilibrium, then we must dispense with eqn [16.3] since this is a condition that ensures equilibrium (i.e. it rules out a state of disequilibrium). We shall replace eqn [16.3] by

$$p_t - p_{t-1} = \beta(d_{t-1} - s_{t-1}) \qquad \beta > 0 \qquad\qquad [16.4]$$

where β is a parameter the size and nature of which we discuss later and p_{t-1}, d_{t-1} and s_{t-1} are respectively price, flow demand and flow supply in period $t-1$; that is, in the 'preceding market period'. Equation [16.4] is in fact merely a mathematical statement of the dynamic assumptions [3.17] and [3.18]. It states that if $d_{t-1} - s_{t-1} > 0$, that is if flow demand exceeds supply in period $t-1$, then $p_t - p_{t-1} > 0$ and price will rise to be higher in period t than it was in period $t-1$. Similarly, if $d_{t-1} - s_{t-1} < 0$, that is if flow demand is less than flow supply, then $p_t - p_{t-1} < 0$ and price will fall. Notice that eqn [16.4] also includes equilibrium as a special case since it implies that if $d_{t-1} = s_{t-1}$, then $p_t = p_{t-1}$ so that price remains unchanged.

Equations [16.1], [16.2] and [16.4] represent a three-equation system in the variables s_t, d_t, p_t, s_{t-1}, d_{t-1} and p_{t-1}. It may appear that we now have too many endogenous variables for us to handle the model, but recall that p_{t-1} represents price in period $t-1$, or the *preceding* market period. If we regard the model as determining price, supply and demand in merely the *current* period, we can treat p_{t-1}, s_{t-1} and d_{t-1} as if they were exogenous.[1] We then have a three-equation model in the three truly endogenous variables s_t, d_t and p_t.

Substituting for d_{t-1} and s_{t-1} in eqn [16.4], using eqns [16.1] and [16.2], we obtain

$$p_t - p_{t-1} = \beta(8400 - 400p_{t-1} + 700 - 300p_{t-1})$$
$$= \beta(9100 - 700p_{t-1})$$

or rearranging,

$$p_t = 9100\beta + (1 - 700\beta)p_{t-1} \qquad [16.5]$$

Since β is a constant, eqn [16.5] expresses p_t in terms of the 'exogenous' p_{t-1} alone and is therefore the reduced form equation for p_t. Reduced form equations for s_t and d_t can be obtained by substituting for p_t in eqns [16.1] and [16.2].

Equation [16.5] is particularly useful because it can be used, firstly, to find the equilibrium price level and, secondly (provided β is known), to determine the time path of the price level when the market is in disequilibrium. Considering the equilibrium position first, this can only occur when $p_t = p_{t-1} = p^*$ where p^* is some constant level of price. Substituting for p_t and p_{t-1} in eqn [16.5] we obtain

$$p^* = 9100\beta + (1 - 700\beta)p^*$$

Hence

$$p^* - (1 - 700\beta)p^* = 9100\beta \quad \rightarrow \quad 700\beta p^* = 9100\beta \quad \rightarrow \quad p^* = 13$$

Equation [16.5] hence yields the new equilibrium price level following the demand shift as 13, the same value as obtained in section 3.4. However, we are now in a position to determine whether, starting from the previous equilibrium price level of 11, this new equilibrium is actually reached. Recall that period $t = 0$ is the last period during which the old equilibrium price level held – that is, period $t = 0$ is the period when the demand curve 'shifted'. We therefore have the *initial condition* $p_0 = 11$. For a given β, and given the initial condition, it is now possible to use eqn [16.5] to calculate the price levels prevailing in succeeding periods – that is, periods $t = 1$, $t = 2$, $t = 3$, etc. Suppose, for example, $\beta = 0.001$. Equation [16.5] then becomes

$$p_t = 9.1 + 0.3p_{t-1} \qquad [16.6]$$

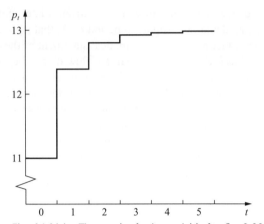

Fig. 16.1(a) Time path of price variable for $\beta = 0.001$

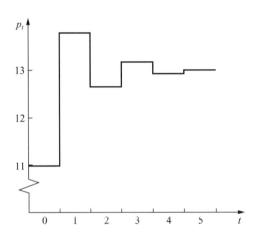

Fig. 16.1(b) Time path of price variable
for $\beta = 0.002$

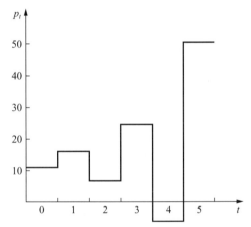

Fig. 16.1(c) Time path of price variable
for $\beta = 0.004$

Setting $t = 1$ in eqn [16.6] we obtain

$$p_1 = 9.1 + 0.3p_0 = 9.1 + 0.3(11) = 12.4$$

Similarly, setting $t = 2$ in eqn [16.6] we have

$$p_2 = 9.1 + 0.3p_1 = 12.82$$

For $t = 3$ we have

$$p_3 = 9.1 + 0.3p_2 = 12.946$$

Clearly by substituting $t = 4$, 5, 6, . . . into [16.6] we can generate the time path of the price variable as far into the future as we wish provided, of course, there are no further shifts in the demand and/or supply curves.

This time path is described in Fig. 16.1(a) from which it should be obvious that the price level converges gradually onto its equilibrium level $p^* = 13$. In this case then the model is stable in the sense that a new equilibrium is eventually reached.

The question naturally arises whether a new equilibrium will always be reached in this gradual way. Suppose instead of $\beta = 0.001$ we have $\beta = 0.002$. Equation [16.5] then becomes

$$p_t = 18.2 - 0.4p_{t-1} \tag{16.7}$$

We can use eqn [16.7] to trace the time path of the price variable, beginning with $p_0 = 11$, just as we did with eqn [16.6]. This yields $p_1 = 13.8$, $p_2 = 12.68$, $p_3 = 13.128$, ... This time path is plotted in Fig. 16.1(b). We see that, although the new equilibrium price level $p = 13$ is again reached, on this occasion price 'overshoots' the new equilibrium price level before converging on it.

Let us examine one further case. Suppose $\beta = 0.004$ in eqn [16.5]. We then have

$$p_t = 36.4 - 1.8p_{t-1} \tag{16.8}$$

Starting with $p_0 = 11$, we now obtain $p_1 = 16.6$, $p_2 = 6.52$, $p_3 = 24.664$, ... This time path is plotted in Fig. 16.1(c). In this case price not only overshoots its equilibrium value, but oscillations are set up which drive price further and further away from its new equilibrium. The market is unstable in the sense that the new equilibrium is never reached. The behaviour when in disequilibrium of the model described by eqns [16.1], [16.2] and [16.4] clearly depends on the value of the parameter β in [16.4]. β measures the responsiveness of price to a disequilibrium in demand and supply. The larger is β, the larger is the rise in price resulting from a given excess demand and the larger is the fall in price resulting from a given excess supply. Provided β is relatively small the market model is stable and moves eventually to a new equilibrium following a disturbance. However, for larger values of β, a disequilibrium in demand and supply leads to such a large response in price that, following a disturbance, not only is the new equilibrium overshot but 'explosive' oscillations are set up similar to those in Fig. 16.1(c).

We would not normally expect to find markets in which β was so large that explosive oscillations about the equilibrium price occurred. However, mathematically, we need to revise the assumptions [3.17] and [3.18] if we are to be certain that eqns [16.1], [16.2] and [16.4] represent a stable market model. We need to specify an appropriate value for β. We shall return to the flow market model later.

Example 16.1

Consider the dynamic flow market model

$$d_t = 5100 - 300p_t$$

$$s_t = -400 + 200p_t$$

$$p_t - p_{t-1} = \beta(d_{t-1} - s_{t-1})$$

(a) If $\beta = 0.001$, trace the future time path for p_t for: (i) $p_0 = 8$; (ii) $p_0 = 12$; (iii) $p_0 = 15$.
(b) If $\beta = 0.005$, trace the future time path for p_t for: (i) $p_0 = 10$; (ii) $p_0 = 11$; (iii) $p_0 = 12$.

A macro-economic example

Equations [16.6]–[16.8] are referred to as *first-order difference equations*. They are 'first-order' equations because they contain the variables p_t and p_{t-1} but not p_{t-2}, p_{t-3}, etc. Difference equations arise quite frequently in economics, specifically when we split time into discrete periods. In this subsection we consider a macro-economic model which leads to a *second-order* difference equation.

Consider the simple Keynesian model given by eqns [2.39]–[2.42]. First let us specify the consumption function [2.39] in more detail. We shall give it a linear form but also let us assume, perfectly reasonably, that consumption plans depend on expected income Y^e rather than actual income, Y. For example, suppose the consumption function is given by

$$C_t = 10 + 0.8Y_t^e \tag{16.9}$$

Where the t subscripts again refer to period t. The *MPC* is therefore 0.8 and 'autonomous' consumption, which is independent of income, equals 10 'units'.

The income expected by a consumer is to a large extent determined by the income the consumer has received in the past. Here we shall assume a very simple expectations-generating mechanism and write

$$Y_t^e = 0.5Y_{t-1} + 0.5Y_{t-2} \tag{16.10}$$

Expected income is thus simply the average income experienced in the previous periods $t-1$ and $t-2$. Substituting for expected income in eqn [16.9], the consumption function then becomes

$$C_t = 10 + 0.4Y_{t-1} + 0.4Y_{t-2} \tag{16.11}$$

Suppose that, just as in section 2.4, the levels of private capital investment and government expenditure are exogenous and given by constants $\bar{I}$ and $\bar{G}$. The equilibrium condition [2.42] then becomes, with t subscripts added,

$$Y_t = C_t + \bar{I} + \bar{G} \tag{16.12}$$

$\bar{I}$ and $\bar{G}$ do not have subscripts because they are constant for all t. Using eqn [16.11] to substitute for C_t in eqn [16.12] we have

$$Y_t = 10 + 0.4Y_{t-1} + 0.4Y_{t-2} + \bar{I} + \bar{G} \tag{16.13}$$

Equation [16.13] is a second-order difference equation in income. It is a *second*-order equation because it contains terms in Y_t, Y_{t-1} and Y_{t-2} but not Y_{t-3}, Y_{t-4}, etc. Just as for the market model of the previous subsection we can use this difference equation both to find the equilibrium level of income for given values of the exogenous $\bar{I}$ and $\bar{G}$ and, also, to trace the time path of income between two such equilibria.

Suppose, for example, $\bar{I} = 120$ and $\bar{G} = 80$. Equation [16.13] then becomes

$$Y_t = 210 + 0.4Y_{t-1} + 0.4Y_{t-2} \tag{16.14}$$

In equilibrium the level of income is constant, so that substituting

$$Y_t = Y_{t-1} = Y_{t-2} = Y^*$$

in eqn [16.14] we obtain

$$Y^* = 210 + 0.4Y^* + 0.4Y^* \quad \rightarrow \quad 0.2Y^* = 210 \quad \rightarrow \quad Y^* = 1050$$

For these values of $\bar{I}$ and $\bar{G}$ the equilibrium level of income is therefore 1050. Suppose now that the level of government expenditure $\bar{G}$ rises to 90 with I unchanged. Equation [16.13] now becomes

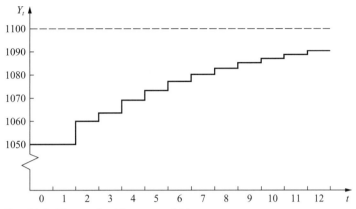

Fig. 16.2 Time path of income variable

$$Y_t = 220 + 0.4Y_{t-1} + 0.4Y_{t-2} \qquad\qquad\qquad\qquad [16.15]$$

Setting $Y_t = Y_{t-1} = Y_{t-2} = Y^*$ we obtain the new equilibrium level of income as 1100. However, will actual income move towards this new equilibrium and if so by what path? We can also use eqn [16.15] to answer these questions. Suppose the old equilibrium level of 1050 has persisted for a number of periods. We can therefore say that

$$Y_0 = Y_1 = 1050$$

are our initial conditions, whereas period $t = 2$ is the first period in which the new level of government expenditure is experienced. Given Y_0 and Y_1 we can now use eqn [16.15] to generate values for Y_2, Y_3, Y_4, etc. Setting $t = 2$ in eqn [16.15] we have

$$Y_2 = 220 + 0.4Y_1 + 0.4Y_0$$
$$= 220 + 0.4(1050) + 0.4(1050) = 1060$$

Similarly

$$Y_3 = 220 + 0.4Y_2 + 0.4Y_1$$
$$= 220 + 0.4(1060) + 0.4(1050) = 1064$$

and

$$Y_4 = 220 + 0.4(1064) + 0.4(1060) = 1069.6$$
$$Y_5 = 220 + 0.4(1069.6) + 0.4(1064) = 1073.44$$

Further income values are $Y_6 = 1077.22$, $Y_7 = 1080.26$, $Y_8 = 1082.99$, ... The time path of income for as many periods as required can be worked out in this manner. The time path is in fact represented in Fig. 16.2 and we see that income does indeed gradually approach its new equilibrium level of $Y = 1100$.

Example 16.2

Consider the Keynesian model

$$C_t = 20 + 0.6Y_t$$

$$I_t = 0.2(Y_{t-1} - Y_{t-2})$$

$$Y_t = C_t + I_t + G_t$$

If $G_t = 80 = $ constant, obtain a second-order difference equation for Y_t. Find the equilibrium value for Y_t. Trace the future time path for Y_t given the initial conditions $Y_0 = 200$, $Y_1 = 220$ and hence determine whether or not the equilibrium is stable.

16.2 Solving difference equations

While it is relatively simple to obtain the equilibrium level of income from equations such as [16.15] it is a tedious affair generating a whole sequence of values for Y in the above manner whenever we wish to determine whether an equilibrium point is ever reached. What we require is a *solution* to the difference equation of the form

$$Y_t = f(t)$$

where $f(t)$ is a function of t, so that we can determine what happens to Y_t as time passes by finding the limit of $f(t)$ as $t \to \infty$. In this section we consider methods of finding such solutions. Before starting, however, we should perhaps warn the reader that some of the procedures followed in this section, although straightforward, may appear a little arbitrary at first glance. The question 'why this?' will come naturally to mind. The answer in all cases is simply 'because it has worked in the past!'

Solutions to first-order linear difference equations

Consider the equation

$$X_t = 3X_{t-1} - 10 \qquad\qquad [16.16]$$

This is an example of a first-order *linear* difference equation – linear because it contains no awkward terms in X_t^2, etc., and because the coefficient on X_{t-1} is a constant and not itself a function of time.

The so-called *general solution* to eqn [16.16] can be shown to be the sum of the *complementary solution* and the *particular solution*.[2] Considering the particular solution first, this is simply what we referred to in section 16.1 as the equilibrium solution. To obtain it we set $X_t = X_{t-1} = X^*$, say, in eqn [16.16]

$$X^* = 3X^* - 10$$

Solving for X^* yields $X^* = 5$, so that this is the particular solution.

The complementary solution is the solution to the equation obtained by suppressing the constant -10 in eqn [16.16]. That is, the solution to

$$X_t = 3X_{t-1} \qquad\qquad [16.17]$$

We require a solution of the kind $X_t = f(t)$, so as a 'trial and error' process, let us try substituting $X_t = Am^t$, where A and m are constants, into eqn [16.17]. This gives

$$Am^t = 3Am^{t-1}$$

or dividing throughout by Am^{t-1}, a value $m = 3$. Hence any solution of the kind

$$X_t = A(3)^t \qquad\qquad [16.18]$$

where A is any arbitrary constant, will satisfy eqn [16.17]. This is the complementary solution referred to earlier.

As noted at the beginning of this subsection, it can be shown that a general solution to the original difference equation [16.16] can be obtained by simply adding together the particular solution $X^* = 5$ and the complementary solution [16.18]. This gives

$$X_t = A(3)^t + 5 \qquad\qquad [16.19]$$

We can easily verify that [16.19] makes LHS = RHS in the difference equation [16.16]. Clearly LHS is given by [16.19], whereas

$$\text{RHS} = 3[A(3)^{t-1} + 5] - 10$$

$$= 3A(3)^{t-1} + 15 - 10 = A(3)^t + 5 = \text{LHS}$$

Notice that the solution [16.19] still includes the arbitrary constant, A. We can find A provided we have an initial condition. That is, providing we have some 'starting value' for X. Suppose, for example, $X_0 = 7$. Letting $t = 0$ in [16.19]

$$X_0 = A + 5 = 7$$

Hence we must make $A = 2$, if the difference equation is to satisfy $X_0 = 7$. The complete solution to [16.16] is therefore

$$X_t = 2(3)^t + 5 \qquad\qquad [16.20]$$

Notice that [16.20] is of the required form $X_t = f(t)$, so that we can determine what happens to X_t as time passes by finding the limit of $2(3)^t + 5$ as $t \to \infty$. Since $(3)^t \to \infty$ as $t \to \infty$ it is clear that

$$X_t \to \infty \quad \text{as} \quad t \to \infty$$

Hence, as time passes, X_t increases without limit and does not tend to its equilibrium level $X^* = 5$. The equilibrium position is not a stable one.

Example 16.3

For the dynamic flow model of Example 16.1, obtain the first-order difference equation for the case $\beta = 0.001$. Find a general solution to this difference equation if $p_0 = 8$.

Example 16.4

Solve the following first-order equations:

(a) $Y_t = 1.5Y_{t-1} - 10$ with $Y_0 = 5$;

(b) $Y_t + 0.6Y_{t-1} = 8$ with $Y_0 = 12$;

(c) $Y_t = 0.9Y_{t-1}$ with $Y_0 = 3$;

(d) $Y_t = 1.2Y_{t-1} - 2$ with $Y_1 = 4$.

We now consider the general first-order difference equation

$$X_t = bX_{t-1} + k \tag{16.21}$$

Given an initial condition X_0, we shall examine the conditions under which the time path of X firstly exhibits cycles and, secondly, is stable in the sense it converges onto some equilibrium value. To solve the difference equation [16.21], we firstly require the particular solution. To obtain it we set $X_t = X_{t-1} = X^*$ in [16.21] in the usual manner. Hence

$$X^* = bX^* + k \quad \rightarrow \quad X^* = \frac{k}{1-b} \tag{16.22}$$

The equilibrium value of X is, as usual, given by the particular solution [16.22]. We now require the complementary solution, that is the solution to $X_t = bX_{t-1}$. Searching for a solution of the form $X = Am^t$, we obtain

$$Am^t = bAm^{t-1} \quad \rightarrow \quad m = b \quad \rightarrow \quad X_t = Ab^t \tag{16.23}$$

where A is an arbitrary constant. Equation [16.23] is the complementary solution.

The complete solution is, as usual, found by adding the particular solution [16.22] and the complementary solution [16.23]:

$$X_t = Ab^t + \frac{k}{1-b} \tag{16.24}$$

Finally, we choose A so that the initial condition X_0 is met. Letting $t = 0$ in [16.24], we have

$$X_0 = A + \frac{k}{1-b} \quad \rightarrow \quad A = X_0 - \frac{k}{1-b} \tag{16.25}$$

Substituting for A into [16.24] gives

$$X_t = \left(X_0 - \frac{k}{1-b}\right)b^t + \frac{k}{1-b} \tag{16.26}$$

The solution [16.26] satisfies both the difference equation [16.21] and the initial condition.

If we examine [16.26], we see that the value of b is crucial for the behaviour of the variable X over time. In particular, it is the value of b that determines whether X moves eventually to its equilibrium value of [16.22]. In fact if $-1 < b < 1$ then, because b^t in [16.26] must therefore tend to zero as t tends to infinity, it follows that X must tend to $k/(1-b)$, its equilibrium value. For these values of b the path of X is therefore stable. That is, we have a difference equation of the kind [16.6] in section 16.1, with a time path similar to Fig. 16.1(a).

However, if b lies outside the above limits, that is if either $b > 1$ or $b < -1$, then X will not move towards equilibrium and the time path of X will be unstable, diverging rapidly from its initial position. For example, if $b = 2$ in [16.26] then b^t will tend to infinity as t tends to infinity, as will the value of X.

Regardless of the stability or instability of X, whether the time path exhibits oscillations/cycles or not also depends on the value of b. If b is negative then X will exhibit oscillations, alternative periods showing rises and falls in its value. For example, the differential equations [16.7] and [16.8] both have $b < 0$ and have oscillating time paths as illustrated in Fig. 16.1(b) and Fig. 16.1(c). However, if b is positive then time paths do not exhibit oscillations.

Solutions to second-order linear difference equations

Consider the second-order equation

$$6X_t = X_{t-1} + X_{t-2} + 11 \qquad [16.27]$$

The solution procedure is no different from that for first-order equations. We first find the equilibrium or *particular* solution by substituting $X_t = X_{t-1} = X_{t-2} = X^*$ in eqn [16.27]. This yields

$$6X^* = X^* + X^* + 11$$

or $X^* = 11/4$ as the particular solution. To determine whether this equilibrium is ever reached, if we start from a non-equilibrium position, we require the complementary solution which is obtained by solving eqn [16.27] with the constant, 11, suppressed. That is,

$$6X_t = X_{t-1} + X_{t-2} \qquad [16.28]$$

Again we look for solutions of the kind $X_t = Am^t$. Substituting this into eqn [16.28] yields

$$6Am^t = Am^{t-1} + Am^{t-2}$$

Dividing throughout by Am^{t-2} we obtain

$$6m^2 - m - 1 = 0 \qquad [16.29]$$

or what is sometimes called the *auxiliary equation*. In this case it is quadratic and can be solved by factorisation to give two solutions for m:

$$(2m - 1)(3m + 1) = 0 \quad \rightarrow \quad m = \tfrac{1}{2} \quad \text{and} \quad m = -\tfrac{1}{3}$$

We therefore obtain two solutions to the difference equation [16.28], $X_t = A(\tfrac{1}{2})^t$ and $X_t = A(-\tfrac{1}{3})^t$. Since both solutions satisfy eqn [16.28], a weighted average of the two must also do so. That is,

$$X_t = w_1 A(\tfrac{1}{2})^t + w_2 A(-\tfrac{1}{3})^t \quad w_1 + w_2 = 1$$

or

$$X_t = A_1(\tfrac{1}{2})^t + A_2(-\tfrac{1}{3})^t \qquad [16.30]$$

where $A_1 = w_1 A$ and $A_2 = w_2 A$. Equation [16.30] is our complementary solution. Notice that it contains two arbitrary constants A_1 and A_2 since we can select w_1 and w_2 arbitrarily.

To find a general solution to the original eqn [16.27] we again just add the particular and complementary solutions to give

$$X_t = A_1\left(\frac{1}{2}\right)^t + A_2\left(-\frac{1}{3}\right)^t + \frac{11}{4} \qquad\qquad [16.31]$$

Since the solution [16.31] contains two arbitrary constants, we need to know two initial conditions if we are to find them. Suppose, for example, $X_0 = 5$ and $X_1 = 7$. Substituting $t = 0$ and $t = 1$ in eqn [16.31] yields

$$X_0 = A_1 + A_2 + \frac{11}{4} = 5$$

$$X_1 = \frac{1}{2}A_1 - \frac{1}{3}A_2 + \frac{11}{4} = 7$$

We therefore have two equations in the two unknowns A_1 and A_2 which can be easily solved to give $A_1 = 6$ and $A_2 = -15/4$. The complete solution to the difference equation [16.27] is therefore

$$X_t = 6\left(\frac{1}{2}\right)^t - \frac{15}{4}\left(-\frac{1}{3}\right)^t + \frac{11}{4} \qquad\qquad [16.32]$$

We can determine the behaviour of X_t as time passes by letting $t \to \infty$ in eqn [16.32]. Since both $(\frac{1}{2})^t$ and $(-\frac{1}{3})^t$ tend to zero as $t \to \infty$ we have that

$$X_t \to \frac{11}{4} \quad\text{as } t \to \infty \qquad\qquad [16.33]$$

Thus X_t gradually approaches its equilibrium value. Notice that this will always be the case whatever the initial conditions, since changing X_0 and X_1 will only affect the constants A_1 and A_2. Hence the equilibrium point $X^* = 11/4$ is a stable one.

Example 16.5

Solve the following second-order equations:

(a) $Y_t - 3Y_{t-1} - 10Y_{t-2} = 24$ with $Y_0 = 0$ and $Y_1 = 1$;
(b) $Y_t - 0.1Y_{t-1} - 0.2Y_{t-2} = 7$ with $Y_0 = 16$ and $Y_1 = 10$;
(c) $Y_t = 7Y_{t-1} + 2Y_{t-2} + 5$ with $Y_0 = Y_1 = 4$.

We now derive the solution for a general second-order difference equation of the type

$$aX_t + bX_{t-1} + cX_{t-2} = k \qquad\qquad [16.34]$$

with given initial conditions X_0 and X_1. We follow the usual procedure. If $X_t = X_{t-1} = X_{t-2} = X^*$, then substituting into [16.34] we have

$$X^* = \frac{k}{a+b+c} \qquad\qquad [16.35]$$

Equation [16.35] is the particular solution, telling us the equilibrium position.

As usual, to find the complementary solution, we look for solutions of the kind $X_t = Am^t$. Dropping k from [16.34], substituting for X_t and then dividing throughout by Am^{t-2}, we obtain the auxiliary equation

$$am^2 + bm + c = \phi \qquad\qquad [16.36]$$

which is a quadratic equation in m. We saw in section 1.5 that quadratic equations such as [16.36] will have two (real) solutions if and only if the condition $b^2 > 4ac$ is satisfied. For the moment we assume that this condition is satisfied and that [16.36] has two solutions $m = m_1$ and $m = m_2$. We shall consider situations where $b^2 < 4ac$ shortly.

Given the two roots m_1 and m_2 we can obtain a complementary solution of the form

$$X_t = A_1(m_1)^t + A_2(m_2)^t \qquad [16.37]$$

where A_1 and A_2 are arbitrary constants.

To find a complete solution to the difference equation [16.34] we add the particular solution [16.35] and the complementary solution [16.37] in the usual manner:

$$X_t = A_1(m_1)^t + A_2(m_2)^t + \frac{k}{a+b+c} \qquad [16.38]$$

Finally we choose the arbitrary constants so that the initial conditions are met. Equation [16.38] then satisfies both the difference equation [16.34] and the initial conditions.

An examination of [16.38] reveals that the values of m_1 and m_2 are crucial for the behaviour of X over time. Provided *both* m_1 and m_2 lie between -1 and $+1$, so that m_1^t and m_2^t both tend to zero as t becomes very large, X_t will converge onto its equilibrium value [16.35]. That is, the equilibrium is stable, no matter what the initial conditions. Note that the initial conditions affect only the values of the arbitrary constants A_1 and A_2 and do not appear in the equilibrium solution.

If *either* m_1 or m_2 or *both* lie outside the range -1 and $+1$, then the time path of X will be unstable, diverging rapidly from its initial position so that an equilibrium position can never be achieved. For example, it is easy to see that, as t tends to infinity, both $(3)^t$ and $(-2)^t$ diverge rapidly from zero.

Some complications

Consider the second-order equation

$$4X_t - X_{t-1} - 3X_{t-2} = 14 \quad \text{with } X_0 = 2, X_1 = 0.5 \qquad [16.39]$$

Suppose we attempt to find the particular solution in the usual manner.
Setting $X_t = X_{t-1} = X_{t-2} = X^*$, we have

$$4X^* - X^* - 3X^* = 14$$

This, unfortunately, just yields the incorrect statement $0 = 14$. In fact X *does not have an equilibrium of the kind* $X^* = constant$. When this happens we have to search for a particular solution of the kind $X_t = X^*t$, that is a 'moving' equilibrium where X changes at a *constant rate* of X^* per period. For example, when in equilibrium over the time periods $t = 10, 11, 12, \ldots$, X takes the values $10X^*, 11X^*, 12X^*, \ldots$ etc. If we substitute $X_t = X^*t$ into [16.39] we obtain

$$4X_t^* - X^*(t-1) - 3X^*(t-2) = 14$$

or

$$X^*t(4 - 1 - 3) + X^* + 6X^* = 14$$

Since the terms in X_t^* cancel out, this gives $X^* = 2$. Hence a particular solution is given by $X_t = 2t$. This implies a moving equilibrium in which X_t grows at a constant rate of 2 per period.

We can find the complementary solution in the usual way. The auxiliary equation is

$$4m^2 - m - 3m = 0 \qquad\qquad [16.40]$$

Factorising into $(4m + 3)(m - 1) = 0$ yields two roots $m_1 = -0.75$ and $m_2 = 1$. The complementary solution is therefore

$$X_t = A_1(-0.75)^t + A_2(1)^t = A_1(-0.75)^t + A_2 \qquad\qquad [16.41]$$

The complete solution to [16.39] can now be found in the usual way by adding on the particular solution $X_t = 2t$:

$$X_t = A_1(-0.75)^t + A_2 + 2t \qquad\qquad [16.42]$$

The arbitrary constants in [16.42], A_1 and A_2, can now be chosen so as to satisfy the initial conditions $X_0 = 2$, $X_1 = 0.5$. Letting $t = 0$ and $t = 1$ in [16.42], we have

$$X_0 = A_1 + A_2 = 2$$

$$X_1 = A_1(-0.75) + A_2 + 2 = 0.5$$

Solving yields $A_1 = 2$ and $A_2 = 0$. Thus [16.42] becomes

$$X_t = 2(-0.75)^t + 2t \qquad\qquad [16.43]$$

Equation [16.43] satisfies both the difference equation [16.39] and its initial conditions.

Investigation of [16.43] reveals that, as t becomes very large, X converges gradually to its moving equilibrium $X_t = 2t$. This is because the root $m_1 = -0.75$ lies within the range -1 and $+1$.

Repeated roots

Consider the equation

$$4X_t = 4X_{t-1} - X_{t-2} + 8 \qquad\qquad [16.44]$$

In this case there is a particular solution $X^* = 8$ and the auxiliary equation is

$$4m^2 - 4m + 1 = 0 \qquad\qquad [16.45]$$

Factorising

$$(2m - 1)(2m - 1) = 0$$

The auxiliary equation [16.45] has only one distinct solution, $m = \frac{1}{2}$. This is referred to as the case of repeated roots. It should be clear from section 1.5 that the general second-order equation [16.34] will have repeated roots whenever $b^2 = 4ac$, as is the case for eqn [16.44]. When we have repeated roots it can be shown that a complementary solution is given by[3]

$$X_t = A_1(m)^t + A_2 t(m)^t \qquad\qquad [16.46]$$

where m is the repeated root. In this case we have $m = \frac{1}{2}$ and the general solution as usual is obtained by adding the particular and complementary solutions yielding

$$X_t = A_1(0.5)^t + A_2t(0.5)^t + 8 \qquad [16.47]$$

Given the initial conditions, we obtain A_1 and A_2 by substituting $t = 0$ and $t = 1$ into [16.47]. Hence

$$X_0 = A_1 + 8 = 12$$

$$X_1 = 0.5A_1 + 0.5A_2 + 8 = 15$$

This gives $A_1 = 4$ and $A_2 = 10$. The complete solution is therefore

$$X_t = 4(0.5)^t + 10t(0.5)^t + 8 \qquad [16.48]$$

Since both $(0.5)^t$ and $t(0.5)^t$ tend to zero as t becomes very large, X_t converges on its equilibrium value of 8. The equilibrium is stable and independent of any initial conditions.

Example 16.6

Find general solutions to the following difference equations:

(a) $2Y_t = 8Y_{t-1} - 8Y_{t-2} + 21$ with $Y_0 = 12.5$ and $Y_1 = 20.5$;
(b) $Y_t = 1.1Y_{t-1} + 0.3Y_{t-2}$ with $Y_0 = 5$ and $Y_1 = 4$;
(c) $2Y_t = Y_{t-1} + Y_{t-2} + 5$ with $Y_0 = Y_1 = 5$;
(d) $3Y_t - 5Y_{t-1} + Y_{t-2} + 10 = 0$ with $Y_0 = 3$, $Y_1 = 5$;
(e) $Y_t - 3Y_{t-1} + 2Y_{t-2} + 4 = 0$ with $Y_0 = 8$, $Y_1 = 10$.

Hence in each case trace the time path of Y_t for $t = 0, 1, 2, 3, 4, 5, 6$.

Complex roots, cycles and stability

Consider the equation

$$X_t + X_{t-1} + 0.8X_{t-2} = 560 \qquad [16.49]$$

The particular solution in this case is $X^* = 200$. The auxiliary equation is

$$m^2 + m + 0.8 = 0 \qquad [16.50]$$

Equation [16.50] is a quadratic equation for which (recall section 1.5) $b^2 < 4ac$. This means it has no solution or, strictly speaking, no *real* solution or root. However, as we briefly noted in section 1.5, such a quadratic equation has what mathematicians call *unreal* or *complex* roots involving the square root of -1. We have not considered the question of complex roots in this book, so we are unable to present the solution of the difference equation [16.49]. However, what we can do is derive the time path for X_t for given initial conditions. This is described in Fig. 16.3 for the initial conditions $X_0 = X_1 = 100$. We see that the time path of X_t exhibits cycles about the equilibrium level of 200. Cycles are to be distinguished from the simple oscillations of Fig. 16.1(c) in that in Fig. 16.1(c) we have values alternatively above and below the equilibrium level. Although X_t cycles about the equilibrium level in Fig. 16.3, in a number of cases successive periods have values either below or above the 200 line.

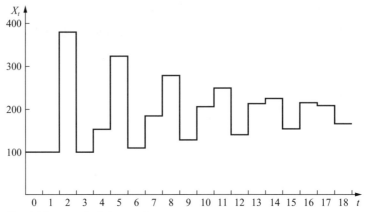

Fig. 16.3 A cyclical time path

It is in fact no coincidence that the first difference equation with complex roots we have considered should imply a cyclical time path. It can be shown that a necessary and sufficient condition for a second-order difference equation to imply cycles is that its auxiliary equation should have complex roots. Considering the general second-order difference equation [16.34], the auxiliary equation is [16.36] which is quadratic. Thus we can see that whenever $b^2 < 4ac$ we will obtain complex roots and hence a cyclical time path for X.

Whether a difference equation implies cycles or not, they can also be divided into those which imply stable time paths and those which imply instability. Stability and instability were illustrated in Fig. 16.1 for a first-order equation. Second-order equations can also imply stable or unstable time paths. Although we shall not prove it here, it can in fact be shown that the second-order equation [16.34] will trace out a stable time path, with X_t converging on its equilibrium value, if and only if

$$-1 < c/a < 1 \quad \text{and} \quad -(1 + c/a) < b/a < (1 + c/a) \tag{16.51}$$

Taking the difference equation [16.49] as an example, in this case $c/a = 0.8$ so the first condition in [16.51] is met and the second condition becomes $-1.8 < -b/a < 1.8$. Since $-b/a = 1$ the second condition is also met so the time path must be stable. Examination of Fig. 16.3 bears this out since the time path clearly converges on the equilibrium level of 200.

Example 16.7

Determine which of the following difference equations imply a stable equilibrium for Y:

(a) $4Y_t = 6Y_{t-1} - 3Y_{t-2} + 12$;

(b) $Y_t - 1.5Y_{t-1} + 0.7Y_{t-2} = 50$;

(c) $5Y_t - 7Y_{t-1} - Y_{t-2} = 80$;

(d) $Y_t + 0.6Y_{t-1} + 0.5Y_{t-2} = 3$.

Which of the above equations imply cycles?

16.3 The dynamic flow market model again

We now return to the flow model of section 16.1. We are now in a position to derive the general solution to the difference equation that arises out of this model. Generalising, suppose the flow supply and flow demand equations are

$$s_t = a_0 + a_1 p_t \tag{16.52}$$

$$d_t = b_0 + b_1 p_t \tag{16.53}$$

Substituting in the disequilibrium equation [16.4] we have

$$p_t - p_{t-1} = \beta(b_0 + b_1 p_{t-1} - a_0 - a_1 p_{t-1})$$

$$= \beta(b_0 - a_0) + \beta(b_1 - a_1) p_{t-1}$$

Hence we obtain the first-order difference equation

$$p_t - [1 + \beta(b_1 - a_1)] p_{t-1} = \beta(b_0 - a_0) \tag{16.54}$$

The particular solution to eqn [16.54] is easily obtained as

$$p^* = \frac{b_0 - a_0}{a_1 - b_1} \tag{16.55}$$

The auxiliary equation yields $m = 1 + \beta(b_1 - a_1)$, so that the complementary solution is

$$p_t = A[1 + \beta(b_1 - a_1)]^t$$

where A is an arbitrary constant. The general solution is therefore

$$p_t = A[1 + \beta(b_1 - a_1)]^t + \frac{b_0 - a_0}{a_1 - b_1} \tag{16.56}$$

The market clearly has an equilibrium price level given by p^* in eqn [16.55] but is the market stable? Will price converge on its equilibrium value, starting from a position of disequilibrium? For this to happen we require that $[1 + \beta(b_1 - a_1)]^t$ should tend to zero as t tends to infinity. This will happen when $1 + \beta(b_1 - a_1)$ lies between 1 and −1, that is

$$1 + \beta(b_1 - a_1) < 1 \quad \text{and} \quad 1 + \beta(b_1 - a_1) > -1$$

or when

$$\beta(b_1 - a_1) < 0 \quad \text{and} \quad \beta(b_1 - a_1) > -2 \tag{16.57}$$

Since $\beta > 0$ we can rewrite these conditions for stability as[4]

$$a_1 > b_1 \quad \text{and} \quad \beta < \frac{2}{a_1 - b_1} \tag{16.58}$$

The first of the conditions [16.58] implies that for stability the slope of the flow demand curve must be less than that of the flow supply curve as it is in Fig. 3.6. If this does not hold then we have a situation as in Fig. 3.7 and the equilibrium given by eqn [16.55] will be an unstable one. In the model at the beginning of this chapter we see from eqns [16.1] and [16.2] that $a_1 = 300$ and $b_1 = -400$, so the condition $a_1 > b_1$ is met.

We also noted in section 16.1 that instability could also occur if β, which measures the responsiveness of price to a disequilibrium in demand and supply, is too large. The second condition in [16.58] tells us exactly what is meant by too large in this case. For the model in section 16.1, β must not exceed

$$\frac{2}{a_1 - b_1} = \frac{2}{300 + 400} = \frac{1}{350}$$

16.4 The simple Keynesian model again

We now return to the simple macro-model of section 16.1 and derive the solution for a general version of the difference equation [16.13].

Suppose the consumption function [16.9] has the general form

$$C_t = \alpha + \beta Y_t^e \quad \alpha > 0, \, 0 < \beta < 1 \tag{16.59}$$

Let the expectations-generating equation [16.10] have the form

$$Y_t^e = \gamma Y_{t-1} + (1 - \gamma)Y_{t-2} \quad 0 < \gamma < 1 \tag{16.60}$$

Thus expected income is a weighted average of past incomes. Thus

$$C_t = \alpha + \beta\gamma Y_{t-1} + \beta(1 - \gamma)Y_{t-2} \tag{16.61}$$

We assume, as in section 16.1, that private and government expenditure are fixed at the levels $\bar{I}$ and $\bar{G}$ respectively. Substituting into [16.12] thus gives

$$Y_t = \beta\gamma Y_{t-1} + \beta(1 - \gamma)Y_{t-2} + E \tag{16.62}$$

where $E = \alpha + \bar{I} + \bar{G}$ is what can be referred to as autonomous expenditure.

Equation [16.62] is a second-order difference equation, for which we can obtain a particular solution in the usual manner. Setting $Y_t = Y_{t-1} = Y^*$ in [16.62] gives

$$Y^* = Y^*(\beta\gamma + \beta - \beta\gamma) + E \quad \rightarrow \quad Y^* = \frac{E}{1 - \beta} \tag{16.63}$$

which is the particular solution. Notice that, since β is the *MPC*, $1/(1 - \beta)$ is the familiar Keynesian expenditure multiplier. For any given value of E, [16.63] tells us the equilibrium level of income.

The auxiliary equation for [16.62] is

$$m^2 - \beta\gamma m - \beta(1 - \gamma) = 0 \tag{16.64}$$

Comparing [16.64] with the general quadratic equation [16.36] we have $a = 1$, $b = -\beta\gamma$ and $c = -\beta(1 - \gamma)$. Since $b^2 = \beta^2\gamma^2$ must be positive, and $4ac = -4\beta(1 - \gamma)$ must be negative since both β and γ lie between zero and unity, it follows that $b^2 > 4ac$. Thus we can rule out both the case of multiple roots and the case of complex roots. The complementary solution must then take the form

$$Y_t = A_1(m_1)^t + A_2(m_2)^t \tag{16.65}$$

where A_1 and A_2 are arbitrary constants and m_1 and m_2 are the two real roots of the auxiliary equation [16.64]. The complete solution to the difference equation [16.62] is therefore

$$Y_t = A_1(m_1)^t + A_2(m_2)^t + \frac{E}{1-\beta} \qquad [16.66]$$

As usual the arbitrary constants A_1 and A_2 will depend on the initial conditions.

Since [16.64] has real roots, we can be certain that the time path for Y will not exhibit cycles. However, will Y converge on its equilibrium position given by [16.63]? That is, will the equilibrium be stable? We can use the conditions [16.51] to check for stability. Since $a = 1$, $b = -\beta\gamma$ and $c = -\beta(1-\gamma)$ the conditions for stability become

$$-1 < -\beta(1-\gamma) < 1 \qquad [16.67]$$

and

$$-[1 - \beta(1-\gamma)] < -\beta\gamma < [1 - \beta(1-\gamma)] \qquad [16.68]$$

We shall now verify that the macro-model of section 16.1 is in fact stable.[5] From [16.9] we have $\beta = 0.8$, while from [16.10] we have $\gamma = 0.5$. Thus $-\beta(1-\gamma) = -0.4$ and $-\beta\gamma = -0.4$. Substituting in [16.67] and [16.68] we can therefore see that the condition [16.67] is met because $-1 < -0.4 < 1$, and the condition [16.68] is met because $-0.6 < -0.4 < 0.6$.

We have now demonstrated that this model has a stable equilibrium income level and that, whatever the initial conditions, income Y converges on this equilibrium without exhibiting cycles. Such behaviour was in fact demonstrated in Fig. 16.2.

Example 16.8

A closed dynamic economic system can be described by the following set of equations:

$$C_t = 200 + 0.65Y_{t-1}$$
$$I_t = 0.3(Y_{t-1} - Y_{t-2})$$
$$G_t = 0.15Y_{t-1}$$

where C_t, I_t and G_t refer respectively to consumption, investment and government expenditure at time t. In addition Y_{t-1} and Y_{t-2} represent income in previous periods.

Assuming that expenditure plans are always realised and given that income in period 0 is $Y_0 = 500$ and income in period 1 is $Y_1 = 550$, find an expression for Y_t in terms of t alone. From your solution, determine the time path of income for $t = 0, 1, 2, 3, 4, 5$. Comment on the stability of the system.

The investment function in the above model is replaced by the form

$$I_t = 3(Y_{t-1} - Y_{t-2})$$

If all other equations in the model remain the same, consider the stability properties of the new system.

Example 16.9

In a simple market model demand in period t is given by

$$d_t = 28 - 2P_t$$

while supply in the same period is given by

$$s_t = 7 - 12P_{t-1} + 18P_{t-2}$$

where P_t, P_{t-1} and P_{t-2} refer to the price levels ruling during current and previous periods. If the market is always cleared such that $d_t = s_t$ and the price levels in periods 0 and 1 are $P_0 = 12.5$ and $P_1 = 20.5$ respectively, find an expression for P_t in terms of t alone.
  Comment on the stability properties of the system.

Higher-order equations

In principle, linear difference equations of an order higher than 2 can be solved in the same way as first- and second-order equations. However, stability conditions and the conditions necessary for cycles are more complicated. Also problems can arise in solving the auxiliary equation. Nowadays computer packages are available to help with the solution of higher-order equations and to trace out implied time paths.

Revision examples

Example R16.1

Flow demand and flow supply equations in a single-good market are

$$d_t = 30 - 6p_t + 10Y_t$$

$$s_t = 10 + 4p_t$$

where p_t is the price of the good and Y_t is consumer income, which is exogenous. If flow equilibrium occurs when $d_t = s_t$, find the reduced equation for p_t. Hence show that when $Y = 8$, the equilibrium level of price $p_t = 10$.
  Suppose that the market is in equilibrium at the above values but income suddenly rises to $Y = 16$. The market is now in disequilibrium and suppose behaviour out of equilibrium can be described by the dynamic equation

$$p_t - p_{t-1} = 0.2(d_{t-1} - s_{t-1})$$

Obtain a difference equation to describe the path of p_t after the change in income. Find a solution to the difference equation, given the initial condition $p_0 = 10$. Hence, find the new equilibrium value for p_t and determine whether the new equilibrium is reached.

Example R16.2

Find complete solutions for the following difference equations:

(a) $Y_t = Y_{t-1} + 6$ with $Y_0 = 2$;

(b) $3Y_t + 7Y_{t-1} - 20Y_{t-2} = 5$ with $Y_0 = 15$, $Y_1 = 20$;

(c) $2Y_t = 2Y_{t-1} - 0.5Y_{t-2} + 8$ with $Y_0 = 24$, $Y_1 = 26$;

(d) $Y_t + 2Y_{t-1} - 3Y_{t-2} = 12$ with $Y_0 = 8$, $Y_1 = 12$;

(e) $5Y_t = 3Y_{t-1} + 3Y_{t-2} + 15$ with $Y_0 = 3$, $Y_1 = 3$.

Example R16.3

Determine which of the following difference equations imply a stable equilibrium for Y. Will the time path for Y exhibit cycles?

(a) $2Y_t + 3Y_{t-1} + 2Y_{t-2} = 15$;

(b) $Y_t = 3Y_{t-1} + 4Y_{t-2} + 10$;

(c) $12Y_t - 13Y_{t-1} + 3Y_{t-2} = 8$.

Example R16.4

Consider the following macro-model:

$$C_t = 0.2Y_t + 0.5Y_{t-1} + 0.3Y_{t-2}$$

$$I_t = 0.2(Y_t - Y_{t-1})$$

$$G_t = 20 + 0.1Y_t$$

$$Y_t = C_t + I_t + G_t$$

C is consumption, Y is income, I is private investment and G is government expenditure. Obtain a difference equation for Y. Given the initial conditions $Y_0 = 30$, $Y_1 = 40$, find a solution for the difference equation, expressing Y_t in terms of t alone. Find the equilibrium value of income and determine whether this solution is stable.

Example R16.5

Solve the following third-order difference equation:

$$6Y_t = 17Y_{t-1} - 11Y_{t-2} + 2Y_{t-3} - 30 \quad \text{with} \quad Y_0 = 11, \; Y_1 = 6, \; Y_2 = 13/3$$

What is the equilibrium value Y? Is the equilibrium stable?
   (*Hint*: $6m^3 - 17m^2 + 11m - 2 = (m - 2)(6m^2 - 5m + 1)$.)

Notes

1. Variables such as p_{t-1} are referred to as lagged endogenous variables. Both lagged endogenous variables and exogenous variables are what are called predetermined variables.
2. See, for example, A. C. Chiang (1984) *Fundamental Methods of Mathematical Economics*, 3rd edn, International Student Edition. McGraw-Hill, Tokyo, p. 554.
3. See, for example, Chiang, op. cit., p. 579.
4. Multiplying an inequality throughout by -1 changes the sign of the inequality. For example, $8 > 6$ but $-8 < -6$.
5. In fact, the conditions for stability [16.51] will always be met provided $0 < \beta < 1$ and $0 < \gamma < 1$.

17 Introduction to matrix algebra

17.1 Vectors and matrices

Almost all economists nowadays need to have some familiarity with vectors and matrices and this final chapter provides an introduction. Matrix algebra is, first and foremost, a convenient shorthand and the rules for handling vectors and matrices, although some at first seem strange, have been designed to make that shorthand as convenient and as powerful as possible.

For example, the 'firms' we have dealt with in this book have normally produced a single good at a single price so that we have been able to write such a firm's total revenue as $R = pq$. But what of the firm that produces, say, six goods with outputs q_1, q_2, q_3, q_4, q_5 and q_6 at prices p_1, p_2, p_3, p_4, p_5 and p_6? While the total revenue of such a firm is clearly

$$R = p_1q_1 + p_2q_2 + p_3q_3 + p_4q_4 + p_5q_5 + p_6q_6 \qquad [17.1]$$

it is tiresome to have to write out eqn [17.1] whenever we wish to refer to an expression for total revenue. Some form of shorthand is obviously desirable.

We shall refer to the firm's six prices as a *vector* of prices p' where

$$p' = (p_1 \quad p_2 \quad p_3 \quad p_4 \quad p_5 \quad p_6) \qquad [17.2]$$

Notice that the prices are *ordered* in a particular manner in [17.2]. The price of the first good is written first, the price of the second next, etc. Thus if we were to write

$$p' = (6 \quad 8 \quad 12 \quad 3 \quad 7 \quad 4)$$

we are in fact saying $p_1 = 6$, $p_2 = 8$, $p_3 = 12$, $p_4 = 3$, $p_5 = 7$ and $p_6 = 4$.

The vector [17.2] is referred to as a *row vector*. It is also possible to stack the firm's prices vertically on top of one another while retaining the same ordering. That is, we can form the *column vector*

$$p = \begin{pmatrix} p_1 \\ p_2 \\ p_3 \\ p_4 \\ p_5 \\ p_6 \end{pmatrix} \qquad [17.3]$$

Notice that it is customary to write a row vector with a 'prime' sign attached to it. Thus the row vector [17.2] is written p' while the column vector [17.3] is written p.

Having written the firm's prices in the form of a vector it is natural to do the same for its six outputs. We can write these outputs either as a row vector q' or as a column vector q. That is,

$$q' = (q_1 \quad q_2 \quad q_3 \quad q_4 \quad q_5 \quad q_6) \quad \text{or} \quad q = \begin{pmatrix} q_1 \\ q_2 \\ q_3 \\ q_4 \\ q_5 \\ q_6 \end{pmatrix} \quad\quad [17.4]$$

Since total revenue is formed by taking the product of outputs and prices, the natural next step is to define a process of *vector multiplication* so that by 'multiplying' our price and output vectors together we obtain a valid expression for the firm's total revenue. Examination of eqn [17.1] indicates that if our vector multiplication is to 'work' then we have to define such multiplication as *taking each element in one of the vectors, multiplying it by the corresponding element in the other vector and then adding up all such products.*[1] For example, if our two vectors were

$$(6 \quad 2 \quad 1 \quad 3 \quad 7 \quad 2) \quad \text{and} \quad \begin{pmatrix} 1 \\ 2 \\ 7 \\ 3 \\ 6 \\ 4 \end{pmatrix}$$

then vector multiplication would yield

$$6(1) + 2(2) + 1(7) + 3(3) + 7(6) + 2(4) = 76$$

Once we accept such a definition of vector multiplication it becomes possible to replace the cumbersome equation [17.1] by the convenient shorthand

$$R = p'q \quad\quad [17.5]$$

Notice that the vector product in [17.5] is written as $p'q$ – that is, a row vector is written first followed by a column vector. As we shall see shortly, there is reason for always regarding vector multiplication as involving the multiplying of a *row into a column*. While it would be equally acceptable to write $R = q'p$, to have written instead pq' and qp' would mean something entirely different to a mathematician!

Example 17.1

Find the products of the following pairs of vectors:

(a) $(-3 \quad 2 \quad 0 \quad 7)$ and $\begin{pmatrix} 5 \\ -3 \\ 4 \\ 0 \end{pmatrix}$ (b) $(a_1 \quad a_2 \quad a_3 \quad a_4 \quad a_5)$ and $\begin{pmatrix} a_1 \\ a_2 \\ a_3 \\ a_4 \\ a_5 \end{pmatrix}$

A further example in this book where some form of shorthand is extremely useful came in Chapter 2 on simultaneous equations. Suppose, for example, we were faced with the following four-equation system in four variables x_1, x_2, x_3 and x_4:

$$a_{11}x_1 + a_{12}x_2 + a_{13}x_3 + a_{14}x_4 = b_1$$

$$a_{21}x_1 + a_{22}x_2 + a_{23}x_3 + a_{24}x_4 = b_2$$

$$a_{31}x_1 + a_{32}x_2 + a_{33}x_3 + a_{34}x_4 = b_3$$
[17.6]

$$a_{41}x_1 + a_{42}x_2 + a_{43}x_3 + a_{44}x_4 = b_4$$

In the equation system [17.6], the a's and b's are all constants. If we wish to write a shorthand version of the system [17.6] an obvious first step is to write the RHS constants in the form of a column vector

$$\boldsymbol{b} = \begin{pmatrix} b_1 \\ b_2 \\ b_3 \\ b_4 \end{pmatrix}$$
[17.7]

Now let us arrange all the LHS constants in [17.6] in the form of an array which we refer to as A

$$\boldsymbol{A} = \begin{pmatrix} a_{11} & a_{12} & a_{13} & a_{14} \\ a_{21} & a_{22} & a_{23} & a_{24} \\ a_{31} & a_{32} & a_{33} & a_{34} \\ a_{41} & a_{42} & a_{43} & a_{44} \end{pmatrix}$$
[17.8]

The array A is known as a *matrix*. Notice that each element in the first row of A comes from the first equation in the system [17.6]. Similarly each element in the second row comes from the second equation etc. Furthermore each element in the first column of A is a coefficient on the variable x_1 in the system [17.6]. Similarly each element in the second column is a coefficient on the second variable x_2 etc. Thus, each element in the matrix A belongs both to a particular row and to a particular column. All matrices involve such a two-way classification.

Given [17.7] and [17.8], all that remain in the equation system [17.6] are the variables. If we arrange these in the form of a column vector

$$x = \begin{pmatrix} x_1 \\ x_2 \\ x_3 \\ x_4 \end{pmatrix} \qquad\qquad [17.9]$$

a natural question to ask now is how matrix–vector multiplication needs to be defined if we are to be able to rewrite the equation system [17.6] in the much more compact shorthand

$$Ax = b \qquad\qquad [17.6a]$$

Clearly the multiplication of the matrix, A, and the vector, x, needs to give rise to another column vector containing as elements the LHSs of eqns [17.6]. That is,

$$\begin{pmatrix} a_{11}x_1 + a_{12}x_2 + a_{13}x_3 + a_{14}x_4 \\ a_{21}x_1 + a_{22}x_2 + a_{23}x_3 + a_{24}x_4 \\ a_{31}x_1 + a_{32}x_2 + a_{33}x_3 + a_{34}x_4 \\ a_{41}x_1 + a_{42}x_2 + a_{43}x_3 + a_{44}x_4 \end{pmatrix} \qquad\qquad [17.10]$$

If each element in Ax is then equated with the corresponding element in the vector b we will indeed obtain the equation system [17.6].

If the multiplication of A and x is to yield [17.10] we must define such multiplication as follows. The matrix A must be regarded as four row vectors stacked on top of each other. That is,

$$A = \begin{pmatrix} a'_1 \\ a'_2 \\ a'_3 \\ a'_4 \end{pmatrix} = \begin{pmatrix} a_{11} & a_{12} & a_{13} & a_{14} \\ a_{21} & a_{22} & a_{23} & a_{24} \\ a_{31} & a_{32} & a_{33} & a_{34} \\ a_{41} & a_{42} & a_{43} & a_{44} \end{pmatrix} \qquad\qquad [17.11]$$

The first element in the resultant vector Ax must then be defined as the quantity obtained by multiplying the row vector a'_1 into the column vector x by the process defined earlier as vector multiplication. Similarly the second, third and fourth elements in Ax must be defined as the quantities obtained by multiplying in turn the row vectors a'_2, a'_3 and a'_4 into the column vector x. That is,

$$Ax = \begin{pmatrix} a_{11} & a_{12} & a_{13} & a_{14} \\ a_{21} & a_{22} & a_{23} & a_{24} \\ a_{31} & a_{32} & a_{33} & a_{34} \\ a_{41} & a_{42} & a_{43} & a_{44} \end{pmatrix} \begin{pmatrix} x_1 \\ x_2 \\ x_3 \\ x_4 \end{pmatrix}$$

$$= \begin{pmatrix} a_{11}x_1 + a_{12}x_2 + a_{13}x_3 + a_{14}x_4 \\ a_{21}x_1 + a_{22}x_2 + a_{23}x_3 + a_{24}x_4 \\ a_{31}x_1 + a_{32}x_2 + a_{33}x_3 + a_{34}x_4 \\ a_{41}x_1 + a_{42}x_2 + a_{43}x_3 + a_{44}x_4 \end{pmatrix} \qquad\qquad [17.12]$$

Only if we define the required multiplication in this way will the equation of each element in Ax with the corresponding element in b replicate the equation system [17.6]. Only then will eqn [17.6a] be a satisfactory shorthand.

Example 17.2

Consider the following systems of equations:

(a) $2x_1 + 3x_2 + x_3 = 5$ (b) $3u + v - 2w = -6$ (c) $x + y = 4$

    $x_1 - 7x_2 + 3x_3 = 2$ $4u + 2w = 6$ $z - 3x = 3$

    $-3x_1 + 4x_2 - x_3 = -4$ $4v - 5w = 4$ $y + 2z = 2$

If the systems are to be written in the matrix form $Ax = b$, how must A, b and x be defined in each case?

When an equation system such as [17.6] is written in the form [17.6a], an intriguing question arises. Is it possible to find some matrix, written A^{-1}, with which we could 'multiply throughout' eqn [17.6a] to yield the following?

$$x = A^{-1}b \tag{17.13}$$

If this were possible then the matrix–vector multiplication process just defined could be used to form a vector $A^{-1}b$ which eqn [17.13] indicates is identical to x, the vector of variables. Once the elements of x arc known we have a solution to the equation system. As we shall see in section 17.4, linear equation systems, however large, can in fact be solved in this way.

Matrix multiplication

The process of *matrix multiplication* is defined simply as an extension of the matrix–vector multiplication just described. Suppose we have two matrices A and B

$$A = \begin{pmatrix} a_{11} & a_{12} & a_{13} & a_{14} \\ a_{21} & a_{22} & a_{23} & a_{24} \\ a_{31} & a_{32} & a_{33} & a_{34} \\ a_{41} & a_{42} & a_{43} & a_{44} \end{pmatrix} = \begin{pmatrix} a'_1 \\ a'_2 \\ a'_3 \\ a'_4 \end{pmatrix}$$

$$B = \begin{pmatrix} b_{11} & b_{12} & b_{13} & b_{14} \\ b_{21} & b_{22} & b_{23} & b_{24} \\ b_{31} & b_{32} & b_{33} & b_{34} \\ b_{41} & b_{42} & b_{43} & b_{44} \end{pmatrix} = \begin{pmatrix} b_1 & b_2 & b_3 & b_4 \end{pmatrix} \tag{17.14}$$

Notice that just as a matrix can be rewritten as a series of row vectors stacked on top of one another so it can also be rewritten as a series of side-by-side column vectors. The matrix B has been rewritten above in this manner.

The matrix product AB is defined as follows. Each element in AB is obtained by the 'row into column' process of vector multiplication defined earlier. For example, the row vector a'_3 in A is multiplied into the column vector b_2 in B to form $a'_3 b_2$, the element in the third row and second column of AB. Similarly, the row vector a'_1 is multiplied into the column vector b_3 to form the element in the first row and third column of AB etc. The matrix product AB is therefore defined as

$$ AB = \begin{pmatrix} a'_1 b_1 & a'_1 b_2 & a'_1 b_3 & a'_1 b_4 \\ a'_2 b_1 & a'_2 b_2 & a'_2 b_3 & a'_2 b_4 \\ a'_3 b_1 & a'_3 b_2 & a'_3 b_3 & a'_3 b_4 \\ a'_4 b_1 & a'_4 b_2 & a'_4 b_3 & a'_4 b_4 \end{pmatrix} \qquad [17.15] $$

Notice that in forming AB we take the *rows* of the *first* matrix A and multiply them into the *columns* of the *second* matrix B. Suppose we were to take the rows of B and multiply them into the columns of A. We would obviously obtain something very different from [17.15]. Mathematicians write the matrix product obtained in this way as BA to distinguish it from AB. Generally

$$ AB \neq BA \qquad [17.16] $$

Thus, although in ordinary algebra $ab = ba$, such a property *does not normally hold for matrices*. To distinguish the two matrix products that can be formed out of A and B, when we form AB we refer to B as being *pre-multiplied* by A. In contrast when BA is formed we refer to B as being *post-multiplied* by A. The two processes have to be clearly distinguished as normally they lead to completely different matrix products. Remember that it is always the *rows* of the *first* matrix which are multiplied into the *columns* of the *second* matrix.

Although both the matrices A and B are *square* in the sense that they contain the same numbers of rows as columns, matrices do not have to be square. In general a matrix with m rows and n columns is knows as an $m \times n$ matrix. For example, P below is a 3×4 matrix and Q a 4×5 matrix. Similarly the square matrices A and B are both 4×4 matrices.

$$ P = \begin{pmatrix} 4 & -1 & 3 & 7 \\ -2 & 5 & 6 & 1 \\ 0 & 2 & -3 & 0 \end{pmatrix} \qquad [17.17] $$

$$ Q = \begin{pmatrix} 2 & 1 & -3 & 2 & 2 \\ -1 & 3 & 0 & 0 & 0 \\ 0 & 3 & 2 & 0 & 0 \\ 1 & -4 & 0 & 1 & 1 \end{pmatrix} $$

It is possible to form matrix products out of non-square matrices by the 'rows into columns' process provided one condition holds. The number of columns in the first matrix must equal the number of rows in the second. Hence, given the matrices P and Q above it is possible to form the product PQ by multiplying rows into columns because each row in P contains the same number of elements as each column in Q.

$$PQ = \begin{pmatrix} 4 & -1 & 3 & 7 \\ -2 & 5 & 6 & 1 \\ 0 & 2 & -3 & 0 \end{pmatrix} \begin{pmatrix} 2 & 1 & -3 & 2 & 2 \\ -1 & 3 & 0 & 0 & 0 \\ 0 & 3 & 2 & 0 & 0 \\ 1 & -4 & 0 & 1 & 1 \end{pmatrix}$$

$$= \begin{pmatrix} 16 & -18 & -6 & 15 & 15 \\ -8 & 27 & 18 & -3 & -3 \\ -2 & -3 & -6 & 0 & 0 \end{pmatrix} \qquad\qquad [17.18]$$

It is not possible to form a matrix product QP, however, because there are five columns in Q but only three rows in P. When it is possible to form a matrix product, the matrices are said to be *conformable*. Otherwise we refer to them as *non-conformable*. The simplest way to check for conformability is to write the dimensions of matrices underneath them. For example, for the matrices P and Q

$$\begin{array}{ccccccc} P & \cdot & Q & = & S & \qquad Q \cdot P & = ? \\ (3 \times 4) & & (4 \times 5) & & (3 \times 5) & \qquad (4 \times 5)\ (3 \times 4) & (\text{—}) \end{array} \qquad [17.19]$$

For two matrices to be conformable the 'middle numbers' must be the same. Thus Q can be pre-multiplied by P to give S but it cannot be post-multiplied by P. When it is possible to multiply two matrices together, notice that the dimensions of the matrix product can be obtained by 'crossing out' the middle numbers. The remaining numbers yield the required dimensions. Thus if an $(n \times k)$ matrix is post-multiplied by a $(k \times m)$ matrix the result is an $(n \times m)$ matrix.

Vectors are, of course, no more than special matrices. A row vector containing n elements is simply a $(1 \times n)$ matrix, while a column vector with n elements is simply an $(n \times 1)$ matrix. We can now see why it was not possible to write the expression [17.5] for a firm's total revenue as pq'. Since p is a (6×1) column vector and q' a (1×6) row vector, the product pq' must be a 6×6 matrix. Applying the normal procedure for matrix multiplication we see that in fact

$$pq' = \begin{pmatrix} p_1 \\ p_2 \\ p_3 \\ p_4 \\ p_5 \\ p_6 \end{pmatrix} (q_1 \quad q_2 \quad q_3 \quad q_4 \quad q_5 \quad q_6)$$

$$= \begin{pmatrix} p_1 q_1 & p_1 q_2 & p_1 q_3 & p_1 q_4 & p_1 q_5 & p_1 q_6 \\ p_2 q_1 & p_2 q_2 & p_2 q_3 & p_2 q_4 & p_2 q_5 & p_2 q_6 \\ p_3 q_1 & p_3 q_2 & p_3 q_3 & p_3 q_4 & p_3 q_5 & p_3 q_6 \\ p_4 q_1 & p_4 q_2 & p_4 q_3 & p_4 q_4 & p_4 q_5 & p_4 q_6 \\ p_5 q_1 & p_5 q_2 & p_5 q_3 & p_5 q_4 & p_5 q_5 & p_5 q_6 \\ p_6 q_1 & p_6 q_2 & p_6 q_3 & p_6 q_4 & p_6 q_5 & p_6 q_6 \end{pmatrix}$$

Example 17.3

Given the following matrices:

$$A = \begin{pmatrix} 6 & 3 & 7 \\ 4 & 5 & -3 \\ 6 & -2 & 1 \end{pmatrix} \qquad B = \begin{pmatrix} 8 & 4 & 2 \\ 3 & 1 & 0 \\ 2 & 5 & 3 \end{pmatrix}$$

$$C = \begin{pmatrix} 4 & -2 \\ 5 & 6 \\ 3 & 5 \end{pmatrix} \qquad D = (10 \quad 3 \quad 1)$$

$$E = \begin{pmatrix} 5 & 3 & -1 & 6 \\ 4 & -2 & 6 & 5 \\ 2 & 0 & 3 & 7 \end{pmatrix}$$

(a) *Where possible* form the following matrix products: (i) AB; (ii) BA; (iii) CA; (iv) DA; (v) CD; (vi) BC; (vii) AE; (viii) EA.

(b) Form the matrix products $(AB)C$ and $A(BC)$ and verify that they are the same.

17.2 Further basic definitions and operations

The element in the ith row and jth column of a matrix such as P in [17.17] is written as p_{ij}. Similarly the element in the ith row and the jth column of a matrix Q is written as q_{ij} etc. For example, in [17.17] $p_{23} = 6$ and $q_{34} = 0$. Two matrices are said to be equal if and only if each element in the one matrix equals the corresponding element in the other matrix. That is,

$A = B$ if and only if $a_{ij} = b_{ij}$ for all i and all j [17.20]

Matrix addition is a simpler process than matrix multiplication and usually seems more logical to the beginner. To add two matrices we simply add the corresponding elements in the two matrices. Thus if $C = A + B$ then the element in the ith row and jth column of C will be

$c_{ij} = a_{ij} + b_{ij}$ [17.21]

Subtraction is performed in a similar way. If a matrix $D = A - B$ then

$d_{ij} = a_{ij} - b_{ij}$ [17.22]

Notice that matrices can only be added and subtracted when they are of the same dimension. It should be obvious that, unlike for matrix multiplication, the order in which matrices are added is not important. That is, for example,

$A + B + C = C + B + A = B + A + C$ etc.   [17.23]

It is sometimes necessary to multiply each element in a matrix by a constant or *scalar*. This process is known as scalar multiplication to distinguish it from matrix multiplication. If λ is any constant then to form the matrix $B = \lambda A$ we use

$b_{ij} = \lambda a_{ij}$ [17.24]

That is, each element in B is formed by multiplying the corresponding element in A by the constant λ.

The *transpose* of a matrix is formed simply by interchanging rows and columns. That is, the first row in the original matrix becomes the first column in the transposed matrix, the second row becomes the second column, etc. The transposed matrix is generally written with a prime sign. Thus the transpose of A is written A'. For example,

$$\text{if } A = \begin{pmatrix} 3 & 1 & 0 & -2 \\ 1 & -3 & 6 & 0 \\ 4 & 7 & -1 & 3 \end{pmatrix} \quad \text{then} \quad A' = \begin{pmatrix} 3 & 1 & 4 \\ 1 & -3 & 7 \\ 0 & 6 & -1 \\ -2 & 0 & 3 \end{pmatrix} \qquad [17.25]$$

Notice that the element in the ith row and the jth column of A becomes the element in the jth row and ith column of A'. That is,

$$a'_{ji} = a_{ij} \qquad [17.26]$$

Obviously the transpose of an $m \times n$ matrix will be an $n \times m$ matrix.

Since a column vector is simply an $n \times 1$ matrix, its transpose will just be a $1 \times n$ row vector. This is why at the beginning of this chapter we wrote row vectors with a prime sign but column vectors without. For example, the row vector [17.2] is the transpose of the column vector [17.3].

The identity matrix

This very special matrix is square and has all elements down its 'main diagonal' equal to unity while all its other elements equal zero. It is usually given the symbol I. For example, a 5×5 identity matrix is

$$I = \begin{pmatrix} 1 & 0 & 0 & 0 & 0 \\ 0 & 1 & 0 & 0 & 0 \\ 0 & 0 & 1 & 0 & 0 \\ 0 & 0 & 0 & 1 & 0 \\ 0 & 0 & 0 & 0 & 1 \end{pmatrix} \qquad [17.27]$$

The identity matrix plays a role in matrix algebra very similar to the role of the number 1 in ordinary algebra. In ordinary algebra $1 \times a = a \times 1 = a$. Similarly in matrix algebra it is not difficult to show that (assuming the matrices are conformable)

$$IA = AI = A \qquad [17.28]$$

For example, if I is a 3×3 identity matrix and A is as given in [17.25] above then

$$IA = \begin{pmatrix} 1 & 0 & 0 \\ 0 & 1 & 0 \\ 0 & 0 & 1 \end{pmatrix} \begin{pmatrix} 3 & 1 & 0 & -2 \\ 1 & -3 & 6 & 0 \\ 4 & 7 & -1 & 3 \end{pmatrix} = \begin{pmatrix} 3 & 1 & 0 & -2 \\ 1 & -3 & 6 & 0 \\ 4 & 7 & -1 & 3 \end{pmatrix} = A$$

Example 17.4

For the matrices in Example 17.3:

(a) Form A', B' and C' and show that $(AB)' = B'A'$ and that $(ABC)' = C'B'A'$.
(b) Verify that $IA = A$, $IC = C$, $AI = A$, $IE = E$ and $DI = D$ where I is a 3×3 identity matrix.
(c) Form the matrix $A + B$ and hence show that $D(A + B) = DA + DB$.

17.3 Inverting a matrix

The *inverse* of a matrix A is defined as that matrix, usually written A^{-1}, for which

$$AA^{-1} = A^{-1}A = I \qquad\qquad [17.29]$$

The inverse matrix is in fact analogous to a reciprocal in ordinary algebra. The reciprocal of x is $1/x$ or x^{-1} and, of course, $xx^{-1} = 1$. Notice, however, that we do not write A^{-1} as $1/A$. One cannot 'divide' one matrix B by another matrix A. The matrix equivalent of division is to form the product of the matrices B and A^{-1}. Indeed, provided the matrices are of the right dimension, it is possible to form either BA^{-1} or $A^{-1}B$. As we have seen, such matrix products are not necessarily the same. Note, also, that *only square matrices have an inverse and that such an inverse is also square*. Equation [17.29] cannot hold for non-square matrices.

The simplest way of finding an inverse of a matrix A is to determine what *row operations* have to be performed on the matrix A to turn it into the identity matrix I. If identical row operations are performed on the identity matrix itself then the required inverse, A^{-1}, is formed.

By row operations we mean either the division of all elements in a row by a constant or the addition/subtraction of multiples of one row to/from another row. An example will make this clearer. Since the row operations to be performed on A and I are the same it is sensible to perform them simultaneously. On the LHS of the first panel in Fig. 17.1 is a 3×3 matrix A to be inverted and on the RHS is the identity matrix.

$$
\begin{array}{ccc|ccc}
6 & 3 & 6 & 1 & 0 & 0 \\
1 & 2 & 0 & 0 & 1 & 0 \\
4 & 5 & 1 & 0 & 0 & 1
\end{array}
\longrightarrow
\begin{array}{ccc|ccc}
1 & \frac{1}{2} & 1 & \frac{1}{6} & 0 & 0 \\
1 & 2 & 0 & 0 & 1 & 0 \\
4 & 5 & 1 & 0 & 0 & 1
\end{array}
\longrightarrow
\begin{array}{ccc|ccc}
1 & \frac{1}{2} & 1 & \frac{1}{6} & 0 & 0 \\
0 & \frac{3}{2} & -1 & -\frac{1}{6} & 1 & 0 \\
0 & 3 & -3 & -\frac{2}{3} & 0 & 1
\end{array}
$$

Fig. 17.1 Matrix inversion I

We wish to transform A into I so as a first step we divide the first row of A by 6, so obtaining a 1 in the top left-hand corner of this matrix. Simultaneously we divide the first row of I by 6. The next step is to turn the remaining elements of the first column of the LHS matrix into zeros. We can do this by subtracting the new first row from the second row and by subtracting four times the new first row from the third row. The same operations are performed simultaneously on the RHS matrix. This yields the third panel in Fig. 17.1.

In Fig. 17.2 the first panel is identical to the third panel in Fig. 17.1. Row operations are then performed on the LHS matrix, firstly to turn the middle element of the second column into a 1, and secondly to turn the remaining elements in that column into zeros. Again identical operations are performed on the RHS matrix.

$$
\left[\begin{array}{ccc|ccc}
1 & {}^{1}/_{2} & 1 & {}^{1}/_{6} & 0 & 0 \\
0 & {}^{3}/_{2} & -1 & -{}^{1}/_{6} & 1 & 0 \\
0 & 3 & -3 & -{}^{2}/_{3} & 0 & 1
\end{array}\right]
\longrightarrow
\left[\begin{array}{ccc|ccc}
1 & {}^{1}/_{2} & 1 & {}^{1}/_{6} & 0 & 0 \\
0 & 1 & -{}^{2}/_{3} & -{}^{1}/_{9} & {}^{2}/_{3} & 0 \\
0 & 3 & -3 & -{}^{2}/_{3} & 0 & 1
\end{array}\right]
\longrightarrow
\left[\begin{array}{ccc|ccc}
1 & 0 & {}^{4}/_{3} & {}^{2}/_{9} & -{}^{1}/_{3} & 0 \\
0 & 1 & -{}^{2}/_{3} & -{}^{1}/_{9} & {}^{2}/_{3} & 0 \\
0 & 0 & -1 & -{}^{1}/_{3} & -2 & 1
\end{array}\right]
$$

Fig. 17.2 Matrix inversion II

Finally in Fig. 17.3 we turn our attention to the third column of the LHS matrix. First the bottom element is turned into a 1 and then by row additions and subtractions the remaining elements are turned into zeros.

$$
\left[\begin{array}{ccc|ccc}
1 & 0 & {}^{4}/_{3} & {}^{2}/_{9} & -{}^{1}/_{3} & 0 \\
0 & 1 & -{}^{2}/_{3} & -{}^{1}/_{9} & {}^{2}/_{3} & 0 \\
0 & 0 & -1 & -{}^{1}/_{3} & -2 & 1
\end{array}\right]
\longrightarrow
\left[\begin{array}{ccc|ccc}
1 & 0 & {}^{4}/_{3} & {}^{2}/_{9} & -{}^{1}/_{3} & 0 \\
0 & 1 & -{}^{2}/_{3} & -{}^{1}/_{9} & {}^{2}/_{3} & 0 \\
0 & 0 & 1 & {}^{1}/_{3} & 2 & -1
\end{array}\right]
\longrightarrow
\left[\begin{array}{ccc|ccc}
1 & 0 & 0 & -{}^{2}/_{9} & -3 & {}^{4}/_{3} \\
0 & 1 & 0 & {}^{1}/_{9} & 2 & -{}^{2}/_{3} \\
0 & 0 & 1 & {}^{1}/_{3} & 2 & -1
\end{array}\right]
$$

Fig. 17.3 Matrix inversion III

We have now transformed the original LHS matrix in Fig. 17.1 into the identity matrix and simultaneously transformed an identity matrix into the final RHS matrix in Fig. 17.3 which is A^{-1}. That is, if

$$
A = \begin{pmatrix} 6 & 3 & 6 \\ 1 & 2 & 0 \\ 4 & 5 & 1 \end{pmatrix} \quad \text{then} \quad A^{-1} = \begin{pmatrix} -2/9 & -3 & 4/3 \\ 1/9 & 2 & -2/3 \\ 1/3 & 2 & -1 \end{pmatrix}
$$

The reader should verify that $AA^{-1} = I$ and $A^{-1}A = I$.

The above procedure for finding an inverse is entirely mechanical and becomes easy with practice. The trick is to concentrate on one column of the original matrix at a time, first getting the 1 in the correct place and then the zeros.

While only square matrices have inverses, *not all square matrices have them*. For example, consider the matrix

$$
B = \begin{pmatrix} 2 & 1 \\ 4 & 2 \end{pmatrix} \tag{17.30}
$$

In Fig. 17.4 we have attempted to follow our usual procedure for finding an inverse. The problem is that in the third panel we obtain a row of zeros and it proves impossible to obtain a 1 in the bottom right-hand corner of the LHS matrix. Our procedure breaks down and in fact there is no matrix B^{-1} such that $BB^{-1} = I$ or $B^{-1}B = I$. The matrix B in [17.30] does not have an inverse.

$$
\left[\begin{array}{cc|cc}
2 & 1 & 1 & 0 \\
4 & 2 & 0 & 1
\end{array}\right]
\longrightarrow
\left[\begin{array}{cc|cc}
1 & {}^{1}/_{2} & {}^{1}/_{2} & 0 \\
4 & 2 & 0 & 1
\end{array}\right]
\longrightarrow
\left[\begin{array}{cc|cc}
1 & {}^{1}/_{2} & {}^{1}/_{2} & 0 \\
0 & 0 & -2 & 1
\end{array}\right]
$$

Fig. 17.4 Breakdown of inversion procedure

The inversion procedure breaks down for the matrix [17.30] because there is an exact relationship between its rows. Each element in the second row equals twice the corresponding element in the first row. It is this relationship that leads to the row of zeros in the third panel of Fig. 17.4. *In fact whenever an exact linear relationship exists between the rows of a matrix the inversion procedure will break down*. For example, consider the matrix

$$C = \begin{pmatrix} 3 & -2 & 1 \\ 1 & 2 & -2 \\ 5 & 2 & -3 \end{pmatrix} \qquad [17.31]$$

In this matrix the third row is equal to the first row plus twice the second row. Such an exact relationship means that the inversion procedure will break down and that C^{-1} does not exist. The reader should confirm that if the inversion procedure is applied to matrix [17.31] a row of three zeros eventually results. Matrices such as B in [17.30] and C in [17.31], which do not have an inverse, are said to be *singular* or of *non-full rank*. A matrix which has an inverse is said to be *non-singular* or of *full rank*.

Example 17.5

Find the inverses, if they exist, of the following matrices:

(a) $\begin{pmatrix} 6 & 4 \\ 3 & 1 \end{pmatrix}$ (b) $\begin{pmatrix} -3 & 2 \\ 4 & -1 \end{pmatrix}$ (c) $\begin{pmatrix} 1 & 2 & 3 \\ 1 & 3 & 5 \\ 1 & 5 & 12 \end{pmatrix}$ (d) $\begin{pmatrix} 3 & 4 & 1 \\ 2 & 1 & 6 \\ 5 & 5 & 7 \end{pmatrix}$

17.4 Determinants

In the previous section we outlined one method of finding the inverse of a matrix. In a moment we will describe another method which provides additional insights. Firstly, however, we need to be able to define and evaluate determinants.

All square matrices A have associated with them a number referred to as the *determinant* of that matrix. The determinant of A is normally written as either det (A) or $|A|$. We begin with 2×2 matrices. The determinant of a 2×2 matrix is *defined* and evaluated as

$$|A| = \begin{vmatrix} a_{11} & a_{12} \\ a_{21} & a_{22} \end{vmatrix} = a_{11}a_{22} - a_{12}a_{21} \qquad [17.32]$$

To evaluate A, we therefore 'cross-multiply'. For example,

if $A = \begin{pmatrix} 2 & 4 \\ -5 & 1 \end{pmatrix}$ then $|A| = \begin{vmatrix} 2 & 4 \\ -5 & 1 \end{vmatrix} = (2)(1) - (4)(-5) = 22$

At first there may seem to be no 'logic' to the definition above. However, as we shall see later, it turns out that evaluating the 'determinant' of a matrix in this way is very useful.

Minors and cofactors

To define the determinant of a square matrix of order greater than 2×2, we need to introduce the concepts 'minor' and 'cofactor'. If we take any element a_{ij} from a square matrix and then delete the ith row and jth column of that matrix, we obtain what is referred to as a sub-matrix. This sub-matrix is also square and its determinant is known as a *minor*, denoted as m_{ij}. For example, if we delete the second row and first column from a 3×3 matrix, in this manner

$$A = \begin{pmatrix} a_{11} & a_{12} & a_{13} \\ a_{21} & a_{22} & a_{23} \\ a_{31} & a_{32} & a_{33} \end{pmatrix}$$

[17.33]

we obtain the sub-matrix

$$\begin{pmatrix} a_{12} & a_{13} \\ a_{32} & a_{33} \end{pmatrix}$$

The minor of a_{21} (the element in the second row and first column of A) is the determinant of the above sub-matrix. It is given by

$$m_{21} = \begin{vmatrix} a_{12} & a_{13} \\ a_{32} & a_{33} \end{vmatrix} = a_{12}a_{33} - a_{13}a_{32}$$

As a numerical example, consider the matrix

$$A = \begin{pmatrix} 2 & -3 & 0 \\ -1 & 4 & -1 \\ 2 & 1 & 2 \end{pmatrix}$$

[17.34]

If we strike out the second row and the second column of A we obtain the minor

$$m_{22} = \begin{vmatrix} 2 & 0 \\ 2 & 2 \end{vmatrix} = 4$$

Similarly, deleting the third row and second column of A yields

$$m_{32} = \begin{vmatrix} 2 & 0 \\ -1 & -1 \end{vmatrix} = -2$$

All the elements in a square matrix will necessarily have minors.

Each minor m_{ij} of a matrix has, closely associated to it, what is referred to as a *cofactor*, c_{ij}. Cofactors are defined as

$$c_{ij} = (-1)^{i+j} m_{ij}$$

[17.35]

for each minor m_{ij}. A cofactor is simply a minor with the appropriate sign attached, according to the relationship [17.35]. Thus if $i + j$ is an even number then the sign attached to the minor is positive and hence $c_{ij} = m_{ij}$. However, if $i + j$ is an odd number, then the sign attached to the minor is negative and in this case $c_{ij} = -m_{ij}$.

For example, if we take the matrix [17.34], then the minor $m_{22} = 4$. Since $i + j = 2 + 2 = 4$ is even, it follows that the cofactor $c_{22} = +4$. Also since the minor $m_{32} = -2$ and $i + j = 3 + 2 = 5$ (an odd number), it follows that the cofactor $c_{32} = -(-2) = +2$.

The evaluation of 3 × 3 determinants

The determinant of a 3×3 matrix can be evaluated in six different ways, each yielding the same result. We simply take any row or any column of elements in the matrix, multiply each such element by its respective cofactor, and sum the resultant products. The sum obtained is defined as the determinant of the matrix. For example, to obtain the determinant of the matrix [17.33], we can 'expand by the first column', obtaining

$$|A| = a_{11}c_{11} + a_{21}c_{21} + a_{31}c_{31}$$

$$= a_{11}m_{11} - a_{21}m_{21} + a_{31}m_{31} \qquad [17.36]$$

Taking the matrix [17.34] as an example, the minors required to evaluate [17.36] are

$$m_{11} = \begin{vmatrix} 4 & -1 \\ 1 & 2 \end{vmatrix} = 9 \quad m_{21} = \begin{vmatrix} -3 & 0 \\ 1 & 2 \end{vmatrix} = -6 \quad m_{31} = \begin{vmatrix} -3 & 0 \\ 4 & -1 \end{vmatrix} = 3$$

Hence, using [17.36],

$$|A| = 2(9) - (-1)(-6) + 2(3) = 18$$

Alternatively, we can expand using the second row, if we wish. Thus

$$|A| = a_{21}c_{21} + a_{22}c_{22} + a_{23}c_{23}$$

$$= -a_{21}m_{21} + a_{22}m_{22} - a_{23}m_{23} \qquad [17.37]$$

Again, taking the matrix [17.34] as the example, this time we require the minors

$$m_{21} = \begin{vmatrix} -3 & 0 \\ 1 & 2 \end{vmatrix} = -6 \quad m_{22} = \begin{vmatrix} 2 & 0 \\ 2 & 2 \end{vmatrix} = 4 \quad m_{23} = \begin{vmatrix} 2 & -3 \\ 2 & 1 \end{vmatrix} = 8$$

Hence, we obtain

$$|A| = -(-1)(-6) + (4)(4) - (-1)(8) = 18$$

It is possible to show that whichever row or column we use to expand the determinant we will always obtain the same value, in this case 18.

The reader should check that the same answer 18 is found when expanding the determinant by, for example, the second column and the first row. Make sure you use the correct signs on the minors.

Note the pattern that arises when we compare cofactors and minors:

$$\begin{pmatrix} c_{11} & c_{12} & c_{13} \\ c_{21} & c_{22} & c_{23} \\ c_{31} & c_{32} & c_{33} \end{pmatrix} = \begin{pmatrix} m_{11} & -m_{12} & m_{13} \\ -m_{21} & m_{22} & -m_{23} \\ m_{31} & -m_{32} & m_{33} \end{pmatrix} \qquad [17.38]$$

Example 17.6

Evaluate the following determinants, first by the second row and then by the third column. Check that you get the same answer in each case.

$$
\text{(a)} \begin{vmatrix} 2 & -3 & 1 \\ 0 & 4 & -2 \\ -5 & 0 & 3 \end{vmatrix} \quad \text{(b)} \begin{vmatrix} -1 & 0 & 5 \\ 10 & -2 & -1 \\ 0 & 5 & 2 \end{vmatrix}
$$

Example 17.7

Evaluate the following determinants by the second row:

$$
\text{(a)} \begin{vmatrix} 4 & 25 & -10 \\ 0 & 0 & 0 \\ -45 & 9 & 24 \end{vmatrix} \quad \text{(b)} \begin{vmatrix} 11 & 3 & -26 \\ 0 & 1 & 0 \\ 1 & -6 & 1 \end{vmatrix}
$$

Given what you should have learnt when tackling (a) and (b) above, evaluate the following:

$$
\text{(c)} \begin{vmatrix} 1 & 0 & 0 \\ -5 & 10 & -6 \\ 7 & 9 & 0 \end{vmatrix} \quad \text{(d)} \begin{vmatrix} 0 & -3 & 5 \\ 0 & 7 & -8 \\ 1 & -3 & 7 \end{vmatrix} \quad \text{(e)} \begin{vmatrix} 7 & -6 & 6 \\ 0 & 3 & -4 \\ 0 & 8 & 0 \end{vmatrix}
$$

Higher-order determinants

Determinants of order 4×4 and higher can be defined in an analogous way to a 3×3 determinant. Their evaluation involves the calculation of minors and cofactors and the use of a pattern very similar to [17.38]. However, the computation required to evaluate a higher-order determinant increases exponentially as the size of the determinant increases. We shall not be concerned with determinants larger than 3×3, because it is impractical to evaluate them by hand calculator. Fortunately computer software is available for this task.

17.5 Alternative method of inverting a matrix

The inverse of a matrix can also found by making use of determinants. The first step in this approach is to form the so-called *adjoint matrix*. Given a 3×3 matrix A, the adjoint of A is obtained by replacing each a_{ij} by its cofactor c_{ij} and then transposing the resultant matrix. Thus we have

$$
\text{adj}\,(A) = \begin{pmatrix} c_{11} & c_{21} & c_{31} \\ c_{12} & c_{22} & c_{32} \\ c_{13} & c_{23} & c_{33} \end{pmatrix} \tag{17.39}
$$

It is possible to show that[2]

$$
A[\text{adj}(A)] = [\text{adj}(A)]A = \begin{vmatrix} |A| & 0 & 0 \\ 0 & |A| & 0 \\ 0 & 0 & |A| \end{vmatrix} = |A|\,I \tag{17.40}
$$

where I is a 3×3 identity matrix. Assuming that $|A|$ is non-zero, we now multiply [17.40] throughout by $1/|A|$ to obtain

$$A(1/|A|)[\text{adj}(A)] = (1/|A|)[\text{adj}(A)]A = I \qquad [17.41]$$

From [17.41] we can now see that, since $A^{-1}A = AA^{-1}$, the inverse of A must be

$$A^{-1} = \frac{1}{|A|}[\text{adj}(A)] = \frac{1}{|A|}\begin{pmatrix} c_{11} & c_{21} & c_{31} \\ c_{12} & c_{22} & c_{32} \\ c_{13} & c_{23} & c_{33} \end{pmatrix} \qquad [17.42]$$

Thus we see that the inverse of a matrix A can be found by taking its adjoint matrix and dividing all its elements by the determinant of A.

Note that, as we saw in section 17.3, not all matrices have inverses. The matrix inversion procedure of section 17.3 broke down whenever an exact linear relationship held between any of the rows in the matrix. In fact, in such a case, it turns out that the determinant of the matrix has a value zero. Any determinant for which there is a linear relationship between rows has a zero value.[3] Hence, the procedure of this section also breaks down because it requires division by $|A| = 0$. Clearly, division by zero is impossible. A matrix that does not have an inverse matrix is said to be singular. A matrix with $|A| \neq 0$, which therefore does have an inverse, is referred to as non-singular.

In section 17.3 we inverted the matrix in the first panel in Fig. 17.1, given here as

$$A = \begin{pmatrix} 6 & 3 & 6 \\ 1 & 2 & 0 \\ 4 & 5 & 1 \end{pmatrix}$$

We now invert the matrix A using the method of the current section. First we find the determinant of A. Expanding by the first column we have

$$|A| = 6\begin{vmatrix} 2 & 0 \\ 5 & 1 \end{vmatrix} - 1\begin{vmatrix} 3 & 6 \\ 5 & 1 \end{vmatrix} + 4\begin{vmatrix} 3 & 6 \\ 2 & 0 \end{vmatrix} = -9$$

The adjoint matrix of A is

$$\text{adj}(A) = \begin{pmatrix} \begin{vmatrix} 2 & 0 \\ 5 & 1 \end{vmatrix} & -\begin{vmatrix} 3 & 6 \\ 5 & 1 \end{vmatrix} & \begin{vmatrix} 3 & 6 \\ 2 & 0 \end{vmatrix} \\ -\begin{vmatrix} 1 & 0 \\ 4 & 1 \end{vmatrix} & \begin{vmatrix} 6 & 6 \\ 4 & 1 \end{vmatrix} & -\begin{vmatrix} 6 & 6 \\ 1 & 0 \end{vmatrix} \\ \begin{vmatrix} 1 & 2 \\ 4 & 5 \end{vmatrix} & -\begin{vmatrix} 6 & 3 \\ 4 & 5 \end{vmatrix} & \begin{vmatrix} 6 & 3 \\ 1 & 2 \end{vmatrix} \end{pmatrix} = \begin{pmatrix} 2 & 27 & -12 \\ -1 & -18 & 6 \\ -3 & -18 & 9 \end{pmatrix}$$

Dividing the adjoint matrix by $|A| = -9$ gives the inverse matrix

$$A^{-1} = \begin{pmatrix} -2/9 & -3 & 4/3 \\ 1/9 & 2 & -2/3 \\ 1/3 & 2 & -1 \end{pmatrix}$$

Notice that the same inverse matrix was obtained in section 17.3.

It is easy to see that, if a matrix A has an inverse A^{-1}, then A^{-1} is unique. Suppose that a matrix B is such that $BA = I$. Then, using the properties of the identity matrix I,

$$A^{-1} = A^{-1}I = A^{-1}AB = B$$

Example 17.8

Find the inverses (if they exist) of the matrices in Example 17.5, using the method of section 17.4.

Example 17.9

Show that the inverse of the matrix

$$A = \begin{pmatrix} a & b \\ c & d \end{pmatrix}$$

is

$$A^{-1} = \frac{1}{ad - bc} \begin{pmatrix} d & -b \\ -c & d \end{pmatrix}$$

17.6 Solution of equation systems by matrix inversion

We saw, in section 17.1, how a simultaneous equation system such as [17.6] could be represented by the matrix equation

$$Ax = b \tag{17.43}$$

We then suggested that provided a matrix A^{-1} could be found, it might be possible to obtain the solution to such an equation system by using eqn [17.13]. We can now see that such a solution procedure is indeed possible. If an inverse matrix A^{-1} exists then we can pre-multiply both sides of eqn [17.43] by A^{-1} obtaining

$$A^{-1}Ax = A^{-1}b \quad \rightarrow \quad Ix = A^{-1}b \quad \rightarrow \quad x = A^{-1}b \tag{17.44}$$

In [17.44] we have first used the definition [17.29] of an inverse matrix and then the basic property [17.28] of the identity matrix. It follows that eqn [17.13] is indeed a valid expression for the solution to a linear equation system.

As an illustration of this method of solution consider the three-equation system

$$6x_1 + 3x_2 + 6x_3 = 9$$
$$x_1 + 2x_2 \quad\quad = 6 \tag{17.45}$$
$$4x_1 + 5x_2 + x_3 = 18$$

If we define the matrices and vectors

$$A = \begin{pmatrix} 6 & 3 & 6 \\ 1 & 2 & 0 \\ 4 & 5 & 1 \end{pmatrix}, \quad x = \begin{pmatrix} x_1 \\ x_2 \\ x_3 \end{pmatrix} \quad \text{and} \quad b = \begin{pmatrix} 9 \\ 6 \\ 18 \end{pmatrix}$$

then the equation system [17.45] can be written in the form [17.43], that is as

$$\begin{pmatrix} 6 & 3 & 6 \\ 1 & 2 & 0 \\ 4 & 5 & 1 \end{pmatrix} \begin{pmatrix} x_1 \\ x_2 \\ x_3 \end{pmatrix} = \begin{pmatrix} 9 \\ 6 \\ 18 \end{pmatrix} \qquad\qquad [17.46]$$

If a solution to the system is to be obtained using [17.44] then we require A^{-1}, the inverse of A. We have in fact already found A^{-1}. A was the matrix inverted in Figs 17.1–17.3. The solution to the equation system [17.45] is therefore

$$\begin{pmatrix} x_1 \\ x_2 \\ x_3 \end{pmatrix} = \begin{pmatrix} 6 & 3 & 6 \\ 1 & 2 & 0 \\ 4 & 5 & 1 \end{pmatrix}^{-1} \begin{pmatrix} 9 \\ 6 \\ 18 \end{pmatrix}$$

$$= \begin{pmatrix} -2/9 & -3 & 4/3 \\ 1/9 & 2 & -2/3 \\ 1/3 & 2 & -1 \end{pmatrix} \begin{pmatrix} 9 \\ 6 \\ 18 \end{pmatrix} = \begin{pmatrix} 4 \\ 1 \\ -3 \end{pmatrix}$$

or $x_1 = 4$, $x_2 = 1$ and $x_3 = -3$.

Example 17.10

Solve the following systems of linear equations by a method of matrix inversion:

(a) $2x_1 + x_2 = 24$ (b) $x_1 + 2x_2 + 3x_3 = 6$ (c) $-x + y + z = a$
$\quad\ 3x_1 - 2x_2 = 8$ $\quad\ x_1 + 3x_2 + 5x_3 = 9$ $\quad\ x - y + z = b$
$\qquad\qquad\qquad\quad x_1 + 5x_2 + 12x_3 = 18$ $\quad\ x + y - z = c$

$(a, b, c$ are constants$)$

We saw in the last subsection that a square matrix does not necessarily have an inverse, that is it may be singular. Obviously, if the matrix A in an equation system such as [17.43] is singular then the above solution procedure will break down. *The matrix A must be non-singular if the equation system is to have a unique solution.*

If the matrix A in a linear equation system is singular then the system has an infinite number of solutions (i.e. is indeterminate in the terminology of Chapter 2) or has no solution at all (i.e. is inconsistent). We shall illustrate these two special cases by means of simple examples. Consider, first, the equation system

$$\begin{array}{l} x + 2y = 3 \\ 2x + 4y = 6 \end{array} \quad \text{that is} \quad A = \begin{pmatrix} 1 & 2 \\ 2 & 4 \end{pmatrix} \quad b = \begin{pmatrix} 3 \\ 6 \end{pmatrix} \qquad\qquad [17.47]$$

The matrix A in [17.47] is singular because the second row equals twice the first row. This system then has no unique solution. Indeed this system has an infinite number of solutions since if we graphed both equations on a two-dimensional coordinate system we would find that they both represented the same straight line. Not only is the second row in A equal to twice the first row but the second element in the vector b equals twice the first element in that vector. Consequently the second equation is an exact multiple of the first. In other words we have just one *independent* equation, not two. Since we really have a one-equation system in two variables we have, not surprisingly, an infinite number of solutions.

Next consider the system

$$\begin{matrix} 2x + y = 4 \\ 6x + 3y = 3 \end{matrix} \quad \text{that is} \quad A = \begin{pmatrix} 2 & 1 \\ 6 & 3 \end{pmatrix} \quad b = \begin{pmatrix} 4 \\ 3 \end{pmatrix} \tag{17.48}$$

The matrix A in [17.48] is also singular. However, this system has no solution at all since if we graphed these equations we would obtain parallel and hence non-intersecting straight lines. The difference between this and the preceding case is that, while the second row of A equals three times the first, causing singularity, this is not also true of the elements in b. Consequently the two equations are, in this case, independent albeit inconsistent.

Similar situations can arise in larger systems with an equal number of variables and equations. When the matrix A is singular no unique solution will exist, either because all the equations are not independent or because two or more equations are inconsistent. In most economic models, however, singularity of the matrix A is an unusual case. As we saw in Chapter 2, we normally expect a linear system in which the number of variables equals the number of unknowns to be determinate – that is, to have a unique solution.

Cramer's Rule

It is also possible to solve a set of equations, for which there is a unique solution, by the use of determinants alone. Consider the three-equation system

$$Ax = b$$

where in the usual notation

$$A = \begin{pmatrix} a_{11} & a_{12} & a_{13} \\ a_{21} & a_{22} & a_{23} \\ a_{31} & a_{32} & a_{33} \end{pmatrix}, \quad x = \begin{pmatrix} x_1 \\ x_2 \\ x_3 \end{pmatrix} \quad \text{and} \quad b = \begin{pmatrix} b_1 \\ b_2 \\ b_3 \end{pmatrix}$$

The matrix A has determinant $|A|$. We define the following further determinants. Firstly, $|A_1|$ is the determinant found by replacing the first column of the determinant $|A|$ by the column vector b. Secondly, the determinant $|A_2|$ is found by replacing the second column of $|A|$ by the column vector b. Finally, we replace the third column of $|A|$ by the vector b to obtain $|A_3|$. Hence

$$|A_1| = \begin{vmatrix} b_1 & a_{12} & a_{13} \\ b_2 & a_{22} & a_{23} \\ b_3 & a_{32} & a_{33} \end{vmatrix} \quad |A_2| = \begin{vmatrix} a_{11} & b_1 & a_{13} \\ a_{21} & b_2 & a_{23} \\ a_{31} & b_3 & a_{33} \end{vmatrix} \quad |A_3| = \begin{vmatrix} a_{11} & a_{12} & b_1 \\ a_{21} & a_{22} & b_2 \\ a_{31} & a_{32} & b_3 \end{vmatrix}$$

It is possible to show that, provided A is non-singular, the solution to the equation system $Ax = b$ is

$$x_1 = \frac{|A_1|}{|A|} \quad x_2 = \frac{|A_2|}{|A|} \quad x_3 = \frac{|A_3|}{|A|} \qquad [17.49]$$

Equation [17.49] is *Cramer's rule*. We shall illustrate the rule by re-solving the system [17.45]. For this system of equations we have

$$|A| = \begin{vmatrix} 6 & 3 & 6 \\ 1 & 2 & 0 \\ 4 & 5 & 1 \end{vmatrix} = -9$$

whereas

$$|A_1| = \begin{vmatrix} 9 & 3 & 6 \\ 6 & 2 & 0 \\ 18 & 5 & 1 \end{vmatrix} = -36 \quad |A_2| = \begin{vmatrix} 6 & 9 & 6 \\ 1 & 6 & 0 \\ 4 & 18 & 1 \end{vmatrix} = -9 \quad |A_3| = \begin{vmatrix} 6 & 3 & 9 \\ 1 & 2 & 6 \\ 4 & 5 & 18 \end{vmatrix} = 27$$

Thus applying Cramer's rule [17.49], we obtain

$$x_1 = (-36)/(-9) = 4 \quad x_2 = (-9)/(-9) = 1 \quad x_3 = (27)/(-9) = -3 \qquad [17.50]$$

As expected the solution is identical to that found in section 17.5.

17.7 Structural and reduced forms again

As has been illustrated on a number of occasions in this book, it is possible to handle an equation system in which the number of variables exceeds the number of equations provided a sufficient number of variables can be treated as predetermined or exogenous. If the number of endogenous variables is kept equal to the number of independent equations, then in principle a reduced form can always be obtained. However, except in the smallest of systems, finding the reduced form can lead to much tedious algebra and a systematic method is needed. Matrix inversion provides such a method.

As an example, suppose we have a three-equation linear system in three endogenous variables y_1, y_2 and y_3 with two exogenous variables x_1 and x_2. The structural equations of such a system can always be written in the form

$$a_{11}y_1 + a_{12}y_2 + a_{13}y_3 + b_{11}x_1 + b_{12}x_2 + c_1 = 0$$
$$a_{21}y_1 + a_{22}y_2 + a_{23}y_3 + b_{21}x_1 + b_{22}x_2 + c_2 = 0 \qquad [17.51]$$
$$a_{31}y_1 + a_{32}y_2 + a_{33}y_3 + b_{31}x_1 + b_{32}x_2 + c_3 = 0$$

where, although many of them may be 0's or 1's, the a's, b's and c's are all constant. The system [17.51] can be rewritten as

$$Ay = -Bx \qquad [17.52]$$

where

$$A = \begin{pmatrix} a_{11} & a_{12} & a_{13} \\ a_{21} & a_{22} & a_{23} \\ a_{31} & a_{32} & a_{33} \end{pmatrix} \qquad y = \begin{pmatrix} y_1 \\ y_2 \\ y_3 \end{pmatrix}$$

$$B = \begin{pmatrix} b_{11} & b_{12} & c_1 \\ b_{21} & b_{22} & c_2 \\ b_{31} & b_{32} & c_3 \end{pmatrix} \qquad x = \begin{pmatrix} x_1 \\ x_2 \\ 1 \end{pmatrix}$$

To find the reduced form of the system [17.51] we need to express the vector of endogenous variables, y, in terms of the vector of exogenous variables, x. To do this we have to premultiply both sides of eqn [17.52] by A^{-1}, the inverse of the matrix A:

$$A^{-1}Ay = -A^{-1}Bx$$

Hence

$$y = -A^{-1}Bx \qquad\qquad [17.53]$$

Equation [17.53] is the reduced form of the equation system [17.52]. As an illustration of this method of finding the reduced form, consider the simple Keynesian macro-model given by eqns [4.48]–[4.50]. The endogenous variables in this model are Y, C and I, whereas G and R are exogenous. Rewriting the three structural equations in the form [17.51] we have

$$
\begin{aligned}
-0.8Y \quad &+ C + 0.5R \quad\quad - 80 = 0 \\
I \quad &+ \quad 2R \quad - 2000 = 0 \\
Y - I - C \quad &\quad\quad - G \quad\quad\quad = 0
\end{aligned}
\qquad [17.54]
$$

Notice that the coefficients of I and G are both zero in the first structural equation in [17.54], the coefficients of Y, C and G are zero in the second equation and the coefficient of R and the constant term are both zero in the third. The matrices A and B of eqn [17.52] are in this case, therefore,

$$A = \begin{pmatrix} -0.8 & 0 & 1 \\ 0 & 1 & 0 \\ 1 & -1 & -1 \end{pmatrix} \qquad B = \begin{pmatrix} 0.5 & 0 & -80 \\ 2 & 0 & -2000 \\ 0 & -1 & 0 \end{pmatrix}$$

while the vectors y and x are

$$y = \begin{pmatrix} Y \\ I \\ C \end{pmatrix} \qquad x = \begin{pmatrix} R \\ G \\ 1 \end{pmatrix}$$

In this case eqn [17.52] is in fact, therefore,

$$\begin{pmatrix} -0.8 & 0 & 1 \\ 0 & 1 & 0 \\ 1 & -1 & -1 \end{pmatrix} \begin{pmatrix} Y \\ I \\ C \end{pmatrix} = - \begin{pmatrix} 0.5 & 0 & -80 \\ 2 & 0 & -2000 \\ 0 & -1 & 0 \end{pmatrix} \begin{pmatrix} R \\ G \\ 1 \end{pmatrix} \qquad [17.55]$$

If we are to make use of the reduced form eqn [17.53] we require the inverse matrix A^{-1}. This is easily obtained in the usual manner:

$$A^{-1} = \begin{pmatrix} 5 & 5 & 5 \\ 0 & 1 & 0 \\ 5 & 4 & 4 \end{pmatrix}$$

Using eqn [17.53] we then have

$$\begin{pmatrix} Y \\ I \\ C \end{pmatrix} = - \begin{pmatrix} 5 & 5 & 5 \\ 0 & 1 & 0 \\ 5 & 4 & 4 \end{pmatrix} \begin{pmatrix} 0.5 & 0 & -80 \\ 2 & 0 & -2000 \\ 0 & -1 & 0 \end{pmatrix} \begin{pmatrix} R \\ G \\ 1 \end{pmatrix}$$

$$= - \begin{pmatrix} 12.5 & -5 & -10\,400 \\ 2 & 0 & -2000 \\ 10.5 & -4 & -8400 \end{pmatrix} \begin{pmatrix} R \\ G \\ 1 \end{pmatrix}$$

$$= \begin{pmatrix} 10\,400 - 12.5R + 5G \\ 2000 - 2R \\ 8400 - 10.5R + 4G \end{pmatrix} \qquad\qquad [17.56]$$

Thus we obtain the same reduced form as that represented by eqns [4.49], [4.51] and [4.52].

Example 17.11

Use the matrix method to find the reduced forms of the systems in Examples 4.3, 4.5, 4.6 and 4.8.

When the simultaneous system under consideration is relatively simple with a small number of equations, finding the reduced form by matrix inversion may seem unnecessarily complicated. However, for large simultaneous systems the matrix method provides a systematic method of finding reduced form equations. The main problem is that for an n-equation system an $n \times n$ matrix has to be inverted. Matrices of dimension greater than $n = 4$ are rarely inverted by hand because of the computational time involved. However, computer programs for the inversion of large matrices are readily available.

Revision examples

Example R17.1

(a) Suppose

$$A = \begin{pmatrix} 3 & 1 & 0 \\ -4 & 2 & -3 \\ 5 & 0 & -1 \end{pmatrix} \quad B = \begin{pmatrix} -4 & 0 & 0 \\ 3 & 1 & -2 \\ 0 & 5 & 2 \end{pmatrix} \quad C = \begin{pmatrix} 1 \\ 2 \\ 1 \end{pmatrix}$$

Show that $(A + B)C = AC + BC$

(b) Let X be any 3×3 matrix. Show that $A = X'X$ is a symmetric matrix. (A is symmetric if $A = A'$.)

Example R17.2

Invert the following matrices by means of row operations, as described in section 17.3:

(a) $\begin{pmatrix} 4 & 2 \\ -3 & 1 \end{pmatrix}$ (b) $\begin{pmatrix} 3 & -2 & 1 \\ -5 & 0 & 2 \\ 0 & 3 & 3 \end{pmatrix}$

Example R17.3

Evaluate the following determinants:

(a) $\begin{vmatrix} 8 & -3 & 1 \\ 2 & 1 & -2 \\ 6 & -4 & 3 \end{vmatrix}$ (b) $\begin{vmatrix} 2 & 10 & -6 \\ 5 & 3 & 0 \\ -2 & 1 & 4 \end{vmatrix}$ (c) $\begin{vmatrix} 4 & 21 & 8 \\ 0 & 0 & 0 \\ -4 & -3 & 6 \end{vmatrix}$

Example R17.4

Consider matrix (b) in Example R17.2.

(i) Find its adjoint matrix and hence its inverse, checking that you obtain the same answer as in Example R17.2.

(ii) By matrix inversion solve the equations

$$3x - 2y + \ z = 5$$
$$-5x + \qquad 2z = 3$$
$$3y + 3z = 4$$

(iii) Re-solve the equations using Cramer's rule.

Example R17.5

Consider the macro-model

$$C = 0.6Y + 0.4W - 0.1R$$
$$I = 0.3Y - 0.4R$$
$$Y = C + I + G$$

where Y is income, C is consumption, W is consumer wealth, R is the rate of interest, I is investment and G is government expenditure. If W, R and G are exogenous, express the model in matrix terms and hence find its reduced form.

Notes

1. Multiplying two vectors together in this way to obtain a single number or *scalar* is some-times referred to as forming the *scalar product*.
2. To obtain the result [17.40] it is necessary to use a property of determinants normally referred to as the 'alien factor' property. See, for example, A. C. Chiang (1984) *Fundamental Methods of Mathematical Economics*, 3rd edn, International Student Edition. McGraw-Hill, Tokyo, pp. 103–4.
3. In fact, it transpires that if there is a linear relationship between any of the rows of a matrix then there must also be a linear relationship between its columns.

Answers to examples

Chapter 1

Examples

1.1 (a) 25, 90, 79 503 (b) $12\frac{1}{2}$, $8\frac{1}{3}$, $10\frac{1}{20}$
(c) 343, −27, 8 365 427

1.2 1594, 7894

1.6 $x = 0.5, x = -4$

1.7 max $y = 5\frac{1}{3}$, $x = 1$, $x = -\frac{5}{3}$

1.8 $q = 3.612$

1.9 (a) 8, 6 (b) $-\frac{8}{3}, \frac{2}{3}$ (c) $\frac{5}{2}, \frac{7}{2}$ $4y = x + 12$

1.10 (a) $x = -1$ (b) identity (c) $x = 3.5$
(d) identity (e) $x = 3$

1.12 (a) $x = 3, x = 2$ (b) $x = 0.5, x = -3$
(c) $x = 0.523, x = -3.189$

1.13 (a) no solutions (b) $x = 1.5, x = -7$
(c) $x = \frac{4}{3}$ (d) $x = 0.886, x = -3.386$
(e) no solutions

1.14 Solutions are $x = 0.5, x = -1, x = 3$.

Revision examples

R1.1 Minimum at $x = -1.5, y = -9.5$.
(b) (i) −3.56, 0.56 (ii) −4, 1
(iii) no solutions

R1.2 (a) (i) $c = 2, m = -3/5$ (ii) $c = 8/3, m = 2/3$
(iii) $c = -5/2, m = -2$
(b) (i) $y = 0.5x - 2.5$ (ii) $y = -1.25x + 5$
(iii) $y = 2$ (iv) $x = 4$

R1.3 (a) (i) equation, $x = -16/3$
(ii) equation, $x = -9/4$
(iii) identity (iv) equation, $x = 15$

(b) The equation is inconsistent and has no
solution.

R1.4 (a) 1/3, −5 (b) 4.62, 2.38 (c) no solutions
(d) −6, −2 (e) −7/2, 1 (f) one solution, 5/3
(g) 1.37, −2.37

Chapter 2

Examples

2.1 (a) $x = 1, y = 2$ (b) $x = 58, y = 35$
(c) $x = 5, y = 3$

2.3 (a) $x = 1, y = 2$ no solutions to (b), (c) and (d)

2.6 (a) $a = 1, b = 2, c = \frac{7}{13}, d = \frac{8}{13}$
(b) $a = -3, b = 10, c = \frac{11}{13}, d = \frac{72}{13}$

2.8 (a) $x = 1, y = 5$ and $x = -\frac{2}{3}, y = -\frac{5}{3}$
(b) no solution

2.9 one solution only, $x = -2, y = -6$

Revision examples

R2.3 (a) two solutions, $x = 0.5, y = -0.5$ and
$x = -2, y = -8$
(b) no solutions ($b^2 < 4ac$)

R2.4 (a) three solutions, −4.85, 0, 1.85
(b) one solution, $x = 4.4, y = 12$

R2.5 min $y = -7$
(a) two solutions, $x = -1/3, y = 4/3$
and $x = -3, y = -4$
(b) no solutions
(c) one solution only, $x = -5/3, y = -20/3$

R2.6 (a) indeterminate (b) determinate
(c) indeterminate

Chapter 3

Examples

3.1 10 000, 9800, 10 408, 10 291.7, 10 480, 10 860.8

3.2 5200, 5380, 5542, 5687.8, 5819, 5937.1

3.3 (a) $p = \frac{25}{3}, d = s = \frac{115}{3}$
(b) $p = 5, d = s = 20$
(c) $p = \frac{3}{2}, d = s = \frac{7}{2}$

3.4 $p = 5, d = s = 35$, yes

3.5 $p = \frac{10}{3}$ $d = s = \frac{80}{3}$, no

3.6 (a) stable (b) unstable (c) stable

Revision examples

R3.1 (a) stock (b) flow (c) flow (d) flow
(e) stock (f) stock (g) flow (h) stock

R3.2 1900, 1820, 1756. Stabilise at 1500.

R3.3 $p = 10, d = s = 150; p = 12, d = s = 160;$
$p = 10, d = s = 180$

R3.4 (a) d falls by 10 (b) d rises by 20

R3.5 $p = 9/2, d = s = 18; p = 41/8, d = s = 79/4$

Chapter 4

Examples

4.2 (a) $p_1 = 5, p_2 = 3, d_1 = s_1 = 9, d_2 = s_2 = 9$
(b) $p_1 = 5.5, p_2 = 3, d_1 = s_1 = 16.5,$
$d_2 = s_2 = 3.5$

4.3 Y falls from 275 to 250, C from 240 to 220, I from 35 to 30

4.4 $p_1 = (\frac{55}{18})y - 5, p_2 = (\frac{40}{9})y - 4,$
$d_1 = s_1 = (\frac{70}{9})y - 13, d_2 = s_2 = -(\frac{5}{18})y + 5$
when $y = 9, p_1 = 22.5, p_2 = 36, d_1 = s_1 = 57,$
$d_2 = s_2 = 2.5$

4.5 $p_1 = -0.4 + 0.4y + 0.8p_2,$
$d_1 = s_1 = 11.2 + 0.8y - 1.4p_2$
(i) $p_1 = 11.6, d_1 = s_1 = 20.2$
(ii) $p_1 = 10.8, d_1 = s_1 = 21.6$
(iii) $p_1 = 8.8, d_1 = s_1 = 17.6$

4.6 p remains unchanged but d and s fall by 28.

4.7 $Y = 300 - 5r, C = 260 - 4r, I = 40 - r$

4.8 $Y = 150 - 500R + 10G,$
$C = 130 - 400R + 8G, I = 20 - 100R + G$
(a) $Y = 300, C = 250, I = 30$
(b) Unit rise in G leads to rises of 10, 8 and 1 in Y, C and I.

Revision examples

R4.1 $p_2 = 3, p_1 = 1, d_1 = s_1 = 5, d_2 = s_2 = 4$

R4.2 $p_2 = 39/2 - (15/2)y, p_1 = 8 - (10/3)y,$
$d_1 = s_1 = -5 + 5y, d_2 = s_2 = 15/2 - (5/6)y$
If $y = 2$, then $p_1 = 4/3, p_2 = 9/2, s_1 = d_1 = 5,$
$s_2 = d_2 = 35/6.$
If $y = 1.5$, then $p_1 = 3, p_2 = 33/4, s_1 = d_1 = 5/2,$
$s_2 = d_2 = 25/4.$

R4.3 $p_2 = 15 - 6y, p_1 = 37/5 - (16/5)y,$
$d_1 = s_1 = 1/5 + (12/5)y, d_2 = s_2 = 16/5 + (2/5)y$
If $y = 2$, then $p_1 = 1, p_2 = 3, d_1 = s_1 = 5,$
$d_2 = s_2 = 4.$
If y rises by 1 then p_2 falls by 0.6, p_1 falls by 0.32, d_1 and s_1 rise by 0.24, d_2 and s_2 rise by 0.04.

R4.4 $p = -26/9 + (8/9)y + (4/9)q,$
$d = s = -64/3 + (16/3)y + (2/3)q$
If y falls by 2 and q rises by 4, then p remains unchanged but d and s fall by 8.

R4.5 $R = 1/3 + (8/3)Y, M = L = 13/3 + (8/3)Y$
If $Y = 4$, then $R = 11, M = L = 15$. If Y falls by 1 then R falls by 8/3.

R4.6 $Y = 250/3 - (1/3)Y_{-1} + (10/3)G,$
$C = 70 - (1/5)Y_{-1} + 2G,$
$I = 40/3 - (2/15)Y_{-1} + (1/3)G$
In 1995, $Y = 190, C = 134, I = 6.$
In 1996, $Y = 186.7, C = 132, I = 4.67.$
In 1997, $Y = 187.78, C = 132.67, I = 5.11.$
In 1998, $Y = 187.41, C = 132.44, I = 4.97.$
Y stabilises at 187.5.

Chapter 5

Examples

5.1 (a) rise 200 (b) unchanged (c) fall 100
(d) rise 100 (e) unchanged

5.2 Full stock equilibrium values are $p = 4$,
$d = s = 7$, $D = S = 10$. Market period
equilibrium values are
  (a) $p = 3.5$, $d = 8$, $s = 5.5$, $D = 12.5$
  (b) $p = 4.5$, $d = 6$, $s = 8.5$, $D = 7.5$
  (c) $p = 3.975$, $d = 7.05$, $s = 6.925$, $D = 10.125$
  (d) $p = 4.025$, $d = 6.95$, $s = 7.075$, $D = 9.875$
  Stock supply next period **(a)** 17.5 **(b)** 2.5
  (c) 10.375 **(d)** 9.625
  Equilibrium appears stable.

5.3 **(a)** $p = 1$, $d = s = 7$, $D = S = 6$
  (b) this period $p = 0.667$, $d = 8$, $s = 6.33$,
  $D = 6.67$; next period $p = 0.806$, $d = 7.58$,
  $s = 6.61$, $D = 6.39$
  (c) No change in full stock equilibrium but
  market period equilibria will differ.

5.4 $p = 2$, $d = s = 10$, $D = S = 10$

5.7 **(a)** $p_1 = 1$, $p_2 = 2$, $d_1 = s_1 = 6$, $d_2 = s_2 = 8$,
  $D_2 = S_2 = 3$
  (b) $p_1 = 0.704$, $p_2 = 1.251$

Revision examples

R5.1 Full stock equilibrium is at $p = 5$, $d = s = 8$,
  $D = S = 12$.
  (a) $S = 8$, $p = 16/7$, $d = 54/7$, $s = 60/7$,
  $D = 80/7$
  (b) $S = 8.857$, $p = 2.224$, $d = 7.776$, $s = 8.448$,
  $D = 11.552$
  End period $S = 9.53$.

R5.2 If $S = 16$, then $p = 37/7$, $d = 150/7$, $s = 160/7$,
  $D = 132/7$.
  Next period, $S = 122/7$, i.e. S is rising.
  If $S = 20$, then $p = 5$, $d = s = 22$, $D = 20$.
  Next period, $S = 20$, i.e. S is unchanged. This
  is stock-flow equilibrium.
  If $S = 24$, then $p = 33/7$, $d = 158/7$, $s = 148/7$,
  $D = 148/7$.
  Next period, $S = 158/7$, i.e. S is falling.

R5.3 **(a)** $p = 4$, $d = s = 10$, $D = S = 4$. No change.
  (b) $S = 28$

R5.4 Red form: $p = 0.8w - 1.2$, $d = s = 23.6 - 2.4w$,
  $D = S = 44.4 - 1.6w$
  (a) when $w = 6$ then $d = s = 9.2$, $D = S = 34.8$,
  $p = 3.6$

  (b) when w rises by 1, d and s fall by 2.4,
  D and S fall by 1.6, p rises by 0.8.

Chapter 6

Examples

6.1 **(a)**, **(b)**, **(c)** are GPs.

6.2 **(a)** 2187, 13.44
  (b) 0.000 033 87, 0.9959
  (c) 0.093 95, 2.353 **(d)** 1024, −22
  (e) −0.097 66, 34.375

6.3 **(b)**, **(c)** and **(e)** are convergent, **(a)** and **(b)**
  are divergent
  (b) 0.999 983, 0.999 999 93, 1
  (c) 3.124, 3.377, 3.5
  (e) 33.301, 33.334, $33\frac{1}{3}$

6.4 **(a)** $1/(1 + x)^2$ **(b)** $(x + 3)/(y - x - 2)$
  progression will converge if $-x^2 < y < x^2$

6.5 **(a)** 1026.23 **(b)** 466.44, 18.9 per cent

6.6 **(a)** 419.8 **(b)** 3327 **(c)** 27 000

6.7 **(a)** 2023.7 **(b)** 12 851.2

6.8 At 5 per cent firm chooses second project but
  at 8 per cent it chooses first project.

6.9 At 10 per cent
  (a) both projects **(b)** second project
  At 5 per cent
  (a) both projects **(b)** first project.

6.10 **(a)** 73 per cent and 55 per cent
  (b) 25 per cent
  (i) At 20 per cent project 2 only. At 35 per
  cent project 1 only. At 60 per cent project
  1 only. At 75 per cent neither project.
  (ii) At 20 per cent both projects. At 35 per
  cent both projects. At 60 per cent project
  1 only. At 75 per cent neither project.

Revision examples

R6.1 **(a)** convergent GP, sum to infinity $= 20$
  (b) not a GP
  (c) divergent GP, sum to 10 is 1023
  (d) convergent GP, sum to infinity $= 256/3$
  (e) convergent GP, sum to infinity $= 3$

R6.2 **(a)** 1800 **(b)** $\dfrac{x^2}{x^2-(y+3)^2}$ **(c)** $\dfrac{pq^7}{q-p}$

R6.4 5 per cent

R6.6 **(a)** 73 per cent and 55 per cent

(b) 25 per cent

When r exceeds 25 per cent, $PV_1 > PV_2$.

When r is less than 25 per cent, $PV_1 < PV_2$.

Chapter 7

Examples

7.1 **(a)** 0 **(b)** 0

7.2 **(a)** 5 **(b)** 4

7.3 14, −4, 8

7.4 **(a)** $-32x^7$ **(b)** $30x^2$ **(c)** 0 **(d)** $126x^{41}$ **(e)** −9

7.5 **(a)** $36x^2$ **(b)** 12 **(c)** 0

7.6 **(a)** $-3/x^4$ **(b)** $1/2\sqrt{x}$ **(c)** $-8/x^3$

(d) $\frac{3}{2}x^{1/2}$ **(e)** $-1/3x^{-4/3}$

7.7 **(a)** $6x-12$ **(b)** $15x^2$ **(c)** $6x^5 - 12x^3 + 16x$

7.8 **(a)** $3x^2 - 6x + 10$ **(b)** $2x - 2/x^3$

7.9 51, 195, 435

7.10 6 at $x = 1$, 0 at $x = 0$

7.11 3 at $x = -1$, −3 at $x = \frac{1}{2}$. Zero gradient at $x = -\frac{1}{4}, y = 1\frac{1}{8}$

7.12 When $q = 10$, $MC = 65$, $AC = 42.5$.

When $q = 20$, $MC = 125$, $AC = 68.75$

$AC = MC$ when $q = 5$.

7.14 0.417, 1.17

7.15 **(a)** 0.615 **(b)** 0.75

7.16 **(a)** $12x^2(5x + 7) + 5(4x^3 + 6)$

(b) $6x(4x^3 + 5x) + 3x^2(12x^2 + 5)$

(c) $(8 - 5x)/x^3$

(d) $(16 + 12x - 16x^3 - 3x^4)/(x^3 + 2)^2$

(e) $16/(2x + 3)^2$

7.17 **(a)** $42x(3x^2 + 5)^6$ **(b)** $30(3x + 4)^9$

(c) $-20x(5x^2 + 4x)^{-3}$ **(d)** $(2x + 4)^{-1/2}$

7.18 **(a)** $8x(x^3 - 3x)^2(x^2 + 4)^3 + 6x^2(x^2 + 4)^4(x^3 - 3x)$

(b) $(1 + x)^2(2x - 7)/(2x - 1)^3$

(c) $-(3x - 10)(3x - 2)/(x + 6)^6$

7.19 $6(6t^3 - t^4 - 6)/(t + 3)^7$

Revision examples

R7.1 **(a) (i)** 2 **(ii)** ∞ **(b) (i)** 6 **(ii)** −0.5

(c) (i) −2 **(ii)** 1/3

R7.3 **(a)** 17, 13. The point is $(-5/6, -61/12)$.

(b) 2, −4 **(c)** When $q = 0$, gradient $= -12$.

When $q = 3/2$, gradient $= 16.5$. When

$q = -4$, gradient $= 44$.

R7.4 **(a)** $-9/x^4$ **(b)** $-1/2x^{3/2}$ **(c)** $1/3x^{2/3}$

(d) $-4/x^3 + 5$ **(e)** $0.75/x^{0.75}$ **(f)** $-0.75x^{-1.25}$

(g) $12/5x^{2/5}$ **(h)** $-4/x^3 + 3/2x^{1/2}$

R7.5 $TR = 2500$, $AR = 25$, $MR = 0$

R7.6 $TC = 2q^2 + 5q + 98$, $AC = 2q + 5 + 98/q$,

$MC = 4q + 5$

When $q = 5$, $TC = 173$, $AC = 34.6$, $MC = 25$.

When $q = 10$, $TC = 348$, $AC = 34.8$,

$MC = 45$. $MC = AC$ when $q = 7$.

R7.7 **(a)** 0.227 **(b)** 1.293

R7.8 **(a)** $30x^2 + 22x - 6$ **(b)** $48(2x + 5)^2$

(c) $\dfrac{21}{(3x+3)^2}$ **(d)** $21(3x^2 + 2x)^6(6x + 2)$

(e) $-\dfrac{2(3x^2 + 12x + 8)}{(3x^2 + 4x)^2}$

R7.9 **(a)** $\dfrac{2(4x - 3)(4x + 7)}{(2x + 1)^2}$ **(b)** $-(2/3)(5x^3 - 2x^2$

$+ 5/x)^{-5/3}(15x^2 - 4x - 5/x^2)$

(c) $(3x - 4)^3(5x + 3)(26x + 4)$

(d) $\dfrac{(1 + x)^2(4x - 5)}{(2x - 1)^3}$

(e) $(4x - 1)^{1/3}(2x - 3)^{1/2}(\frac{26}{2}x + \frac{11}{2})$

R7.10 **(a) (i)** $\dfrac{1}{2x(16x^2 + 3)}$ **(ii)** $\dfrac{1}{9(3x + 6)^2}$

(b) (i) $-\dfrac{(3y - 1)^2}{10}$ **(ii)** $\dfrac{1}{64y(2y^3 + 3)^3}$

Chapter 8

Examples

8.1 **(a)** $6x + 2$, 6 **(b)** $-2x^2/(x^2 + 3x)^2$, $4x^3/(x^2 + 3x)^3$

(c) $21(3x - 5)^6$, $378(3x - 5)^5$

8.3 **(a)** $f(x)$ has minimum of 9.8 when $x = 0.2$

(b) $f(z)$ has minimum of 9 when $z = 1$.

(c) $f(x)$ has local minimum of 12 when $x = 1.5$ and local maximum of -12 when $x = -1.5$

(d) $f(x)$ has maximum of $\frac{1}{12}$ when $x = 6$.

8.4 **(a)** minimum at $x = -2$ **(b)** point of inflection at $x = -2$ **(c)** point of inflection at $x = 4$

8.6 $q = 6.96$, $p = 19.78$, profit $= 44.5$

8.7 **(i)** $q = 40$ **(ii)** $q = 10$ **(iii)** $q = 20$
(a) $TR = 1200$ **(b)** $p = 30$ **(c)** $\Pi = 450$
(d) $p = 45$

8.9 $Q = 5(2 - W)/(1 + W)$, $P = 5(2 + W)/2(1 + W)$, $\Pi = 5(5W^2 - 24W + 16)/2(1 + W)$

Revision examples

R8.1 **(a)** local min at $x = -2$
(b) local min at $x = 2$, local max at $x = -5$
(c) local min at $x = 3$, local max at $x = -1$
(d) local min at $x = 8$, local max at $x = 0$

R8.2 **(a)** point of inflection at $x = 2$, $y = 0$
(b) point of inflection at $x = -3$, $y = -23$

R8.3 Fixed costs $= 200$. Min point of AC curve is at $q = 7.07$, $AC = 66.57$. When $q = 7.07$, $MC = 66.57$.

R8.4 Profit $\Pi = 10q - 1.25q^2 - 5$. Maximised when $q = 4$ and $p = 12$. To maximise revenue, $q = 26$. When $q = 4$, $\Pi = 15$. When $q = 26$, $\Pi = -590$ (i.e. firm makes loss).

R8.5 Profit max at $q = 25$, $p = 475$, $\Pi = 5595$. With tax, $q = 19.355$, $p = 503.2$. Government revenue $= 2879$.

R8.6 Profit max at $q = 10$, $p = 45$. With tax $q = 8.75$, $p = 45.62$. Government revenue $= 43.75$.

Chapter 9

Examples

9.1 **(a)** $x^5 + c$ **(b)** $\frac{3}{2}x^4 + c$ **(c)** $10x + c$ **(d)** $\frac{1}{3}x^9 + c$

9.2 **(a)** $\frac{4}{3}x^3 + 5x^2 + 3x + c$ **(b)** $2x^4 - \frac{5}{2}x^2 + c$
(c) $\frac{9}{5}x^5 + \frac{5}{3}x^3 - 3x + c$

9.3 **(a)** $-3/x + c$ **(b)** $1.875x^{1.6} + c$
(c) $0.8x^{1.25} - 0.6x^{-5} + c$

9.4 $TC = 0.25q^3 - 3q^2 + 20q + 50$

9.5 **(a)** $\frac{1}{7}(2x + 3)^6(4x - 1) + c$
(b) $\frac{1}{6}(x + 10)^8(4x - 5) + c$
(c) $\frac{1}{99}(x + 5)^9(9x^2 - 9x + 5) + c$
(d) $\frac{2}{5}(x + 5)^{3/2}(3x - 10) + c$

9.6 **(a)** $\frac{1}{4}(x^4 + 3)^6 + c$ **(b)** $\frac{1}{24}(x^3 + 5)^8 + c$
(c) $-1/2(2x^2 + 4)^2 + c$
(d) $-1/3(x^3 + 5)^5 + c$

9.7 **(a)** $-\frac{1}{2}x^{-2} + c$ **(b)** $\frac{3}{2}x^{3/2} + c$ **(c)** $\frac{8}{3}x^3 - \frac{5}{x} + c$
(d) $\frac{2}{7}(x + 4)^{5/2}(5x - 8) + c$
(e) $3(x^2 + 2)^{1/2} + c$

9.8 **(a)** 165 **(b)** -4.5 **(c)** 208 **(d)** 1

9.9 $5\frac{1}{6}$

9.10 500

Revision examples

R9.1 **(a)** $2x^4 + x^3 + c$ **(b)** $6x^2 + 15x + c$
(c) $-3/x + c$ **(d)** $-\frac{8}{3}(\sqrt{x})^3 + c$ **(e)** $\frac{8}{3}x^{3/2} + c$

R9.2 $TC = 2q^3 + 4q^2 + 10q + 860$. Fixed cost $= 860$.
$TR = 50q - 0.5q^2$

R9.3 **(a) (i)** $\frac{5x}{18}(3x + 4)^6\left(\frac{6}{7}x - \frac{4}{21}\right) + c$

(ii) $\frac{-3}{(x + 3)^2} + c$

(b) (i) $(3/56)(2x^4 + 3)^7 + c$

(ii) $-\frac{1}{8(4x^2 + 3)^4} + c$

R9.4 **(a)** 504 **(b)** -0.5 **(c)** 2145/4

R9.5 **(a)** 63/4 **(b)** 22/3

R9.6 440

Chapter 10

Examples

10.3 **(a)** 1104, 864 **(b)** 912, -18

10.4 **(a)** $40x^4y^2 + 10xy^2 + 12x + 3y$, $16x^5y + 10x^2y + 3x$
(b) $-48x^{-5}y^{-2}$, $-24x^{-4}y^{-3}$
(c) $6(x^2 + 2y^2x)^3(3x + y) + 6(3x + y)^2$ $(x^2 + 2y^2x)^2(x + y^2)$, $2(x^2 + 2y^2x)^3$ $(3x + y) + 12xy(3x + y)^2(x^2 + 2y^2x)^2$

(d) $7(3x^2y^2 + 5x)^6(6xy^2 + 5)$,
$42x^2y(3x^2y^2 + 5x)^6$

(e) $\dfrac{(12x^2y + 8xy^2 - 10x - 15y)}{(x^2 + y^2 + 3xy)^2}$,

$-\dfrac{(4x^2 + 5)(2y + 3x)}{(x^2 + y^2 + 3xy)^2}$

10.5 $3bcd + 4ba + 6a^2c^3$, $3acd + 2a^2$,
$3abd + 8cd + 9a^3c^2$, $3abc + 4c^2$

10.6 0.147, 1.103, 0.956. Substitutes.

10.9 1088

10.10 $2uv^2 + 2uw^2$, $2u^2v - 2w$, $2u^2w - 2v + 2w$,
$4uv$, $4uw$, -2

Revision examples

R10.1 **(a)** 252, 20 **(b)** 1224, −18

R10.2 **(a)** $8xy - 3y$, $4x^2 - 3x$ **(b)** $16x^3y^3$, $12x^4y^2$
(c) 3, 8 **(d)** $4x + 2y$, $8y + 2x$ **(e)** 0, $14y$
(f) $-8y/x^3$, $4/x^2$

R10.3 $\partial z/\partial a = bc^2 + 8c^3a^3$, $\partial z/\partial b = ac^2 + 10cb$
$\partial z/\partial c = 2abc + 3d^2c^2 + 5b^2 + 6c^2a^4$,
$\partial z/\partial d = 2dc^3$
$\partial^2 z/\partial a\partial c = 2bc + 24c^2a^3 = \partial^2 z/\partial c\partial a$,
$\partial^2 z/\partial b\partial d = 0 = \partial^2 z/\partial d\partial b$

R10.4 **(a)** $\partial z/\partial x = 30x(3x^2 + 2y)^4$,
$\partial z/\partial y = 10(3x^2 + 2y)^4$
(b) $\partial z/\partial x = ?(5x + 3y)^7(85x + 3y + 160)$,
$\partial z/\partial y = 24(2x + 4)(5x + 3y)^7$

R10.5 Own-price elasticity = 8.09, income
elasticity = 7.36, cross-price elasticity =
−1.82. Goods are complements.

R10.6 **(a)** $APL = 800(K/L)^{0.4}$, $MPL = 480(K/L)^{0.4}$
(b) $MPK = 320(L/K)^{0.6}$.
When $K = 4$ and $L = 10$, $MPL = 332.7$ and
$MPK = 554.5$.

Chapter 11

Examples

11.1 **(a)** $10xyw^3\,dx + 5x^2w^3\,dy + 15x^2yw^2\,dw$
(b) $(15x^2y + 4y^3)\,dx + (5x^3 + 12xy^2)\,dy$
(c) $2(u + 4)(v + 3)^3\,du + 3(u + 4)^2(v + 3)^2\,dv$

11.2 180 000 000

11.3 $\dfrac{2Y^2 - 5p_1^2 + 6p_2}{Y + 10p_1p_2}$, $\dfrac{4Yp_2 - p_1}{Y + 10p_1p_2}$

11.4 $1/(1 - b)$, $-b/(1 - b)$ where $b = \partial C/\partial Y^d$
If $G = T$ then $\partial Y/\partial G = \partial Y/\partial T = 1$.

11.7 **(a)** $15y^4(4y + 6)^2$, $6y^4(14y + 15)(4y + 6)$
(b) 3, $64y^3 + 3$

11.8 **(a)** $750w^4$ **(b)** $75vw^2$ **(c)** $3500w^6 + 14vw$
(d) $2w + 100w^3v^2$

11.9 **(a)** $-3x/y$ **(b)** $-3y/2x$ **(c)** $(y^2 + 7)/xy$ **(d)** $3/y$

11.11 **(a)** **(i)** z is multiplied by 4 **(ii)** z is increased
by 12.36 per cent **(iii)** z is divided by 4
(iv) z falls by 51 per cent
(b) **(i)** z is halved
(ii) z is increased by 10 per cent

11.12 **(a)** degree 3 **(b)** degree 0
(c) non-homogeneous
(d) non-homogeneous
(e) degree $\alpha + \beta$ **(f)** degree 0.

11.14 **(a)** degree 4 in x and y
(b) degree 0 in x and y
(c) degree 0 in u and v

Revision examples

R11.1 **(a)** 518
(b) **(i)** $dz = 2(3x + 2y)\,dx + 2(2x + 5y)\,dy$
(ii) $dz = 0.3(z/w)\,dw + 0.2(z/x)\,dx +$
$0.5(z/y)\,dy$ **(iii)** $dz = -\dfrac{dx + dy}{(x + y)^3}$

R11.2 $\dfrac{\partial p_1}{\partial p_2} = -\dfrac{2p_1}{5 + 2p_2}$, $\dfrac{\partial p_1}{\partial Y} = \dfrac{4}{5 + 2p_2}$

R11.3
$$\dfrac{\partial Y}{\partial M} = $$
$$\dfrac{\partial I/\partial R}{(\partial L/\partial R)(1 - \partial C/\partial Y - \partial I/\partial Y) + (\partial I/\partial R)(\partial L/\partial Y)}$$

$$\dfrac{\partial Y}{\partial W} = $$
$$\dfrac{\partial C/\partial W}{1 - \partial C/\partial Y - \partial I/\partial Y + (\partial I/\partial R)(\partial L/\partial Y)/(\partial L/\partial R)}$$

R11.4 **(a)** $\partial z/\partial x = 150/x^3$, $dz/dx = -150/x^3$
(b) $dz/dw = (20/3)w^4$
(c) **(i)** $dy/dx = 3/(2 - 2y)$
(ii) $dy/dx = -2(1 + x)/4y^3$

R11.5 **(a)** **(i)** non-homogeneous
       (ii) homogeneous of degree -2
       (iii) homogeneous of degree 0
   (b) **(i)** homogeneous of degree 5 in x and
       y only **(ii)** homogeneous of degree 0 in
       x and y only

Chapter 12

Examples

12.1 **(a)** no turning-points
   (b) local minimum at $u = 2$, $v = 1$
   (c) local minimum at $x = 0$, $y = 0$ and at
      $x = -1.278$, $y = -1.065$

12.2 $q = 625$, $k = 625/4$, $l = 625/16$

12.3 $q_1 = 25$, $q_2 = 22$, $p_1 = 165$, $p_2 = 59$,
   profit $= 4118$

12.4 $q_1 = 2$, $q_2 = 3$, $p = 44$

12.5 local minimum at $x = 3$, $y = 1$

12.7 **(a)** local max at $x = -2.659$, $y = -0.532$
   and local min at $x = 2.659$, $y = 0.532$
   (b) local max at $x = 0.707$, $y = 0.707$
   and local min at $x = -0.707$, $y = -0.707$
   (c) local min at $x = 0$, $y = 0$ and local max
   at $x = 4$, $y = -2$

Revision examples

R12.1 **(a)** local min at $x = 2$, $y = -1$
   (b) local max at $x = 2$, $y = 0$ and saddle
   point at $x = -2$, $y = 0$
   (c) no stationary points exist
   (d) local min at $u = 0$, $v = 0$

R12.2 $q_1 = 12.5$, $q_2 = 7.5$, $p = 161$, $\Pi = 2528$

R12.3 $q_1 = 16$, $q_2 = 12$, $p_1 = 108$, $p_2 = 84$,
   $TC = 1396$. With constant average variable
   costs, $q_1 = 17.67$, $q_2 = 14.5$.

R12.4 **(a)** $x = 2.74$, $y = 1.37$, $z = 5.477$. Local
   minimum. **(b)** $x = 1.35$, $y = 0.95$,
   $z = 3.225$. Local maximum.

R12.5 For max output, $x = 9$, $y = 81$. For min cost,
   $x = 9$, $y = 81$. Min cost $= 378$. MC is given
   by $\lambda = \sqrt{9}$.

R12.6 $q_1 = 6$, $q_2 = 2$. $\lambda = 2880 =$ marginal utility of
   expenditure. With total expenditure 540,
   $q_1 = 60$, $q_2 = 20$.

Chapter 13

Examples

13.1 **(a)** $q = 105\,004$
   (b) $q = 50\,667$, $x_1 = 0.444$, $x_2 = 16$

13.2 $MRTS = 1/k$

13.4 Optimality condition is $k = 4l$. Max $q = 100$,
   $l = 5$, $k = 20$. $\lambda = 0.625 =$ extra output
   obtained from unit increase in TC.

13.5 Min cost $= 160$, optimality condition is $k = 4l$.

13.6 $k = 4l$

13.7 Expansion path is $k = 3.75l$.
   Max $q = 1.58 \times 10^9$, $l = 10$, $k = 37.5$.

13.8 $q = 0.624p^4$.
   $k = 15\,983.3$, $l = 6393.1$, $q = 15\,983.3$
   $q = 2548(p/m)^2(p/w)^2$,
   $k = 1019(p/m)^3(p/w)^2$, $l = 1019(p/m)^2(p/w)^3$

13.9 **(a)** $q = 1\,287\,000$
   (b) $x_1 = 0.444$, $x_2 = 16$, $q = 50\,665$

13.11 **(a)** $C = 0.003\,38q^2$ **(b)** $q = 147.9p$

13.12 **(a)** $C = w_1 \bar{x}_1 + 2\bar{x}_1^{-1/2} w_2^{1/2} w_3^{1/2} q^{3/2}$
   (b) $C = 3(w_1 w_2 w_3)^{1/3} q$

Revision examples

R13.1 **(a)** $MRTS = 6L/7K$, $TC = 5K + 6L$
   (b) max $Q = 64\,527$, $L = 507.7$, $K = 493.6$,
   $\lambda = 15.73$
   (c) $K = 6C_0/13p_1$, $L = 7C_0/13p_2$ are output-
   maximising factor demand equations.

R13.2 Expansion path is $l = 0.91k$.
   Minimum cost $= 298.9$.

R13.3 **(a)** $x = 54$, $y = 30$, $\lambda = MC = 0.9$, $AC = 0.66$
   (b) $x = 0.134(p_2/p_1)^{0.454} q^{0.909}$,
   $y = 0.112(p_1/p_2)^{0.546} q^{0.909}$.
   x and y are cost-minimising factor
   demand equations. Substituting x and
   y into $C = p_1 x + p_2 y$ gives firm's long-
   run cost curve.

R13.4 (a) $q = 38.44$, $k = 57.67$, $l = 57.67$

R13.5 $x = 0.0517(p_2/p_1)^{0.6}(p_3/p_1)^{0.2}Q$,
$y = 0.155(p_1/p_2)^{0.4}(p_3/p_1)^{0.2}Q$,
$z = 0.0517(p_2/p_1)^{0.6}(p_1/p_3)^{0.8}Q$.
Long-run cost curve is $C = 1.575Q$. Short-run cost curve is $C = 384 + 0.386Q^{1.25}$.

Chapter 14

Examples

14.1 (a) $MRS = q_1^3/q_2^3$
(b) $MU_1 = U^3/q_1^3$, $MU_2 = U^3/q_2^3$; yes

14.2 $8q_1 + 4q_2 = 500$, $q_1 = 38.34$, $q_2 = 48.31$

14.3 0.060

14.5 $q_1 = \dfrac{-Y/p_1}{1 + (p_2/p_1)^{2/3}}$, $q_2 = \dfrac{Y/p_2}{1 + (p_1/p_2)^{2/3}}$

14.6 $q_1 = 2Y/9p_1$, $q_2 = Y/3p_2$, $q_3 = 4Y/9p_3$,
$\lambda = 2q_1 q_2^3 q_3^4 /p_1$

14.7 $c_1 = 4.5$, $c_2 = 2.25$. With $r = 0.2$, $c_1 = 4.29$,
$c_2 = 2.34$. Rise in r leads to substitution of c_2 for c_1.

14.8 $c_1 = 0.5(w/p)$, $c_2 = 0.333(1 + r)(w/p)$,
$c_3 = 0.167(1 + r)^2(w/p)$

Revision examples

R14.1 $y = (15 - x^{0.5})^2$, $MRS = (y/x)^{0.5}$, $x = 100$,
$y = 25$

R14.2 (a) $q_1 = 53.2$, $q_2 = 47.9$, $\lambda = 1.10 \times 10^{12} =$
marginal utility of total expenditure

(b) $q_1 = \left(\dfrac{a}{a + b}\right)\left(\dfrac{Y}{p_1}\right)$, $q_2 = \left(\dfrac{b}{a + b}\right)\left(\dfrac{Y}{p_2}\right)$

The functions have unit elasticity with respect to income and own-price but cross-price elasticities are zero.

R14.3 $q_1 = 2 + m/3p_1 - 5p_2/3p_1$,
$q_2 = 5/3 + 2m/3p_2 - 2p_1/p_2$

R14.4 $Y = 3q_1 + 5q_2$
(a) $q_1 = 3.84$, $q_2 = 3.06$, min $Y = 26.82$
(b) $q_2 = 1.13(p_1/p_2)^{3/7}U_0^{1/7}$,
$q_1 = 0.848(p_2/p_1)^{4/7}U_0^{1/7}$.
These functions are Hicksian compensated demand equations.

R14.5 $x_1 = \dfrac{Y/p_1 - (5/3)(p_2/p_1) - (5/2)(p_2/p_1)^2}{1 + (1/2)(p_2/p_1)^2}$

$x_2 = \dfrac{Y/p_2 - 5(p_1/p_2) - (10/3)(p_1/p_2)^2}{1 + 2(p_1/p_2)^2}$

Chapter 15

Examples

15.4 $x = (1/b)\log_a(y/c)$

15.5 (a) 3 (b) 3 (c) 0 (d) -3 (e) 1/3 (f) 0
(g) -5 (h) -4

15.6 (a) $\log A = \log 5 + 2 \log d + 4 \log e - 3 \log b$
$\qquad - 4 \log c$

(b) $\log K = \log 3 - 3 \log w + 3 \log x + 6 \log y$
$\qquad - 4 \log z$

15.7 (a) 2.01 (b) 6.545 (c) -3.517 (d) 3.387

15.8 (a) 147.78 (b) 100 281.1 (c) 3.508×10^8

15.9 (a) 0.063 (b) 0.061

15.11 33.52, 30.45, 63.56

15.12 (a) $y = (1/3)e^{x/4}$ (b) $x = (1/6)e^{y/3}$ (c) $x = e^{y/2}$

15.13 (a) $5e^x$ (b) $10x/(5x^2 + 6)$ (c) $xe^x(x + 2)$
(d) $3e^{-5x}(1 - 5x)$ (e) $16e^{4x}(2 \ln 3x^2 + \frac{1}{x})$

15.15 $q = 0.012$

15.16 $p = (A/B)Y^2$, $d = s = (A^2/B)Y^4$. p grows at rate $2g$, d and s at rate $4g$.

Revision examples

R15.1 (a) $x = (1/6)\ln(y/4)$ (b) $x = 0.2e^{y/3}$

R15.2 (a) (i) 3 (ii) 5 (iii) 0 (iv) 2 (v) -7 (vi) 4
(vii) -3 (viii) 1/2
(b) (i) 1.422 (ii) 3.332 (iii) 2.618
(iv) 0.8155 (v) 5.513
(vi) $\log_{10}(-5.3)$ does not exist.

R15.3 $P = 173.15$ in 1985, $P = 63.67$ in 1965;
$g = 0.0253$ between 1985 and 1995;
$P = 300$ by 2007

R15.4 (a) $20xe^{2x^2}$ (b) $1/x$ (c) $5x^2[3 \ln(3x) + 1]$
(d) $2xe^{3x}(2 + x)$

R15.5 W grows exponentially if elasticities are constant, that is if W_1/W and W_2/W are constants. $g = (W_1/W)\alpha g_1 + (W_2/W)(1 - \alpha)g_2$

Chapter 16

Examples

16.2 $Y^* = 250$, stable

16.3 $p_t = 5.5 + 0.5p_{t-1}, p_t = -3(0.5)^t + 11$

16.4 (a) $Y_t = -15(1.5)^t + 20$ (b) $Y_t = 7(-0.6)^t + 5$
(c) $Y_t = 3(0.9)^t$ (d) $Y_t = -5(1.2)^t + 10$

16.5 (a) $Y_t = (5)^t + (-2)^t - 2$
(b) $Y_t = 2.67(0.5)^t + 3.33(-0.4)^t + 10$
(c) $Y_t = 0.786(7.275)^t + 3.839(-0.275)^t$
$\quad - 0.625$

16.6 (a) $Y_t = (2 + 3t)(2)^t + 10.5$
(b) $Y_t = 3.305(1.326)^t + 1.695(-0.226)^t$
(c) $Y_t = 3.89(1)^t + 1.11(-0.5)^t + 1.67t$
(d) $Y_t = -2.809(1.434)^t - 4.191(0.232)^t + 10$
(e) $Y_t = 10 - 2(2)^t + 4t$

16.7 All equilibria are stable except for (c).
Only equation (a) implies cycles.

16.8 $Y_t = -2000(0.6)^t + 1500(0.5)^t + 1000$.
Stable, unstable.

16.9 $p_t = (9.875 - 3.917t)(3)^t + 2.625$, unstable

Revision examples

R16.1 $p_t = 2 + Y_t$. Difference equation is
$3p_t - p_{t-1} = 36$ with $p_0 = 10$. Solution to
difference equation is $p_t = -8(1/3)^t + 18$.
As $t \to \infty$, $p_t \to 18$, its equilibrium value.

R16.2 (a) $Y_t = 2 + 6t$
(b) $Y_t = 0.94(-4)^t + 14.56(5/3)^t - 0.5$
(c) $Y_t = 8(0.5)^t + 12t(0.5)^t + 16$
(d) $Y_t = 8.25 - 0.25(-3)^t + 3t$
(e) $Y_t = 16.58(1.131)^t + 1.42(-0.531)^t - 15$

R16.3 (a) Unstable with cycles
(b) Unstable without cycles
(c) Stable without cycles

R16.4 Difference equation is
$Y_t - Y_{t-1} - Y_{t-2} + 40 = 0$. Solution is
$Y_t = 7.24(3.236)^t + 2.76(-1.236)^t + 20$.
The equilibrium level of Y is 20 but the
equilibrium is unstable.

R16.5 $Y_t = -5(2)^t - 3(1/3)^t + 4(1/2)^t + 15$.
Unstable.

Chapter 17

Examples

17.1 (a) -21 (b) $a_1^2 + a_2^2 + a_3^2 + a_4^2 + a_5^2$

17.2 (a) $A = \begin{pmatrix} 2 & 3 & 1 \\ 1 & -7 & 3 \\ -3 & 4 & -1 \end{pmatrix}$

$x = \begin{pmatrix} x_1 \\ x_2 \\ x_3 \end{pmatrix}$ $b = \begin{pmatrix} 5 \\ 2 \\ -4 \end{pmatrix}$

(b) $A = \begin{pmatrix} 3 & 1 & -2 \\ 4 & 0 & 2 \\ 0 & 4 & -5 \end{pmatrix}$ $x = \begin{pmatrix} u \\ v \\ w \end{pmatrix}$ $b = \begin{pmatrix} -6 \\ 6 \\ 4 \end{pmatrix}$

(c) $A = \begin{pmatrix} 1 & 1 & 0 \\ -3 & 0 & 1 \\ 0 & 1 & 2 \end{pmatrix}$ $x = \begin{pmatrix} x \\ y \\ z \end{pmatrix}$ $b = \begin{pmatrix} 4 \\ 3 \\ 2 \end{pmatrix}$

17.3 (a) $AB = \begin{pmatrix} 71 & 62 & 33 \\ 41 & 6 & -1 \\ 44 & 27 & 15 \end{pmatrix}$

$BA = \begin{pmatrix} 76 & 40 & 46 \\ 22 & 14 & 18 \\ 50 & 25 & 2 \end{pmatrix}$

$DA = (78 \quad 43 \quad 62)$ $BC = \begin{pmatrix} 58 & 18 \\ 17 & 0 \\ 42 & 41 \end{pmatrix}$

$AE = \begin{pmatrix} 56 & 12 & 33 & 100 \\ 34 & 2 & 17 & 28 \\ 24 & 22 & -15 & 33 \end{pmatrix}$

Other products do not exist.

(b) $(AB)C = A(BC) = \begin{pmatrix} 693 & 395 \\ 191 & -51 \\ 356 & 149 \end{pmatrix}$

17.5 (a) $\begin{pmatrix} -\frac{1}{6} & \frac{2}{3} \\ \frac{1}{2} & -1 \end{pmatrix}$ (b) $\begin{pmatrix} \frac{1}{5} & \frac{2}{5} \\ \frac{4}{5} & \frac{3}{5} \end{pmatrix}$

(c) $\begin{pmatrix} \frac{11}{3} & -3 & \frac{1}{3} \\ -\frac{7}{3} & 3 & -\frac{2}{3} \\ \frac{2}{3} & -1 & \frac{1}{3} \end{pmatrix}$ (d) Inverse does not exist.

17.6 (a) 14 (b) 249

17.7 (a) 0 (b) 37 (c) 54 (d) –11 (e) 224

17.8 (a) $x_1 = 8$, $x_2 = 8$ (b) $x_1 = 1$, $x_2 = 1$, $x_3 = 1$

(c) $x = \dfrac{b+c}{2}$, $y = \dfrac{a+c}{2}$, $z = \dfrac{a+b}{2}$

Revision examples

R17.1 $(A + B)C = \begin{pmatrix} 1 \\ 0 \\ 16 \end{pmatrix} = AC + BC$

R17.2 (a) $\begin{pmatrix} 0.1 & -0.2 \\ 0.3 & 0.4 \end{pmatrix}$

(b) $\begin{pmatrix} 2/21 & -1/7 & 4/63 \\ -5/21 & -1/7 & 11/63 \\ 5/21 & 1/7 & 10/63 \end{pmatrix}$

R17.3 (a) 0 (b) –418 (c) 0

R17.4 (i) Adjoint matrix is $\begin{pmatrix} -6 & 9 & -4 \\ 15 & 9 & -11 \\ -15 & 9 & -10 \end{pmatrix}$

Inverse is as in R17.2(b).

(ii) $x = 19/63$, $y = -58/63$, $z = 142/63$

R17.5 $\begin{pmatrix} Y \\ C \\ I \end{pmatrix} = \begin{pmatrix} 4W - 5R + 10G \\ 2.8W - 3.1R + 6G \\ 1.2W - 1.9R + 3G \end{pmatrix}$

Index

abscissa   3
algebra
  brackets   xxiv–xxv
    multiplication   xxix
    powers   xxviii–xxix, xxx
  division   xxv
  fractions   xxxi–xxxvi
    division   xxxv–xxxvi
    multiplication   xxxi–xxxv
    reciprocals   xxxiv–xxxv
    simplification   xxxiii–xxiv
  multiplication   xxiv
  power notation   xxiv
algebra shorthand
  basic rules   xxiv–xxv
  examples of use   xxvi–xxviii
annuities   101–2
  perpetual   102
arithmetic operations, use of brackets   xiv–xv
average cost   122–3
average product of capital   187
average product of capital curves   187
average product of labour, definition   187
average product of labour curves   187

brackets
  in algebra   xxiv–xxv
  use in arithmetic operations   xiv–xv

capital stock   90
ceteris paribus assumption   47, 58, 60, 62, 78, 87,
  181–4
co-ordinate systems   3–4, 176
Cobb-Douglas production function   242–4, 279
  profit-maximisation model   242–3
column vector   303
common ratio   94, 98, 101
complex roots   15, 295–6

compound interest   93, 100
constant, definition   1
constrained optimisation problems
  solution
    by calculus   220–1
    graphical   219–20
constraints   218–28
  budget   250, 251, 252, 255–6, 259, 260
  cost   235–6
  output   236–8
consumer surplus   172–3
consumption, marginal rate of substitution of
    current for future   260
consumption function   35–8, 73–4, 89, 90,
  199–201, 286, 298
coordinate systems, graphing of functions   4–9
cost (functions)
  average   9, 147–8
  marginal   109–10, 122–3, 147–9, 163, 164, 244
  short versus long run   244–6
  total   8, 109–10, 122–3, 147–58, 163–4
cost minimisation model   240–1
  Cobb-Douglas production function   243
cycles   295–6

demand
  excess flow   50
    definition   45
  excess market   81, 83–4
    definition   46
  flow   48–9, 58–72, 78–90, 123, 195–8, 282–5
    definition   45
  functions   252–7
  market   58, 82, 256–7
    definition   45–6
  price elasticity   133–4
  stock   78–90
    definition   45

dependent variable, definition   2
depreciation   90
derivatives   117
  first order   138, 139, 140, 146
  higher order   138–59, 188–90
  partial   178–84
    first-order   190
    second-order   188–90
  second order   138–40, 146
  third-order   146
  total   201–2
  see also differentiation
difference equations   282–302
  first order   285, 288–91
  higher order   300
  second order   286–8, 291–4
  solutions   288–96
    complex roots, cycles and stability
      295–6
    first-order linear equations   288–91
    repeated roots   294–5
    second-order linear equations
      291–4
differentials   193–5
  total   193–210
differentiation   114–37, 175–92
  addition rule   120–1
  chain rule   130–2
  definition   117
  of exponential functions   276–7
  implicit   202–4
  inverse function rule   133
  of logarithmic functions   276–7
  partial   178–84, 181–4
  power rule   118–20
  product rule   128–9
  quotient rule   129–30
  subtraction rule   120–1
discounted cash flow   103–4
domain   8
dynamic analysis   53, 68, 282–302

economic models   35–8
elasticity of demand
  constant   126–7
  cross-price   184, 198–9
  income   183, 198–9
  price   126–7, 133–4, 182–3, 198–9
elasticity of supply   127–8, 198–9
equation of exchange   13

equations   1–22
  cubic   17
  linear   9–13
    solution   12–13
  polynomial   16–18
  quadratic   7, 13–16
  simple, solution   xxxvi–xxxviii
  simultaneous   23–41, 195–201
  simultaneous with more than two variables
      27–9
    algebraic solution   27–9
    graphical solution   27
  simultaneous with two variables   23–6
    algebraic solution   23–4
    graphical solution   24–6
equilibrium
  flow   58–72, 80–1, 89–90
    determination   49–51
    relationship with full stock   82–6
  full stock   49, 81–6, 87, 88, 91–2
  market period   82, 282–5
  stable   54–5, 282–5, 295–6
  unstable   54–5, 282–5, 295–6
Euler's theorem   207–8, 209
expansion path   238
exponential constant   273
exponential functions   265–6, 271–4, 276–9
  differentiation   276–7
exponential growth rate   278–9
exponents   xix
exports   43–4

factorisation   13–14
foreign exchange reserves   43–4
fractions   xv–xvii
  addition   xvi
  denominator   xv
  division   xvi
  multiplication   xvi
  numerator   xv
  simplification   xv
  subtraction   xvi
full employment   37, 89
functional relationship, definition   1
functions
  continuous   110
  exponential   265–6, 271–4, 276–9
  graphing   4–9
  inverse   18–20, 266–7
  linear   9–11

logarithmic   266–8, 276–7
of more than one variable   175–8
quadratic   6–9

general equilibrium analysis   62
geometric progressions   93–108, 102
convergent   97–9, 102
definition   94
divergent   97, 99
nth term   94
sum to infinity   96–9
sum to n terms   94–5
Giffen good   54
government expenditure   35–8, 73–4, 89–90,
189, 199–201, 286, 298–9
gradient
of non-linear function   109–10, 114–17
of straight line   10, 109
graphing of functions   4–9
growth   273, 276, 278–9

homogenous functions   204–7, 239, 240, 242,
252, 256

i   15
identities   12
imports   43–4
income
distribution   257
effect   57
national   35–8, 73–4, 89–90, 199–201, 279,
286–7, 298–9
net fixed   92
inconsistent system   28, 31
independent variable, definition   2
indices   xix
indifference curve   249–51, 258
inferior good   57
inflection, point of   144–5, 146–7
integers, basic operations   xiii–xiv
integrals
definite   168–71
indefinite   168
integration   160–74
additional rule   162
area under curve   169–71
by parts   164–6
by substitution   166–8
constant of   160, 165, 166, 167, 169
notation and terminology   160–1

power rule   161–2
subtraction rule   162
intercept   10
interest rate   36–8, 73–4, 89, 93, 100–4,
199–201, 258–9, 260, 271–3
investment
private capital   35–8, 73–4, 89–90, 199–201
in stocks   46, 78–80
IS-LM model   37, 200–1
iso-cost lines   233–5, 234–5, 236
iso-value curves   176–8
isoquants   233–5
convexity of   233, 242

Keynesian models   35–8, 73–4, 89, 90, 199–201,
286, 298–9, 323–4

labour market   37–8, 56
Lagrange multiplier   221, 235, 236, 237, 251,
255, 259
use and interpretation   222–5
Lagrangian   221–5, 235–7, 251, 255, 259
limits   97, 110–14, 273, 288
linear functions   9–11
definition   9
logarithmic functions   266–8
differentiation   276–7
logarithms   268–70
natural   275
and negative numbers   268
of unity   269

marginal cost   122–3
marginal product
of capital   207
curve   186, 236, 242
definition   186
diminishing   186, 242
of labour   207
curve   186–7, 236, 242
definition   186
marginal productivity, law of diminishing
47
marginal propensity
to consume   74
to save   74
marginal rate of substitution   249–51
capital for labour   234–8
marginal utility   188, 251, 256, 258
of income   251

market
  definition   45
  flow   46–51
  multi-good flow   58, 60–2
  period   82
  stock-flow   78–92
market period, equilibrium   282–5
matrices
  addition   310
  adjoint   317
  conformable   309
  description   305
  determinants   314–19
    4×4 and higher-order   317
    cofactors   315
    definition   314
    evaluation   314, 316–17
    matrix inversion   317–19
    minors   315
    solution of equation systems   321–2
  identity   311
  inversion   312–14
    Cramer's Rule   321–2
    solution of equation systems   319–22
    use of determinants   317–19
  multiplication   307–10
  non-conformable   309
  scalar multiplication   310–11
  subtraction   310
  transpose   311
matrix-vector multiplication   306–8
maxima and minima
  global   142–4, 146, 211, 227, 235, 251
  local   140–4, 146, 211–15, 225, 226, 230–1,
    235
money   37
multipliers   68, 74, 195, 199–200

natural logarithms   275
negative numbers   xviii–xix, xxii, 268
non-linear system   195–201
  definition   33
  solution
    algebraically   33
    graphically   33–4

optimisation
  constrained   218–28, 235–8
  unconstrained   211–15
ordinate   3

origin   3
own-price substitution effects   233–4

partial adjustment coefficient   80
perpetual annuities   102
powers of numbers   xix–xxiv
  calulation using calculator   xix
  division   xx
  fractional or decimal   xxii–xxiii
  handling rules   xx–xxi
  multiplication   xx
  negative   xxi–xxii
  negative numbers   xxii
  zero   xxi
present value   100–4, 259
price elasticity of demand   133–4
prices   46–9, 52–3, 58–72, 78–90, 252–7, 259,
    260, 282–5
  factor   236, 239–40, 244
producer surplus   173
production function   184–7, 206, 207, 233–48
  Cobb Douglas   242–4, 279
profit, definition   215
profit function   149
profit maximisation   149–58, 215–18, 238–41
  cost and revenue functions   244–6
  first order conditions   150, 153, 216
  model, Cobb-Douglas production function
    242–3
  second order conditions   150–2, 153, 216,
    217–18
  and taxation   152–6

quadratic equations   7
  general form   6
  solution   13–16
    formula   14
    number of   15–16
quadratic functions
  graphs   6–9
  representation of total cost curve   8–9
quasi-concavity   226–8
  strict   226, 233, 249, 255, 258

reduced form   62–74, 156–7, 252, 256, 261,
    322–4, 339–44, 345
  coefficients   68
  of non-linear system   195–201
  obtaining   66–7
  uses of   67–8, 70, 74

repeated roots 294–5
returns to scale 206, 242
revenue (function)
  average 124–5
  marginal 123, 124, 134, 149–58, 164, 244
  total 123–4, 133–4, 149–58, 164
row vector 303

saddle points 231–2
saving 89–90, 258–9
simultaneous linear equations *see* equations,
    simultaneous
static analysis 51–2, 68, 282
  comparative 52
  definition 51
stationary points 140–7
  global maxima and minima 142–4, 146
  local maxima and minima 140–4, 146
  point of inflection 144–5, 146–7
  see also maxima and minima
stock adjustment coefficient 79, 92
stock investment 46, 78–80
stock-flow markets
  macro-economic example 89–90
  for more than one good 878
straight line 9–11
structural coefficients 68
structural form 62–74, 156–7, 322
substitution effect 57, 253
supply
  curve 240
  elasticity 127–8
  flow 47–8, 58–72, 78–90, 195–8, 282–5
    definition 45
  market 58, 82
    definition 46
  stock 78–90
    definition 45
systems of equations
  determinate 30, 36, 50, 60, 64, 320–1
  indeterminate 31–2, 37, 58–60, 320–1
  linear 30–2
    representation by matrices 305–7
    solution by matrix inversion 319–22

non-linear 32–5, 195–201
overdeterminate (inconsistent) 31, 38,
    320–1

taxation
  and profit-maximisation 152–6
  of profits 152–3
  of revenue 153–6
  of sales 153–6
total cost curve, representation by quadratic
    functions 8–9
total product curves 185
turning-points 140–4, 213

utility functions 187–8, 249–52, 255–6, 257
utility maximisation 249–52, 256
  overtime (intertemporal) 257–62

variables
  definition 1
  endogenous 63, 64–7, 68, 69, 70, 73
  exogenous 63, 64–7, 68, 69–70, 71, 73
  flow 42–4, 101
    examples 42
    measurement 42
  independent 2
  pre-determined 63
  stock 42–4, 101
    examples 42
    measurement 42
vector
  column 303
  description 303–4
  multiplication 304
  row 303

Walras, L. 62
wealth 89–90, 92

x-axis 3
x-coordinate 3

y-axis 3
y-coordinate 3